British Muslims in the Neoliberal Empire

OXFORD BRITISH MUSLIM STUDIES

General Editors
Yahya Birt, Sophie Gilliat-Ray, and Shamim Miah

British Muslims in the Neoliberal Empire

Resisting, Healing, and Flourishing in the Metacolonial Era

WILLIAM BARYLO

Great Clarendon Street, Oxford, OX2 6DP,
United Kingdom

Oxford University Press is a department of the University of Oxford.
It furthers the University's objective of excellence in research, scholarship,
and education by publishing worldwide. Oxford is a registered trade mark of
Oxford University Press in the UK and in certain other countries

© William Barylo 2025

The moral rights of the author have been asserted

All rights reserved. No part of this publication may be reproduced, stored in a retrieval system, transmitted, used for text and data mining, or used for training artificial intelligence, in any form or by any means, without the prior permission in writing of Oxford University Press, or as expressly permitted by law, by licence or under terms agreed with the appropriate reprographics rights organization. Enquiries concerning reproduction outside the scope of the above should be sent to the Rights Department, Oxford University Press, at the address above.

You must not circulate this work in any other form
and you must impose this same condition on any acquirer

Published in the United States of America by Oxford University Press
198 Madison Avenue, New York, NY 10016, United States of America

British Library Cataloguing in Publication Data
Data available

Library of Congress Control Number: 2024951006

ISBN 9780198924944

DOI: 10.1093/9780198924975.001.0001

Printed and bound by
CPI Group (UK) Ltd, Croydon, CR0 4YY

The manufacturer's authorised representative in the EU for product safety is
Oxford University Press España S.A. of El Parque Empresarial San Fernando de Henares, Avenida de Castilla, 2 – 28830 Madrid (www.oup.es/en or
product.safety@oup.com). OUP España S.A. also acts as importer into Spain
of products made by the manufacturer.

'... for the growing good of the world is partly dependent on unhistoric acts ... and is half owing to the number who lived faithfully a hidden life, and rest in unvisited tombs.'

George Eliot, *Middlemarch*

Acknowledgements

In the name of God, the Lord of Mercy, the giver of Mercy, I express my gratitude to God for giving me the strength, the resources, and the support to accomplish this work. I seek forgiveness and mercy from God, and all those involved in this work, their families, and their ancestors.

Thanks to the British Academy who trusted me by awarding the highest possible grant in Europe at my career stage to this research (PF2\180037), especially Ken Emond and Peris Thuo, who allowed me to give back and participate in the wonderful community behind the scenes.

Thanks to the University of Warwick who hosted me and supported my teaching and public engagement endeavours. Thanks to Sophie Gilliat-Ray, Shamim Miah, Yahya Birt, Rachel Atkins, and Tom Perridge at Oxford University Press for the support and guidance during the production process of this book.

Thanks to my academic mentors Fauzia Ahmad and Virinder Singh Kalra who convinced me that I was not an impostor, who guided and supported me through the murky waters of academia. I would also like to thank the brilliant academics Su'ad Abdul Khabeer, Yahya Birt, Esra Özyürek, Asim Qureshi, Konrad Pędziwiatr, and Mario Peucker for their invaluable guidance in my professional and personal journey.

I acknowledge this research has been undertaken in the United Kingdom and France, centres of colonial empires built on racial, class, gender, and religious divides, exploitation, theft, and genocide across the globe. I acknowledge I have a responsibility for the stewardship of the land on which I live and work, and that I strive for the healing, growth, and self-determination of all those affected and the generations to come.

The fieldwork included the San Francisco Bay Area, the ancestral homeland of the Ramaytush Ohlone; Los Angeles, homeland of the Tongva, Tataviam, Serrano, Kizh, and Chumash; Austin, Texas, land of the Carrizo, Comecrudo, Coahuiltecan, Caddo, Tonkawa, Comanche, Lipan Apache, Alabama-Coushatta, Kickapoo, and Tigua Pueblo; Toronto, territory of the Mississaugas, Anishnabeg, Chippewa, Haudenosaunee, and the Wendat.

Thanks to Rumi's Cave, the Muslim Vibe, especially Salim Kassam, Haseeb Rizvi, and Nouri Sardar and to Professor Hatem Bazian at Zaytuna College for helping me to disseminate the findings of this research in its earliest stages.

Thanks to Apne Film Club, British Muslim TV, CAGE, Cambridge Muslim College, Cambridge Central Mosque, The Cambridge Crescent, Children of Adam, the City Circle, the Concordia Forum, Everyday Muslim Heritage, the

Green Deen Tribe, the Herbal Blessing Clinic, the Halal Monitoring Committee UK, Healing Justice London, Human Appeal, the Institute for Strategic Dialogue, Islah LA, MADE, Mansheds, MEND (since when I knew you as iEngage!), Mu'allif, Muslamic Makers, Muslim Charity, the Muslim Entrepreneur Network, the Muslim Influencer Network, Muslim Hands, Muslim History Tours, Muslim Space, the Muslim Youth Helpline, Muzz (formerly Muzmatch), the National Zakat Foundation, the New Crescent Society, Penny Appeal, the Rabbani Project, Rumi's Cave, Sacred Footsteps, the Tesselate Institute, and the Urban Equestrian Academy for either your insights or allowing me to participate in some of your projects.

I would like to thank Abbas Zahedi, AbdulMaalik Tailor, Ameen Kamlana and Farah Elahi, Aminah Babikir, Aziza ElHarchi and Chems Hadj, Dawuud Loka, Engie Salama, Fahad Khalid, Farah Soobhan and Matthew Robinson, Farrah Azam, Fatima Khemilat, Farzana Khan, Fawad Shaikh, Fozia Latif, Hamja Ahsan, Hassan Vawda, Hawa N'Dongo, Henrietta Szovati, Ibrahim Bechrouri, Imad Ahmed, Janna Bouhassoun and Yacine Madi Saïd, Jayde Russell and Hamid Senni (rest in peace), Jessica Harn, Jeyda Hammad, Josue Comoe, Juma Harding Dimmock and Warren Clementson, Jumana Moon, Khalidah Ali, Khurram Malik, Luqman Ali, Maaida Noor, Matthew Philip Long and Miriam Abdulla, Medina Whiteman, Minhaaj Khan, Nuria, John and Bushra Dunne, Rizwan Hussein, Razwan Faraz, Roshan Jahangeer, Sabre Bougrine, Sadia Habib and Ghulam, Sadiya and Irfan Ahmed, Sahar Al Faifi, Sakinah LeNoir and Rabiah Mali, Salahuddin Ahmed Mazhary, Sanah Ahsan, Shemiza Rashid, Shamsher Singh, Shareefa Energy, Shuranjeet Singh Thakar, Sultanah Parvin, Syed Mustafa Ali, Tanya Muneera Williams, Tarek Younis, Tony Salih Whelbourne, Umair Saeed, Umar Atallah Khan, Undleeb Iqbal, Yasmeen Rasheed, Yasmine Ahmed, Zahra Latif, Zain Dada, and Zara Choudhary.

Not only do you shine a light in the darkness; you also have reminded me that I am not crazy for seeing the things I see and thinking the way I think. When I felt I had no one, you were my family. Thank you for your guidance, advice, and support. Our encounters, conversations, and stay-overs have shaped my thoughts and focused my aims in life. Thank you for inspiring me, healing me, and giving me hope. Thanks to my students at Warwick and those here because of YouTube, as you are the actual teachers!

Finally, thanks to Javayria Masood who has allowed me to recover, heal, and flourish, and to rebuild a life after I had lost everything.

I dedicate this book to people of all faiths and none who consider their resources, be these wealth, knowledge, visibility, or networks, as trusts to be used for good, and who consider their role on Earth as stewards for harmony. You don't run after medals but you are the real heroes.

I dedicate this book to those who run after medals too, who prioritize their own liberation through material possessions, oppression, and symbols of power. May your illusions shatter and open a path to service.

This book is for those seeking alternatives to current hegemonies, different ways of doing and being. My work is a homage to those who taught me how to resist, heal, and flourish. I believe that my knowledge is not valid if it is not shared. Therefore, this book is, in a written form, the settlement of my knowledge tax duty towards society.

Contents

Detailed Contents — xiii
Transliterations and Blessings — xv

   Introduction — 1

1. Hair Straighteners — 23
2. Faithfolk Ain't Kinfolk — 45
3. Making Muslims Great Again: Alt-Bros, Alpha Muslims, and Supremacists — 70
4. Wounds and Helplines — 93
5. Green Deen and Stewardship — 115
6. Praying Alone: Collapse and Revival of the Muslim Community — 136
7. I Was Just Following the Trend: Art of the Oppressed or Oppressive Culture? — 158
8. Spaces of Nurture and Resistance — 189

   Conclusion — 213

Index — 219

Detailed Contents

Transliterations and Blessings   xv

    Introduction   1
       I.1. Muslim Community Spaces: A Genesis   4
       I.2. Metacolonialism: From 1492 to Islamic Decoloniality   7
       I.3. Methodology and the Field   10
       I.4. A Metacolonized Sociologist   13
       I.5. Overview of the Book   15

1. Hair Straighteners   23
       1.1. De-diasporization, WesTernization, and Metacolonization   25
       1.2. Conformity Is Safety   29
       1.3. Temporarily Embarrassed White People   32
       1.4. The Internalization of White Oppression   36

2. Faithfolk Ain't Kinfolk   45
       2.1. Securitization and Control of Dissent   47
       2.2. Deprivation and Theology of Liberation   51
       2.3. Engineering the New Muslim Elite   54
       2.4. Representation Is Not Liberation   58

3. Making Muslims Great Again: Alt-Bros, Alpha Muslims, and Supremacists   70
       3.1. The Alphas and Betas of Male Crisis   72
       3.2. Make Muslims Great Again   75
       3.3. Make Islam White Again   79
       3.4. When Muslim Men Want to Be Western Boys   83
       3.5. Comrades in Struggle?   86

4. Wounds and Helplines   93
       4.1. The State Is an Abuser   95
       4.2. Spiritual Abuse and Unsafe Spaces   98
       4.3. Community Healing Initiatives   101
       4.4. Reframing Narratives from Pain to Power   107

5. Green Deen and Stewardship   115
       5.1. The Disease of Leadership: Modernity and Its Disconnections   117
       5.2. Hikers and Healers: From Leadership to Stewardship   120
       5.3. Ramadan as a Decolonial Month   125
       5.4. Rabiah Mali: The Hijra of Muslim Liberation   129

6. Praying Alone: Collapse and Revival of the Muslim Community 136
   6.1. Can the Muslim Speak? 137
   6.2. 'The *Ummah* Is People's Gangs' 141
   6.3. Muslim History Tours and Archives: The Ecosystem of
        the Past and Present 147
   6.4. Sacred Footsteps and Film Clubs 150
   6.5. Is There a British Islam? 152

7. I Was Just Following the Trend: Art of the Oppressed or
   Oppressive Culture? 158
   7.1. Allah for Sale 160
   7.2. Oppression Sold as Resistance 166
   7.3. Colonial Charities 170
   7.4. Twilight of the Idols 173
   7.5. Muslim Culture or Islamic Culture? 177

8. Spaces of Nurture and Resistance 189
   8.1. Nurturing Spaces: Come Whoever You Are 191
   8.2. Funding, Perseverance, *Sabr*, and Imagination 195
   8.3. Moses and Pharaoh: Resistance and Rehabilitation 199
   8.4. Islamic Decoloniality 203

   Conclusion 213

Index 219

Transliterations and Blessings

Most translations from Arabic and Urdu, Punjabi, Bangla, and Farsi to English are mine, unless specified otherwise. I use spellings that are commonly used in English, loosely following the guidelines of the *International Journal of Middle Eastern Studies* for languages based on the Arabic script, and Hunterian transliterations for language based on Devanagari and similar—all without diacritics except for the Arabic letters 'ayn (') and hamza (').

I use the Qur'anic translation by M.A.S. Abdel Haleem (Oxford University Press, 2010 edition) unless specified otherwise.

In quoted text, I follow transliterations by a contextual translation conveying the specific meaning they express, and what is understood by their audiences.

Blessings upon the Prophet Muhammad, usually following each mention of his name in many Muslim traditions, just like blessings upon his family, his companions, or ancestors, do not appear unless in a quote. Feel free to pause and extend blessings to them after each reference.

Introduction

> Today I learnt that I am a second-class citizen. Today I learnt my parents were right when they said that we will never be accepted. Today I learnt that I can lose my citizenship because I have dual nationality by descent. (Iqbal 2019)

On 19 February 2019, the lives of millions of migrants or descendants of immigrants in the UK took one of the sharpest turns ever. On that day, 19-year-old Shamima Begum had lost her appeal against the Home Office's decision to revoke her British citizenship, for being groomed and joining the terrorist group ISIS at the age of 15, in 2015. Although she only held a British passport, the government argued that, because she was born from Bangladeshi parents, she thus held Bangladeshi citizenship—despite the government of Bangladesh unequivocally stating that she was not a Bangladeshi citizen and that she has never applied to become one.[1] The Home Office, stripping her from her British citizenship, would make her stateless, contrary to international conventions.[2] For context, three years before, the UK voted its withdrawal from the European Union and the US elected Donald Trump as president, both the result of campaigns fuelled by anti-immigrant sentiments. As an immigrant to the UK myself, born from Polish parents who migrated to France, I was trying to reassure myself, thinking that Britain would never dare to take the same route as France or Poland, internationally notorious for their cuisine, landscapes, and their vocal manifestations of racism. After all, Britain was the country of 'multiculturalism' where diversity, through 'protected characteristics', was enshrined in the law. I was mistaken. The decision of revoking one's citizenship pretexting ancestry, signified, for millions, that they had become de facto foreigners 'by descent'[3] who could see their citizenship being cancelled at any time, should the Home Office decide so,[4] and potentially be deported to a country they barely knew and had likely never visited. Since Britain could not be 'home' any more, where was 'home' supposed to be?

For many British Muslims, another problem was Sajid Javid, the Home Secretary at the time. He was instrumental in stripping Begum from her citizenship, born from Pakistani working-class immigrant parents, previously a victim of racism, but targeting a teenager with a similar upbringing with more verve and passion than the most racist voices in England. Many within minoritized groups expect that people from their own communities share some solidarity against structural adversity. From the perspectives of many community organizers, it was a betrayal. Betrayal by England, and by Javid, marked by the bitter realization that not all South Asians, not all working-class people, not all Muslims are 'in this together' and will show solidarity. 'Skinfolk ain't kinfolk': people who share the same skin colour are not necessarily those who will support you (see chapter 2).

This book was written at the dawn of the 2020s, which some call the new 'roaring twenties'[5] (more because of social activism than the economic growth of the 1920s), a decade following various waves of social justice movements across Euro-America (a generalizing term for the socio-economically privileged and white-dominated modern societies in Europe, North America, and Australasia), which some also call the Wild White West. The most remarkable ripples of this wave are movements such as Black Lives Matter, in reaction to police brutality against Black people, Me Too, in reaction to the abuse of women, Rhodes Must Fall, contesting the celebration of colonization and slavery, or the several worldwide protests to stop the Palestinian genocide. In the UK, they rippled through protests following the killing of seventy-two people trapped in the Grenfell tower block in 2017, the Windrush scandal in 2018, and the Goldsmiths Anti-Racist Action blockade in 2019.

At the same time, this book is located at the turn of an era for Muslim diasporas in the Wild White West. Muslims, targeted as a suspect demographic since 9/11, have been facing an unprecedented wave of violence ranging from criminal damage to mosques, attacks on individuals to the institutionalized surveillance, control, and criminalization of citizens through counter-extremism strategies such as CVE (Countering Violent Extremism) in the US and PREVENT in the UK, using native informants, infiltrators, or social engineering. Many Muslims have since been seeking collaboration with this multi-million-pound industry complicit with human rights violations (Lean 2012) in search of financial stability and political or media representation (see chapter 2). In the absence of alternative funding streams, collaboration with oppressive systems poses the dilemma of ethical poverty: shall people submit in order to thrive individually and sacrifice collective interest; or, by respecting human rights, are they condemned to stay at the margins, deprived from visibility, representation, and opportunities? Because of this apparent lack of choice, many Muslims amongst my respondents feel sandwiched between racism and Islamophobia on the one hand, and, on the other, members of their own communities supporting structures of oppression, in an invisible prison where the oppressed of yesterday could become the oppressors of tomorrow.

During the era of European colonial empires, oppression was synonymous with violence. In the age of social media, oppression has become convincing people to adopt certain behaviours, looks, ways of speaking, dressing, spending, voting, and thinking. In the same way the British, Spanish, and French empires asserted control through the occupation of lands and resources, white supremacy, neoliberalism, and patriarchy, and other hegemonies have found novel ways of making their way through the colonization of a new frontier: the occupation of minds. Looking at the inadequacy of Eurocentric models of mental health care in Sudan, this observation led Hussein Bulhan (2015), to coin the term 'metacolonization', describing how market trends, trade regulations, business models, bureaucratic processes, and culture worldwide are insistently suggested or pressured to adopt Eurocentric standards. 'A socio-political, economic, cultural and psychological system that comes after, along with, or among the earlier stages of colonialism' (Bulhan 2015, 244), metacolonization is a global and decentralized form of colonization, a form of soft occupation of the social, economic, political, and cultural universes that deprives its inmates from civic, social, and economic opportunities should they step outside.

This book offers an examination of the interpenetrations, clashes, and resistances between the new empires and Muslim communities from various diasporas in the twenty-first century in modern Euro-America, those who collaborate, and those building alternatives. Academics, artists, and community organizers have for decades documented, analysed, and established a comprehensive diagnosis of the *modus operandi* of structures of oppression—what hurts people and how. The question is therefore: what are the next steps? This work posits that there are many ways out.

This research has three major aims. First, understanding: how did the oppressed turn into oppressors? Why are there Muslims supporting racist policies and narratives portraying them as suspects by default? Second, mapping and assessing the various modes of Muslim positive agency, resistance, healing, experimenting, and self-determination designed, crafted, and experimented by those advocating a decolonization of the dominant structures of power, despite lacking in support and resources, motivated by their culture and Islamic ethics. Third, providing a toolbox for community organizers and stakeholders to assess the impact of certain choices and showcasing the multiple ways for projects to flourish outside the usual power structures.

This book offers three central arguments. First, that Britain and other centres of power resulting from European colonization are still colonial. By projecting hegemonic normative powers, and presenting neoliberalism, patriarchy, whiteness, and others (as structures of authority rooted in colonial and racial capitalist forms of property (Harris 1995; Moreton-Robinson 2015)) as theologies of liberation, they divide citizens along the lines of race, class, gender, and belief, and shape how citizens should look, speak and behave. Second, people navigate. Post-colonial literature used to revolve around three main types of response of minorities to hegemonies: assimilation, rejection, and negotiation (see chapter 1). This work focuses on a fourth posture: navigation, the ability not to compromise and draw solid boundaries, refusing harmful opportunities and crafting their own terms for existing. Finally, I argue that decolonization is possible and effectively under way by comparing and assessing how various Muslim grass-roots initiatives across

Euro-America are proactively organizing in the fields of arts, education, environmentalism, heritage, health care, and more. They show that it is possible to resist, to heal, and to flourish.

I.1. Muslim Community Spaces: A Genesis

The first modern Muslim organizations in Euro-America would be small and local, exclusively for managing mosques. In the 1990s, bigger structures emerged, which would either work on the representation of Muslims such as the Muslim Council of Britain (MCB, in 1997), the Union des Organisations Islamiques de France (UOIF, Union for the Islamic Organisations of France, 1983), the Council on American-Islamic Relations (CAIR 1994), or international humanitarian aid (Islamic Relief 1984, Muslim Aid 1985, Human Appeal 1991, Muslim Hands 1993). The 1990s also mark the spreading of religious education in faith-based schools (*madrassa*) and the beginning of political activism.

The events of 9/11, the war on terror, and the subsequent wave of Islamophobia led many young Muslims to pursue formal Islamic theology and jurisprudence degrees with the goal of responding to racist arguments, in institutes such as the Institut Européen des Sciences Humaines (IESH), Al Maghrib Institute, or the International Institute of Islamic Thought (IIIT). The same period saw the creation of organizations for the defence of Muslim rights such as the CCIF in France and MEND (formerly iEngage) in the UK. These were the years when Tariq Ramadan (1999) rose to fame with his affirmation that one can be Muslim and European citizen at the same time, a narrative that inspired a whole generation to get involved into small acts of civic engagement (Barylo 2017a), in parallel with the emergence of more educated, financially and socially privileged individuals (Pędziwiatr 2010; Ahmad 2012).

During the 2010s, the Muslim charity sector in the UK mushroomed dramatically. As of 2020, there were 1,026 Muslim charities with humanitarian objects (Mohammed and Bianchi 2023). With an average of £371 of donations per head per year, multiplied by an estimated 3.9 million of Muslims in the UK,[6] the total in donations comes to just over £1.4 billion in the UK alone.[7] In 2020, figures went to £708 million for humanitarian charities alone (Mohammed and Bianchi 2023). The UK charity Commission estimates British Muslims have donated around £100 million during the sole month of Ramadan 2013.[8] According to the statistics of the Charities Aid Foundation based on official data of the Charities Commission,[9] large Muslim humanitarian NGOs such as Islamic Relief can receive on average millions of pounds in voluntary donations per year (Islamic Relief recorded more than £50 million in 2012). However, many of these multi-million-pounds charities embraced the functioning of large multinational business ventures where the race for profit, results, and competition was justified with the distortion of the Qur'an into a management handbook (Barylo 2016, 2017a). Many of these were criticized for their aggressive and guilt-driven fundraising techniques, the appropriation of community spaces, their colonial-era style of quasi-missionary operations abroad, and abusive treatment of partners (see chapter 7.3).

In the midst of the emergence of social justice movements, the 2010s saw celebrity religious scholars come under fire: Hamza Yusuf for his political stances,[10] and Nouman Ali Khan, Tariq Ramadan, and Usama Canon in 2019 for their inappropriate conduct with women. Although their actions were not criminal, many younger Muslims lost trust in these traditional role models, soon replaced by social media 'influencers' (see chapter 7). While Islam might be the 'fastest growing religion on the planet', religiosity figures (such as mosque attendance) which peaked in the 2010s, were on the decline globally by the dawn of the 2020s:[11] there are more people who identify as Muslim, but among those, fewer people are practising the religion. From a moral and ethical framework, Islam became reduced to a cultural heritage or an identity label. As of 2024, Muslim initiatives and organizations are atomized and far from being united.

However, the 2010s also saw a very different set of organizations emerge, breaking away from neoliberal models, founded mainly by young Muslims born in the 1980s and the 1990s (millennials), a response to precise, local, social problems such as homelessness, student poverty, complementary education, or alternative media (Barylo 2017a). These include names such as Children of Adam (UK), Averroès, and Amatullah (in France). Limited in scale, independent from larger Muslim organizations or religious currents, with a core team not exceeding a dozen volunteers (but with networks comprising hundreds of sympathizers), they function more like small families exempt from bureaucratic procedures. Most of these groups, made up of unpaid volunteers, rely not on institutional funding but on private contributions from members and benefactors. They are not competing with larger or older charities. Some of them evolve in hubs offering isolated urban Muslims a community and diverse activities ranging from charity works to artistic events, film nights, talks, creative skills workshops, and more. These hubs include names such as Ta'leef Collective (San Francisco Bay Area), Rumi's Cave (London, UK), Maison Soufie (France), Café Floraison (Canada), Benevolence (Melbourne, Australia), and Muslim Space (Austin, Texas).

They are the manifestation of the era of post-conventional politics, whereby concepts such as nation-state and party politics lose their relevance, and more personalized, flexible, and informal forms of extra-institutional engagement emerge (Meyer and Tarrow 1998; Wieviorka 2005; Blühdorn 2006; McDonald 2006; Feixa et al. 2009; Kennelly 2011; Langman 2013; Keck and Sikkink 2014). They do not take part in the management of their localities nor replace public services, although they are essential components for the democratic life of societies. In that sense, they are 'infrapolitical' structures (Chanial 2003). These organizations understand citizenship as a positive, proactive engagement at different levels of politics and society also called 'active citizenship' (Mouffe 1992; Adler and Goggin 2005; Hoskins and Mascherini 2009; O'Toole and Gale 2010; Harris and Roose 2014; Peucker and Akbarzadeh 2014; Roose and Harris 2015; Peucker and Ceylan 2016; Vergani et al. 2017; Oskooii and Dana 2018; Peucker 2018), thus 'transforming the public sphere' (Soliman 2017).

However, globalization, neoliberalism, and mass consumerism have emerged as some of the strongest forces shaping how Muslims practise Islam in the twenty-first century (Haenni 2005; Janmohammed 2016; Shirazi 2016; Nilan 2017; O'Brien 2017; Lewis and Hamid 2018). The younger generation have been engaging in new modes of cultural hybridation through carefully curated expressions of piety around food and fashion. They embody the new Muslim 'cool' (Boubekeur 2005; Herding 2013); they don't shy from buying designer brands, and aspire to fame, physical attractiveness, wealth, and influence while fostering inequalities and overlooking human rights violations (see chapter 7). However, more people are becoming aware that begging for recognition, visibility, power, and fame are limited strategies for minorities and have thus started focusing on unquantifiable values such as meaning, quality, intentions, and long-term thinking. My work thus focuses on the un-cool Muslims, the statistical anomalies proof that 'the impetus for change in Islam has more often come from the bottom than from the top, from the edge than from the centre' (Lewis and Hamid 2018).

The initiatives presented in this work are not charities in a classic sense, nor volunteers are a pair of helping hands, but informal, self-organized groups of friends or individuals committed to the betterment of the society. They do not aim at making a measurable impact or participate in traditional activism such as campaigns, protests, and mass mobilization. I thus describe their work not as *activism* but *community organizing*. They are mostly young people between the ages of 25 and 35, and work or study alongside their activities. Although not everyone in my study had access to higher education, they articulate their feelings, experiences and understand the injustices they observe through reading and watching online conferences or social media discussion groups, paintings, photography, live performance, or films through an ecosystem merging of academics, artists, and community organizers. Some of them have attended retreats such as the Granada Summer School or Critical Muslim Studies.

Most of them are the children of immigrant parents of modest background from colonial diasporas. Their cultural roots hail from South Asia, North Africa, the Caribbean, East and West Africa, the Middle East, and the Far East, not forgetting Europe or North America. Often from mixed backgrounds, their roots comprise multiple points of origins from a Saidian perspective (Said 1984). Although the majority have been brought up in Sunni Islam and a minority in Shi'a Islam, some of them refuse to use religious labels; they don't necessarily rely on one specific religious scholar to guide them but use the diversity of religious opinion as tools for reflection and self-development. However, many are wounded by disillusions from their own community and the trauma of racism and other oppressions, struggling financially or encountering glass ceilings. They are familiar with the consequences of globalization and neoliberalism, the rise in social inequalities, gender issues, racism, poverty, and other issues such as healthier food, local entrepreneurship, and environmentally friendly behaviours. Rather than leaders, they see themselves as stewards (see chapter 5), actively restoring justice in the sense of Ruha Benjamin's *Viral Justice* (2020), amplifying 'small efforts … and … spread[ing] them, like a life-sustaining virus' (Benjamin 2020, 28) and 'dismantling harmful systems, providing for people's immediate needs, and creating alternative structures that can meet those needs based on values of care, democratic participation, and solidarity' (Benjamin 2020, 22).

I.2. Metacolonialism: From 1492 to Islamic Decoloniality

The development and expansion of colonialism, which started with the invasion of what has become known as the Americas (Quijano 2007), affected the thought, behaviour and the life of colonized peoples, the way they acquire knowledge, understand their history, comprehend their world, and define themselves. The erosion of indigenous social bonds, beliefs, values, and identities (Alcoff 2007; Maldonado-Torres 2010) was achieved with the help of different agents such as missionaries, anthropologists, medical doctors, and journalists, and the education of local agents through colonial schools, disseminating Eurocentric epistemology, ontology, and ideology validating the hegemonic European monopoly of power, knowledge, and truth (Dussel 1985, 1996; Mignolo 2000; Quijano 2000; Mignolo 2007). As a result, what started with the occupation and control of land and populations resulted in a sustained occupation of beings (Bulhan 2015) which left behind political, economic, cultural, intellectual, and social enduring legacies that keep alive the European hegemony.

Although the fall of the European empires has birthed what was labelled the 'post-colonial era' (Said 1984; Spivak 1988; Bhabha 1994), local elites inherited colonial states, not to serve the colonized but to exploit them—a stage called 'neocolonialism' (Nkrumah 1965; Bulhan 2008). Consequently, many object to the use of the term 'post-colonial' (McClintock 1992; San Juan 1998; King 2001), arguing that the world hasn't moved past colonialism, it has only taken a different shape (Lugones 2007; Quijano 2007; Mignolo 2010; Grosfoguel 2011).

Coloniality is a global matrix of power (Hill Collins 2008; D'Ignazio and Klein 2023) still emanating from the same former colonial centres of power that emerged during the Atlantic slave trade (Parenti 1995), that operates through military control (imperialism), through macro structures (nation state, law, policies, economic system), disciplinary (administration, law enforcement, labour), hegemony (culture, media, subjective world views, including through technology (Ali 2019)), and interpersonal dimensions (individual experiences, sexuality, reproduction, and family structures). Consequently, empires are not local any more, but global, immaterial, conceptual, and virtual. This results in the formation of racial, gender, sexual, spiritual, epistemic, linguistic, aesthetic, pedagogical, media, age, ableist, ecological, and spatial hierarchies with racism as the structural organizing principle, and works with the exclusion, domination, selectivity of beings, and the depoliticization or decontestation of its effects. Concepts such as misogyny, neoliberalism, and white supremacy—the unfair domination of white people and cultural norms over ethnically minoritized people and the oppression of the latter—are only the tip of the iceberg.

While Fanon (1967) and Memmi (1965) have operated clear distinctions between colonizers and the colonized, in the post-9/11 era of globalized uniform financial, education, health care, and cultural systems, Bulhan (2015) argues that such distinctions are no longer adequate. Whether it is the adoption of maladapted Eurocentric models of health care in Sudan, the global obsession for fair skin or China employing British counter-extremism strategies to repress Muslims in the Xinjiang,[12] the boundaries between empires and margins, oppressor and oppressed have become more porous than ever. Metacolonialism is a form of colonization that is not forced upon people, but is a set of strongly suggested economic, social, political, and cultural conventions which:

1. people have to adopt in order to be perceived as legitimate in a given society; and
2. leaves no space to local, individual, economic, social, and cultural identities or uniqueness. It is a culture of conformation that makes identities redundant—unless commodified.

In Paulo Freire's (1993, 47) words, it is when 'the oppressed have internalised the image of the oppressor and have adopted his guidelines'. It is, for example, the UK Conservative Home Secretary Suella Braverman declaring in 2023 that 'multiculturalism has failed'—while herself being a child of British multiculturalism, born from immigrant South Asian parents, married to a Jewish husband and serving under a Hindu prime minister. It is ethnically minoritized people supporting the pro-white narrative about 'taking control of our borders', 'taking our country back', or making 'America great again' (subtext: 'make America white again' (Morrison 2016)), calling for the rebuilding of a hypothetically lost golden age of a white civilization. I therefore use white supremacy interchangeably with the expression 'white civilizational project' in the Latin sense of *projicio* (to throw ahead). Metacolonialism has merged the best of authoritarian repression and softer measures of control under the guise of aspiration and entertainment, in a powerful Orwellian-Huxleyan double punch. Metacolonialism has also contaminated the very Eurocentric structures it emanated from, whether it is politics to research and education: how much of modern research methods, concepts, and theories have been polluted with neoliberal ideas—such as, in sociology, 'social capital' instead of 'network'?

While postcolonialism remains a critique of colonial dynamics, decolonial scholars such as Quijano, Maldonado-Torres, Mignolo, Lugones, and Grosfoguel advocate a multi-dimensional work of resistance and liberation from epistemological dominance, a 'critical thinking emerging in the colonies and ex-colonies', 'a trans-disciplinary horizon ... at the service of the regeneration of life' (Mignolo 2010, 11) aiming at healing and self-determination. While works around decoloniality have largely covered knowledge and culture (Bhambra 2014), only a few have explored the religious perspective (Mandair 2009, focusing on Sikhi). Various Muslim academics and thinkers have formulated either Islam as a liberation theology (Farid Esack, Tariq Ramadan (2008), Abdennur Prado, or Asma Lamrabet) or a decolonial approach based on Islam such as Salman Sayyid (2014) and the Critical Muslim Studies movement and the journal *Re-Orient* (different to the *Critical Muslim* journal by the Muslim Institute, also worth mentioning), American-Palestinian scholar Hatem Bazian, or the Neo-Kalam movement, trying to reverse the epistemic colonization of the Muslim imagination (Birt 2022), or, further, an 'Islamic decoloniality': a spiritual-political project aimed at resisting and replacing modern hegemonies with a pluriversal system informed by Islam, free from man-made supremacies (see chapter 8). Muslim decolonial movements in Euro-America have been mainly emerging from English-speaking societies (the UK and the US), but also in France with, for example, the Parti des Indigènes de la République (Party of the Indigenous of the Republic), founded in 2005—and later in the 2010s with younger figures such as Assa Traoré, Hanane Karimi, Fatima Khemilat, Sihame Assbague, and Fatima Ouassak. The Muslim actors of decolonial thought find many crossovers with the Latin American pioneers of the field, to the point of organizing yearly joint events and conferences (Dialogo Global, Critical Muslim Studies conferences, etc).

Decolonization comes from the margins, in thirdspaces (Soja 1996), borderlands (Anzaldúa 1987), or heterotopias (Foucault 1971). In this work, these are geographical or virtual spaces of faith when society pushes for secularism (Cloke et al. 2013); community spaces of solidarity in a society of individualism and competition; spaces of care, trust, love, and conviviality (Illich 1973) when the dominant society pushes people to devalue and hate themselves. Spaces that value the non-numerable, emotions, and the non-profitable in times of neoliberalism, consultation, and consensus in times of authoritarianism; giving and nurturing in a society that takes and exploits. The organizations and individuals I mention in this research do not label themselves as 'decolonial'. However, because of their work of critical thinking, delinking, and counter-acting the dominant power structures on the one hand, and their efforts in healing, restoring, and nurturing on the other, I consider them decolonial.

I.3. Methodology and the Field

This work is based on more than ten years of research mainly with Muslims in the UK. My research interests and relationships I have built took me to London, the Midlands, Scotland, Wales, Paris, its banlieue, San Francisco, Los Angeles, New York, Toronto, French Guyana, Suriname, Dubai, Iceland, Sri Lanka, and Poland. It all started in 2009 in France for my master's degree, after France banned hijabs in schools in 2004. Most academic works about Muslims revolved around violence, extremism, poverty, immigration, and the 'compatibility' of Islam with Europe. I wanted to show the daily Muslim life that I was observing around me: student organizations which, despite the climate of hatred, continued with preparing soup kitchens for the homeless, supporting students from underprivileged backgrounds, or setting up their own media outlet. My pool of respondents comes from the fieldwork I have undertaken since my enrolment as a PhD student in 2011 and with whom I have kept contact until the present day. I started fieldwork as a volunteer for different organizations, meeting people through film making, talking about my research, facilitating workshops, and organizing events before developing rhizomatically my own networks built from attendance to common events, common workplaces, or common affinities.

The data stems from ethnographic observations, interviews, informal conversations, and biographical trajectories collected from 2012 to 2022 from 126 people aged 21–65, identifying as Muslims, with an equal proportion of males and females, independent or affiliated to eighteen different organizations. These include academics, artists, activists, students, parents, community organizers, grass-roots and large charities, mental health hotlines, informal healing initiatives, students' associations, intellectual online forums, activist spaces, informal archival initiatives, community hubs and artists' collectives, and more. They all hail from different cultural, ethnic, religious, and socio-economic backgrounds, and are of various genders and sexual orientations. Through trusted contacts, I was also able to interview people on 'the other side of the fence': people who make the choice of supporting Islamophobic, anti-Black or misogynistic narratives. During the 2020 pandemic, a lot of my data stemmed also from digital ethnography: engagement on social media accounts, comments, posts, websites, and podcasts.

This long-term project's participant observation involved sharing time and space, speaking with, eating with, and also feeling with people, in times of joy and times of grief, in a way knowledge is shared and produced intersubjectively (Abdul Khabeer 2016). I have witnessed charities setting up and closing down, social media influencers rising and falling, people getting married, divorced, raising kids, parents and family members passing away, people embracing Islam, and leaving Islam: 'being is always a becoming' (Heckert 2016, 43). Islam is a lived experience (Asad 2003; Mahmood 2004; Fadil 2006), encompassing all spheres of human life.

I consider Islam in this work as a complex system (Morin 1977, 1986), a matrix, or an ecosystem (Barylo 2017a, 2017b), a material and immaterial environment made of beliefs, scriptures, written and oral traditions, rituals, daily life actions, values, ethics, a vision of life, people whether they are scholars or family members influential to the subjects, places of worship, spaces, times, symbolic items, items conferred with religious meaning, and all the various subjective interpretations of the aforementioned, the subsequent thoughts and observable actions, where God is considered as a real actor in the lives of those who believe.

This research prioritizes the respondents' own subjectivity and describes phenomena with the subjects' own words, references and meanings, using them as a basis for analysis, following methods of social phenomenology (Husserl 1982; Cope 2005), narrative inquiry (Connelly and Clandinin 2006), and Dubet's sociology of experience (1994). When my respondents identify as Muslims, regardless of their level of orthodoxy, I call them Muslims. When people follow a moral compass antithetic to Islam, this choice might produce oxymorons such as *Muslim criminals*. Therefore, I use *Muslim* as an identity label which doesn't mean they follow Islam, and I use 'Islamicate' (Hodgson 1977) to refer to what revolves around Islam while not representing the religion—Islam is not what Muslims do. This work analyses both religious and racial dynamics as Muslim, despite being heterogeneous and extremely diverse in their cultures, beliefs, traditions, and relationship to Islam, are racialized as a homogeneous non-white 'other' (Lloyd 2013, 80) and therefore a 'political category' (Jenkins 2014; Younis and Hassan 2018). For this work, I adopt an analysis based on an anti-utilitarian sociology of action (Caillé 2009) where beyond power dynamics, non-quantifiable elements such as affect (Ahmed 2014), gift (Mauss 2007), and emotions are part of the grammar of human relations (Chanial 2011): what is given and taken? Consequently, I am trying to find proclivities (tendencies to do something particular) and common narratives through their works, biographies, faith journeys and other life experiences (Josselson 2011).

Insider ethnography or ethnography 'close to home' (Caputo 2000, 22) is an investigation within the researcher's own social circles or touching at the researcher's own life, where their friends, family, partners (Behar 1996), and their own biographies are enmeshed in the fieldwork, the data, and the analysis—achieved through long-term relationships with the respondents (Lucia and Amritanandamavi 2014), travelling along with them (Connors Jackman 2016). Building on pioneers like Limón (1994) as a member of the Chicano culture or Williams (1991) finding the deed of sale of her own great-great-grandmother as a slave, I am walking in the footsteps of the likes of Muslim anthropologist, artist, and community organizer Su'ad Abdul Khabeer (2016) who considers her respondents as her teachers, with whom she often has pre-existing long-term connections and strong bonds of trust, or Mohammed Qasim (2018) going back to the criminal gangs of Bradford with which he spent his younger years.

My choice is pragmatic and at the same time circumstantial: ethnography requires trust, and not anyone can be granted trust within Muslim circles in a post-9/11 context of securitization and criminalization. Trust means interacting as a person and not a scientific instrument, making myself vulnerable. People trusted me not only because of shared beliefs (as a Muslim since 2008), geographical location (in the UK since 2013), but because of shared personal struggles, concerns, life situations (migrating to the UK, divorcing, facing rejection, struggling with mental health, healing, and later getting married again), shared workload, and aims (offering my help, asking for help). To paraphrase Muñoz (2016), I didn't choose the field; my networks, my identity, and my journey placed me in the field.

Muslim community spaces are a realm where, coming from a foreign white man in a privileged social position, the formalities of questionnaires, consent forms and other traditional means for data collection break trust, overburden participants (Behar 1996), and ultimately alienate the researcher (Bledsoe et al. 2007; Detamore 2016). It is a work of emotional intelligence and commitment. It also includes brief situations, so quick they are impossible to transcribe; thus, I incorporate material from anecdotes, memories, informal conversations, and encounters of the 'footnote kind' (Weston 1998). Therefore, I work with quotations in a consultative feedback loop process, where anything I put into writing is submitted first to my respondents for them to approve. My ethnography was not only conducted when I had a paid job as a researcher but also when I was jobless and, over two years, homeless. I didn't see sociology as my job; it was my life.

My methods include auto-ethnography, meaning I am 'one of many characters acting in the field' (Lucia and Amritanandamavi 2014), where my personal experiences, field notes, thoughts, emotions, and reactions are data to be critically analysed to extract meaning and contextualizing them to understand broader social, cultural, and political issues (Harding 1987; Ronai 1995; Bochner 2000; Slattery 2001; Spry 2001; Koro-Ljungberg 2004; Dowling 2005; Plummer 2005; Anderson 2006; Hilfrich 2006; Holman Jones and Adams 2016). Just like Behar's (1996) research helped her to process her grief, this research is a formalized and theorized journey for me to understand and process my traumas of displacement, separation, abuse, rejection, and my quest for belonging. My research questions are a co-production with my respondents, trying to solve challenges we share in common, in a push-pull dynamic where the research is a product of the field and the field is shaped by the research in a process of co-construction (Heckert 2016).

I consider all of the participants as repositories of knowledge and experts by experience and practice. They are my teachers and I am their student (Abdul Khabeer 2016). This participatory action-research project is a multi-disciplinary co-creation *with* as opposed to research *on* people (Pain 2004; Blake 2007; Bradley 2007; Cahill et al. 2007; Elwood 2007; Chambers 2008; Reason and Bradbury 2008; Chevalier and Buckles 2013) 'committed to making community' (Dahl 2016, 165), aiming at a transformative social action (Lewin 1946; Freire 1982).

I organized workshops at Rumi's Cave with artists, academics, activists, and community organizers from France, the US, the UK, and Canada for starting conversations sharing our respective strategies for resisting, healing, and eventually flourishing. In the spirit of performance ethnography (Abdul Khabeer 2016), I have used visual sociology as both a research method and an outlet for the findings of this research. I have examined visual production made by others and how they were received, and also have released my own fictions, mini-documentaries, and informative videos on social media, and analysed their reception.[13] The data is not only produced by the subjects but also embodied and enacted by the visual production (Madison 2005; Abdul Khabeer 2016).

This project and its method, however, bear limitations such as sample bias. I cannot be a complete insider: in some circles with a strong ethno-cultural baggage, my French accent, passport, or my parents' Polish origins were enough for some people to close their doors, sometimes brutally. 'Anthropology that doesn't break your heart just isn't worth doing' (Behar 1996, 158). Consequently, despite interviewing people in polar opposition with many community organizers, some may find a lack of tension and disagreements and see it as a shortcoming of insider research. However, truth is not always antagonistic and antagonisms don't always add to the analysis. Second, this research is not replicable. It gives an *instantané* of an ecosystem at specific locations and times, a barometer of where the society is headed. The subjects that once were, are no more, as per the Persian adage: *yeki bud, yeki nabud* (once there was, once there was not). Although history doesn't repeat itself, it rhymes: this work is still relevant for movements which share similar challenges, dynamics, and motivations. Finally, it is not a how-to manual. This work rather maps ideas to serve as an inspiration for future and more adapted tools.

I.4. A Metacolonized Sociologist

I am a child of metacolonialism. My identity, merging both privileges and marginality, has undergone phases of erasure for the sake of validation, by my parents, others, and myself. As ethnography is always subjective (Devereux 1967), I must locate my own position and trajectory for the reader (Constanza-Chock 2020). As I write these words, I am a married white cis heterosexual male occupying a position at a British university, I run two small businesses, own a flat and a car, have no debt, and enjoy a good physiological and mental health in a country with free health care. Since I couldn't have even dreamed of having any of these only a few years ago, I have a responsibility towards those who are in the position I once was. Although I benefit from this location from the systems of whiteness, neoliberalism, patriarchy, ableism, and others, some of my characteristics played to my disadvantage in both my fieldwork and the wider society I navigate.

I am born from Polish parents who fled communism and migrated to France in the 1980s. My mum, who grew up on a small farm in the Świętokrzyskie province in southern Poland, always aspired to study literature but became a supermarket cashier and still is. My dad, born from a construction worker and housewife in the industrial region of Śląsk (Silesia), aspired to become a computer engineer. After a short career, he became long-term unemployed and developed health problems due to alcoholism. While they held to their Polish roots by cooking *kluski śląskie* (potato dumplings) and *gołąbki* (cabbage rolls), decorating the living room with pictures of John Paul II and the *Czarna Matka* (Polish representation of Mary as a Black woman), they gave English names to my sister and I, 'because anywhere you go in the world, people will pronounce your names correctly'. They refused to speak Polish to us, fearing we would be bullied if we had any trace of that accent. They pushed me to become an engineer, as they believed that happiness meant money. I grew up believing what they, and school, taught me: that France was the beacon of civilization, democracy, and human rights, that all Muslims were Arab terrorists, Black people were thieves and that I should marry a blonde German wife with blue eyes because 'Germans work hard'.

They wilfully erased the Polish in us for us to assimilate, for the French 'meritocracy' to work for us. It cost us language, knowledge of history, geography, cooking recipes, family ties, and more. Each election, they would express their fears of the Front National (the main far-right party); they would always tell us that 'if they succeed, they will send us all back to Poland'. My parents were Catholics more by culture and therefore didn't care about my faith until I embraced Islam in 2008, when they felt I was betraying my Polish roots, even though I tried to explain it was more like a software update—and made a documentary about Poland's Muslims settled in the country since the fourteenth century. In 2013, I went through the trauma of an involuntary divorce after five years of a physically and emotionally abusive marriage. Facing the subsequent depression and suicidal thoughts, I migrated to the UK at the same time, without a penny to my name, in debt, in a country where I didn't know a single person and I had no family.

The UK is where, paraphrasing Malcolm X, I was taught to hate myself. My skin colour, my education, and my French accent had people thinking I would find it easy in the UK, especially in the 'Muslim community'. However, when I applied for jobs with Muslim charities or when I was looking for someone to get married to, I would get systematic rejections because I had the wrong passport, the wrong parents, I was too practising, I had a beard, I didn't wear designer clothes, I was too quiet, and most importantly, I was 'the wrong kind of doctor'. When I looked at the men who would get the jobs I applied for, and marry the women who rejected me, I wanted to embrace the traits they all had in common: the arrogance, the loudness, the egoism. I contemplated shaving my beard, stopping praying, starting smoking shisha, taking out loans so I could buy the designer clothes they were wearing or the German saloons they were driving. Despite my PhD, I couldn't find work, became homeless, and squatted in a derelict house in London for two years, eventually working as a waiter in restaurants and markets. I hated myself, and felt guilty about my invalid identity. I was in a situation where I would have sold my soul, my faith, and my core principles to get a glimpse of acceptance.

Thankfully, I came across wonderful people who like me, didn't tick the right boxes and accepted me as I was. I realized that I was not an anomaly per se—only relatively to certain circles. They, and this work of research, helped me understand that it wasn't my fault; I was a victim of the victims of a mental prison system; and unlike my parents did, or the workplaces and people who rejected me, the way out was not to conform but to navigate.

I.5. Overview of the Book

Chapter 1, 'Hair straighteners', begins with exploring whiteness as a spectrum which is not solely defined by skin colour. A reference to the symbolic tool for European beauty standards, the chapter draws an inventory of other physical and metaphorical tools with which colonial powers assert their domination. Focusing on these tools of control, chapter 2 explores how government strategies are evolving from the criminalization of Muslims towards socially engineering a new Muslim elite, and what motivates those who collaborate with oppressive structures in the name of 'representation'. On the other end of the spectrum of conformation to dominant structures, chapter 3 focuses on Muslims joining the alt-right, the Muslim manosphere, those advocating misogynistic and anti-Black narratives or white-Muslim-only spaces. I explore their grievances and attempt to see them as hurting 'comrades in struggle', which leads me to dig deeper into individual and collective trauma in chapter 4. This chapter focuses on the growing number of faith- and culture-based mental health initiatives for helping Muslims to make sense of their pain and eventually heal. Many Muslims increasingly connect healing with a growing concern about the protection of the environment and their responsibility of stewardship (*khilafa*) towards society, which is the subject of chapter 5. More than a way to reconnect to their faith and roots, the relationship between Islam and nature also serves as a detoxification (read decolonization) of the mind. Decolonization supposes reflecting on the past to build a brighter future. Chapter 6 thus sheds light on initiatives testing institutions and documenting British Muslim history. Through archival work or guided tours on red double-deckers, they excavate local stories and organize film clubs to uncover the work of previous generations. This chapter also covers the breakdown of the British Muslim *ummah* (community) and examines whether a 'British Islam' is possible. Chapter 7 is about the emerging Euro-American Muslim art scene, with collectives and artists using visual arts and culture, whether it is through Islamic pop-art or community open-mics, as a form of expression for their spirituality, and ways to subvert and contest dominant structures. The chapter also explores the world of social media 'influencers', the commodification of religion and 'humanitarian' charities converted into colonial missionary business ventures. However, places of hope exist. Chapter 8 refers to nurturing spaces displaying unconventional methods of community organizing and governance by consultation and consensus, and their strategies of survival despite a lack of resources that exemplifies the movement for Islamic decoloniality amongst Muslims in the Wild White West. However, first I needed to understand the implications and ramifications of the white-dominated hegemonies in Euro-American Muslim communities in which I have been immersed for the past sixteen years.

Notes

1. Ministry of Foreign Affairs of Bangladesh, 'Bangladesh's position on the report of revoking Ms Shamima Begum's citizenship by the British Government in connection with her involvement in ISIS in Syria' (14 February 2019). https://web.archive.org/web/20190514004618/https://mofa.gov.bd/site/press_release/a5530623-ad80-4996-b0b4-f60f39927005
2. 'Text of the 1954 Convention Relating to the Status of Stateless Persons', UNHCR, accessed 1 February 2024.
3. Frances Webber, *Citizenship: From Right to Privilege* (London: Institute of Race Relations 2022).
4. Esther Addley, 'Shamima Begum: decision risks "creating second class of citizenship"', *The Guardian*, 22 February 2019. https://web.archive.org/web/20190222214206/https://www.theguardian.com/politics/2019/feb/22/shamima-begum-decision-risks-creating-second-class-of-citizenship
5. Roaring 20s Radio [Twitter] (2019). https://archive.is/5HiNM
6. 2021 Census. Office for National Statistics, accessed 1 February 2024. https://www.ons.gov.uk/census
7. Ruth Gledhill, 'Muslims 'are Britain's top charity givers', *The Times*, 20 July 2013. https://web.archive.org/web/20170419100834/https://www.thetimes.co.uk/article/muslims-are-britains-top-charity-givers-c7w0mrzzknf
8. Jenna Pudelek, 'UK Muslims expected to raise more than £100m for charity during Ramadan', *Third Sector*, 9 July 2013. https://web.archive.org/web/20180802092916/https://www.thirdsector.co.uk/uk-muslims-expected-raise-100m-charity-during-ramadan/fundraising/article/1189642
9. 'Britain's top 1,000 charities ranked by donations. Who raises the most money?', *The Guardian*, 24 April 2012. https://web.archive.org/web/20130826215719/https://www.theguardian.com/news/datablog/2012/apr/24/top-1000-charities-donations-britain
10. Abdulrazaq, Tallha. 'Hamza Yusuf is no brother to the Muslim Brotherhood', *Middle East Monitor*, 9 January 2017. https://web.archive.org/web/20170110034436/https://www.middleeastmonitor.com/20170109-hamza-yusuf-is-no-brother-to-the-muslim-brotherhood; Maha Hilal, 'It's time for Muslim Americans to condemn Hamza Yusuf', *AlJazeera*, 15 July 2019. https://web.archive.org/web/20190715205738/https://www.aljazeera.com/indepth/opinion/time-muslim-americans-condemn-hamza-yusuf-190715130254222.html
11. 'Religious landscape study', Pew Research Center, 2007–14, accessed 1 February 2024. https://www.pewresearch.org/religion/religious-landscape-study/#religions; Dalia Mogahed and Youssef Chouhoud, 'American Muslim Poll 2017: Muslims at the crossroads' (Dearborn: Institute For Social Policy And Understanding 2017); Jennifer Holleis, 'Middle East: are people losing their religion?', *Deutsche Welle*, 2 April 2021. https://web.archive.org/web/20210204124859/https://www.dw.com/en/middle-east-are-people-losing-their-religion/a-56442163; Peter Kenyon, 'Turks examine their Muslim devotion after poll says faith could be waning', *NPR*, 11 February 2019. https://web.archive.org/web/20190211165811/https://www.npr.org/2019/02/11/692025584/turks-examine-their-muslim-devotion-after-poll-says-faith-could-be-waning; 'U.S. Muslims concerned about their place in society, but continue to believe in the American dream', Pew Research Center. 26 July 2017. https://web.archive.org/web/20220428165106/https://www.pewr

esearch.org/religion/2017/07/26/religious-beliefs-and-practices/#many-muslims-attend-mosque-weekly-but-most-say-they-pursue-spiritual-life-mainly-outside-the-mosque
12. 'Project Hunter: the UK programme exporting its border abroad', Privacy International, 9 April 2019. https://web.archive.org/web/20191030032936/https://privacyinternational.org/longread/2780/project-hunter-uk-programme-exporting-its-border-abroad; 'Countering the root causes of violent extremism undermining growth and stability in China's Xinjiang Region by sharing UK best practice', Development Tracker, 29 September 2020. https://web.archive.org/web/20200929200036/https://devtracker.fcdo.gov.uk/projects/GB-GOV-3-PAP-CNF-002340
13. William Barylo, Video Series with the Muslim Vibe. https://web.archive.org/web/20240216092114/https://mne.williambarylo.com

References

Abdul Khabeer, Su'ad. 2016. *Muslim Cool: Race, Religion and Hip Hop in the United States*. New York: New York University Press.
Adler, Richard and Judy Goggin. 2005. 'What do we mean by "civic engagement?"' *Journal of Transformative Education* 3(3), 236–53.
Ahmad, Fauzia. 2012. '"Growing up under lockdown" or "educational pioneers"? Challenging stereotypes of British Muslim women in education.' In *Muslim Youth: Challenges, Opportunities and Expectations*, edited by Fauzia Ahmad and Mohammed S. Seddon. London: Continuum, 119–43.
Ahmed, Sara. 2014. *The Cultural Politics of Emotion*. Edinburgh: Edinburgh University Press.
Alcoff, Linda. M. 2007. 'Mignolo's epistemology of coloniality.' *The New Centennial Review* 7(3), 79–101.
Ali, Syed Mustafa. 2019. 'White crisis and/as existential risk, or the entangled apocalypticism of artificial intelligence.' *Zygon* 54, 207–24.
Anderson, Leon. 2006. 'Analytic autoethnography.' *Journal of Contemporary Ethnography* 35(4), 373–95.
Anzaldúa, Gloria. 1987. *Borderlands/La Frontera: The New Mestiza*. San Francisco: Lute Books.
Asad, Talal. 2003. *Formations of the Secular: Christianity, Islam, Modernity*. Stanford: Stanford University Press.
Barylo, William. 2016. 'Neo-liberal not-for-profits: the embracing of corporate culture in European Muslim charities.' *Journal of Muslim Minority Affairs* 36(3), 383–98.
Barylo, William. 2017a. *Young Muslim Change-Makers*. London: Routledge.
Barylo, William. 2017b. 'Islam as a matrix: young Muslim volunteers blurring the lines between mundane and sacred.' *Method and Theory in the Study of Religion* 29(2), 181–204.
Behar, Ruth. 1996. *The Vulnerable Observer: Anthropology that Breaks Your Heart*. Boston: Beacon Press.
Benjamin, Ruha. 2020. *Viral Justice: How We Grow the World We Want*. Princeton: Princeton University Press.
Bhabha, Homi. 1994. *The Location of Culture*. London: Routledge.
Bhambra, Gurminder K. 2014. 'Postcolonial and decolonial dialogues.' *Postcolonial Studies* 17(2), 115–21.
Birt, Yahya. 2022. *Ummah at the Margins: The Past, Present and Future of Muslim Minorities*. London: Ayaan Centre.
Blake, Megan. 2007. 'Formality and friendship: research ethics and review and participatory action research.' *ACME: An International E-Journal for Critical Geographies* 6(3), 411–21.
Bledsoe, Caroline, Bruce Sherin, Adam Galinsky, et al. 2007. 'Regulating creativity: research and survival in the iron cage.' *Northwestern University Law Review* 101(2), 593–642.
Blühdorn, Ingolfur. 2006. 'Self-experience in the theme park of radical action? Social movements and political articulation in the late-modern condition.' *European Journal of Social Theory* 9(1), 23–42.
Bochner, Arthur. 2000. 'Criteria against ourselves.' *Qualitative Inquiry* 6(2), 266–72.

Boubekeur, Amel. 2005. 'Cool competitive Muslim culture in the West.' *ISIM Review* 16, 12–13.
Bradley, Matt. 2007. 'Silenced for the own protection: how the marginalizes those it feigns to protect.' *ACME: An International E-Journal for Critical Geographies* 6(3), 340–9.
Bulhan, Husein. A. 2008. *Politics of Cain—One Hundred Years of Crises in Somali Politics and Society.* Bethesda: Tayosan International Publishing.
Bulhan, Hussein A. 2015. 'Stages of colonialism in Africa: from occupation of land to occupation of being.' *Journal of Social and Political Psychology* 3(1), 239–56.
Cahill, Caitlin, Farhana Sultana, and Rachel Pain. 2007. 'Participatory ethics: politics, practices, institutions.' *ACME: An International E-Journal for Critical Geographies* 6(3), 304–18.
Caillé, Alain. 2009. *Théorie Anti-Utilitariste de l'Action et du Sujet.* Paris: La Découverte.
Caputo, Virginia. 2000. *Constructing the Field: Ethnographic Fieldwork in the Contemporary World.* New York: Routledge.
Chambers, Robert. 2008. 'PRA, PLA and pluralism: practice and theory.' In *The Sage Handbook of Action Research: Participative Inquiry and Practice*, edited by Peter Reason and Hilary Bradbury. London: Sage, 297–318.
Chanial, Philippe. 2003. 'La culture primaire de la démocratie : Communautés locales, publics démocratiques et associations.' In *Les Sens du public. Publics politiques, publics médiatiques*, edited by Daniel Cefaï and Dominique Pasquier. Paris: Presses Universitaires de France, 269–89.
Chanial, Philippe. 2011. *La sociologie comme philosophie politique et réciproquement.* Paris: La Découverte.
Chevalier, Jacques and Daniel Buckles. 2013. *Participatory Action Research: Theory and Methods for Engaged Inquiry.* London: Routledge.
Cloke, Paul, Justin Beaumont, and Andrew Williams. 2013. *Working Faith: Faith-based Organisations and Urban Social Justice.* Milton Keynes: Paternoster.
Connelly, Michael and D. Jean Clandinin. 2006. 'Narrative inquiry.' In *Handbook of Complementary Methods in Education Research*, edited by Judith L. Green, Gregory Camilli, and Patricia Elmore. Mahwah: Lawrence Erlbaum, 447–87.
Connors Jackman, Michael. 2016. 'The trouble with fieldwork: queering methodologies.' In *Queer Methods and Methodologies: Intersecting Queer Theories and Social Science Research*, edited by Kath Browne and Catherine J. Nash. New York: Routledge, 113–29.
Constanza-Chock, Sasha. 2020. *Design Justice: Community-led Practices to Build the Worlds We Need.* Cambridge: MIT Press.
Cope, Jason. 2005. 'Researching entrepreneurship through phenomenological inquiry: philosophical and methodological issues.' *International Small Business Journal* 23(2), 163–89.
Dahl, Ulrika. 2016. 'Femme on femme: reflections on collaborative methods and queer femmeinist ethnography.' In *Queer Methods and Methodologies: Intersecting Queer Theories and Social Science Research*, edited by Kath Browne and Catherine J. Nash. New York: Routledge, 143–67.
Detamore, Mathias. 2016. 'Queer(y)ing the ethics of research methods: toward a politics of intimacy in researcher/researched relations.' In *Queer Methods and Methodologies: Intersecting Queer Theories and Social Science Research*, edited by Kath Browne and Catherine J. Nash. New York: Routledge, 167–83.
Devereux, George. 1967. *From Anxiety to Method in the Behavioral Sciences.* The Hague: De Gruyter Mouton.
D'Ignazio, Catherine and Lauren F. Klein. 2023. *Data Feminism.* Cambridge: MIT Press.
Dowling, Robyn. 2005. 'Power, subjectivity, and ethics in qualitative research.' In *Qualitative Research Methods in Human Geography*, edited by I. Hay. South Melbourne: Oxford University Press, 19–29.
Dubet, François. 1994. *Sociologie de l'expérience.* Paris: Seuil.
Dussel, Enrique. 1985 [1977]. *Philosophy of Liberation.* New York: Orbis.
Dussel, Enrique. 1996. 'Modernity, Eurocentrism, and trans-modernity: in dialogue with Charles Taylor.' In *The Underside of Modernity: Apel, Ricoeur, Rorty, Taylor, and the Philosophy of Liberation*, edited by Eduardo Mendieta. Atlantic Highlands: Humanities Press, 129–59.

Elwood, Sarah. 2007. 'Negotiating participatory ethics in the midst of institutional ethics.' *ACME: An International E-Journal for Critical Geographies* 6(3), 329–38.

Fadil, Nadia. 2006. 'We should be walking Qurans: the making of an Islamic political subject.' In *Politics of Visibility. Young Muslims in European Public Spaces*, edited by Gerdien Jonker and Valérie Amiraux. Bielefeld: Transcript Verlag, 53–78.

Fanon, Franz. 1967 [1952]. *Black Skin, White Masks*. New York: Grove Press.

Feixa, Carles, Inês Pereira, and Jeffrey Juris. 2009. 'Global citizenship and the "new, new" social movements Iberian connections.' *Young* 17(4), 421–42.

Foucault, Michel. 1971 [1966]. *The Order of Things*. New York: Vintage Books.

Freire, Paulo. 1982. 'Creating alternative research methods. Learning to do it by doing it.' In *Creating Knowledge: A Monopoly*, edited by Budd Hall, Arthur Gillette, and Rajesh Tandon. New Delhi: Society for Participatory Research in Asia, 29–37.

Freire, Paulo. 1993 [1968]. *The Pedagogy of the Oppressed*. New York: Continuum.

Grosfoguel, Ramon. 2011. 'Decolonizing post-colonial studies and paradigms of political-economy: transmodernity, decolonial thinking, and global coloniality.' *Journal of Peripheral Cultural Production of the Luso-Hispanic World* 1(1), 1–37.

Haenni, Patrick. 2005. *L'islam de marché: l'autre révolution conservatrice*. Paris: Seuil.

Harding, Sandra. 1987. *Feminism and Methodology*. Bloomington: Indiana University Press.

Harris, Anita, and Joshua Roose. 2014. 'DIY citizenship amongst young Muslims: experiences of the "Ordinary".' *Journal of Youth Studies* 17(6), 794–813.

Harris, Cheryl. 1995. 'Whiteness as property.' In *Critical Race Theory: The Key Writings that Formed the Movement*, edited by Kimberlé Crenshaw, Neil Gotanda, Kendall Thomas, et al. New York: The New Press, 276–91.

Heckert, Jamie. 2016. 'Queer experiences of social research.' In *Queer Methods and Methodologies: Intersecting Queer Theories and Social Science Research*, edited by Kath Browne and Catherine J. Nash. New York: Routledge, 41–55.

Herding, Maruta. 2013. *Inventing the Muslim Cool: Islamic Youth Culture in Western Europe*. Bielefeld: Transcript-Verlag.

Hilfrich, Carola. 2006. '"The self is a people": autoethnographic poetics in Hélène Cixous's fictions.' *New Literary History* 37(1), 217–35.

Hill Collins, Patricia. 2008. *Black Feminist Thought: Knowledge, Consciousness, and the Politics of Empowerment*. New York: Routledge.

Hodgson, Marshall G. S. 1977. *The Venture of Islam (Vol. 1): The Classical Age of Islam*. Chicago: University of Chicago Press.

Holman Jones, Stacy and Tony E. Adams. 2016. 'Autoethnography is a queer method.' In *Queer Methods and Methodologies: Intersecting Queer Theories and Social Science Research*, edited by Kath Browne and Catherine J. Nash. New York: Routledge, 195–215.

Hoskins, Bryony and Massimiliano Mascherini. 2009. 'Measuring active citizenship through the development of a composite indicator.' *Social Indicators Research* 90(3), 459–88.

Husserl, E. 1982 [1960]. *Cartesian Mediations: An Introduction to Phenomenology*. The Hague: Martinus Nijhoff.

Illich, Ivan. 1973. *Tools for Conviviality*. New York: Harper & Row.

Iqbal, Siema. 2019. [Twitter] 19 February. https://web.archive.org/web/20220801201316/https://twitter.com/siemaiqbal/status/1097967526062051329

Janmohammed, Shelina. 2016. *Generation M*. London: IB Tauris.

Jenkins, Richard. 2014. *Social Identity* (4th ed.). London: Routledge.

Josselson, Ruthellen. 2011. 'Narrative research: constructing, deconstructing, and reconstructing story.' In *Five Ways of Doing Qualitative Analysis*, edited by F. J. Wertz, K. Charmaz, L. M. McMullen, R. Josselon, R. Anderson, and E. McSpadden. New York: Guilford Press, 224–42.

Keck, Margaret. E. and Kathryn Sikkink. 2014. *Activists beyond Borders: Advocacy Networks in International Politics*. Ithaca: Cornell University.

Kennelly, Jacqueline. 2011. *Citizen Youth: Culture, Activism, and Agency in a Neoliberal Era*. Basingstoke: Palgrave Macmillan.

King, C. Richard (ed.) 2001. *Postcolonial America*. Urbana: University of Illinois Press.

Koro-ljungberg, Mirka. 2004. 'Impossibilities of reconciliation: validity in mixed theory projects.' *Qualitative Inquiry* 10(4), 601–21.
Langman, Lauren. 2013. 'Occupy: a new new social movement.' *Current Sociology* 61(4), 510–24.
Lean, Natahan. 2012. *The Islamophobia Industry: How the Right Manufactures Fear of Muslims*. London: Pluto Books.
Lewin, Kurt. 1946. 'Action research and minority problems.' *Journal of Sociological Issues* 2(4), 34–46.
Lewis, Phillip and Sadek Hamid. 2018. *British Muslims: New Directions in Islamic Thought; Creativity and Activism*. Edinburgh: Edinburgh University Press.
Limón, José E. 1994. *Dancing with the Devil: Society and Cultural Poetics in Mexican-American South Texas*. Madison: University of Wisconsin Press.
Lucia, Amanda J. and Mata Amritanandamayi. 2014. *Reflections of Amma: Devotees in a Global Embrace*. Berkeley: University of California Press.
Lloyd, Vincent. 2013. 'Race and religion: contribution to symposium on critical approaches to the study of religion.' *Critical Research on Religion* 1(1), 80–6.
Lugones, María. 2007. 'Heterosexualism and the colonial/modern gender system.' *Hypatia* 22(1), 186–209.
Madison, Soyini, D. 2005. *Critical Ethnography: Method, Ethics and Performance*. Thousand Oaks: Sage.
Mahmood, Saba. 2004. *Politics of Piety: The Islamic Revival and the Feminist Subject*. Princeton: Princeton University Press.
Mandair, Arvind-Pal. 2009. *Religion and the Specter of the West: Sikhism, India, Postcoloniality and the Politics of Translation*. New York: Columbia University Press.
Maldonado-Torres, Nelson. 2010. 'On the coloniality of being: contributions to the development of a concept.' In *Globalization and The Decolonial Option*, edited by Walter D. Mignolo and Arturo Escobar. London: Routledge, 94–124.
Mauss, Marcel. 2007 [1924]. *Essai sur le don*. Paris: Presses Universitaires France.
McClintock, Anne. 1992. 'The angel of progress: pitfalls of the term "post-colonialism".' *Social Text* 31(32), 84–98.
McDonald, Kevin. 2006. *Global Movements: Action and Culture*. Hoboken: Wiley.
Memmi, Albert. 1965 [1957]. *The Colonizer and the Colonized*. Boston: Beacon Press.
Meyer, David S. and Sidney. G. Tarrow. 1998. *The Social Movement Society: Contentious Politics for a New Century*. Lanham: Rowman & Littlefield.
Mignolo, Walter D. 2000. *Local Histories/Global Designs: Coloniality, Subaltern Knowledges, and Border Thinking*. Princeton: Princeton University Press.
Mignolo, Walter D. 2007. 'DELINKING.' *Cultural Studies* 21(2–3), 449–514.
Mignolo, Walter D. 2010. 'Introduction: coloniality of power and decolonial thinking.' In *Globalization and the Decolonial Option*, edited by Walter D. Mignolo and Arturo Escobar. London: Routledge, 1–21.
Mohammed, Jahangir and Beatrice Bianchi. 2023. *Aiding the Ummah: Analysing the Muslim Humanitarian Charity Sector in the UK*. London: Ayaan Institute.
Moreton-Robinson, Aileen. 2015. *The White Possessive: Property, Power, and Indigenous Sovereignty*. Minneapolis: University of Minnesota Press.
Morin, Edgar. 1977. *La Méthode: La nature de la Nature*. Paris: Seuil.
Morin, Edgar. 1986. *La Méthode: La vie de la Vie*. Paris: Seuil.
Morrison, Toni. 2016. 'Making America white again.' *The New Yorker*, 21 November. https://web.archive.org/web/20161117155227/https://www.newyorker.com/magazine/2016/11/21/making-america-white-again
Mouffe, Chantal. 1992. *Dimensions of Radical Democracy: Pluralism, Citizenship, Community*. London: Verso.
Muñoz, Lorena. 2016. 'Brown, queer and gendered: queering the latina/o "street-scapes".' In *Queer Methods and Methodologies: Intersecting Queer Theories and Social Science Research*, edited by Kath Browne and Catherine J. Nash. New York: Routledge, 55–69.

Nilan, Pam. 2017. *Muslim Youth in the Diaspora: Challenging Extremism through Popular Culture*. London: Routledge.
Nkrumah, Kwame. 1965. *Neocolonialism: The Latest Stage of Colonialism*. New York: Routledge.
O'Brien, John 2017. *Keeping It Halal: The Everyday Lives of Muslim American Teenage Boys*. Princeton: Princeton University Press.
O'Toole, Therese and Richard Gale. 2010. 'Contemporary grammars of political action among ethnic minority young activists.' *Ethnic and Racial Studies* 33(1), 126–43.
Oskooii, Kassra and Karam Dana. 2018. 'Muslims in Great Britain: the impact of mosque attendance on political behaviour and civic engagement.' *Journal of Ethnic and Migration Studies* 44(9), 1479–505.
Pain, Rachel. 2004. 'Social geography: participatory research.' *Progress in Human Geography* 28(5), 652–63.
Parenti, Michael. 1995. *Against Empire*. San Francisco: City Lights Books.
Pędziwiatr, Konrad. 2010. *The New Muslim Elites in European Cities: Religion and Active Social Citizenship amongst Young Organized Muslims in Brussels and London*. Saarbrücken: VDM Verlag.
Peucker, Mario and Shahram Akbarzadeh. 2014. *Muslim Active Citizenship in the West*. Oxon and New York: Routledge.
Peucker, Mario and Rauf Ceylan. 2016. 'Muslim community organizations: sites of active citizenship or self-segregation?' *Ethnic and Racial Studies* 40(14), 2405–25.
Peucker, Mario. 2018. 'On the (in)compatibility of Islamic religiosity and citizenship in Western democracies: the role of religion for Muslims' civic and political engagement.' *Politics and Religion* 11(3), 553–75.
Plummer, Ken. 2005. 'Critical humanism and queer theory: living with the tensions.' In *The Landscape of Qualitative Research: Theories and Issues*, edited by N. Denzin and Y. Lincoln. Thousand Oaks: Sage, 357–73.
Qasim, Mohammed. 2018. *Young, Muslim and Criminal: Experiences, Identities and Pathways into Crime*. Bristol: Policy Press.
Quijano, Anibal. 2000. 'Coloniality of power, Eurocentrism, and Latin America.' *Nepantla: Views from South* 1(3), 533–80.
Quijano, Anibal. 2007. 'Coloniality and modernity/rationality.' *Cultural Studies* 21(2–3), 168–78.
Ramadan, Tariq. 1999. *To Be a European Muslim*. Leicester: The Islamic Foundation.
Ramadan, Tariq. 2008. *Islam, la réforme radicale: Ethique et libération*. Paris: Presses du Châtelet.
Reason, Paul and Hilary Bradbury (eds). 2008. *The Sage Handbook of Action Research: Participative Inquiry and Practice*. Newbury Park: Sage.
Ronai, Carol R. 1995. 'Multiple reflections of child sex abuse.' *Journal of Contemporary Ethnography* 23(4), 395–426.
Roose, Joshua and Anita Harris. 2015. 'Muslim citizenship in everyday Australian civic spaces.' *Journal of Intercultural Studies* 36(4), 468–86.
Said, Edward. 1984. *The World, the Text and the Critic*. Cambridge: Harvard University Press.
San Juan Jr., Epifanio. 1998. *Beyond Postcolonial Theory*. New York: St. Martin's Press.
Sayyid, Salman. 2014. *Recalling the Caliphate: Decolonisation and World Order*. London: Hurst.
Shirazi, Faegheh. 2016. *Brand Islam: The Marketing and Commodification of Piety*. Austin: University of Texas Press.
Slattery, Patrick. 2001. 'The educational researcher as artist working within.' *Qualitative Inquiry* 7(3), 370–98.
Soja, Edward W. 1996. *Thirdspace*. Malden: Blackwell.
Soliman, Asmaa. 2017. *European Muslims Transforming the Public Sphere: Religious Participation in the Arts, Media and Civil Society*. London: Routledge.
Spivak, Gayatri C. 1988. 'Can the subaltern speak?' In *Marxism and the Interpretation of Culture*, edited by Cary Nelson and Larry Grossberg. Chicago: University of Illinois Press, 271–313.
Spry, Tami. 2001. 'Performing autoethnography: an embodied methodological praxis.' *Qualitative Inquiry* 7(6), 706–32.

Vergani, Matteo, Amelia Johns, Michelle Lobo, et al. 2017. 'Examining Islamic religiosity and civic engagement in Melbourne.' *Journal of Sociology* 53(1), 63–78.
Weston, Kath. 1998. *Long Slow Burn: Sexuality and Social Science*. London: Routledge.
Wieviorka, Michel. 2005. 'After new social movements.' *Social Movement Studies* 4(1), 1–19.
Williams, Patricia J. 1991. *The Alchemy of Race and Rights*. Cambridge: Harvard University Press.
Younis, Tarek and Ghayda Hassan. 2018. 'Second-generation Western Muslims: a qualitative analysis of multiple social identities.' *Transcultural Psychiatry* 56(6), 1155–69.

1
Hair Straighteners

MEHDI: I don't see whiteness as literal whiteness. Like with Spanish white [Muslim] converts for example, the way they chat to me, I always see there's a difference between them . . . and English white converts . . . I used to work with Romanians, Polish people . . . The interactions I had with them were different from those I have with Tom or Wayne who are English, as if they were not white.

JAVAYRIA (Nodding at Mehdi): my colleague Irena who's Ukrainian, in my head she's not white. White Polish people who come here, are seen in a different way than white Polish people in Poland. They don't have the cultural, social capital a southern English white man or woman will have. There's at gradation, 'white' doesn't work all the time.

MEHDI: True, some people don't mind Asians, there are fine with having Asian neighbours, but not Romanian neighbours. It's like they say: 'you haven't stayed long enough, you haven't contributed enough to earn your right to be here', and contribution is linked to neoliberalism.

JAVAYRIA: Superficially you benefit, but as soon as they know you're Polish and Muslim, will they give you a job? But I would argue, on the other end, even Asians can benefit from white supremacy. Even some Asians try to become white.

MEHDI: True. I have a colleague, his name is Ali, and at work, you have his white colleagues, they've asked him: 'can we start calling you Alistair?' He confronted the guy about it—he then refers to his second name but again anglicising it. At work, you have to adapt and it can lead you to become manipulative—not in a wrong way, I would never use it to hurt anyone—but I have a white middle class colleague at work and I have to be extra nice, do extra smiling for him not to be offended. Because when it's a white colleague joking with him, it's fine, but if I make a joke, he always takes it personally. So, you have to change your behaviour. I'm scared that this could make me conform and lose my identity.

JAVAYRIA: Conformity is safety. No one wants to be left outside. For them, you're never good enough. You need to behave in such a way, dress a certain way to be human. When I think of all these YouTubers, these politicians . . .

MEHDI (Interrupts Javayria): These coconuts!

JAVAYRIA: I feel sad, I pity them, that they had to go through so much pain that they are doing these things. People don't make me feel human. I wish there was a space for being human...

MEHDI: I am sick of being in servitude to white people—and the point about having to code switch, getting called nicknames, dressing and behaving in a certain way is because we fall into the old colonial trap of master and servant. We always want to please, not upset, keep the peace and not rock the boat. How sad. Sorry another trailing off rant.

Mehdi and Javayria's conversation triggered so many questions in my mind. For them, whiteness is a spectrum with a hierarchy of validity. As a white researcher, is my whiteness complicated because of my Polish parents? Second, how and why do ethnically minoritized actually aspire at being white?

Mehdi and Javayria are both friends in their early thirties, volunteering for the same Muslim grass-roots organization in London, working on questions of racism and Islamophobia. I met Javayria through common friends and she introduced me to Mehdi when we started volunteering for his organization three years ago. We are now married. We were having a conversation at mine around some home-baked pizza where we exchanged reflections about race and class dynamics at work, three years after the Brexit referendum. Mehdi works for a trade union and Javayria works in higher education. Their workplaces are predominantly staffed with English white middle-class people. Before the Brexit vote, a huge amount of campaigning revolved around the slogan 'taking back our borders', which numerous anti-racist campaigners saw directed towards ethnically minoritized people and Eastern-European workers.

Both observe that being valid as a brown person in white-dominated spaces is subject to a performance which can include adopting nicknames, changing one's behaviour or adapting one's looks in order to keep relations peaceful. Mehdi describes those who push this performance too far as 'coconuts', a derogatory term like 'Oreo' or 'Magnum', because of their white inside surrounded by a brown outside. These are used by and for ethnically minoritized people to describe the performance of whiteness. Other terms such as *deriyaon* (deniers) are used for people from humble backgrounds turning their back on their culture, faith and the struggle of migration, or *sepoy*, referring to the Indian soldiers serving the British Raj. In a later text conversation with Mehdi, he also mentions that:

> Coconut is a term that has been used against brown people who are seen to be different, for example... LGBT Muslims... who have had other South Asians bully or target them for not being brown enough... The kind of coconut I am talking about here—are the people who strip their identity for success/profit... who take positions of power but never really help change the structures at the top... who

never open up those spaces for other brown people . . . they want to be the only uncle tom—in total servitude to the white man.

This is how community organizers would describe Sajid Javid, Priti Patel, or Suella Braverman for their support of racist policies, despite themselves being children of immigrants. Many see in this support a denial of their non-white origins and an aspiration at or embracing white supremacy. However, as Mehdi states, these terms have complex and different usages alluding to compromises with both culture and power. Since metacolonialism is located in the twilight zone between oppressed and oppressor, where do the boundaries lie between abandoning one's culture and actively feeding systems of injustice?

1.1. De-diasporization, WesTernization, and Metacolonization

When Javayria gets ready to go to work, she uses a hair straightener. She plugs the tool in, commenting cynically: 'colonial tool of power . . . This is how they want us to look like.' Although she often goes to her parents' house wearing *shalwar kameez* (South Asian attire), in which she feels more 'like [her]self', she comments about her dark-coloured corporate clothes: 'I grew up feeling very insecure. The reason for choosing these clothes is because I want to blend in, I don't want anyone to notice me or to say anything about me . . . I've understood I need to mimic them to stay there. So I just mimic them to get my paycheck. I turn it on and off.' *Professionalism* is an unspoken rule about putting forth an 'appropriate' workplace identity for members of minorities (Gulati and Carbado 2000; Evetts 2014) which reinforces racial, social, and gender hierarchies by giving managers the right to police behaviours, looks, and discourses.

Javayria is conscious that the society she lives in expects her to dress and look a certain way at work, and in counterpart, expects her to give up her curly hair. Her brother-in-law, a senior civil servant in his forties, decided to avoid tensions at work by not completely shaving his hair as part of the rituals of *umrah* (minor pilgrimage), thus invalidating it out of fear: 'I didn't complete my *umrah*. I didn't shave it to the bone. I couldn't go to work like this. Some people at work would have got scared.' Javayria's brother on the other hand, now a social worker in his thirties living in Surrey, was bullied in childhood by other Muslims shaming him for going to the mosque. My respondents relate similar experiences, like Tayyibah: 'you're trained to blend, you're told at school subtly. Our parents told us: "go out with the jeans, not with your *shalwar kameez*, it's for home." It's how you're trained.' However, Javayria's younger cousins, now at university, would happily adopt trainers and skinny jeans not because of pressures but because they felt comfortable in. To what extent does each scenario reflect a play or compromise with their roots?

Literature around cultural dynamics within diasporas (people dispersed from their original lands), has been revolving around two major concepts: de-diasporization and westernization. Werbner (2009) conceptualizes the 'segmented' South Asian diasporas as people, who share similar 'vernacular tastes, cuisines, music, sport, poetry, fashion and film but also diverge in other contexts, such as religion' (Werbner 2009, 114). Islam adds a layer of complexity: although Muslims share no common homeland, they have a shared orientation (*qiblah*) towards Makkah, a shared faith, scripture, prophets (Birt 2022, 9), a sense of belonging to a global *ummah* (community) as a 'transnational Islamic homeland' (Sayyid 2010, 129–46; Mandaville 2001), sharing a common spiritual capital in the form of meanings, values, purposes, and motivations (Zohar and Marshall 2000) (see chapter 6.2). Although my respondents identify as belonging to the 'Muslim diaspora', there can be tensions between various communities and ethnicities—like the issue of anti-Blackness. Diasporas across the globe do not hold to their heritage in similar ways. Javayria, after a trip to Suriname, comparing the retention of Hindustani language between there (Hassankhan 2013, 2016) and in her family, observed: 'why is it that people in Suriname have been speaking Hindi for eight generations? Why is there in the UK people from the second generation who can't speak Urdu anymore? Is it because there is no white dominant society [in Suriname]?' However, the opposite is also true: Akala (2018) observes how Jamaicans in Jamaica are less into Jamaican culture because they don't feel the need to prove themselves, as opposed to British Jamaicans. Diaspora dynamics also change depending on the host country: while Javayria's parents, born in Pakistan, find British Pakistanis 'cold, arrogant and flashy', they find Spanish Pakistanis 'humble and hospitable'.

Diasporic culture is a site of melancholia (Mishra 2007; Hassankhan 2013; Lallmahomed-Aumeerally 2014), a site of 'impossible mourning' (Derrida 1986, 6). Migration has produced a trans-generational trauma of loss, and diasporic communities are faced with the inability to make up for it, leading to an impoverished sense of self that is compensated by latching onto cultural elements such as cuisine, language, music, and essentialist or romanticized narratives such as the concept of Indianness as depicted in Bollywood movies (Lallmahomed-Aumeerally 2014) or in Pakistani *dramai* (soap operas). This is one reason why a plethora of diasporic artistic, charitable, and business initiatives in Britain are re-appropriating their Asian, African, and Middle Eastern cultures (see chapters 6 and 7). Many Muslims I've encountered also feel nostalgic about romanticized ideas of a twelfth-century Andalusia, often described as 'the Golden Age of Islam' or even towards the early years at the beginning of the Qur'anic Revelation in the seventh century. In some cases, this melancholia can lead some Muslims to isolate themselves in a protectionist move, build an interpretation of Islam disconnected from the contemporary context, and develop an exclusionary discourse (see chapter 3).

De-diasporization occurs when people no longer experience this nostalgia (Mehta 2010) or, for Bal and Sinha-Kherkoff (2007), when people no longer see their parents' or ancestors' country as their homeland. De-diasporization is the loss of elders' generations' distinctive culture, of the Saidian point of origin (Said 1984). This loss occurs partly because of the geographic distance to this point of cultural origin (Lallmahomed-Aumeerally 2014). However, Lallmahomed-Aumeerally's or Hassankhan's works and other analysis of (de-)diasporization are specific to former colonies resulting from the Indian indenture: Mauritius, Suriname, Trinidad, Fiji, and others, where any narrative of sending people 'back home' wouldn't make sense, since both people in power and citizens share a similar history. From that perspective, Javayria's hypothesis of the impact of a white-dominant culture makes sense. In Mauritius or Suriname, no government has ever used the narrative of assimilation nor academics or the media ever questioned the compatibility of Islam or Hinduism with 'Mauritian' or 'Surinamese values'. Lewis and Hamid (2018) also suggest that de-diaporization in a white-dominated society can be explained by the domination of English as a *lingua franca*. In Mauritius, while French and English are official languages, people speak Kreol at home. Same in Suriname, where Dutch is the official administrative language while people of South Asian descent speak *Hindoestani*. The loss of language is a powerful indicator of the coloniality of being since language is not only something humans *have*, but something of what people *are* (Mignolo 2003; Maldonado-Torres 2007). While in Bal and Sinha-Kherkoff's work (2007), Muslims in Mauritius consider themselves Mauritian, the British and French governments have been, since the 1990s, questioning the belonging of Muslims to the country: people are being tribalized as per Modood's post-immigration difference (2012), just like in some countries in the Arab Gulf where the tribe's lineage must figure on identity papers. Paradoxically, conservative policies and hatred discourse against minorities have played an unexpected role in keeping the diaspora 'diasporized'; by reminding them that no matter how hard they try to blend in, they are still 'from somewhere else'.

The romanticization of their parents' culture can lead people to unconsciously replicate cultural stereotypes (casually wearing clothes and accessories reserved only for festivals and weddings) or conform to racial stereotypes such as men organizing belly dancing shows in shisha cafés in London, which Aly (2015) calls ethnonormativity. The desire for self-preservation can lead to ethnosectarianism: when diasporic communities co-exist along others without interacting or mixing (Kasenally 2011) or, when people seek a hypothetical cultural purification, to the loss of parts of their heritage and traditions. Jahangeer-Chojoo (2004) notices how, in the span of a few decades, Muslims in Mauritius stopped welcoming *qawwalis* (South Asian devotional music) and *ghazals* (poems) at weddings and for Eid, as local imams embraced the Wahhabi view, saying that music is forbidden in Islam. At school, while Hindu children usually learn Hindi, Muslim students learn Arabic and not Urdu. Similarly, in the UK, some South Asian Muslims now prefer the Arabic *akhi* for brother instead of *bhai*. Eisenlohr explains that many Muslims have sought to relocate themselves within a

Middle-Eastern qua Arabic imaginary, having appropriated Arabic as their 'ancestral language' (Eisenlohr 2006).

However, younger generations are more inclined to interject elements belonging to their contemporary context (Ali et al. 2006), which some describe as westernization (Gillespie 1995): the adaptation or appropriation of Euro-American cultural codes out of appreciation, with no agenda. Some of my respondents calls overly westernized South Asians *burger bacche* (burger kids). Criticized by the elders' generation, younger ones argue back that acculturation is not assimilation: 'Jeans don't make me "white"' (Preetha 2017). Perhaps what the elders fear is a 'westoxification': 'the fascination with and dependence upon the West to the detriment of traditional, historical, and cultural ties to Islam and Islamic world ... Implies a sense of intoxication or infatuation that impairs rational judgment' (Esposito 2003, 1).

Lewis and Hamid (2018) see these cultural dynamics as a historical process of hybridization which has always been a feature of Muslim societies through history, and a cradle for cultural innovation and creation. Although they describe insiders becoming outsiders, de-diasporization, westernization, westoxification, or Bhabha's (1994) mimicry do not bear the power dynamics and the external forces implied by Bulhan's metacolonialism. Nobody at work has explicitly asked Javayria to give up her look but she would put herself at risk of conflict with her hierarchy and of discrimination from her colleagues. Metacolonization is when the loss and the adaptation come from external pressures to conform and fit in, under the suggestion or the threat of social and economic difficulties. Metacolonialism isn't just about creating a 'white habitus, whites' racial tastes, perceptions, feelings, and emotions and their views on racial matters' (Bonilla-Silva 2010), but rather using them to discriminate and reject, if not harm, those who do not abide by the same norms. For Dustin Craun (2013), it re-joins the crux of coloniality as a form of supremacy—and the will to belong to this supremacy. Metacolonialism is a form of deep acting: 'deceiving oneself as much as deceiving others' (Hochschild 1983, 33).

Where do Javayria's hair straighteners sit? The answer depends on the intentionality of the person using it, their awareness of any external agency and of their cultural and historical context. If we hypothetically reduce Javayria's Muslim Punjabi identity to her hair in an effort of simplification, we would have the following different scenarios:

Westernization: Javayria uses hair straighteners out of taste.
De-diaporization: She can only imagine herself with straight hair.
Westoxification: Javayria is obsessed with straight hair.
Metacolonialism: Javayria is legally allowed not to straighten her hair but if she doesn't, her work colleagues will likely develop animosity. In some instance, she is made to believe that straight hair will liberate her and make her happy; therefore, she urges others to do the same.

During my research, I noticed various kinds of metaphorical hair straighteners. In Bulhan's (2015) work, it is the Eurocentric mental health system. In Fanon's work, it is the French language. They can be economic, disciplinary, cultural, and more.

1.2. Conformity Is Safety

Muneera, a poet, hip-hop artist, and educator from Bristol, in her thirties who I met through Rumi's Cave, recalls how during her school and university years, peer pressures affected her as a Black Muslim woman:

> Loathsome, disgusting, repulsive, dirty, stupid, ugly, prone, to rape, below, unclean, addicted, undeserving of all good and deserving of all negativity. That was the voice that followed me around daily as a child, so it's no wonder in later life I developed complications with my self-worth ... I had already grown a disdain for my body ... It was at this point I had my real first bout of what I now know to be depression. Feelings of worthlessness combined with thoughts of not wanting to exist consumed me. (Williams 2017)

The addition and accumulation of repetitive overt and covert forms of abuse led her to suffer to the point of self-harm. Similar forms of harm hide behind subtle challenges to legal boundaries that are often not clear to decipher. In the case of Mehdi's friend, how harmful is it to suggest jokingly that he adopts the nickname 'Al'? When does *free speech* become racism? How do we draw the line between *cultural appropriation* and *cultural appreciation*? Are these micro-aggressions (or 'subtle act of exclusions' (Jana and Baran 2020)), or is it that people are 'oversensitive'? Is this organization's idea of *professionalism* legitimate or does it deprive its worker of basic human rights? Whether it is through racist comments passed as a joke, the tokenization, the fetishization of the Other (Said 1978), or repeated small violations of personal dignity, metacolonialism eventually manages to create a narrative accepted in the mainstream that can eventually become law.

The challenge with these violations resides in two major facts. First, determining from a legal perspective whether a perceived violation is racist or not depends on the intentions of the perpetrators and their knowledge: was this action intended to harm? Was the perpetrator aware that their action was harmful? Back to Mehdi's friend Ali, surely wanting him to adopt an English nickname is rooted in layers of racist thinking, but what tells us that his colleagues wanted to inflict pain? Second, as intentionality and awareness can be easily masked by the excuse of ignorance, law doesn't consider the structural power that class, gender or race can have. Even if it didn't inflict pain, Mehdi recognized this seemingly innocent joke was perpetuating a system of thinking that diminishes the identity of ethnically minoritized people by negating their right to be called by their name. However, exposing these acts as racist aggressions is only possible if the law considers a system, the framework, matrix, or ecosystem that has permitted the legitimization of doing harm to others. But then comes a paradox: how is it possible to reform the law when law is an essential part to this very same matrix of power? Thus, metacolonialism has been able to thrive by pushing oppression into legal vacuums and grey areas, while it produces tangible consequences. While Muneera has been struggling with her mental health as she couldn't change her appearance, other people try to police their looks, behaviours, and thoughts for various reasons, from the fear of being singled out to the desire to climb the social ladder, or just to survive.

Like Mehdi and Javayria, many respondents self-censor themselves, being 'careful' about what they say and 'keeping [their] head down'. Not only they take on duties at work far beyond their job description to avoid any tensions, they also would never ask for a pay rise or flexible working in fear of being seen as 'too demanding' and seeking 'exclusive treatment'. Mehdi tells Javayria: 'our parents told us keep your head down and work hard, be nice, keep quiet. White middle-class people are taught: "go and ask, you deserve it."' Self-censorship is fuelled by the fear of losing the very little stability they have acquired. Expressing opinions perceived as political can prove risky for Muslims. Footballer Mesut Özil faced criticism and threats from China when denouncing the oppression of Uyghurs in the Xinjang,[1] YouTuber and celebrity Amena Khan had to end her contract with l'Oréal after tweets in support for Palestine were found on her account.[2] Academics Sadek Hamid and Tahir Abbas attempted to engage constructively with government counter-extremism commissions, before having their contributions declared non-compliant[3] for having previously engaged with community organizations labelled as 'extremist'. How is it possible to sustain a career or a public presence while remaining faithful to one's values?

Change in behaviours or appearance, the presentation of a 'low-key' Islamic, South Asian or non-white self (O'Brien 2017) in this context are a consequence of yielding to group pressures (Eysenck 2004; Breckler et al. 2006). Cultural mimesis can be used as a protection mechanism, similar to what Black Americans perform by dressing up.[4] These changes can be either normative (from a desire to avoid punishments), ingratiational (in order to gain rewards (Mann 1969)), or informational (Deutsch and Gerard 1955), which is the case when a person lacks knowledge and looks to the group for information and direction (Lacan's *sujets supposés savoir* (1981)). Some social psychologists have shown that assimilation can be used as a mechanism, to minimize cognitive dissonance between one's values and those displayed by the dominant group (Festinger and Carlsmith 1959). British Muslim activist and thinker Asim Qureshi (2017, 214) expresses what many echoed in my fieldwork: 'people of colour know they cannot make mistakes, for they are punished in a way that others are not'. These are the consequences of the post-9/11 and 7/7 securitization of Muslims: the 'good' Muslims are the depoliticized and obedient ones, those who don't make waves and cannot threaten the structures of power hoping for social and financial mobility (see chapter 2).

Friedman and Laurison's study (2019), demonstrates how finding a job in Britain is not a matter of talent, skills, qualifications or 'legitimate fortune'. Progress on the career ladder is conditioned to finding 'mentors' and 'sponsors' who will broker job opportunities (Friedman and Laurison 2019, 211), which is only possible through 'cultural matching', whether the candidate fits into class expectations and behaviours:

> Top firms eliminate nearly every applicant who did not attend an elite college or university. They then put applicants through a series of 'informal' recruitment activities, such as cocktail parties and mixers, that are generally uncomfortable and unfamiliar to those from working-class backgrounds. Finally, when formal interviews happen, selectors often eschew formal criteria and evaluate candidates more on how at ease they seem, whether they build rapport in the interview, and whether they share common interests. (Friedman and Laurison 2019, 211–16)

Esra, one of my respondents in the UK, an executive in her thirties, recalls an encounter with a colleague who abruptly told her: 'you should drink. Most of my business has been made over drinks.' She acknowledges that in British workspaces: drinking is a strong builder of social capital. Hawa, another of my respondents, a professional in her twenties in France, relates similar observations: 'the number of things that you learn at the pub or during cigarette breaks is insane. This is when everything, every key decision happens. But then, it excludes non-smokers and non-drinkers like me from key social times.' The quest for 'cultural matching' partners creates cognitive apartheids where pubs and cocktail receptions make absent Muslims subject to negative judgement. Even if working-class candidates attend top universities, they are less likely to be selected: 'Bangladeshi people from working-class backgrounds, for example, are only half as likely as working-class white people to make it into top jobs, despite attending university at much higher rates' (Ibid). Rizvi (2019) gives an example of cultural triage at Cambridge:

> It's easier to 'become one of the good ones' if you talk like them. I remember trying to convince my bursar there was in issue with racism at Cambridge and he only listened to me when he discovered that I like Schubert's string quartet.

The pressure to conform can be internalized to modify individuals' value systems and aspirations (Kelman 1958, 53). Some respondents would say or post statements such as 'we need a Muslim Mark Zuckerberg', 'we need a Muslim Richard Branson', or 'we need a Muslim Rupert Murdoch'. Why do these Muslims idolize white secular rich males with a record of exploitation and racism instead of imagining a British Malcolm X, an American Al Ghazali, a European Rabia Al 'Adawiyya? This is what Malcolm X described in the lost chapter from his autobiography[5] as 'aspirational whiteness' and which Fanon (1967) calls wearing 'white masks'.

1.3. Temporarily Embarrassed White People

Adam is a white Muslim in his early thirties, having embraced Islam a few years ago. Of mixed Irish and Catalan descent, he is a former activist now working for a school in East London, and someone who grew to become very critical about his whiteness since being othered at school for not being English. After a filmed interview of him, we were discussing about why people would aspire to embrace whiteness:

ADAM: Have you heard of this idea, "Temporarily Embarrassed Millionaires"?
WILLIAM: No, what is it about?
ADAM: It's about why working-class white people have no solidarity with each other because everyone wants to be a millionaire. It's like they're supposed to be there, they feel entitled, this is who they should be, millionaires . . . distancing themselves from those who are worse off. There is shame with the fact they're not rich. It's like how everyone outside London wants to get this London accent.
WILLIAM: What does it have to do with whiteness?
ADAM: We can say the same thing about some Muslims and victims of racism: many feel they're temporarily embarrassed white people. Rich white people.

Adam was referring to a quote by Ronald Wright (2004, 124): 'socialism never took root in America because the poor see themselves not as an exploited proletariat but as temporarily embarrassed millionaires'. In Adam's discourse, whiteness is an aspiration that comes with domination over non-white cultures, hatred towards the other, the non-white or the poor, and denial, rejection of one's own poverty or non-whiteness. I have observed similar trends with some Muslim 'influencers' (see chapter 7) who would rather identify as 'third-culture kids', instead of 'children of immigrants'. *Third-culture kids* usually refers to children of Euro-American upper-class diplomats, academics military personal, missionaries, and businesspeople in the Global South who mostly go to international schools and live with their parents in gated communities. *Third-culture kid* serves as a barrier, a lexical differentiation from the inferior non-white *migrant*: while the former is exoticized for their English accent with a touch of foreign language, the latter are mocked for the same, even if they come from similarly privileged families (Khosroshahy 2016). While one can be 'citizens of the world', the others are pushed to renounce their roots.

Sharma (2010) and AbdulKhabeer (2016) observe similar stereotypical appearances and lifestyles of Muslims in the United States, conflated with being South

Asian. Sharma (2010) terms it 'hegemonic desiness', referring to South Asians displaying exceptional financial and educational success and ethnic insularity, coming from or aspiring toward middle-class consumptive practices such as suburban living and dressing in designer clothes (Sharma 2010). In his ethnography of shisha cafés on Edgware Road in London, Aly (2015), following Butler's (1993) analysis of gender mimicry, argues that mimicry of race and class belonging are a regulated mode of conformity, for the survival of the self in a racially and socio-economically regulated culture.

Javayria's contention is when people cannot imagine themselves outside of dominant norms, this leads to the death of collective cultural and moral standards:

> South Asian families' conventions are replicated for an illusional feeling of safety—which makes someone feel ok to sacrifice their identity for the sake of keeping everyone pleased. But Nature produces by essence non-conventional people... I find the British Muslim articulation of Islam suffocating. Why does it have to be centred around food, wealth and fashion? Historically, it was about arts, culture, poetry, philosophy, scientific progress. We had Iqbal, why is the standard now Kash and Shabs? [two brothers who became TV celebrities for their love of flashy cars]

Multi-disciplinary scholar Saaleh Baseer from the Bay Area echoes these thoughts in what he calls the 'Muslim American Nightmare': 'Are Muslim normies?': 'your ancestors have erected *waqfs* [eternal charitable trusts], patronized *masajid* [mosques] as art, and then you're exiled to migrate from your land. You move to Dallas or Chicago. You say you're coming from education. Your son goes to college and becomes a third-rate tiktok influencer-dancer.'[6]

Although state structures push towards assimilation, the ethnicization of Islam and Muslims has remained useful for consumerism. Muslim-led marketing agencies such as Ogilvy Noor are trying to 'help brands to tap into the Muslim market', playing on racial capitalism (Robinson 1983). They turn the month of Ramadan into the secular and consumerist equivalent of Christmas season and commodify Muslim women into palatable and digestible items by promoting those who abide by European beauty standards and marginalizing the rest (see chapter 7.2). Some Muslims openly play this same game with books such as *Generation M* (Janmohammed 2016), which 'reads like a marketing guide on how to sell products to young Muslims and uncritically endorse consumerist culture' (Lewis and Hamid 2018, 210). This trend has been particularly visible on social media (see chapter 7).

Wandering on my Instagram feed, the content suggested by the algorithm displays almost identical pictures of Muslims: women who have undergone nose, breast, and bottoms enhancements,[7] loosely copying the racially ambiguous appearance of Kim Kardashian;[8] men who have undergone liposuction and steroid injections trying to become clones of Drake.[9] The modifications undergone by these ordinary social media users have in common the hyper-sexualization of male and female characteristics. People's facial features and appearance are important signifiers of social status. In the collective imaginary, people with smoother facial features are perceived to have struggled less in life, and therefore are perceived as financially successful (Bjornsdottir and Rule 2017). Moreover, those who bear facial features that fit dominant norms and expectations are allowed further privileges such as job opportunities (Peterson and Palmer 2017). These factors illustrate the working of metacolonialism, pressuring people to fit in in order to stay socially and professionally valid.

Farrah, a mixed-media henna artist in her early thirties, has around 80,000 followers on Instagram, which is one of her main income streams as a single mother. Farrah posts mostly about her art designs, commissions for well-known cosmetics brands, cosy London locations, skin care products, and occasionally, pictures of herself. Farrah is one of the rare people I met who witnessed both sides of social media culture, first caught in a race for followers, and she later stopped caring about it.

> I felt I was never good enough... How I would I feel about myself or a certain piece would be quite dependent on how many likes it would get or how many comments it would get... I always wanted to be accepted by people, like my family or my extended family, I wanted them to be happy with me... I tried to look like them... talk like them... be in the same things they were into, even if it was things I wasn't even necessarily interested in such as fashion... I tried to put filler in my lips for me to look like these Instagram models... I looked at myself and I thought: this is not me, this is not who I am. I felt that the more I tried, the less I was actually accepted... No matter how hard you try, you cannot be somebody you're not... Since, I've been experiencing anxiety and I have a very low self-esteem.

Her journey for acceptance, which lasted until her late twenties when she experienced her divorce, illustrates how peer pressure impacted her identity to the point that she wouldn't recognize herself in the mirror, and the subsequent damage to her mental health (see chapter 4). She is an example of the *Lonely Crowd* effect, where people seek to adapt and please (Riesman et al. 1950) because they want to belong. The *Lonely Crowd* study demonstrates that people who adhere to similar norms of looks and behaviours are easier to identify in industries looking for smooth functioning. Consequently, a considerable number of Muslims on social media drink, boast their material wealth, have multiple partners outside marriage, reveal their bodies, and boast about money earned through drugs,[10] forex trading, or producing adult content on OnlyFans. They are mostly fair-skinned, tall, slim, with straight hair, muscular, wearing designer clothes, driving in expensive cars, flying to holidays at the other end of the world, and are politically silent. There are almost no Black Muslims. A lot of this online display is also moulded into a certain performance of Britishness: shedding a tear for Queen Elizabeth II's passing, decorating one's house for Christmas, pursuing imperial titles such as OBEs. As much as they are called 'stories', social media videos and pictures, never tell any stories; they just *feature* Muslims. They create an aesthetic lifestyle coded by fashion choices, pastel colours, buzzwords, stimuli, strongly shaped by market forces and dominant power dynamics. As said in the movie *Fight Club* (1999): 'everything is a copy, of a copy, of a copy'.

Neoliberalism, an economic system turned into a life ethic (Harvey 2005), offers a theology of liberation relying on empowerment (Fisher 2013): the promise of escaping racism and poverty if people compete with each other for wealth and fame and conform to dominant norms and moral frameworks. Displaying hyper-sexualized pictures of them online, along with symbols of wealth and captions such as 'daydreaming about you', men and women not only signal that they are fit for sexual reproduction; they signal that they are socially and economically fit for the reproduction of the same *safe* structures of power. Because, at its core, coloniality looks for the sustenance and the reproduction of its hegemonic powers: the physical appearance of the successful is copied in hope that modifying their physical appearance will make them successful in turn: 'fake it until you make it' (Marwick 2013) (see chapter 7). Neoliberalism thus creates a form of social Darwinism, a survival-of-the-fittest mindset where not only to be poor is to fail, but also to be different. In the era of neoliberalism, the human reaches another evolutionary step: the *homo oeconomicus*—who earns, possesses, and consumes. Islam is reduced to a fashion statement, a commodity, a consumable, a superficial brand of coolness defined by pride and privilege in a wider theology of aesthetics: 'the route to freedom and happiness lay not in winning political freedoms but in material possessions' (Fisher 2013, 27). American historian of West African Islam Rudolph Ware III comments on modern Euro-American Muslims: 'for a lot of Muslims, capitalism is their religion and Islam their ritual observance'.

Brands in the era of racial capitalism 'want the face, but they don't want the complex politics or the identity or the voice behind it' (Kumar 2018), as a device to assert their idea of belonging to the white-neoliberal-patriarchal-supremacy. By encouraging racial capitalism, colonial agents encourage the economic rape of Muslims. Just like Farrah, people will continue to feed these structures as long as the power imbalance will make them crave for a hypothetical validation. This is what the Pakistani feminist collective Girls at Dhabas (2018) expressed with a tweet: 'the colonisers might have exited this country decades ago, but our need to seek validation from them still hasn't left our veins': despite the end of geographical empires, the minds of the diaspora have remained occupied and tweaked to seek validation from the dominant powers.

Social control implies discipline and curation or selection of *valid* citizens (see chapter 2). Since the wider society allows only certain types of Muslims to be recognized—those who are economic participants, who aspire to the modern aesthetics and white patriarchal neoliberal ideas of success; it is also the case that Muslims will close the doors to their own peers if they don't tick the right boxes. Valid Muslims are the cool ones, part of an adjust-to-fit neo-theo-tribalism (Nilan 2017) defined by consumerism and the adoption of certain aesthetic norms. However, the internalization of dominant norms also leads to the creation of a hierarchy of validity, making Muslims exclude if not oppress other kinds of Muslims deemed less valid.

1.4. The Internalization of White Oppression

Umair, a psychotherapist and trekking enthusiast of Indian descent in his mid-thirties who I have met through Rumi's Cave, recalls:

> I was invited for *rishta* [face-to-face traditional matchmaking involving the families] once, at the house of a renowned geneticist. He was a geneticist, so I was expecting he was a man of great education and of great knowledge. The first thing he said to me was: 'are you Pakistani? I don't want my daughter to marry a Pakistani.' I said to him I was Indian, he says 'ok.' Then, he looks out of the window and asks me 'is this your car?' I said 'yes.' I had the same as now, my Vauxhall Astra. Then the *rishta* ends, I go back home but I didn't get any messages from the girl anymore. I message her, asking 'what's going on?' She says this to me: 'My dad said to me: I don't want my daughter to marry someone who has less than a Mercedes.'

On the other end, numerous women have been struggling with similar issues of rejection because of their education level and them pursuing careers, perceived as threatening for some men, as many of my respondents relate. Many expand on the problem that people in general want to marry those who abide by 'European beauty standards' and 'Western' ideas of 'success' (see chapter 7): wealth, fame and influence. British Sociologist Fauzia Ahmad also backs these statements with her observations: lots of men will never get married 'because they don't look like George Clooney' (Ahmad in The Muslim Vibe 2020). Similarly, another of my respondents, Tarek, a consultant in the City, summarizes: 'if you're a Muslim in London and you want friends in the [Muslim] community, you're either an accountant, a banker, a GP or a lawyer, or you're nobody'. This can affect white Muslims too.

Many people in the UK had a problem with my parents being Polish. It cost me job opportunities in the Muslim charity sector, and several potential marriage partners. My own current father-in-law, before meeting me, thought I was like 'these dodgy people who build a shoddy driveway and run away with the money' despite me having a PhD in sociology and no driveway building experience. However, my Polishness, although a problem in the UK, was not an issue for Muslims I met in France, in the US, in India, and in Pakistan. Similarly, while my PhD was perceived as a liability in the UK (the 'wrong kind of doctor'), it was seen as an asset in the countries mentioned above. I've never encountered, observed, heard, or read about any anti-Polish sentiment amongst Muslims in these countries, or in their societies at large. Since anti-Polish rhetoric was one of the hallmarks of the Brexit debates, I can only theorize that these discourses must have been embraced by mimesis.

When it comes to the recognition of talent and job opportunities, why have artists like Pearls of Islam or Poetic Pilgrimage, who have been performing for more than ten years, not risen to the status of global celebrities, while, within a few months, the world erected idols out of Mona Haydar or Harris J (nicknamed 'the Muslim Justin Bieber')? Pearls of Islam and Poetic Pilgrimage have been critically acclaimed and internationally recognized for their musical skills and the depth of their lyrics. While Muslim charities and conferences would court Mona Haydar or Harris J for being present at their fundraisers or performing at their events, and would offer the costs of making their music videos, the Pearls or Poetic Pilgrimage never had a fraction of this level of attention, only being used occasionally as token Black female hip-hop or *nasheed* (acapella devotional music) artists. Besides the impact on self-esteem, the comparison with people who abide by dominant standards and seeing the consequent financial stability, amount of recognition, and the doors it unlocks makes them question their validity (see chapter 4).

A similar kind of discrimination happens to Shi'as, Ahmadis, Ismailis in Sunni circles, working-class Muslims, and disabled, non-British, and non-binary Muslims. Author Medina Whiteman calls 'Muslim Misfits' those who don't tick the right boxes, those invalid for either the dominant institutional structures, and the majority of British South Asian Hanafi Muslims. These exclusionary dynamics are part of what causes some Muslims to distance themselves from the British *ummah* (see chapter 6.2). Selecting people from dominant structures by 'cultural matching' produces what Mills calls 'white ignorance' (2015): knowledge is not necessary valued anymore since applying to positions of power does not rely on credentials other than class and ethnicity privileges. Talking to elders who got involved in Muslim charities in the 1990s, it was not always the case. When I did my fieldwork in France in the late 2000s and early 2010s, such discriminations didn't exist in the Muslim charity sector either. So, what has changed?

The murder of George Floyd on 25 May 2020 echoed loudly within Muslim communities worldwide for one particular reason: on social media, people circulated the alleged fact that the grocery store that called the police was owned by Arabs, which forced Muslim across the globe to face the issue of anti-Blackness in their communities and families. Social media was soon flooded by calls to 'anti-Blackness is *haraam*' (religiously not permissible), making anti-racism a religious duty and racism a major sin. The issue has been for long documented in the US (Abdul Khabeer 2016) and in the UK (Nurein and Iqbal 2021). Community polls, while limited by their sampling, found that 63% of Black British Muslims felt they did not belong in the UK Muslim community and that nearly 50% of participants had experienced racism and discrimination within a religious setting (Black Muslim Forum 2020). For more than half a decade Muslims have set up initiatives for combatting racism and anti-Blackness in their own communities such as the Muslim Anti-Racism Collaborative in the US[11] or putting Black Muslims at the centre of the narrative such as Black and Muslim in Britain[12] or Sapelo Square[13] in the US. In a series of tweets, famous Muslim poet, author, and community organizer Suhaiymah Manzoor Khan (also known as The Brown Hijabi) links anti-Blackness to the aspiration of whiteness:

> One of the most subtle of these is the internalised desire to be closer to whiteness. If we look at the likes of Patel & Javed we see how Asians are able to access power through performing proximity to whiteness THROUGH their internalised racism... South Asians are often intent on lightening their gene pool through marriage choices in this almost dystopian 'breeding' of skin colour that goes into partner choices. All resting on hating dark skin. (Manzoor-Khan 2020)

Some of the discriminations, racism, and anti-Blackness present within Muslim communities stem from social divisions established during the colonial-era, further exacerbated post-9/11 through the good/bad Muslim narrative (see chapter 2). Through her assertion, Suhaimah posits that oppressed people are not only buying into a narrative of acculturation, they are active in replicating the agenda of white supremacy, a continuation already explored by Fanon (1967), Memmi (1965), or Freire (1993) writing about how the oppressed have internalized the image and adopted the guidelines of the oppressor. In the matrix of coloniality, white supremacy and its offshoots such as Eurocentric education or beauty standards work together in an ecosystem with neoliberalism (when the free market becomes an organizing framework for human lives resulting in an economic and social deregulation coupled with the competition for power, wealth, and influence), patriarchy (male domination), gender normativity, and other systems such as ableism. Anibal Quijano (2007) refer to these as a package which bell hooks call 'white supremacist capitalist patriarchy' (hooks 2004, 17), which here we could name 'white neoliberal patriarchal supremacy'. In the present-day consumerist culture, whiteness has become a brand, a goal to achieve. There is no clear distinction between colonizer and colonized anymore. White people do not necessarily abide by whiteness and white supremacy, just like whiteness and white supremacy are not traits exclusive to white people. As one of my respondents sums it up, paraphrasing bell hooks: 'patriarchy has no gender, it affects both, but men benefit from it. White supremacy has no race or ethnicity, but white people benefit from it. Neoliberalism has no class either.'

Whiteness as a set of norms, and white supremacy as the endeavour of imposing whiteness, help understanding forms of oppression inherited from the historic belief in Europe—and by extension white people—as the centre of the world and the beacon of human civilization. Although both white and non-white people can abide by white supremacy, it serves only the narrative of whiteness. Metacolonization is not only a passive *internal colonization*; its distinctive strategy is to turn the oppressed into the oppressor in hope for acceptance by the dominant society. It could be compared to a collective Stockholm syndrome where the colonial abductor deprives its victims to the point where they believe that marrying their abuser (embracing oppressive powers in this metaphor) is the only option. Vulnerable populations are too weakened to contest power and instead, are fighting to have their slice of it, with in mind the illusory horizon that liberation only resides in building empires in turn. Although, in the UK, white supremacy has been associated with stereotypes like the football hooligans or landowners from the South East, metacolonialism shows that there is another type of white supremacy that can be enacted by non-white subjects.

Mignolo (2007) understands coloniality as modernity, constructed as a marker of the 'civilized' in opposition to traditional or 'savage' societies (Lévi Strauss 1962). Touraine (1992) defines modernity as a culture of separation which, with an increased reliance on technology making one of the landmarks of the modern Eurocentric civilization (Sztompka 1993): the modern project aims at the crafting of a self-reliant and a-historical individual, therefore disconnected from others and disconnected from nature. The symptoms of modernity include an increasing isolation of people, the atomization and individualization of societies (Riesman et al. 1950; Tönnies 1957; Bellah et al. 1985), the formalization, depersonalization and instrumentalization of interpersonal relations (Weber 1968; Bauman 1988) and the alienation from political and economic governance (Seeman 1959). Exponential development of these characteristics coupled to an increased volatility (Beck 1992) of values, finances, and social positions led Giddens (1991) to suggest that we have entered an era of hyper-modernity or liquid modernity (Bauman 2000). Modernity is the concretization of a Promethean race for power: the (white) man against the gods and the odds, embodying domination and will as pillars of Western thought and culture (Hodge at al. 1975).

One evening, the BBC was playing Muzlamics, a satirical series featuring two Muslim comedians, caricaturing Muslim South Asians navigating various spaces in society. Javayria and one of her friends comment:

HARRIS: The sketch idea from Muzlamics that I enjoyed the most was the brown competition over white credentials in the workplace [the two characters compete to find out who is the whitest of them by, for example, enjoying English food or not washing themselves with water after using the toilet].

JAVAYRIA: But not everyone is like that.

HARRIS: Not all Asians have the same mindset than us. People of colour are not in together, that's complete bollocks. It's like lots of people at work who are working class who happily vote Tory. We have a bunch of second-generation Muslims replicating white power structures. It's people who think gentrification is fine, we've worked hard, we don't live in council estates, we can move out of Aldgate East. They don't realise that the people who suffer are the poor Black people, the poor white people, the poor Bangladeshis. It's like Shabnam's [his wife] friends. Very practicing, borderline salafi [religiously conservative], vote Labour, involved in the community, but they send their kids to private schools. It's aspirational. If you send your kids to private school, there's a massive issue with your understanding of religion and justice.

Harris links copying cultural norms and aspiration to replicating systems of oppression. What infuriates him is the lack of solidarity (see chapters 2 and 6.2) between people sharing a same skin colour, the same social, economic, and cultural background and Islam, which Harris understands as a moral frame of reference standing against inequalities. However, are Shabnam's friends who value private schools not simply embracing their idea of a typical British lifestyle? Aren't they only adapting to the local context to give more chances to their kids? While aspiring to more privileges is understandable for Adam, moving in the direction of whiteness supposes to engage with structures replicating inequalities. But where does aspiration turn itself into losing one's culture and into oppression?

Social psychologist Solomon Asch (1951) has demonstrated how group pressure pushes in certain cases individuals to act against logic or against their own interests: 'if everyone else does it, I should do it too and if I don't, I must be wrong'. Milgram demonstrated that in these contexts, ethics and morals could easily be overridden by authority or by accessing positions of power (Blass 2004). However, psychology doesn't explain on a collective level what enables whole groups at the margins to harm other people perceived as more marginal. The next chapter explores situations when people actively try to work for oppressive structures in the hope of acceptance, and the limits of such strategies.

Notes

1. Lily Kuo, 'Mesut Özil row: China's Arsenal fans burn shirts in anger at Xinjiang post', *The Guardian*, 16 December 2019. https://web.archive.org/web/20191216073044/https://www.theguardian.com/world/2019/dec/16/mesut-ozil-row-chinas-arsenal-fans-burn-shirts-in-anger-at-xinjiang-post

2. William Barylo, 'What Amena Khan's apology tells us about the limits of Muslim "success"', *Middle East Eye*, 8 February 2018. https://web.archive.org/web/20210613145358/https://www.middleeasteye.net/opinion/what-amena-khans-apology-tells-us-about-limits-muslim-success
3. Sadek Hamid, 'The perils of engaging CVE policy making: a British case study', *The Maydan*, 4 December 2019. https://web.archive.org/web/20191213230513/https://themaydan.com/2019/12/the-perils-of-engaging-cve-policy-making-a-british-case-study/#_ftn14
4. David Yi, 'Black armor', *Mashable*, 8 August 2015. https://web.archive.org/web/20200530051053/https://mashable.com/2015/08/08/black-men-dressing-up-police/?europe=true#wy8Tm1N.eGq1
5. Missy Sullivan, 'The explosive chapter left out of Malcolm X's autobiography', *History*, 28 February 2019. https://web.archive.org/web/20190301030449/https://www.history.com/news/malcolm-x-autobiography-lost-chapter
6. Saaleh Baseer, 'Are Muslim normies?', Instagram story, 24 July 2022.
7. Ruqaiya Haris, 'Why cosmetic surgery can be complex when you're Muslim', *Dazed Digital*, 17 October 2018. https://web.archive.org/web/20181022025722/https://www.dazeddigital.com/beauty/head/article/41850/1/cosmetic-surgery-muslim-beauty-modesty
8. Jia Tolentino, 'The age of Instagram face', *The New Yorker*, 12 December 2019. https://web.archive.org/web/20191212122807/https://www.newyorker.com/culture/decade-in-review/the-age-of-instagram-face
9. Hussein Kesvani, 'Why South Asian men are so obsessed with Drake', *MEL Magazine*, 2 July 2019. https://web.archive.org/web/20190819125257/https://melmagazine.com/en-us/story/why-south-asian-men-are-so-obsessed-with-drake
10. Yahya Birt. 'Being a real man in Islam: drugs, criminality and the problem of masculinity', Masud Blog, 2014. https://web.archive.org/web/20150905145519/http://masud.co.uk/being-a-real-man-in-islam-drugs-criminality-and-the-problem-of-masculinity
11. The Muslim Anti-Racism Collaborative. https://web.archive.org/web/20210602194711/https://www.muslimarc.org
12. Black and Muslim in Britain. [YouTube] 2016. https://web.archive.org/web/20200611135659/https://www.youtube.com/channel/UC9nJ7cqWZvB2VDdDhQFGCkg
13. Sapelo Square. https://web.archive.org/web/20201029042247/https://sapelosquare.com/about-us

References

Abdul Khabeer, Su'ad. 2016. *Muslim Cool: Race, Religion and Hip Hop in the United States*. New York: New York University Press.

Akala. 2018. *Natives: Race and Class in the Ruins of Empire*. London: John Murray Press.

Ali, Nasreen, Virinder Kalra, and Salman Sayyid (eds). 2006. *A Postcolonial People: South Asians in Britain*. London: Hurst.

Aly, Ramy M. K. 2015. *Becoming Arab in London: Performativity and the Undoing of Identity*. London: Pluto Press.

Asch, Solomon. E. 1951. 'Effects of group pressure upon the modification and distortion of judgment.' In *Groups, Leadership and Men*, edited by H. Guetzkow. Pittsburgh: Carnegie Press, 177–90.

Bal, Ellen and Kathinka Sinha-Kherkoff. 2007. 'Separated by partition: Muslims of British Indian descent in Mauritius and Suriname.' In *Global Indian Diasporas: Exploring Trajectories of Migration and Theory*, edited by Gjisbert Oonk. Amsterdam: Amsterdam University Press, 90–120.

Bauman, Zygmunt. 1988. 'Sociology and postmodernity.' *The Sociological Review* 36(4), 790–813.

Bauman, Zygmunt. 2000. *Liquid Modernity*. Cambridge: Polity Press.

Beck, Ulrich. 1992. *Risk Society: Towards a New Modernity*. London: Sage Publications.

Bellah, Robert N., Richard Madsen, William M. Sullivan, et al. 1985. *Habits of the Heart: Individualism and Commitment in American Life*. Berkeley: University of California Press.

Bhabha, Homi. 1994. *The Location of Culture*. London: Routledge.

Birt, Yahya. 2022. *Ummah at the Margins: The Past, Present and Future of Muslim Minorities*. London: Ayaan Centre.

Bjornsdottir, R. Thora and Nicholas Rule. 2017. 'The visibility of social class from facial cues.' *Journal of Personality and Social Psychology* 113(4), 530–46.

Black Muslim Forum. 2020. 'They had the audacity to ask me if I was Muslim, when they saw me—a black woman in Niqab—report on the experiences of Black British Muslims.' https://web.archive.org/web/20200414115016/https://blackmuslimforum.org/2020/04/05/they-had-the-audacity-to-ask-me-if-i-was-muslim-when-they-saw-me-a-black-woman-in-niqab-experiences-of-black-british-muslims

Blass, Thomas. 2004. *The Man Who Shocked the World: The Life and Legacy of Stanley Milgram*. New York: Basic Books.

Bonilla-Silva, Eduardo. 2010. *Racism without Racists: Color-Blind Racism and the Persistence of Racial Inequality in the United States*. Lanham: Rowman and Littlefield.

Breckler, Steven, James Olson, and Elizabeth Wiggins. 2006. *Social Psychology Alive*. Boston: Thomson Wadsworth.

Bulhan, Hussein A. 2015. 'Stages of colonialism in Africa: from occupation of land to occupation of being.' *Journal of Social and Political Psychology* 3(1), 239–56.

Butler, Judith. 1993. *Bodies that Matter: On the Discursive Limits of 'Sex'*. New York: Routledge.

Craun, Dustin. 2013. 'Exploring pluriversal paths toward transmodernity: from the mind-centered egolatry of colonial modernity to Islam's epistemic decolonization through the heart.' *Human Architecture: Journal of the Sociology of Self-Knowledge* 11(1), 91–113.

Derrida, Jacques. 1986. *Memoires for Paul de Man*. New York: Columbia University Press.

Deutsch, Morton and Harold Gerard. 1955. 'A study of normative and informational social influences upon individual judgment.' *The Journal of Abnormal and Social Psychology* 1(3), 629–36.

Eisenlohr, Patrick. 2006. 'The politics of diaspora and the morality of secularism: Muslim identities and Islamic authority in Mauritius.' *Journal of Royal Anthropological Society* 12(2), 395–412.

Esposito, John L. 2003. 'Westoxification.' *The Oxford Dictionary of Islam*. Oxford Islamic Studies. https://web.archive.org/web/20141026095053/http://www.oxfordislamicstudies.com/article/opr/t125/e2501

Evetts, Julia. 2014. 'The concept of professionalism: professional work, professional practice and learning.' In *International Handbook of Research in Professional and Practice-based Learning*, edited by S. Billett, C. Harteis, and H. Gruber. Dordrecht: Springer, 29–56.

Eysenck, Michael. 2004. *Psychology: An International Perspective*. New York: Psychology Press

Fanon, Franz. 1967 [1952]. *Black Skin, White Masks*. New York: Grove Press.

Festinger, Leon and James Carlsmith. 1959. 'Cognitive consequences of forced compliance.' *Journal of Abnormal and Social Psychology* 58, 203–10.

Fight Club. 1999. [Film]. David Fincher (dir.). Los Angeles: Fox 2000, Regency and Linson.

Fisher, Rebecca (ed.). 2013. *Managing Democracy, Managing Dissent: Capitalism, Democracy and the Organisation of Consent*. London: Corporate Watch.

Freire, Paulo. 1993 [1968]. *The Pedagogy of the Oppressed*. New York: Continuum.

Friedman, Sam, and Daniel Laurison. 2019. *The Class Ceiling: Why It Pays to Be Privileged*. Bristol: Policy Press.

Giddens, Anthony. 1991. *The Consequences of Modernity*. Stanford: Stanford University Press.

Gillespie, Marie. 1995. *Television, Ethnicity, and Cultural Change*. New York: Routledge.

Girls At Dhabas. 2018. [Twitter] 14 November. https://web.archive.org/web/20210209050529/https://twitter.com/girlsatdhabas/status/1062741569076453377

Gulati, Mitu and Devon Carbado. 2000. 'Working identity.' *Cornell Law Review* 85(4), 1259–308.

Harvey, David. 2005. *A Brief History of Neoliberalism*. Oxford: Oxford University Press.

Hassankhan, Mauritz S. 2013. 'Kahe Gaile Bides—why did you go overseas? An introduction in emotional aspects of migration history: a diaspora perspective.' In *Caribbean Issues in The Indian Diaspora*, edited by Kumar Mahabir. New Delhi: Serials Publications, 3–35.

Hassankhan, Maurits S. 2016. 'Islam and Indian Muslims in Suriname: a struggle for survival.' In *Indentured Muslims in the Diaspora Identity and Belonging of Minority Groups in Plural Societies*, edited by Maurits Hassankhan, Goolam Vahed, and Lomarsh Roopnarine. Oxon: Routledge, 181–226.

Hochschild, Arlie R. 1983. *The Managed Heart: Commercialisation of Human Feeling.* London: UCL Press.
Hodge, John L., Donald K. Struckmann, and Lynn Dorland Trost. 1975. *Cultural Bases of Racism and Group Oppression: An Examination of Traditional 'Western' Concepts, Values and Institutional Structures Which Support Racism, Sexism and Elitism.* Berkeley: Two Riders.
hooks, bell. 2004. *The Will to Change: Men, Masculinity and Love.* Washington: Washington Square Press.
Jahangeer-Chojoo, Amena. 2004. *La Rose et le Henné: Une Etude des Musulmans de Maurice.* Moka: Mahatma Gandhi Institute.
Jana, Tiffany and Michael Baran. 2020. *Subtle Acts of Exclusion: How to Understand, Identify, and Stop Microaggressions.* Oakland: Berrett-Koehler.
Janmohammed, Shelina. 2016. *Generation M.* London: IB Tauris.
Kasenally, Roukaya. 2011. 'Mauritius: paradise reconsidered.' *Journal of Democracy* 22(2), 160–9.
Kelman, Herbert. C. 1958. 'Compliance, identification, and internalization: three processes of attitude change.' *Journal of Conflict Resolution* 2(1), 51–60.
Khosroshahy, Paniz. 2016. 'Immigrant vs. expatriate: on being a third culture kid.' *Gal Dem*, 23 May. https://web.archive.org/web/20160527054838/http://www.gal-dem.com/third-culture-kid
Kumar, Rashmee. 2018. 'Marketing the Muslim woman: hijabs and modest fashion are the new corporate trend in the Trump era.' *The Intercept*, 29 December. https://web.archive.org/web/20181229140116/https://theintercept.com/2018/12/29/muslim-women-hijab-fashion-capitalism
Lacan, Jacques. 1981 [1973]. 'Of the Subject who is Supposed to Know.' In *The Four Fundamental Concepts of Psychoanalysis—Book XI of the Seminar of Jacques Lacan,* edited by Jacques-Alain Miller, translated by Alan Sheridan. New York: W. W. Norton, 230–43.
Lallmahomed-Aumeerally, Naseem. 2014. 'A reading of Bollywood cinema as a site of melancholia for Indo-Mauritian Muslim female youth.' *South Asian Popular Culture* 12(3), 149–62.
Lévi-Strauss, Claude. 1962. *La pensée sauvage.* Paris: Plon.
Lewis, Phillip and Sadek Hamid. 2018. *British Muslims: New Directions in Islamic Thought; Creativity and Activism.* Edinburgh: Edinburgh University Press.
Maldonado-Torres, Nelson. 2007. 'On the coloniality of being: contributions to the development of a concept.' *Cultural Studies* 21(2–3), 240–70.
Mandaville, Peter. 2001. *Transnational Muslim Politics: Reimagining the Umma.* London: Routledge.
Mann, Leon. 1969. *Social Psychology.* New York: Wiley.
Manzoor-Khan, Suhaiymah. 2020. [Twitter] 28 May. https://web.archive.org/web/20200529172105/https://twitter.com/thebrownhijabi/status/1265923953954115584
Marwick, Alice E. 2013. *Status Update: Celebrity, Publicity, and Branding in the Social Media Age.* New Haven: Yale University Press.
Mehta, Binita. 2010. 'Memories in/of diaspora: Barlen Pyamootoo's Bénarès (1999).' *L'Esprit Créateur* 50(2), 46–62.
Memmi, Albert. 1965 [1957]. *The Colonizer and the Colonized.* Boston: Beacon Press.
Mignolo, Walter D. 2003. *The Darker Side of the Renaissance: Literacy, Territoriality, and Colonization* (2nd edn). Ann Arbor: University of Michigan Press.
Mignolo, Walter D. 2007. 'DELINKING.' *Cultural Studies* 21(2–3), 449–514.
Mills, Charles W. 2015. 'White ignorance.' In *Race and Epistemologies of Ignorance,* edited by Shannon Sullivan and Nancy Tuana. Albany: SUNY Press, 13–38.
Mishra, Vijay. 2007. *The Literature of the Indian Diaspora: Theorising the Diasporic Imaginary.* London: Routledge.
Modood, Tariq. 2012. *Post-immigration 'Difference' and Integration: The Case of Muslims in Western Europe.* London: The British Academy.
Nilan, Pam. 2017 *Muslim Youth in the Diaspora: Challenging Extremism through Popular Culture.* New York: Routledge.

Nurein, Sheymaa and Humera Iqbal. 2021. 'Identifying a space for young Black Muslim women in contemporary Britain.' *Ethnicities* 21(3), 433–53.

O'Brien, John. 2017. *Keeping it Halal: The Everyday Lives of Muslim American Teenage Boys.* Princeton: Princeton University Press.

Peterson, Rolfe. D. and Carl Palmer. 2017. 'Effects of physical attractiveness on political beliefs. Politics and the life sciences.' *The Journal of the Association for Politics and the Life Sciences* 36(2), 3–16.

Preetha, Christina. 2017. 'Jeans don't make me "white".' *Burnt Roti*, 30 April. https://web.archive.org/web/20171022231414/http://www.burntroti.com/blog/jeans-dont-make-me-white

Quijano, Anibal. 2007. 'Coloniality and modernity/rationality.' *Cultural Studies* 21 (2–3), 168–78.

Qureshi, Asim. 2017. *A Virtue of Disobedience.* London: Byline Books.

Riesman, David, Nathan Glazer, and Reuel Denney. 1950. *The Lonely Crowd: A Study of the Changing American Character.* New Haven: Yale University Press.

Rizvi, Husna. 2019. 'A FLY girl's guide to Cambridge—a new book on women of colour navigating, and resisting, elite power.' *New Internationalist*, 1 January. https://web.archive.org/web/20190206181848/https://newint.org/features/2019/02/01/how-survive-elite-institutions-cambridge-woman-colour

Robinson, Cedric 1983. *Black Marxism: The Making of the Black Radical Tradition.* London: Zed Books.

Said, Edward. 1978. *Orientalism.* New York: Pantheon Books.

Said, Edward. 1984. *The World, the Text and the Critic.* Cambridge: Harvard University Press.

Sayyid, Salman. 2010. 'The homelessness of Muslimness: the Muslim umma as a diaspora.' *Human Architecture: Journal of the Sociology of Self-Knowledge* 8(2), 129–46.

Seeman, Melvin. 1959. 'On the meaning of alienation.' *American Sociological Review* 24(6), 783–91.

Sharma, Nitasha. 2010. *Hip Hop Desis: South Asian Americans, Blackness, and a Global Race Consciousness.* Durham: Duke University Press.

Sztompka, Piotr. 1993. *The Sociology of Social Change.* Hoboken: Wiley-Blackwell.

The Muslim Vibe. 2020. 'The CHALLENGES of marriage and relationships!' [YouTube] 3 April. https://archive.org/details/practical-solutions-to-muslim-marriage-problems-1080p

Tönnies, Ferdinand. 1957. *Community and Society.* East Lansing: Michigan State University Press.

Touraine, Alain. 1992. *Critique de la Modernité.* Paris: Fayard.

Weber, Max. 1968 [1922]. *Economy and Society.* New York: Bedminster.

Werbner, Pnina. 2009. 'Paradoxes of postcolonial vernacular cosmopolitanism in South Asia and the diaspora.' In *The Ashgate Research Companion to Cosmopolitanism*, edited by Maria Rovisco and Magdalena Nowicka. Surrey: Ashgate, 107–23.

Williams, Tanya Muneera. 2017. 'We are valuable.' I Am Not What Is Broken. https://web.archive.org/save/https://iamnotbroken.williambarylo.com/?p=41

Wright, Ronald. 2004. *A Short History of Progress.* Toronto: House of Anansi.

Zohar, Danah, and Ian Marshall. 2000. *Spiritual Intelligence: The Ultimate Intelligence.* London: Bloomsbury.

2
Faithfolk Ain't Kinfolk

Nadeem was breathing heavily, wiping his sweat with a tissue every two seconds, visibly anxious. He was twenty-seven, of Bangladeshi background, and grew up in a council estate in Tower Hamlets. A SOAS[1] graduate, he now works for a mainstream youth organization, and is an active participant in elitist and secretive organizations promoting the narrative of 'Muslim leadership' (see section 2.3). He was renowned amongst my respondents for being a sexual predator and for having accepted a medal of the Order of the British Empire (OBE). I wanted to ask him about his thoughts on power.

WILLIAM: What do you think of people in the community who attain positions of power and don't share their power or don't use it for the community?
NADEEM: Selfishness is just another kind of leadership. I'm a pragmatist: if ego drives the success of an organization, it's not necessarily a bad thing.
WILLIAM: What do you think of organizations at the grassroots then, how can they survive if no one supports them?
NADEEM: I don't believe in the grassroots, that's very exclusionary. The grassroots never achieved anything. If we want change, it's top down or nothing.
WILLIAM: Do you then think that social media influencers can change things?
NADEEM: These people try to normalize the presence of Muslims. If we can drive a brand like Nike to issue a sports hijab, it's a victory for us.

Nadeem defines change through power, money, and influence. He believes that more representation in the market and in politics will curb racism, and dismisses grass-roots movements as useless. The problem is, while grass-roots organizations have a reputation for being inefficient and prone to mismanagement, the larger multi-million-pound charities with which he does business are far from being safe from the same problems (see section 7.3). Nadeem echoes some of my other Muslim respondents who lean toward Conservative sayings: 'there's no structural inequalities, some Muslims make it to Oxford and Cambridge'; 'if there is few it's because Muslims are lazy'. He doesn't believe in the accountability of the state and echoes the neoliberal narrative saying that if poor people are poor, it's because they don't work hard enough, which denotes a lack of understanding of socio-economic structures, even though, paradoxically, he had grown up in a council-housed, working-class family. He believes in the Great Man theory—a concept attributed to Thomas Carlyle circa 1840 positing that history can be explained by the impact of a few influential and charismatic men—and talks about Muslims using the generalizing plural 'us' (see section 6.2). When I talk about sharing power, he immediately jumps to 'selfishness' and 'ego' as positive values, echoing Margaret Thatcher's and Boris Johnson's remarks about how 'greed' can be a driver of success (Allegretti and Elgot 2021). For most of my respondents, particularly in Sufi circles, the ego (*nafs*) is an enemy, if not the main one, of the believer. Scholars like Craun (2013) locate in ego the root of all supremacies and therefore colonialism. Islamic scholar Abdal Hakim Murad (2020, 50) sees in behaviour such as Nadeem's participation in elitist private clubs mingling with people of high wealth, fame or power not only an un-Islamic behaviour but the expression of an 'inferiority complex' inherited from the colonial era's Darwinist doctrines, whose 'highest ambition is to have their photograph taken beside an MP ... hoping to find healing in what on some level they still know to be treason' (Murad 2020, 50).

According to goal-content theory (Kasser and Ryan 1996), Nadeem's views fit into the frame of extrinsic goals and values—concerned with status, image, fame, power, financial success, and prestige, and not interested in cooperation or community (as opposed to intrinsic goals, concerned with personal growth, empathy, community intimacy, and self-acceptance). The acquisition of such values is rooted in feelings of insecurity (Kasser et al. 2004)—which I argue are created by an environment of deprivation (see section 2.2)—and from exposure to social models that encourage these values (Kasser et al. 2004), especially in an individualistic society where performance, ego, and Machiavellianism are necessary to survive and are rewarded (Marwick 2013). 'Success' is worth the compromise, even when it means climbing the pyramid of white supremacy[2]—as for many community organizers, echoing a tweet by the collective No White Saviors (2019): 'white supremacy performed in Black or Brown skin is still white supremacy'.

Collaborators are replicating the same oppressive dynamics under the guise of 'representation' and 'empowerment'. However, the collaborators I have interviewed are pragmatic, as also observed by Qureshi (2017); they don't see the state as a threat but know it can harm (Qureshi 2017, 120).

Nadeem mirrors this character from John Carpenter's movie *They Live* (1988). At the beginning, he is a homeless man. Toward the end of the film, he is seen in a tuxedo, having sold out to the aliens who control humanity. When threatened, he justifies himself: 'it's just business ... We sell out every day, might as well be on the winning team.' It's an 'if you can't beat them, join them' mindset. Nadeem's interview and trajectory, along with others in this chapter, have been pivotal for me to understand the metacolonial phenomenon about why there is no shared solidarity in some Muslim circles and why so many Muslims support counter-extremism strategies, despite the fact that these policies erect Muslims as a suspect demographic and depict Islam as a religion of violence.

2.1. Securitization and Control of Dissent

In the aftermath of the 9/11 attacks, media scrutiny on Muslims increased disproportionately to the point where terror attacks by Muslims received 357% more press attention than attacks by non-Muslims (Kearns et al. 2018), although Muslim attacks in Western countries only accounted for 0.5% of all attacks (Institute for Economics and Peace 2015). This scrutiny led to overwhelmingly long-lasting perceptions in the public consciousness of Muslims as terrorists (Allen 2012; Sharma and Nijjar 2018) and Islam being perceived as a 'religion of intolerance' (Zick et al. 2011, 61), leading to the reawakening of Islamophobia (a term coined in 1904 by Ivan Agueli[3]), as defined by a fear, hatred of, or prejudice against the Islamic religion, Muslims, and those mistaken for Muslims.[4] Global debates in Europe and North America started revolving around the 'compatibility' of Islam and Muslim traditions with Western democracies (Bowen 2011), while most Muslims themselves didn't perceive any conflict between practicing Islam and living in a Western society (Pew 2016; Jakubowicz et al. 2012; Environics Institute 2016). As of 2019, a third of Britons believe that Islam threatens the 'British way of life' (Perraudin 2019). The other contention with counter-extremism policies is that they threaten political divergence of opinions, since anyone who expresses views conflicting with 'the existing order' can be catalogued as an 'extremist' (Dalgaard-Nielsen 2010, 798). In 2020, controversy arose when the environmentalist movement Extinction Rebellion was classified as an extremist group for its 'anti-establishment philosophy' (Dodd and Grierson 2020).

The global context of Islamophobia has led the public opinion and state structures to perceive Muslims as suspects by default and as a risk-prone demographic (Pantazis and Pemberton 2009, 2011; McGovern and Tobin 2010; Hickman et al. 2012), and ultimately to marginalize them (Sayyid and Vakil 2010; Hajjat and Mohammed 2013; Tyrer 2013; Kundnani 2014; Massoumi et al. 2017). The UK and US governments deployed an arsenal of strategies in an attempt to prevent Muslim attacks on their soil through strategies such as CVE (Countering Violent Extremism) in the US and PREVENT in the UK. These are part of former Prime Minister Theresa May's 'hostile environment policy', a set of legal requirements and administrative practices designed to make living in Britain for a subset of immigrants as burdensome as possible so that they voluntarily leave. Counter-extremism strategies have had tangible consequences for Muslims who can find themselves put on a no-flight list, blacklisted,[5] and unable to apply for jobs, and in more extreme cases they have had their houses searched even in the absence of criminal evidence (Cohen and Tufail 2017; Versi 2017). These policies, also partly because they are pushing people to suppress their identities, have had adverse effects on people's mental health (Mythen et al. 2009; Brown and Saeed 2015; see also chapter 4).

Fatima, a university researcher in France, observes how the police and the intelligence services regularly attend her conferences and once searched her flat. Hawa, a community organizer, describes how being a Muslim organization in France makes it nearly impossible to set up a business bank account. Farhan, who is preparing his PhD on police informants, talks about how his PhD supervisor warned him: 'if you work on this topic it will put off potential recruiters'. Walid, who works as a media officer in the charity sector in the UK, has been made aware that he can't apply for certain civil service jobs or sit on panels at certain events organized by a public body, despite having no criminal record and his DBS (Disclosure and Barring Service) check coming out clear. These policies are sometimes used by Muslims to criminalize other Muslims as a means to oust business competitors or for having different political opinions. Sahar, a long-term critic of the Saudi regime's handling of human rights, relates in a post how she was put on a blacklist preventing her from taking part in a public scheme by a Muslim PREVENT coordinator (Al Faifi 2019). However, the very low ratio of arrests and the poor value for money of counter-extremism strategies (Lomborg 2008) and their negative public impact led to criticisms in academia, education, the media,[6] and the health sector (Kundnani 2014; Blackbourn and Walker 2016; Mastroe 2016; Open Society 2016) and from the United Nations due to infringements of human rights (UN 2020).

Counter-extremism strategies relied primarily on being 'pre-criminal' (Goldberg et al. 2017; Qureshi 2019), based on the assumption that violent behaviour could be predicted. Early visuals for PREVENT depict a pill with the caption 'prevention is better than cure' (Younis 2020). Identifying 'presymptomatic individuals' has been a target for centuries in the UK and the US to prevent threats to the social order (Rose 1999). Consequently, public bodies across the UK, teachers, social, youth, and health workers, and universities are required by law to report people displaying these suspicious behaviours (DCSF 2008; Coppock and McGovern 2014; HMSO 2015). Pre-criminal identification would rely on changes in appearance, behaviour, and religious practice, although the methodology lacks research-based evidence and relies heavily on subjectivity (Jackson 2009; HM Government 2011, 2020a; Kundnani 2012; Coppock and McGovern 2014; Peatfield 2016; Elshimi 2017; Bechrouri 2018: Pettinger 2020). In France, state structures interpret wearing hijabs or long dresses as 'having a political agenda' and 'calculated motives'. Suddenly deciding to stop listening to music or making changes in one's dress code, vocabulary, or friendship group (as per British[7] and French[8] guidelines found in pamphlets) can trigger a series of red flags that would cause some Muslims to be put under electronic surveillance, or, in the most extreme cases, potentially to lose the right to see their own children.[9] The pathologization of religiosity has meant that Muslims developing mental health issues are also prime targets. These strategies led banks and governments, based on suspicion alone, to freeze the accounts of several Muslim charities, including Islamic Relief,[10] and to dissolve the humanitarian charity Barakacity and the CCIF (Collective Against Islamophobia in France, a pro-bono lawyer collective with a UN consultant status), despite having no proof of wrongdoing.[11] These narratives deny the existence of Islamophobia or hatred against Muslims, adopting victim-blaming discourses as in France or Belgium: religious clothing is regulated allegedly for people to be visibly neutral so they *won't* be targets of discrimination—in other words, 'if you don't want to face racism, remove your hijab'.

Second, counter-extremism strategies rely on differentiating between 'good' and 'bad' Muslims by setting limits on how Muslims should behave (Mamdani 2005). The 'good' and 'bad' Muslim dichotomy, racially constructed (Howell and Richter-Montpetit 2020), originates in British colonial Africa where the 'good' Muslims would cooperate with colonial authorities and 'bad' ones would be those threatening the status quo (Reynolds 2001). The dichotomy was used in two major reports (Al-Arian and Kanjwal 2018) by the RAND Corporation's National Defense Research Institute conducting research and analysis for the US Department of Defense: *The Muslim World after 9/11* (RAND 2004) and *Building Moderate Muslim Networks* (RAND 2007). These reports draw a typology determining who qualifies as a 'moderate' Muslim (Modood 2005) or potential allies to American interests: secularists, liberals, moderate Sufis, religious scholars, academics and intellectuals, community activists, journalists, and writers. Nowadays, a 'good' or 'moderate' Muslim is not simply one 'who rejects violence and fundamentalism . . . , but one who is also uncritical of empire, liberalism, and neoliberal economic policies . . . and situates blame entirely on other Muslims' understanding or interpretation of Islam' (Al Arian and Kanjwal 2018, 22). Hence, governments widened their strategies to target not only terrorists but Islam, establishing Islamophobia as an institutionalized norm (DCSF 2008; Mirza 2010, 22; Richards 2011; Warsi 2017).

The work of depoliticization and the management of dissent was brought into focus when the British government published official guidelines for schools classifying anti-capitalist ideas as 'extreme' ideologies (HM Government 2020b). Younis (2020) and Abbas (2019) see counter-extremism policies as a powerful psychological weapon to mollify resistance by pathologizing Muslim political dissent, similar to how 'disobedient housewives' in the Victorian era were thought by many to be schizophrenic. The expectation for non-white people to 'acclimate if not assimilate to whiteness' (Sharma 2010, 72) serves as an enabler for the access to and control of natural resources and consumer markets (see chapter 1). It is also operated by a subtle consolidation of nationalism: Younis (2020) argues that it is not a coincidence that PREVENT has introduced Fundamental British Values (FBV) into school curriculums. Because conversion to Christianity is a factor that can weight toward granting asylum in the UK (even despite past criminal offenses), in 2024, forty refugees changed their religion.[12]

In Euro-America, in addition to the deployment of infiltrators and covert police officers (Bechrouri 2018; Qurashi 2018), some initiatives made business out of flagging Muslim individuals and organizations as 'extremist', such as the Henry Jackson Society, resulting in the establishment of an entire *Islamophobia Industry* (Lean 2012). In the US, seven right-wing foundations spent $42.6 million between 2001 and 2009 (Ali et al. 2011) on creating a support network of politicians, media companies, bloggers, and other news outlets which would disseminate anti-Muslim rhetoric (Ernst 2013, 3), following a 'Cheshire-Cat logic'—that is, for Muslims to commit acts of violence, there must be something wrong with Islam (Younis 2020). The discourse echoes far-right narratives romanticizing the Crusades, depicting Muslims as a bloodthirsty arch-enemy, and painting movements like Salafism or the Muslim Brotherhood as political projects aiming at destroying European civilization. These forms of exclusion are racially specific and rely on the imaginary of the colonial past on both sides of the Atlantic (Meer 2014, Hajjat and Mohammed 2013). At the same time, these strategies across the Atlantic included a number of American Muslims who were expected to play the role of 'native informants' (Al-Arian and Kanjwal 2018; Bechrouri 2018; Abbas 2019). As Sahar mentioned, these networks include Muslims referring other Muslims to PREVENT or CVE, which some respondents compare to World War II kapos (concentration camp prisoners carrying out orders of Nazi camp officers).

The advent of social media led counter-extremism strategies to turn to digital data collection and intelligence gathering rather than direct contact with communities (Qurashi 2018). The Institute of Strategic Dialogue (ISD), funded by the UK Home Office and the US Department of State, staffed with ex-Quilliam Foundation and ex-Henry Jackson Society staff members, is a specialist in data harnessing, marketing tactics, and the creation of 'grassroots networks'[13] (see astroturfing in section 2.2). Although not participating openly in the PREVENT strategy, in 2020, the ISD secured a £800,000 partnership as a 'delivery partner' with the Mayor of London and Google to 'counter violent extremism' (Mayor of London 2020). In 2018, the ISD used Facebook Messenger,[14] in a project funded by Facebook, to spot and intervene in private conversations where the subjects were suspected to be at risk of extremism. The cooperation of tech giants with counter-extremism in order to monitor minorities is not new (Younis 2020). Google was a key partner for initiatives like Imams Online,[15] the company Moonshot CVE has been using Google analytics to detect online suspicious activities related to religious extremism, and the company DataMinR has been used to monitor Black Lives Matter protests with the help of Twitter.[16] Beyond raising issues about data privacy and security, scandals around the racially biased development of artificial intelligence by companies such as Google[17] or the implementation of racially biased facial recognition systems by the governments, such as with the UK Home Office,[18] are eerie reminders of Eugenics and Race Science—and frame tech giants as arms of colonial powers (Ali 2017; Benjamin 2019; Kwet 2019).

2.2. Deprivation and Theology of Liberation

In the UK, Muslims are hit by the most severe unemployment rates, obtain lower educational qualifications, are less likely than other groups to own a property, and are hit most severely by ill health.[19] Racism and Islamophobia, combined with a volatile job market and the lack of representation in politics or the media, has put Muslims in a situation of deprivation and pessimism, particularly impacting less financially well-off organizations and individuals. This has nurtured a self-esteem crisis, feelings of powerlessness, and alienation from the media and political sphere (Khan 2012; DeHanas 2016). Thus, many Muslims find themselves at a point where they are ready to compromise on their culture, faith, values, ethics, and identity in exchange of a quantum of financial stability or representation, reaching a point of moral resignation. One of my respondents who joined a counter-extremist think tank told me: 'I can't struggle all my life, I have a wife, I have kids, I need a secure income. I prefer that to compromising my mental health and not being able to secure my children's future.' This is a justification also observed in the US amongst those taking part in CVE programs or becoming informants (Bechrouri 2021).

In the UK, PREVENT officers exploit the financial insecurity of organizations to exert pressure (Qurashi 2018), thus holding a monopoly over the funding available for cultural and social initiatives, and including non-negotiable conditions such as spying on students and volunteers. Survival was made possible by submitting to whiteness and abiding by its norms, creating a sense of dependence. This cultural resignation is illustrated by the words of Saima Mir, a journalist and participant of the 2019 Bradford Literature Festival, in a conversation with Suhaymah Manzoor Khan (who boycotted the festival which was funded by counter-extremism money, along with fifteen other artists[20]). Mir admitted that 'having principles is a privilege not everyone can afford' (Mir in Manzoor-Khan and Mir 2019). Mir's words vocalize that the racist climate in the UK has led Muslims to ethical poverty: the lack of funding opportunities makes ethical decisions privileges held by those with enough wealth and influence to bypass institutional funding.

Her evocation of ethical poverty echoes Qasim's works around young Muslim criminals in Bradford (Qasim 2018; Qasim and Webster 2020): the climate of austerity, unemployment, and social and economic deprivation pushes some young Muslims, in order to survive financially, to resort to trading drugs, despite the risks. Umar, who has grown up in Luton and is now in his early thirties, has seen how his friends, because of deprivation and lack of opportunities, felt 'imprisoned' and has observed 'too many people going to extremes, but [who] then lost their identity', referring to friends who sought refuge in either criminality, religious conservatism, or the banking sector. People experience a scarcity mindset; they are in survival mode, focused on the short term, and experience cognitive overload, tunnelling, and goal inhibition: 'focusing on something that matters to you makes you less able to think about other things you care about' (Mullainathan and Shafir 2013,

13). As Paulo Freire (1993, 47) words it, 'the oppressed . . . have become resigned to [structures of oppression], are inhibited from waging the struggle for freedom so long as they feel incapable of running the risks it requires', and consequently, giving up the fight for liberation, they allow themselves to become oppressors or 'sub-oppressors' (Freire 1993, 45). However, Manzoor-Khan posits that ethical poverty is an illusion, as the boycotting artists organized a parallel, free event:

> I hope my withdrawal may also inspire others out of the scarcity mindset—as artists, writers, creatives or activists we sometimes act if any chance to share our work is the last chance, but the choice of where and when and who we perform for is just as important as the content itself.

The popularity of watchdog organizations and those specialized in advocacy and legal support, such as CAIR (in the US) and CAGE, HHUGS, or MEND (in the UK), conjugated with the loss of credibility of think tanks like the Henry Jackson Society or 'native informant' structures such as the Quilliam Foundation (Abbas 2019)—which closed down in 2021—suggests that antagonistic and confrontational strategies were not the most effective. When France enforced compliance through the law, it attracted condemnations by European and international human rights courts[21] and was internationally ridiculed when making the wearing of face masks compulsory for Muslim women during the pandemic, as in 2010 the government had banned masking of the face in public (Roy in McAuley 2020). These policies caused a 'brain drain' of engineers, academics, and health care professionals leaving France for the UK or Canada, where they could find jobs according to their skills and experience.[22]

Consequently, research and think tanks argued for more inclusive strategies.[23] In the mid-2010s, the UK and the US shifted from discipline-and-punish strategies (Foucault 1977) to a society of control (Deleuze 1992), enforcing compliance without pressure (Fraser and Freedman 1966). However, compliance needs a myth, which I frame as a theology of liberation: the promise of escaping racism and poverty if people conform to dominant norms and moral frameworks. However, communications were not always subtle, as with an associate of the RUSI (Royal United Services Institute) think tank trying to rebrand 'PREVENT as a site of resistance' to patriarchy and power.[24] Neoliberalism, relying on a similar empowerment narrative, has been pivotal for stirring the collective Muslim psyche in a certain direction—otherwise known as social engineering.

Neoliberalism in the age of social media has become a powerful force shaping the Muslim psyche: most humanitarian charities and YouTube religious figures have adopted a neo-Pentecostal (or prosperity gospel) model (Burity 2013; Martikainen 2013): valorizing pragmatism and financial success, using business management techniques, and turning the Qur'an into a management handbook (Barylo 2016, 2017). Before traditional religious authorities such as Hamza Yusuf,

Tariq Ramadan, and Nouman Ali Khan lost their monopoly, young Muslims would elect role models amongst social media influencers (see chapter 7) to the point where members of the public would consult them for religious rulings.[25] Early figures such as Rumena Begum, Amena Khan, or Adam Saleh, displaying Eurocentric beauty standards and showcasing a luxurious lifestyle where religion was nothing more than a cultural marker, have shown that it is possible to influence the thoughts and behaviours of Muslims through aspiration.

The consumerist Islam disseminated by social media celebrities has made the UK and the US succeed where France failed: people stop wearing the hijab not because of legal pressures, but because Islam has lost its meaning; Islam has become a cultural label and the hijab a mere fashion accessory. To paraphrase Postman (1985), there are no reasons to ban the hijab, for there is no one who wants to wear one. Both neoliberalism and counter-extremism are two facets of the same hegemony, in Gramsci's (1971, 263) sense of a 'consensus protected by the amour of coercion'. Both produce vulnerability and create structural pessimism: they make people believe that there is no other way of surviving than by abiding by the dominant system while giving them the illusion of choice (Mac an Ghaill and Haywood 2017)—as Thatcher said regarding neoliberalism: 'there is no alternative'. Just like neoliberalism sells people stories of liberation based on financial success and hard work, metacolonialism sells liberation through stories of assimilation.

Social engineering has been a pillar for counter-extremism strategies (Abbas 2019), specifically when it comes to the engineering of fake Muslim grass-roots groups pretending to be organically created (Qurashi 2018), otherwise called 'astroturfing'. 'Astroturfing is designed to give the appearance of "grass roots" mobilisation, or community-led bottom-up civil society initiatives, when in fact it is driven from above by state funding, patronage, training, in-kind services, etc. channelled through proxies... [subverting] the normal, healthy and authentic development of Muslim youth cultures by chaining it to the War on Terror logic of the good/bad Muslim binary' (Birt 2019). These strategies aim at 'effect[ing] behavioural and attitudinal change'[26] in young Muslims. In the UK, some of these proxies have been exposed such as Ummahsonic, Breakthrough Media, This is Woke, or Zinc Media.[27] In these regards, community-based programs in the US have received more than $10 million, despite the strategy violating civil rights (Al-Arian and Kanjwal 2018). These fake initiatives were quickly exposed by community watchdogs such as CAGE and MEND in the UK or the news outlet 5Pillars, and forced to close down. However, these organizations have limitations; CAGE and MEND, although popular in the 2010s amongst those who witnessed 9/11 and the war on terror unfold, struggle to reach younger, politically disinvested audiences born after these events or who were too young to understand them. Outlets like 5Pillars, although effective interrupters, reach more of a young, working-class, religiously conservative audience rather than older, liberal, financially comfortable Muslims in positions of power or influence. Muslim watchdogs are constantly playing catch-up with the newer counter-extremism strategies such as the selection of vetted exemplars.

2.3. Engineering the New Muslim Elite

A nod to Konrad Pędziwiatr's *New Muslim Elites* (2010), the term originally refers to young Muslims in the early 2000s actively taking part in the political, intellectual, and community life of their societies and creating vibrant hubs for ideas, hopes, activism, and creativity. In this section, this yesteryear's vibrant elite has been replaced by a different, unorganic one, sat on mountains of wealth and power, having disproportionate control over social and economic resources (Khan 2011), politically apathetic, engineered by a system that has designed a set of gears to run the machine.

Al-Arian and Kanjwal (2018) observed the erection of an 'official Islam' by governments, represented by a select pool of Muslims presented as new '*sujets supposés savoir*' (Lacan 1981) (subjects supposed to know better) or models of reference. These are those invited to the White House or 10 Downing Street in 'gestures of relationship building through culture and civil society—gaining hearts and minds' (Abdul Khabeer 2016, 212). However, under the illusion of political establishments becoming accommodating for a new social reality, these initiatives reward the accommodation of the 'good' half of the good-bad Muslim divide. The most famous examples cited by my respondents include, in the US, Zayd Shakir or Hamza Yusuf (the latter having being selected for Trump's human rights panel in 2019), in France, imam Hassen Chalghoumi, or, in the UK, figures like native informant Maajid Nawaz, London Mayor Sadiq Khan, Member of the House of Lords Baroness Sayeeda Warsi, social media celebrity Amena Khan, or actor Riz Ahmed. These exceptional citizens are a modern iteration of Soviet-era Stakhanovism, perpetuating the illusion that adopting the 'right' discourse, looks, and behaviours will free Muslims from racism, poverty, and exclusion. In the media, the BBC used presenter Mehreen Baig as a 'native informant' host of a programme titled: 'Lost boys? What's going wrong for Asian men', constructing Asian men as problematic (Manzoor-Khan 2018). Consequently, Muslim communities witness the emergence of a version of Islam not emerging organically from communities but 'manufactured in offices' in Washington, DC, New York, California, and London (Mahmood 2006; Al-Arian and Kanjwal 2018). In 2016, the ISD partnered with YouTube Creators for Change to create the program 'Be Internet Citizens'[28] (including influencers such as Dina Tokio, Humza Arshad,[29] or Nadir Nahdi[30]), promoting select influencers from minoritized demographics to 'teach teenagers about media literacy, critical thinking and digital citizenship'. These Muslims engaging in the spheres of power often blur the line between being 'Muslim professionals' and 'professional Muslims' (Kanjwal 2018): 'individuals whose career trajectory ... largely relies on the utilization and profession of some part of their Muslim identity'.

A few Muslim-led organizations in the UK and North America, working with government officials, have followed a similar strategy of engineering global Muslim 'leaders'. Amongst these are the Muslim Leadership Initiative (MLI), Emgage (US), and the Muppies (US), gathering the wealthiest Muslims in Silicon Valley or the Concordia Forum (UK/US). While Emgage and the Muppies focus respectively on voters' participation in American elections and Muslims in executive roles in high-profile companies, the MLI has attracted distrust from a wide array of Muslims for being a one-way 'exercise of power' (it invites Muslims to learn about Judaism but not Jews to learn about Islam) and a 'neo-colonial project' for creating cohorts of 'Good Muslims who could be publicly and privately pitted against the Bad Muslims' (Ziad 2018). By hinting at the promise of financial success, fame, and political power, these clubs and their relationship with governments and counter-extremism think tanks 'sell the dream of a future world in which one day there will be salvation' (Qureshi 2017, 128). While these organizations provide access to political and professional circles, secure publishing and business contracts, jobs in mainstream outlets such as the *New York Times*, and fellowships with leading neoliberal political think tanks, historian Hafsa Kanjwal questions the 'Muslimness' of the initiative (Kanjwal 2018) in the sense that the initiative, instead of creating 'leaders' as its claims, rather enslaves US American Muslims into the same structures of power that oppress them.

Elitist clubs like the Concordia Forum, which have strong ties to British and US politicians, gather Muslims who enjoy some degree of fame, wealth, or power such as Muslim MPs, entrepreneurs, media personalities, or those with imperial titles such as OBEs. One can find two videos of Hillary Clinton delivering messages of congratulations to the forum,[31] including one on the US Department of State official channel.[32] On their website, one can find that the Forum, which shares a senior executive with the aforementioned counter-extremism think tank ISD,[33] describes itself as 'a ground-breaking transatlantic network for leaders of Muslim backgrounds' and aims at 'promoting social justice'. The Concordia Forum has been running since 2009 in the form of yearly retreats in luxury resorts in Europe and North America. The Forum is invitation-only and abides by the Chatham House rules (no pictures and no communication are allowed about the content of the retreats). This model is similar to other exclusive networking retreats like Summit[34] for Silicon Valley entrepreneurs; however, it is one example amongst many others.

Some respondents who were invited to some of these elitist clubs mentioned that the invitation is not enough: they had to pay between £1,200 and £2,200 ($1,500–$2,800) to take part, excluding plane tickets. Some people call them sarcastically 'Muslim Opus Dei' or 'Muslim Illuminati'. John, a UK resident and artist in his fifties, has been attending every single retreat of one of these clubs since the beginning, in the hope of changing them from the inside:

JOHN: They initiated it to build trust and confidence among Muslim 'leaders'. They've helped a number of marriages ... But they lack of values, they're very distant from Prophetic values and lack of diversity, it's very Indo-Pak dominated. It's very exclusionary, it's for those in professional circles and the entry ticket is prohibitive.

WILLIAM: Why do you keep going to their retreats?

JOHN: It was a tough decision, but I decided to continue to engage because I had two options: leave and then things will get worse, or stay and try to do something. There is already little attention payed to congregational prayers. *jumuah* [Friday congregation] is ok, people go. [Someone] offered to the group to have *zikr* [devotional remembrance in congregation] one evening, and [they] came under attack. People have a bad image of *tasawwuf* [sufis]. There's lots of head of charities there, they're operating behind the layer of humanitarian action but are promoting capitalist ideas.

One of the founders and senior executives of one of these clubs, based in the UK, expanded on his intentions in one of my interviews: 'my intention was to create a Muslim Davos Forum, so people can strike business deals, political alliances, and we've even facilitated some marriages'. I asked him about the prohibitive price of the entry fees excluding working-class Muslims, the lack of representation of Black Muslims, and them giving a platform to the MLI and their partnership with the ISD: 'we really want everyone to participate. We can help people with a part of the entry fee and last year we've given awards to five Black people from America. We believe in free speech, no matter if you're from the right or the left, we want everyone to participate.' Bringing together the wealthiest, powerful and famous to build a Muslim elite in times of Islamophobia and under-representation of Muslims doesn't seem, at first sight, opposed to the betterment of the social and political situation of a minority. However, when questioned, some organizers are on the defensive, such as another senior executive based in the UK. On on-line platforms, in response to criticisms, he would post links and pictures of the 'achievements' of the club (mainly pictures of its members with famous politicians or business people), and use foul language: 'motherfucker', 'members of our network contributed thousands of dollars and people power to get them re-elected in the past few weeks', 'whatever you have been doing for the past 10 years to oppose what the UK government has done [is not working]'.

This is a behaviour I have observed, and have been on the receiving end of, when analysing and interviewing other people in positions of fame, wealth, and power such as charity magnates or influencers (see chapter 7), which happen to gather often in these elite clubs. Conjugated with the search for wealth and power, the rejection of community organizing, and the obsessive posting of 'achievements', the display of rudeness, anger, denial, dismissiveness, and patronization are all hallmarks of extrinsic values and goals, making them more likely places for people to objectify and exploit other people to behave rudely and aggressively (Kasser et al. 2004). When questioning smaller structures or people more at the margins, they were more ready to acknowledge their weaknesses and take on board criticism.

As observed by Al-Arian and Kanjwal (2018) and myself, not everyone who attended these events knew their agenda and only formed an opinion after attending. The very rare Black Muslims who attended felt isolated amongst an overwhelmingly South Asian crowd. The participants to these retreats are, however, of similar working-class background, some having achieved financial stability through high-paying jobs or business investments; some others are still struggling financially but aspire to the same goals. Through my personal network, I interviewed people who attended some of the retreats, like Salah, in his late twenties, working in media:

> It's all behind closed doors. It feels like a boys' club at some times. I disagree with the establishment and their views, lots of people attend once and never go back, they've been really put off. The establishment is not interested about Islamic values, it's really more about power and financial interests . . . but I've met good people there.

A few people I interviewed eventually got excluded and blacklisted; the reasons for their exclusion ranged from 'arbitrary' to 'their politics don't align' to 'their business was seen as a competitor with [one of the founder's] communication company'. Kanjwal (2018) criticizes the exclusionary and secretive nature of these clubs and the Concordia Forum specifically, noting that the reports and findings of the forum are not made public and that they are driven by 'insatiable desire for political 'relevance', and ultimately, power itself, at any cost'.

While these groups would organize events around issues such as anti-Blackness, the main contention my respondents have is that they just 'talk' without influencing. Fisher (2013) suggests that the power of hegemonies resides in their ability to tolerate and accommodate or even tokenize a shifting range of values always with the agenda of eventually recuperating if not neutralizing these. This is an observation backed by anthropologist Nazia Kazi, which calls these groups 'US Empire's Good Muslim Cheerleaders' (Kazi 2018): 'Muslims who silence, sidestep or disregard tackling the most egregious elements of American imperialism in exchange for visibility and legitimacy in the US racial order' (Kazi in Essa 2020). In his sermons, Khaled Abou El Fadl (2019), an American scholar popular in activist circles, calls out Muslims using similar strategies, like Hamza Yusuf, for being 'more lethal than islamophobes'. Judge and Brar (2017) analysed, for Sikhs in the US, how the acceptance of similar awards and official forms of recognition, seen as opportunities to escape the 'waiting room of history', implies forgetting genocide, indentured labour, and slavery that undergirds the empires while fastening a community to 'whiteness and its violent moorings' (Judge and Brar 2017, 148). Another symptom of this collective low self-esteem are the various awards ceremonies such as British Muslim Awards or Muslim Women Awards – which aim at celebrating achievements not recognised in mainstream society, but ultimately embrace the same neoliberal fallacy and culture of competition implying that one person must be better than the others.

Alternatives to elitist groups like the Muppies, however exist. Muslamic Makers, originating from London, gathers Muslims across the tech sector in the UK and globally. Holding workshops and panels such as 'AI and Ethics',[35] they do not gather solely around shared ethnic background or profession but consider Islam as a framework for fairer designs, offering pro-bono networking, mentoring, and training services, aware that a huge demographic doesn't have access to the resources, tools, and knowledge to enter the sector. In their defence, elitist clubs are working top-down to erect new Muslim exemplars (archetypes that people associate with Muslims), trying to shift the public perception of Muslims from being terrorists or immigrants. However, for the public to perceive Muslims as fame-thirsty celebrities, power-hungry businesspeople, or apathetic politicians seems to replicate other age-old stereotypes. Furthermore, public image doesn't automatically improve the socio-economic conditions of minorities.

2.4. Representation Is Not Liberation

Shareefa, an award-winning poet popular in activist circles, performed in Parliament for the launch of the South Asian Heritage Month in 2019 in a stance questioning the implementation of anti-immigration policies by Asian members of the government:

> It is vital South Asian communities do not fall into naive fantasies assuming the rise of South Asians in positions of power in Britain's cabinet who support right wing rhetoric and push for policies that dehumanise their own and fellow marginalised communities is in anyway shape or form progressive or inspiring worth celebrating... It is appalling when people would accept anything as visibility applauding those who firmly seek to uphold draconian laws as 'representation' for having seats at the table. (Shareefa Energy 2019)

Community historian Yahya Birt (2022, 38) roots the colonization of political engagement in a 'pragmatic negotiation for rights and recognition of the Muslim minority, which has led to an integration into local political party structures', which had no outcomes in terms of the betterment of their social, economic, and political condition. American blogger and lawyer Ahmed Shaikh identifies six categories of people he deems responsible for the 'complete failure' of American Muslim organizing: 'foreign Agents, Table-Or-Menu people, Careerists, Astroturf Scammers, Vassal Coalitionists and Professional Activists',[36] pointing out that Muslims accessing centres of power often act out of individual rather than collective interest. In my observations in the UK, I found that MPs who identify as Muslims, although increasingly numerous, rarely enjoy a large support network within their own parties or constituencies, and thus are pressured to disregard the interests of the wider Muslim communities and compromise on their initial ethical stances. A notable exception is Zarah Sultana, MP for Coventry South since 2019, who has been uncompromisingly transparent and vocal about her experience and against injustices toward marginalized groups. An initiative called The Muslim Vote,[37] established in 2023, claiming to be a coalition of British Muslim grass-roots initiatives, calls to Muslim voters whom it depicts as 'a powerful, united force of 4 million acting in unison'. However, some critics argue that unity is perhaps the main challenge for British Muslim communities (see section 6.2). Decolonial computer scientist Syed Mustafa Ali wants to leave the door open to partisan politics open under certain conditions: 'the question should be: I'm joining a club, what are the rules of the club?' (Ali in The Muslim Vibe 2020). He encourages people to examine the history and governance of any party and whether or not they fit into one's ethics and values, rather than vice versa. However, he is doubtful about the ability of parties to offer an ethical mode of governance, mentioning that the Qur'an is anti-elitist by essence and that, contrary to modern party politics, the early Islamic tradition was not to give power to those who want it[38] (see chapter 5).

While Muslim celebrities like Mohamed Salah were found to reduce hate speech amongst football fans and local crime rates (Alrababa'h et al. 2019), it remains to be proven whether these also affect higher circles of power, such as business and politics, and if these trends are not reversed over time. For example, the 1998 'Black White and Brown' euphoria consequent to France's first World Cup victory suddenly vanished after 9/11: what impact on racism and Islamophobia had Zidane and his team when, six years later, France banned the hijab in high schools? While popular culture has a constitutive effect on the self (Markus and Kitayama 2010), diversity and inclusion policies in business and politics act only as inventories which manage race in a way that sustains existing power relations: 'diversity is a technology of power, a means of managing the very difference it expresses' (Gray 2016, 242). Asim Qureshi (2017) highlights how Barack Obama's presidency illustrates the 'lie that representation can save us' (Qureshi 2017, 96) since his presidency didn't stop the shooting of innocent Black people or drone strikes over Afghanistan and Pakistan. Qureshi notes that 'most of Muslim politicians do not particularly represent Muslims' (Qureshi 2017, 98). Representation only works when there is organization and redistribution of power, as Al-Arian and Kanjwal write (2018), describing how US organizations like CAIR, MPAC, and others organized demonstrations, founded dedicated charitable institutions, built coalitions, and reached out to policy makers, despite finding many doors closed. Representation works when people adopt an attitude of service, just like Zarah Sultana exposes how companies tried to bribe her just after being elected.[39]

A consensus was reached by people from various community spaces, that representation and diversity apply more for values, ethics, and traditions than for colour: ethnically minoritized people in power don't mean anything if they do not tackle injustices that their communities are suffering. As Shareefa Energy (2019) sums up: 'Priti Patel is no sister of mine, Sajid Javed is no uncle of mine either.'

Being oneself is turning into the 'bad' category of Muslimness; it is becoming one of Fanon's *damnés* (wretched or doomed) and bears a huge social, financial, and sometimes legal cost. Although accepting positions of power or trying to change one's looks or behaviour to limit the damages are tempting, they have only limited effectiveness, especially when people trade respect for validation. This quest for validation cripples people's capacity of being who they most want to be (Bellah et al. 1991), putting oneself at the mercy of the group that validates. People with extrinsic values are more likely to suffer from frustration, dissatisfaction, stress, anxiety, anger, and compulsive behaviour (Kasser et al. 2004): personal well-being declines as the likelihood of having experiences that satisfy important psychological needs decreases. Respect implies boundaries, otherwise, one can suddenly lose approval and find themselves othered and made redundant; for example, social media celebrity Amena Khan was made obsolete when the public decided that her political opinions were worth terminating her contract with L'Oréal. It takes sometimes events such as global financial crises or pandemics for a community to lose their status of 'model minority', as happened during the 2020 coronavirus outbreak, when East Asians in the US came to be seen as the 'Yellow peril'.

In the UK, badges of approval, 'honours' such as Member or Commander of the British Empire (MBE or CBE), illustrate the uselessness of validation. These medals, granting no formal rights or privileges (apart, perhaps, from facilitating access to certain social circles), reading the inscription 'For God and The Empire', have been controversial within diasporas for their reference to the colonial era. Many Muslims, including some of my respondents, have justified their acceptance, saying, 'I want to make my parents proud' and 'we need to recognise Muslims' achievements'. In France, similar honours have existed since the nineteenth century such as the *Légion d'Honneur* (Legion of Honor). Ironically, French Emperor Napoléon Bonaparte, who implemented the *Légion d'Honneur*, acknowledged that the sole purpose of the honours system was the sustenance of his own power through control. He famously said to his critics: 'you call them toy rattles and indeed, it is by toy rattles that men are ruled' (Lavisse and Pariset 1921, my translation).

Elitist Muslim clubs are spaces at the apex of social Darwinism. They are not aiming at challenging the 1% (wealthiest people on Earth) or the establishment on their unfair treatment of minorities; instead, they aim at making Muslims part of the 1% and staying there. They are part of gated social communities which seem to have forgotten that 9/11 happened and that their very own communities have been the victims of the war on terror, waged by the very powers they are striving to serve. They are pessimistic initiatives that believe in the narrative of becoming Hercules, while in reality, they embody the Greek myths of Tantalus and Sisyphus at the same time, thirsty for a water they will never drink and pushing the rock that will lead to their own downfall. Falling into the traps of self-objectification, commodification, and orientalization, they end up navigating on the *Radeau de la Méduse* (reference to a classical painting by Géricault depicting the aftermath of the wreck of the French frigate Méduse), where castaways eventually eat each other for survival. Salim shared with me the lyrics of American Latinx rapper Immortal Technique who in 2001 wrote about these very issues regarding Black and Latinx Americans:

> when you try to change the system from within; it's not you who changes the system, it's the system that will eventually change you. No matter how much you want to dye your hair blonde... how many diamonds you buy from people who exploit your own brutally to get them, ... you will never be them. They're always gonna look at you as nothing but a little monkey. (Immortal Technique 2001)

By joining the elite, they feed the machine that will subjugate them in turn. However, no matter how high people rise on the ladder of power, people will still remain the non-white 'other'; as Baroness Warsi publicly declared about Sajid Javid: 'however much he panders to the right of our party, sadly the right of our party still believes he is far too Muslim to be leader'.[40] They earn the ability to oppress without the privileges and thus losing on all fronts: losing their identity, their community, and their legitimacy. Even the shield of MPs and other people of influence secured by the millionaires of the Muslim Entrepreneur Network didn't protect them from arrest when a coalition of former clients accused them of fraud.[41] As put by Hatem Bazian: 'we're negotiating a place on America's power dining table despite constantly being on the menu' (Bazian 2014), in an infinite Möbius loop of oppression and domination. On the other end of the spectrum, the metacolonization of the Muslim political imagination leads to the creation of chimera such as the Muslim alt-right.

Notes

1. School of Oriental and African Studies, University of London.
2. The graphic was originally produced by the Safehouse Progressive Alliance for Nonviolence in 2005 and since adapted in many variants, the most popular of which was adapted by Ellen Tuzzolo in 2016.
3. Abdal Hadi Ivan Agueli was Swedish by birth, a convert to Islam, and a Sufi with anarchist and anti-imperialist politics. He coined the term Islamophobia in 1904 in a piece written in Italian, called *The Enemies of Islam*. See Mark Sedgwick (ed.) *Anarchist, Artist, Sufi: The Politics, Painting, and Esotericism of Ivan Agueli* (London: Bloomsbury, 2021).
4. 'Islamophobia', Oxford Dictionaries. 2022; 'Islamophobia', Dictionary.com Unabridged. Random House. 2022; 'Islamophobia', Collins Dictionary. 2022.

5. Jamie Grierson, 'Counter-terror police running secret Prevent database', *The Guardian*, 6 October 2019. https://web.archive.org/web/20191007020647/https://www.theguardian.com/uk-news/2019/oct/06/counter-terror-police-are-running-secret-prevent-database
6. Jamie Grierson, 'Prevent figures show only one in 10 anti-radicalisation referrals need acute support', *The Guardian*, 19 December 2019. https://web.archive.org/web/20191219124222/https://www.theguardian.com/uk-news/2019/dec/19/prevent-figures-show-only-one-in-10-anti-radicalisation-referrals-need-acute-support; Richard Adams, 'Teachers back motion calling for Prevent strategy to be scrapped', *The Guardian*, 28 March 2016. https://web.archive.org/web/20160328125455/https://www.theguardian.com/politics/2016/mar/28/teachers-nut-back-motion-calling-prevent-strategy-radicalisation-scrapped; Jamie Grierson, '"My son was terrified": how Prevent alienates UK Muslims', *The Guardian*, 27 January 2019. https://web.archive.org/web/20190127164535/https://www.theguardian.com/uk-news/2019/jan/27/prevent-muslim-community-discrimination; Alice Ross, 'Academics criticise anti-radicalisation strategy in open letter', *The Guardian*, 29 September 2016. https://web.archive.org/web/20160930162234/https://www.theguardian.com/uk-news/2016/sep/29/academics-criticise-prevent-anti-radicalisation-strategy-open-letter; 'PREVENT will have a chilling effect on open debate, free speech and political dissent', *The Independent*, 10 July 2015. https://web.archive.org/web/20150713000351/https://www.independent.co.uk/voices/letters/prevent-will-have-a-chilling-effect-on-open-debate-free-speech-and-political-dissent-10381491.html
7. 'Who is vulnerable to radicalisation', Hertfordshire Constabulary. Accessed 1 February 2024. https://archive.is/KFWUy
8. 'Premiers signes', Préfet de l'Aisne. Accessed 1 February 2024. https://archive.is/U6y1u
9. Rivais, Rafaële. 2017. 'Le père qui se radicalise perd son droit de visite', *Le Monde*, 23 June 2017. https://web.archive.org/web/20200302105113/https://www.lemonde.fr/vie-quotidienne/article/2017/06/23/le-pere-qui-se-radicalise-perd-son-droit-de-visite_6004433_5057666.html
10. Simon Hooper, 'Palestinian campaign group's UK bank account shut down', *Middle East Eye*, 5 January 2016. https://web.archive.org/web/20200923110137/https://www.middleeasteye.net/news/palestinian-campaign-groups-uk-bank-account-shut-down
11. Simon Dawes, 'The Islamophobic witch-hunt of Islamo-leftists in France', *Open Democracy*, 2 November 2020. https://web.archive.org/web/20201102175624/https://www.opendemocracy.net/en/can-europe-make-it/islamophobic-witch-hunt-islamo-leftists-france
12. Charles Hymas, 'Forty Bibby Stockholm asylum seekers converting to Christianity', *The Telegraph* (4 February 2024). https://web.archive.org/web/20240205005021/https://www.telegraph.co.uk/news/2024/02/04/bibby-stockholm-asylum-seekers-converting-christianity
13. 'Approach'. Institute of Strategic Dialogue. Accessed 1 February 2024. https://web.archive.org/web/20201213192024/https://www.isdglobal.org/isdapproach
14. Catrin Nye and William Kremer, 'Facebook Messenger used to fight extremism', *BBC News*, 27 February 2018. https://web.archive.org/web/20180227020012/http://www.bbc.com/news/technology-43170837
15. 'Imams online or "imams in line"?', *5Pillars*, 25 January 2017. https://web.archive.org/web/20170127064054/https://5pillarsuk.com/2017/01/25/imams-online-or-imams-in-line
16. Sam Biddle, 'Police surveilled George Floyd protests with help from Twitter-affiliated startup DataminR', *The Intercept*, 9 July 2020. https://web.archive.org/web/20200709181717/https://theintercept.com/2020/07/09/twitter-dataminr-police-spy-surveillance-black-lives-matter-protests
17. Maggie Zhang, 'Google photos tags two African-Americans as gorillas through facial recognition software', *Forbes*, 1 July 2015. https://web.archive.org/web/20150702044556/https://www.forbes.com/sites/mzhang/2015/07/01/google-photos-tags-two-african-americans-as-gorillas-through-facial-recognition-software/#477420bc713d
18. Charles Hymas, 'Home Office under fire over face recognition technology that fails to recognise very dark or light faces', *The Telegraph*, 10 October 2019. https://web.archive.org/web/20191011133204/https://www.telegraph.co.uk/politics/2019/10/10/home-office-fire-face-recognition-technology-fails-recognise
19. Office for National Statistics, 2011 Census. https://www.ons.gov.uk/census/2011census
20. Nathan Atkinson, 'Bradford Literature Festival has 15 withdrawals over fund source', *Telegraph and Argus*, 26 June 2019. https://web.archive.org/web/20220618170525/https://www.thetelegraphandargus.co.uk/news/17729465.bradford-literature-festival-15-withdrawals-fund-source
21. 'France: banning the niqab violated two Muslim women's freedom of religion', UNHCR, 2018. https://web.archive.org/web/20201101044129/https://www.ohchr.org/EN/NewsEvents/Pages/DisplayNews.aspx?NewsID=23750; Dil Neiyyar, 'UN human rights body backs French Sikhs

on turbans', *BBC News*, 13 January 2012. https://web.archive.org/web/20120116105606/https://www.bbc.co.uk/news/world-europe-16547479; 'European Court of Human Rights condemns France over 'inhuman' living conditions for asylum-seekers', *France 24*, 2 July 2020. https://web.archive.org/web/20200703122945/https://www.france24.com/en/20200702-european-court-of-human-rights-condemns-france-over-inhuman-living-conditions-for-asylum-seekers
22. Donia Ismail, 'Ces musulmanes portant le voile qui quittent la France pour trouver du travail en Angleterre', 30 November 2020. https://web.archive.org/web/20201130061916/http://www.slate.fr/story/197507/france-femmes-musulmanes-voile-foulard-islam-trouver-travail-emploi-angleterre-royaume-uni
23. Sarah Lyons-Padilla, Michele Gelfand, Hedieh Mirahmadi, et al. 'Belonging nowhere: marginalization and radicalization risk among Muslim immigrants'. *Behavioral Science & Policy* 1(2) (2015), 1–12; Clara Pretus, Hamid Nafees, Sheikh Hammad, et al. 'Neural and behavioral correlates of sacred values and vulnerability to violent extremism'. *Frontiers in Psychology* 9(1) (2018), 24–62; Harith Hasan Al-Qarawee. *Iraq's Sectarian Crisis: A Legacy of Exclusion* (Carnegie Middle East Center 2014). https://web.archive.org/web/20191112043129/https://carnegie-mec.org/publications/55372
24. Elizabeth Pearson [Twitter], 18 May 2020. https://web.archive.org/web/20200518090607/https://twitter.com/lizzypearson/status/1262306160201347073
25. Omar Shahid, 'Keeping in check: maintaining spirituality in the influencer space', The Muslim Vibe Podcast, 28 June 2020. https://archive.org/details/Omarshaheed
26. Ian Cobain, '"This is woke": the media outfit that's actually a UK counter-terror programme', *Middle East Eye*, 15 August 2019. https://web.archive.org/web/20190815114705/https://www.middleeasteye.net/news/revealed-woke-media-outfit-thats-actually-uk-counterterror-programme
27. Simon Hooper, 'UK government "running covert counter-extremism propaganda campaign"', *Middle East Eye*, 23 December 2016. https://web.archive.org/web/20190709051121/https://www.middleeasteye.net/news/uk-government-running-covert-counter-extremism-propaganda-campaign
28. 'Be Internet Citizens', Institute of Strategic Dialogue. Accessed 1 February 2024. https://web.archive.org/web/20190112061833/https://www.isdglobal.org/programmes/education/internet-citizens-2; 'Be Internet Citizens', YouTube. Accessed 1 February 2024. https://web.archive.org/web/20170424131002/https://internetcitizens.withyoutube.com
29. 'Catching up with YouTube's Muslim creators for change', *Ummahsonic*. 2017. https://web.archive.org/web/20171120055456/https://ummahsonic.com/catching-youtubes-muslim-creators-change
30. 'Be Internet Citizens policy', YouTube. Accessed 1 February 2024. https://web.archive.org/web/20170424171656/https://internetcitizens.withyoutube.com/policy; 'Creators for change yearly report 2016–2017', YouTube. Accessed 1 February 2024. https://web.archive.org/web/20200509170430/https://kstatic.googleusercontent.com/files/7b8ee6bc5ac50d52d5634d45248383eb3112770f7cee6013b6d6437827dce956131c47ea17daacbb1b156ce064c7ceefdaf6cf32e69956764749ba163e4f39d9
31. 'Hillary Clinton on the 10th anniversary of the Concordia Forum', The Concordia Forum [YouTube], 7 November 2018. https://archive.org/details/hillary-clinton-on-the-10th-anniversary-of-the-concordia-forum-you-tube-1080p
32. 'Secretary Clinton delivers a video message to the Concordia Summit', US Department of State [YouTube], 1 October 2012. https://archive.org/details/secretary-clinton-delivers-a-video-message-to-the-concordia-summit-you-tube-360p
33. 'Zahed Amanullah', Institute of Strategic Dialogue. Accessed 1 February 2024. https://web.archive.org/web/20200219064632/https://www.isdglobal.org/isd_team/zahed-amanullah
34. Paul Lewis, 'Welcome to Powder Mountain—a utopian club for the millennial elite', *The Guardian*, 16 March 2018. https://web.archive.org/web/20180316144515/https://www.theguardian.com/technology/2018/mar/16/powder-mountain-ski-resort-summit-elite-club-rich-millennials
35. 'AI Ethics Panel @ Muslim Tech Fest 2023', Muslamic Makers [YouTube], 4 June 2023. https://archive.org/details/ai-ethics-panel-muslim-tech-fest-2023-360p
36. Ahmed Shaikh. '6 ways American Muslim political organizing has been a comprehensive failure', Ehsan blog, 6 December 2023. https://web.archive.org/web/20240129222713/https://ehsan.substack.com/p/6-ways-american-muslim-political
37. The Muslim Vote. 2023. https://web.archive.org/web/20231219193320/https://themuslimvote.co.uk
38. Imam Ghazali, *Ayyuhal Walad*, translated by Irfan Hasan (Pakistan, Dar-al Ishaat [no date]).

39. Zarah Sultana. [Twitter], 25 February 2020. https://web.archive.org/web/20200922160816/https://twitter.com/zarahsultana/status/1232396880866398210?lang=en; Double Down News. [Facebook], 24 February 2020. https://archive.org/details/10000000-597229150945051-5701560766986463051-n; Zarah Sultana, 'I didn't realise how many gifts politicians were sent until I became an MP', *Metro*, 17 February 2020. https://web.archive.org/web/20200218174536/https://metro.co.uk/2020/02/17/didnt-realise-many-gifts-politicians-sent-became-mp-12240994
40. Bill McLoughlin, '"Sajid Javid too MUSLIM to be leader" says Tory peer in SHOCKING Islamophobia claim', *Express*, 6 March 2019. https://web.archive.org/web/20190306095800/https://www.express.co.uk/news/uk/1096204/Conservative-party-news-sajid-Javid-islamophobia-baroness-Warsi-tory-peer-bbc-newsnight
41. Hannah Somerville, 'Self-styled entrepreneur and Instagram "influencer" reportedly arrested after get-rich-quick scheme collapse', *Ilford Recorder*, 4 November 2019. https://web.archive.org/web/20191104232730/https://www.ilfordrecorder.co.uk/news/crime-court/com-mirza-reportedly-arrested-in-dubai-1-6356408; Hannah Somerville, 'Investors who lost thousands in Muslim entrepreneur scheme rally at Barking mosque', *Barking and Dagenham Post*, 13 December 2019. https://web.archive.org/web/20191213235950/https://www.barkinganddagenhampost.co.uk/news/business/muslim-entrepreneur-network-protest-in-barking-1-6424887

References

Abbas, Tahir. 2019. 'Implementing "Prevent" in countering violent extremism in the UK: A left-realist critique.' *Critical Social Policy* 39(3), 396–412.

Abdul Khabeer, Su'ad. 2016. *Muslim Cool: Race, Religion and Hip Hop in the United States*. New York: New York University Press.

Abou El Fadl, Khaled. 2019. 'More lethal than Islamophobes—the modern day Murji'ah,' The Usuli Institute, 20 September. https://web.archive.org/web/20200806214556/https://www.usuli.org/2019/09/20/more-lethal-than-the-islamophobes-the-modern-day-murji-ah

Al-Arian, Abdullah, Kanjwal, Hafsa. 2018. 'The perils of American Muslim politics.' In *With Stones in Our Hands: Writings on Muslims, Racism, and Empire*, edited by Sohail Daulatzai and Junaid Rana. Minneapolis: University of Minnesota Press, 16–34.

Al-Faifi, Sahar. 2019. [Facebook] 14 July. https://archive.is/dR6Z8

Ali, Syed Mustafa. 2017. 'Transhumanism and/as whiteness.' *Proceedings of the IS4SI 2017 Summit Digitalisation for A Sustainable Society* 1(3), 244.

Ali, Wajahat, Eli Clifton, Matthew Duss, et al. 2011. *Fear, Inc. the Roots of the Islamophobia Network in America*. Washington, DC: Centre for American Progress.

Allegretti, Aubrey and Jessica Elgot. 2021. 'Covid: "greed" and capitalism behind vaccine success, Johnson tells MPs.' *The Guardian*, 24 March. https://web.archive.org/web/20210323231331/https://www.theguardian.com/politics/2021/mar/23/greed-and-capitalism-behind-jab-success-boris-johnson-tells-mps

Allen, Chris. 2012. 'A review of the evidence relating to the representation of Muslims and Islam in the British media.' Written evidence submitted to the All Party Parliamentary Group on Islamophobia, University of Birmingham.

Alrababa'h, Ala', William Marble, Salma Mousa, and Alexandra A. Siegel. 2019. 'Can exposure to celebrities reduce prejudice? The effect of Mohamed Salah on Islamophobic behaviors and attitudes.' *American Political Science Review* 115(4), 1111–28.

Barylo, William. 2016. 'Neo-liberal not-for-profits: the embracing of corporate culture in European Muslim charities.' *Journal of Muslim Minority Affairs* 36(3), 383–98.

Barylo, William. 2017. *Young Muslim Change-Makers*. London: Routledge.

Bazian, Hatem. 2014. [Facebook] 12 September. https://archive.is/lNB8W

Bechrouri, Ibrahim. 2018. 'The informant, Islam and Muslims in New York city.' *Surveillance & Society* 16 (4), 459–72.

Bechrouri, Ibrahim. 2021. *Approche géopolitique des stratégies de lutte antiterroriste du New York Police Department: une analyse multi-scalaire*. PhD thesis. 8 July, Université Paris 8.

Bellah, Robert, Steven Tipton, Ann Swidler, et al. 1991. *The Good Society*. New York: Knopf.
Benjamin, Ruha. 2019. *Race after Technology*. Cambridge: Polity Press.
Birt, Yahya. 2019. 'Astroturfing and the rise of the secular security state in Britain.' *Medium*, 17 April. https://web.archive.org/web/20191211210630/https://medium.com/@yahyabirt/astroturfing-and-the-rise-of-the-secular-security-state-in-britain-cd21c5005d43
Birt, Yahya. 2022. *Ummah at the Margins: The Past, Present and Future of Muslim Minorities*. London: Ayaan Centre.
Blackbourn, Jessie and Clive Walker. 2016. 'Interdiction and indoctrination: the Counter-Terrorism and Security Act 2015.' *Modern Law Review* 79(5), 840–70.
Bowen, John R. 2011. *Can Islam Be French? Pluralism and Pragmatism in a Secularist State*. Princeton: Princeton University Press.
Brown, Katherine E. and Tania Saeed. 2015. 'Radicalization and counterradicalization at British universities: Muslim encounters and alternatives.' *Ethnic and Racial Studies* 38(11), 1952–68.
Burity, Joanildo A. 2013. 'Entrepreneurial spirituality and ecumenical alternglobalism: two religious responses to global neoliberalism.' In *Religion in the Neoliberal Age: Political Economy and Modes of Governance*, edited by Tuomas Martikainen and François Gauthier. Farnham: Ashgate, 21–36.
Cohen, Barbara and Waqas Tufail. 2017. 'Prevent and the normalization of Islamophobia.' In *Islamophobia: Still a Challenge for Us All*, edited by Farah Elahi and Omar Khan. London: Runnymede, 41–5.
Coppock, Vicki and Mark McGovern. 2014. '"Dangerous minds"? Deconstructing counter-terrorism discourse, radicalisation and the "psychological vulnerability" of Muslim children and young people in Britain.' *Children Society* 28(3), 242–56.
Craun, Dustin. 2013. 'Exploring pluriversal paths toward transmodernity: from the mind-centered egolatry of colonial modernity to Islam's epistemic decolonization through the heart.' *Human Architecture: Journal of the Sociology of Self-Knowledge* 11(1), 91–113.
Dalgaard-Nielsen, Anja. 2010. 'Violent radicalization in Europe: what we know and what we do not know.' *Studies in Conflict and Terrorism* 33(9), 797–814.
DCSF. 2008. *Learning Together to Be Safe: A Toolkit to Help Schools Contribute to the Prevention of Violent Extremism*. Nottingham: DCSF.
DeHanas, Daniel. 2016. *London Youth, Religion, and Politics: Engagement and Activism from Brixton to Brick Lane*. Oxford: Oxford University Press.
Deleuze, Gilles. 1992. Postscript on the Societies of Control. *October*, Vol. 59 (Winter), 3–7.
Dodd, Vikram and Jamie Grierson. 2020. 'Terrorism police list Extinction Rebellion as extremist ideology.' *The Guardian*, 10 January. https://web.archive.org/web/20200110172313/https://www.theguardian.com/uk-news/2020/jan/10/xr-extinction-rebellion-listed-extremist-ideology-police-prevent-scheme-guidance
Elshimi, Mohammed. 2017. *De-Radicalisation in the UK Prevent Strategy: Security, Identity and Religion*. London: Routledge.
Environics Institute. 2016. *Survey of Muslims in Canada 2016*. Toronto: Environics Institute.
Ernst, Carl (ed.). 2013. *Islamophobia in America: The Anatomy of Intolerance*. New York: Palgrave Macmillan.
Essa, Azad. 2020. 'Joe Biden, Emgage and the muzzling of Muslim America.' *Middle East Eye*, 9 October. https://web.archive.org/web/20201010074302/https://www.middleeasteye.net/big-story/joe-biden-emgage-muslim-america-us-elections
Fisher, Rebecca (ed.). 2013. *Managing Democracy, Managing Dissent: Capitalism, Democracy and the Organisation of Consent*. London: Corporate Watch.
Foucault, Michel. 1977 [1975]. *Discipline and Punish*. New York: Pantheon Books.
Fraser, Freedman. 1966. 'Compliance without pressure: the foot in the door technique.' *Journal of Personality and Social Psychology* 4(2), 155–202.
Freire, Paulo. 1993 [1968]. *The Pedagogy of the Oppressed*. New York: Continuum.
Goldberg, David, Sushrut Jadhav, and Tarek Younis. 2017. 'Prevent: what is pre-criminal space?' *BJPsych Bulletin* 41(4), 208–11.

Gramsci, Antonio. 1971. *Selections from the Prison Notebooks*, edited and translated by Quintin Hoare and Geoffrey Nowell Smith. New York: Lawrence and Wishart.
Gray, Herman. 2016. 'Precarious diversity: representation and demography in precarious creativity global media.' In *Local Labor*, edited by Michael Curtin and Kevin Sanson. Berkeley: University of California Press, 241–54.
Hajjat, Abdellali and Marwan Mohammed. 2013. *Islamophobie: Comment les élites françaises fabriquent le 'problème musulman'*. Paris: La Découverte.
Hickman, Mary, Lyn Thomas, Henri Nickels, et al. 2012. 'Social cohesion and the notion of communities: a study of the experiences and impact of being suspect for Irish communities and Muslim communities in Britain.' *Critical Studies on Terrorism* 5(1), 89–106.
HM Government. 2011. *Prevent Strategy*. London: Crown Copyright. https://web.archive.org/web/20130616194314/https://www.gov.uk/government/uploads/system/uploads/attachment_data/file/97976/prevent-strategy-review.pdf
HM Government. 2020a. *E-Learning Training on PREVENT*. London: Crown Copyright. https://web.archive.org/web/20160612084224/https://www.elearning.prevent.homeoffice.gov.uk
HM Government. 2020b. *Plan Your Relationships, Sex and Health Curriculum*. London: Crown Copyright. https://web.archive.org/web/20201001141000/https://www.gov.uk/guidance/plan-your-relationships-sex-and-health-curriculum
HMSO. 2015. *Revised 'Prevent' Duty Guidance: for England and Wales*. London: Crown Copyright. https://web.archive.org/web/20231231001453/https://www.gov.uk/government/publications/prevent-duty-guidance-england-scotland-and-wales-2015/revised-prevent-duty-guidance-for-england-and-wales-2015
Howell, Alison and Melanie Richter-Montpetit. 2020. 'Is securitization theory racist? Civilizationism, methodological whiteness, and antiblack thought in the Copenhagen School.' *Security Dialogue* 51(1), 3–22.
Immortal Technique. 2001. 'The poverty of philosophy.' *Revolutionary Vol. 1*. New York: Viper Records.
Institute for Economics and Peace. 2015. *Global Terrorism Index: Measuring and Understanding the Impact of Terrorism*. Sydney: Institute for Economics and Peace.
Jackson, Richard. 2009. 'The study of terrorism after 11 September 2001: problems, challenges and future developments.' *Political Studies Review* 7(2), 171–84.
Jakubowicz, Andrew, Jock Collins, and Wafa Chafic. 2012. 'Young Australian Muslims: social ecology and cultural capital.' In *Muslims in the West and the Challenges of Belonging*, edited by F. Mansouri and V. Marotta. Melbourne: Melbourne University Press, 34–59.
Judge, Rajbir Singh and Jasdeep Singh Brar. 2017. 'Guru Nanak is not at the White House: an essay on the idea of Sikh-American redemption.' *Sikh Formations* 13(3), 147–61.
Kanjwal, Hafsa. 2018. 'What is "Muslim" about the Muslim Leadership Initiative?' *Muftah Special Collection: Examining American Islam*, 9 July.
Kasser, Tim, and Richard Ryan. 1996. 'Further examining the American dream: differential correlates of intrinsic and extrinsic goals.' *Personality and Social Psychology Bulletin* 22(3), 280–7.
Kasser, Tim, Richard Ryan, Charles Couchman, et al. 2004. 'Materialistic values: their causes and consequences.' In *Psychology and Consumer Culture: The Struggle for a Good Life in a Materialistic World*, edited by T. Kasser and A. D. Kanner. Worcester: American Psychological Association, 11–28.
Kazi, Nazia. 2018. *Islamophobia, Race, and Global Politics*. Lanham: Rowman & Littlefield.
Kearns, Erin, Allison Betus, and Anthony Lemieux. 2018. 'Why do some terrorist attacks receive more media attention than others?' *Justice Quarterly* 36(6), 985–1022.
Khan, Saeed A. 2012. 'The phenomenon of serial nihilism among British Muslim youth of Bradford, England.' In *Muslim Youth: Challenges, Opportunities and Expectations*, edited by Fauzia Ahmad and Mohammad Siddique Seddon. London: Bloomsbury, 15–31.
Khan, Shamus. 2011. *Privilege: The Making of an Adolescent Elite at St. Paul's School*. Princeton: Princeton University Press.
Kundnani, Arun. 2012. 'Radicalisation: the journey of a concept.' *Race and Class* 54(2), 3–25.

Kundnani, Arun. 2014. *The Muslims Are Coming: Islamophobia, Extremism, and the Domestic War on Terror*. New York: Verso.
Kwet, Michael. 2019. 'Digital colonialism: US empire and the new imperialism in the Global South.' *Race & Class* 60(4), 3–26.
Lacan, Jacques. 1981 [1973]. ' Of the Subject who is Supposed to Know.' In *The Four Fundamental Concepts of Psychoanalysis—Book XI of the Seminar of Jacques Lacan*, edited by Jacques-Alain Miller, translated by Alan Sheridan. New York: W. W. Norton, 230–43.
Lavisse, Ernest and Georges Pariset. 1921. *Histoire De France Contemporaine Depuis La Révolution Jusqu'à La Paix De 1919, Tome 3: Le Consulat et l'Empire (1799–1815)*. Paris: Hachette.
Lean, Natahan. 2012. *The Islamophobia Industry: How the Right Manufactures Fear of Muslims*. London: Pluto Books.
Lomborg, Bjorn. 2008. 'Is counterterrorism good value for money?' *NATO Review*, 8 April. https://web.archive.org/web/20200923101628/https://www.nato.int/docu/review/articles/2008/04/08/is-counterterrorism-good-value-for-money/index.html
Mac an Ghaill, Máirtín and Chris Haywood (eds.). 2017. *Muslim Students, Education and Neoliberalism: Schooling a 'Suspect Community'*. London: Palgrave.
Mahmood, Saba. 2006. 'Secularism, hermeneutics and empire: the politics of Islamic Reformation.' *Public Culture* 18(2), 323–47.
Mamdani, Mahmood. 2005. *Good Muslim, Bad Muslim: America, the Cold War, and the Roots of Terror*. New York: Harmony.
Manzoor-Khan, Suhaiymah and Saima Mir. 2019. 'Does Bradford festival's counter-extremism funding warrant a boycott?' *The Guardian*, 24 June. https://web.archive.org/web/2019062 4130059/https://www.theguardian.com/commentisfree/2019/jun/24/bradford-literary-festi val-counter-extremism-funding-boycott
Manzoor-Khan, Suhaiymah. 2018. 'The story of British Pakistani men, told by a native informant.' *AlJazeera*, 16 August. https://web.archive.org/web/20201109041334/https://www.aljazeera.com/opinions/2018/8/16/the-story-of-british-pakistani-men-told-by-a-native-informant
Markus, Hazel Rose and Shinobu Kitayama. 2010. 'Cultures and selves: a cycle of mutual constitution.' *Perspectives on Psychological Science* 5(4), 420–30.
Martikainen, Tuomas. 2013. *Religion in the Neoliberal Age: Political Economy and Modes of Governance*. Farnham: Ashgate.
Marwick, Alice E. 2013. *Status Update: Celebrity, Publicity, and Branding in the Social Media Age*. New Haven: Yale University Press.
Massoumi, Narzanin, Tom Mills, and David Miller. 2017. *What is Islamophobia? Racism, Social Movements and the State*. London: Pluto Press.
Mastroe, Caitlin. 2016. 'Evaluating CVE: understanding the recent changes to the United Kingdom's implementation of Prevent.' *Perspectives on Terrorism* 10(2), 50–60.
Mayor of London. 2020. 'Mayor launches new fund to counter violent extremism and hate crime.' 14 January. https://web.archive.org/web/20200706151615/https://www.london.gov.uk/press-releases/mayoral/mayors-new-fund-to-counter-violent-extremism
McAuley, James. 2020. 'France mandates masks to control the coronavirus. Burqas remain banned.' *The Washington Post*, 10 May. https://web.archive.org/web/20200511010233/https://www.washingtonpost.com/world/europe/france-face-masks-coronavirus/2020/05/09/6fbd50fc-8ae6-11ea-80df-d24b35a568ae_story.html
McGovern, Mark and Angela Tobin. 2010. *Countering Terror or Counter-Productive: Comparing Irish and British Muslim Experiences of Counterinsurgency Policy and Law*. Ormskirk: Edge Hill University.
Meer, Nasar. 2014. 'Islamophobia and postcolonialism: continuity, Orientalism and Muslim consciousness.' *Patterns of Prejudice* 48(5), 500–15.
Mirza, Heidi. 2010. *Multicultural Education in England*. London: Institute of Education.
Modood, Tariq. 2005. *Multicultural Politics: Racism, Ethnicity, and Muslims in Britain*. Minneapolis: University of Minnesota Press.

Mullainathan, Sendhil and Eldar Shafir. 2013. *Scarcity: Why Having So Little Means So Much*. London: Penguin.

Murad, Abdal Hakim. 2020. *Travelling Home: Essays on Islam in Europe*. Cambridge: The Quilliam Press.

Mythen, Gabe, Sandra Walklate, and Fatima Khan. 2009. '"I'm a Muslim but I'm not a terrorist": victimisation, risky identities and the performance of safety.' *British Journal of Criminology* 49(6), 736–54.

No White Saviors. 2019. [Twitter] 17 November. https://archive.is/OLc1A

Open Society Justice Initiative. 2016. *Eroding Trust, the UK's Prevent Counter-Extremism Strategy in Health and Education*. New York: Open Society Foundations.

Pantazis, Christina and Simon Pemberton. 2009. 'From the "old" to the "new" suspect community: examining the impacts of the recent UK counter-terrorist legislation.' *British Journal of Criminology* 49(5), 646–66.

Pantazis, Christina and Simon Pemberton. 2011. 'Restating the case for the "suspect community".' *British Journal of Criminology* 51(6), 1054–62.

Peatfield, Elizabeth-Jane. 2016. 'Making vulnerable: the effect on minority communities of the identification of vulnerability within PREVENT.' In *Muslims in the UK and Europe II*, edited by Yassir Suleiman and Paul Anderson. Cambridge: Centre of Islamic Studies, 48–53.

Pędziwiatr, Konrad. 2010. *The New Muslim Elites in European Cities: Religion and Active Social Citizenship amongst Young Organized Muslims in Brussels and London*. Saarbrücken: VDM Verlag.

Perraudin, Frances. 2019. 'Third of Britons believe Islam threatens British way of life, says report.' *The Guardian*, 17 February. https://web.archive.org/web/20190217120446/https://www.theguardian.com/world/2019/feb/17/third-of-britons-believe-islam-threatens-british-way-of-life-says-report

Pettinger, Tom. 2020. 'British terrorism preemption: subjectivity and disjuncture in Channel "deradicalization" interventions.' *British Journal of Sociology* 71(5), 970–84.

Pew Research Center. 2016. *Religion in Everyday Life*. Washington, DC: Pew Research Center.

Postman, Neil. 1985. *Amusing Ourselves to Death*. Methuen: Viking Penguin.

Qasim, Mohammed. 2018. *Young, Muslim and Criminal: Experiences, Identities and Pathways into Crime*. Bristol: Policy Press.

Qasim, Mohammed and Colin Webster. 2020. '"Prisons were made for people like us": British Pakistani Muslim experiences upon release from prison.' *The Prison Journal* 100(3), 399–419.

Qurashi, Fahid. 2018. 'The Prevent strategy and the UK 'war on terror': embedding infrastructures of surveillance in Muslim communities.' *Palgrave Communications* 4, 17.

Qureshi, Asim. 2017. *A Virtue of Disobedience*. London: Byline Books.

Qureshi, Asim. 2019. *The 'Science' of Pre-Crime: The Secret 'Radicalisation' Study Underpinning Prevent*. London: CAGE.

RAND 2004. *The Muslim World after 9/11*. Santa Monica: RAND Corporation. https://web.archive.org/web/20240130203520/https://www.rand.org/content/dam/rand/pubs/monographs/2004/RAND_MG246.pdf

RAND 2007. *Building Moderate Muslim Networks*. Santa Monica: RAND Corporation. https://web.archive.org/web/20240116103101/https://www.rand.org/content/dam/rand/pubs/monographs/2007/RAND_MG574.pdf

Reynolds, Jonathan. 2001. 'Good and bad Muslims: Islam and indirect rule in northern Nigeria.' *The International Journal of African Historical Studies* 34(3), 601–18.

Richards, Anthony. 2011. 'From terrorism to "radicalization" to "extremism": counterterrorism imperative or loss of focus?' *International Affairs* 91(2), 371–80.

Rose, Nikolas. 1999. *Governing the Soul: Shaping of the Private Self*. London: Free Association Books.

Sayyid, Salman and AbdoolKarim Vakil (eds.). 2010. *Thinking through Islamophobia: Global Perspectives*. London: Hurst.

Shareefa Energy 2019. [Facebook], 26 July. https://web.archive.org/web/20200929102123/https://www.facebook.com/shareefa.human/posts/10162172570545473

Sharma, Nitasha. 2010. *Hip Hop Desis: South Asian Americans, Blackness, and a Global Race Consciousness.* Durham: Duke University Press.

Sharma, Sanjay and Jasbinder Nijjar. 2018. 'The racialized surveillant assemblage: Islam and the fear of terrorism.' *Popular Communication* 16(1), 72–85.

The Muslim Vibe. 2020. 'Should Muslims engage in politics?' [YouTube] 8 March. https://archive.org/details/should-muslims-engage-in-politics-or-not-1080p

They Live. 1988. [Film]. John Carpenter (dir.). USA: Alive Films and Larry Franco.

Tyrer, David. 2013. *The Politics of Islamophobia: Race, Power and Fantasy.* London: Pluto Press.

UN Special Rapporteur. 2020. *Human Rights Impact of Policies and Practices Aimed at Preventing and Countering Violent Extremism.* https://web.archive.org/web/20231219235039/https://digitallibrary.un.org/nanna/record/3872336/files/A_HRC_43_46-EN.pdf?withWatermark=0&withMetadata=0&version=1&registerDownload=1

Versi, Miqdad. 2017. 'The latest Prevent figures show why the strategy needs an independent Review.' *The Guardian*, 10 November. https://web.archive.org/web/20171110131506/https://www.theguardian.com/commentisfree/2017/nov/10/prevent-strategy-statistics-independent-review-home-office-muslims

Warsi, Sayeeda. 2017. *The Enemy within: A Tale of Muslim Britain.* London: Allen Lane.

Younis, Tarek. 2020. 'The psychologisation of counter-extremism: unpacking PREVENT.' *Race & Class* 62(3), 37–60.

Ziad, Homayra. 2018. 'Why I left the Muslim Leadership Initiative.' *Muslim Matters*, 6 June. https://web.archive.org/web/20180622225017/https://muslimmatters.org/2018/06/06/why-i-left-the-muslim-leadership-initiative

Zick, Andreas, Beate Küpper, and Andreas Hövermann. 2011. *Intolerance, Prejudice and Discrimination. A European Report.* Berlin: Friedrich-Ebert Foundation.

3

Making Muslims Great Again

Alt-Bros, Alpha Muslims, and Supremacists

> The child who is not embraced by the village will burn it down to feel its warmth. (African proverb)

'Men age like wine. Women age like milk.' 'Women! As long as you feed us, you frack us, and . . . shut the frack up, we're ok' (Azeez 2020). Nabeel Azeez presents himself to his tens of thousands of followers as 'the voice of the silent majority on Muslim Social Media' (Becoming the Alpha Muslim 2018). Founder of the podcast, blog, and YouTube channel 'Becoming the Alpha Muslim',[1] he became popular for his views on women's rights, Trump, and the Black Lives Matter movement. His channel targets 'millennial Muslim men who are raised and live in a globalized World where Euro-American popular culture is dominant' (Becoming the Alpha Muslim 2018). On his YouTube channel, he covers various topics such as 'the Cat and Mouse game of Male Female Interaction', 'How to make a side income', and 'Trump: Year 1—The Alt-Bro Perspective'. He invites supporters and advisors to Donald Trump,[2] uses vocabulary such as Antifa, SJW (Social Justice Warriors, a pejorative designating people vocal against oppression), and 'fake news', claims that Black Lives Matters have a 'hidden agenda' (Azeez 2017), and mentions often the problem of 'the decline of testosterone in men'. Nabeel Azeez defines himself as being an 'alt-bro',[3] a Muslim 'not subscribing to any political party', who 'can be liberal on some issues and I can be conservative on other issues', as a reaction to the global 'Muslim leftist bandwagon'.

In the wake of Me Too and Black Lives Matter, very few Muslims expected that some fellow believers would publicly take position against these movements. Nabeel Azeez is not an isolated figure. Part of a heterogeneous movement, a number of prominent anti-feminist, homophobic and sometimes anti-Black figures have sparked controversy such as Daniel Haqiqatjou, Abdullah Al-Andalusi, Gabriel Al-Romaani, YouTuber Saajid Lipham, or Joe Bradford, the latter dismissing attacks on whiteness as a conspiracy theory and Andrew Tate, wrestler and reality-TV star who embraced Islam in late 2022, whose views have been labelled as 'extreme misogyny' by UK domestic abuse charities.[4] Ghumkhor and Mir (2022) also note that the narrative of 'crisis of masculinity' and the decline of traditional Islam is found in more mainstream scholars such as Jonathan Brown or Abdal Hakim Murad.

The popularity of anti-feminist figures has shocked many Muslims sympathetic to the well-established discourse on women's rights in Islam. Post-9/11, as a reaction to Islamophobia, numerous young Muslims in Europe and America had undertaken Islamic jurisprudence courses (*ijaza*, see introduction), in order to refute Islamophobic arguments such as Islam being inherently misogynistic. Muslim women would defend the hijab as their choice, sometimes against their own families, and would mention examples of women at the time of the Prophet, running businesses like Khadija, taking part in battles like Nusaybah bint Ka'ab at Uhud, travelling on their own like Umm Salama, who set out on Hijra alone with her child, being teachers, scholars, poets, and more. Instead of showing solidarity with Muslim women victim of sexual abuse (their 'sisters' in faith), popular online debaters not necessarily qualified in jurisprudence, were seen as denying the oppression of women and using victim-blaming rhetoric: '90% of cases of abuse is them [women] being emotional and whining about having to do a little bit of work around the house' (Becoming the Alpha Muslim 2018).

Azeez embraced the label 'alt-bro' originally used in a 2017 Al Madina podcast, defining 'alt-bros' as a movement of 'reactionary hyper-masculinity' that has developed to counter feminism, and using power to 'control, exploit, denigrate our partners amongst the female gender' (ImanWire Podcast 2017). Some others call them the 'akhi-right' (from the Arabic *akhi*, brother) or the alt-*wallah* (Ghumkhor and Mir 2022). Alt-bro' is derived from the US American 'alt-right', a loosely connected network of white nationalists, supremacists, and separatists, advocating for tight immigration restrictions, racism, xenophobia, antisemitism, antifeminism, homophobia, and islamophobia (Heikkilä 2017). Due to their strong opposition to feminism, some of these 'men's rights activists' have been labelled as the 'manosphere' (Hodapp 2017; Marwick and Lewis 2017; Lumsden 2019), with Nabeel Azeez including himself in the 'Muslim manosphere' (Kesvani 2019; Ghumkhor and Mir 2022). Amongst Muslim voices against feminism some advocates have emerged for the creation of white-Muslim-only spaces and white Muslims marrying each other, such as Islam4Europeans.com[5] or Maliki Clique.[6]

This chapter analyses their background story, grievances, and contentions in an attempt at positioning these figures in the wider social landscape of Muslim activism in Euro-America. My fieldwork is based on people in my own circles who adhere to these views and on the elements of the main tenets of the movement have shared online. This chapter argues that sexism, misogyny, and anti-Blackness are not issues inherent to Islam, Muslims, or South Asians. In the framework of metacolonialism, they are the symptoms of wider, global issues inherited from dominant systems, which some Muslims adopt as liberation theologies out of a feeling of powerlessness. Although the alt-bros constitute one marginal extreme of the spectrum of political engagement of Muslims, I found that similar narratives are echoed by more mainstream privileged Muslim figures. Ultimately, using the framework of affect and looking at the movement from the perspective of trauma and diasporic melancholia, this chapter analyses the alt-bros from bell hooks' concept of 'comrades in struggle'.

3.1. The Alphas and Betas of Male Crisis

The few people I met who support alt-bros figures share mixed views. They would acknowledge the mistreatment of women, but would question the validity of feminism. Saleh, in his mid-twenties, who frequents the same London hubs as many of my respondents, doesn't agree with the term 'toxic masculinity': 'it's a blanket term, it pathologises men, but I agree that it's useful to describe something rampant... There's really bad behaviour such as guys sending pictures of their penises on social media, but it's not all men.' At the same time, he would post on social media thoughts about how soft a man his father is, or that in the Middle East, male friends would hold hands publicly, and how it can seem shocking according to Eurocentric heterosexual norms. Haroon, in his early thirties, whom I know from the same social circles, is an orthodox young man who would use expressions such as 'don't tell stories like women, go to the point'; he believes that gender roles are biologically defined, that governments disseminate female hormones in tap water, and would respond in disbelief when hearing direct testimonies of women victims of sexual abuse on public transport. However, when prompted to comment on Nabeel Azeez's views, he distances himself: 'that's completely wrong, that's not Islamic'.

Yaqoob, a marketing coach in his late thirties in the Midlands, expands on his clients: 'these entrepreneurs who come to see me for advice, all of them struggle with their masculinity and end up being tyrants'. Salim, a marriage coach from London in his forties, points at the parental education at home which makes men suppress their emotions and their pain instead of learning how to manage them: 'a lot of these guys, because of the restrictions in their parents' home, in their childhood, experience delayed adolescence. This is why, when they leave their parents' home, they sleep with so many women and do all sorts of things.' Salim continues: 'men have to be the bread earner and equally... he has to be helping at home [with the parents]. It really affects us and wears down on us.' bell hooks (2004, 91) names this phenomenon 'male crisis': 'men are told that money offers fulfilment and that work is a way to acquire money', but at the same time, neoliberalism makes it much more difficult for men to become the breadwinners. While there is no crisis or threat of masculinity, she argues, these men are in distress.

Some of my younger respondents recall adopting certain behaviours at university to fit in their friends' circles, such as going to the gym or making sexist jokes. Many men I spoke with, both younger and older, being single or rejected multiple times, would also express some grievances against women, especially for those in their mid-thirties or older, deploring that 'women would go only for certain men' who go by the modern ideals of wealth and stereotypical looks dictated by social media. These frustrations can lead to resentment towards the female gender as a whole as in incel (involuntary celibates) culture in the US. In one of his first videos, *Why Muslim Men Should Stop Getting Married*, Nabeel Azeez offers his explanation to the marriage crisis: 'women have too high expectations' (Azeez 2020). However, he gives some advice to the men who are not deemed acceptable: 'become wealthy, successful, go lift weights, once you achieve these things, you can marry any women you want'. He implies that men should 'man up' in the sense of gaining more power.

In the climate of deprivation that Muslims experience (chapter 2), the societal expectation both outside and within the community makes men experience a crisis on many fronts with heavy consequences for their mental health (see chapter 4). Mohammed Qasim, in his research around Muslim boys' gangs in Bradford, argues that consequently, the boys acquire a 'siege mentality' where they feel 'locked out of society' (Qasim 2018, 149–50). Hidayat (2015, 218) observes in Australia that the 'awareness of being a minority', 'different', and Islamophobia 'weakens the core component of Muslim masculinity that is the Muslim men's religiously justified status as the leader or imam of the family', and therefore, Muslim men encountered 'a crisis of authority', leading them to compensate by employing their piety as a marker of masculinity and by creating all-male networks that in counterpart restricts the position of women in religious spaces. As observed by hooks (2004), hypermasculine narratives and behaviours compensate for the insecurities created by neoliberal hyper-modern society as an attempt at regaining a sense of control over their lives. In that context, Me Too and feminism, and the increased scrutiny on men, perceived as an attack on the male gender, triggered a widespread reaction in the Muslim manosphere.

Daniel Haqiqatjou, one of the most prominent figures of the manosphere, a Harvard physics and philosophy graduate who, at the time of writing, didn't have a formal qualification in Islamic theology or jurisprudence, acknowledges that cases of abuses against women exist amongst Muslims, but believes that feminism is a 'medicine worse than the disease' (5Pillars 2020). Like many other alt-bros commenters, he shares the conviction that women are 'indoctrinated' and that Islam is incompatible with feminism. These words might seem contradictory when recalling that Islam forbade the pagan practice of burying daughters alive. Haqiqatjou describes feminism as an anti-men movement encouraging women to use violence to gain visibility and repeating all day '"Men are trash!"' (Haqiqatjou 2018a). Zara Faris, a female figure popular amongst alt-bros, argues that 'women's rights' are different from 'feminism',[7] and since the former are included in Islam, Muslims don't need the 'gender-centric' concept of feminism that she dismisses because rooted in Eurocentric secular culture: 'Muslim "Feminists" do not subscribe to the values of Feminists at all, but actually the values of Islam ... would it not be more rational, and a more decisive call to justice, to just call themselves "Muslim"?'

(Faris 2014). Therefore, it appears that the Muslim manosphere has become engaged in a Don Quixotean fight against an imagined feminism constructed as a destructive entity and invalid because of its Eurocentric roots.

Paradoxically, many in the Muslim manosphere would frame their discourse with Eurocentric ideologies such as the red pill (a reference to the 1999 movie *The Matrix*) or the concept of the alpha male. Taking the red pill is synonymous with experiencing an awakening to the truth and a narrative of male empowerment about regaining control over one's life. The concept is widely used amongst coaches promising men recipes to seduce potentially any women. Some Muslim figures, however, distance themselves from the red pill movement, arguing that its philosophy of promiscuity is incompatible with Islam: 'Muslims can't be "Red Pill" ... Mainstream Red-Pillers are Machiavellian hedonists ... [it] is mostly used for fornication' (Azeez [no date]). Ali Al Norweji of Maliki Clique is critical of the movement too: 'you can't beat your wife in Islam ... A red pill movement against women is simply not fair' (Al Norweji 2020a). The alpha-beta dichotomy is used to justify a male-female hierarchy using biological determinism (Ghumkhor and Mir 2022), such as on Azeez's website, 'Becoming the Alpha Muslim', or Gabriel Al Romaani's concept of the Muslim alpha male. The scientifically debunked alpha-beta binary comes from a study on wild dogs and was later refuted by the very researcher who coined it.[8] By applying the alpha-beta dichotomy, the manosphere ironically argues (like its imagined feminist counterpart), that men are wild dogs. The alpha, Al Norweji (2019) argues, is a 'proud' lion which doesn't know fear, 'he just fights'.

Although the alpha concept is scientifically baseless, many insist that it describes biologically determined social roles: 'since the beginning of time, there was always alpha men and beta men ... The beta is inferior and weak—mama's special little boys' (Al Norweji 2019). 'The good mother and wife love to serve her husband and children. That's her nature' (Haqiqatjou 2020a). 'The least his wife can do is be devoted, loving, and obedient' (Haqiqatjou 2018b). They describe the Alpha male as someone wealthy and physically fit, and who has unquestioned authority over others. In examples of alpha males, apart from the Prophet Muhammad, Azeez mentions Donald Trump: 'he's the consummate Alpha Male—a man's man' (Azeez [no date]), as if the President of the United States was therefore a prophetic figure, very similarly to when Hamza Yusuf qualified Trump as a 'servant of God'.[9] While there is in their discourses a strong emphasis on male appearance and physical fitness, I wonder: how does Donald Trump fit into their model?

While some like Haqiqatjou justify these concepts with Islam by selecting marginal interpretation of some verses (e.g. Qur'an (4:34) where he interprets the word *qawwamuna* as 'authority' while mainstream translations use 'support', 'care', or protection[10]), the manosphere's philosophy is rooted in ideas of control which do not belong to Islamic frameworks. They correspond to the idea of hegemonic masculinity (Connell 1987, 1995; Connel and Messerschmidt 2005), a specific form of masculinity that legitimates unequal gender relations between men and women, between masculinity and femininity, and among masculinities. In her analysis, Abdul Khabeer traces these exclusionary conceptions to white American ideals of masculinity: 'the grown man is who has power and dominates. Strength, courage, bravery, might, rationality and valor are highly prized characteristics of a man who acts for the nation, enabling US success and the country's ability to dominate' (Abdul Khabeer 2016, 172). The idea of American masculinity echoes bell hooks' (2004, 116) definition of the 'dominator model', seeing human relations based on power struggles: the dominating man is strong, a provider; it is not his role to nurture or take care of others; it is not his role to express his feelings; and rage and violence are the tools that help him protect home and nation (hooks 2004, 18–19). bell hooks' dominator model is also helpful to understand the complex relationship that the alt-bros entertain with mainstream far-right narratives.

3.2. Make Muslims Great Again

Daniel Haqiqatjou's concern is that 'authentic Islam is facing extinction in the United States'.[11] Ghumkhor and Mir (2022) label this narrative Islamic declinism (believing that Islam/the Islamicate is in terminal decline). However, the alt-bros posit that the main reason for the supposed decline of Islam and the biggest threat to Muslims are not Islamophobia, racism, dominant political powers, or the neoliberal market, but rather the 'dilution' of Islam by 'western', 'liberal' ideas which is the fault of 'feminism', 'degenerate liberal Muslims', and 'compassionate imams' (5Pillars 2020), referring to the likes of American imams Omar Suleiman or Suhaib Webb. The endangerment argument is coupled with a revivalist narrative (an equivalent of 'Make Muslims Great Again'). Similar to the European or American far-right, the alt-bros' discourse is fuelled by nostalgia towards a lost past. They mourn a romanticized idea of the 'golden ages' of Muslim societies; such as twelfth-century Andalusia, the Moghul era, the Ottoman Empire, and the Arabian Peninsula at the times of the Revelation, advocating the return to an 'authentic' Islam.

However, the alt-bros do not abide by Euro-American left-right binaries. While the alt-bros do not stand for the same things, they clearly define themselves by what they are not. They are against secularism, feminism, liberalism, media corporations, counter-extremism funding, police informants, global corporations, Marxism, Eugenics, Darwinism, homosexuality, the distortion of Islamic texts, the mixing of genders in public, mingling with governments, women pursuing a career, the genocide of the Palestinians, the Uyghurs, and the Rohingyas, people insulting the Prophet, and men shaving their beards (Haqiqatjou 2020b). When criticizing the media corporations as propaganda, the rich and powerful elite, counter-extremism strategies, the oppression of Muslims around the globe, a lot of the discourse of the alt-bros could be mistaken for a radical left textbook. When advocating Islam as the main reference framework, critiquing liberalism, Marxism, and secularism, Haqiqatjou shares a lot on common with Islamic decolonial scholars.

However, one of the points of rupture between the alt-bros and the wider Muslim communities is their critique of modern movements against oppression such as Black Lives Matter. As Ghumkhor and Mir (2022) pinpointed, corroborating my observations, their thesis of the 'crisis of Islam' is articulated through the problematization of Muslim women and other marginalized groups (Black and LGBT Muslims) whom they accuse of spreading *fitna* (division) through 'identity politics'. Haqiqatjou fears that support groups such as for Black Muslims are 'dividing the *Umma* by race' (Haqiqatjou 2019b), and that Black Lives Matter is a 'Trojan horse for a LGBT agenda, wanting the 'normalization of *fahisha* [indecency]' (Haqiqatjou 2017a), thus not recognizing the need for intra-community solidarity, sharing of experiences, strategies, and healing. He recognizes, however, the existence of 'a prison and military industrial complex that disproportionately profits from the militarizing police and locking up Black people' (Haqiqatjou 2017b).

My respondent Haroon agrees with Hamza Yusuf's statement that the problem with Black Americans is not police brutality but rather with Black on Black violence.[12] Quoting a proverb attributed to Al Ghazali—'better one hundred years of the Sultan's tyranny than one year of people's tyranny over each other' (Lambton 1981, 124)—he argues that Muslims shouldn't revolt against politicians and representatives of the state. Nabeel Azeez argues similarly that the Black community should 'sort themselves out' first and posits that police brutality is the result of the behaviour of Black Americans in the first place, and that structural oppression doesn't exist (Azeez 2017). I have come across posts shared by Muslims on social media after the murder of George Floyd qualifying the murderer as 'an innocent man doing his job'. Although anti-Blackness is not new in Muslim communities (chapter 1), and compared in the Islamic tradition to pre-Islamic days of ignorance,[13] the alt-bros use narratives similar to those of the UK Conservatives or US Republicans criticizing anti-racism activists for spreading 'cancel culture', 'threatening free speech', and 'photoshopping our history',[14] thus delegitimizing opposing opinions and revolts against oppression—which Haqiqatjou dismisses as 'all about shutting down, throwing milkshakes, harassing and abusing' (The Muslim Skeptic 2019).

Just like feminism has been useful to understand the logic of exclusion and targeting of Muslim women by Islamophobes, critical race theory (CRT, see chapter 8) has been vital for understanding situations like Palestine or Kashmir (Muhammad 2019) and the racial logics of Islamophobia (Wheeler 2020). However, the alt-bros are vocal against an imagined definition of CRT, perceived as an anti-white sentiment (Haqiqatjou 2020c), echoed by some prominent scholars like Hamza Yusuf, upset upon finding that students at Zaytuna College were reading Fanon in Zaid Shakir's Islamic history classes (Kashani 2023). They see critical theories as non-metaphysical, deconstructive, and godless, and encouraging alliances with people of other faiths and none (Kashani 2023, 188).

Abdullah Al-Andalusi would give a lecture about how Islam abolished slavery,[15] but at the same time would disapprove of critical race theory. Haqiqatjou is not in favour of laws against homophobic slurs in the name of free speech, but at the same time advocates blasphemy law for people not to insult the Prophet (5Pillars 2020). He is in favour of religious-based discrimination in the workplace, but opposes discrimination against Muslims at the same time. Neoliberal statements such as 'becoming the Alpha Muslim is an aspirational brand' (Azeez [no date]) play the same game of branding as the Instagram celebrities they despise (see chapter 7). This shows the paradoxical selectivity of alt-bros politics, acknowledging structural forces when it comes to Islamophobia, or a fantasized global feminist-LGBTQ agenda, but ignoring their existence when it comes to anti-Blackness and misogyny (Muhammad 2020)—in a similar fashion to right-wing politics imagining Muslim-led conspiracies to take over Euro-America.

Although Haqiqatjou doesn't support the far-right, he builds bridges between his interpretation of Islam and far-right rhetoric:

> The far-right is definitely sympathetic to Islamic values, as I have written before. So much of the right wing consists of people who are sick and tired of the leftist cultural project that pushes feminism, homosexuality, and cross-dressing on society . . . In terms of online white supremacist culture, you even have the most hardcore neo-Nazi's calling for 'White Sharia' . . . These white supremacists correctly identify the Sharia as the cure for this cancer. (Haqiqatjou 2019a)

In podcasts, he amalgamates LGBTQ with paedophiles, sex offenders, incest, and bestiality (5Pillars 2020), a common far-right trope, and prides himself for voicing what is 'politically incorrect' (a synonym for hate-mongering). Muslims finding commonalities with the far-right is nothing new; in their analysis of Muslim public intellectuals in the German far right, Göpffarth and Özyürek (2020) observe how by critiquing liberal rationalism, Muslim far-right sympathizers help to legitimize far-right discourses which are paradoxically anti-Islam by spiritualizing nationalist narratives. In the 2010s, these bridges have been highlighted with Muslims supporting Islamophobic thinkers such as Jordan Peterson (Ghumkhor and Mir 2022) or Donald Trump,[16] despite his anti-Muslim policies such as the 'Muslim ban'. Ghumkhor and Mir (2022) point at the paradox between this sympathy to the far-right and the re-appropriation of an Eurocentric 'heroic masculinity' offered by femonationalism (an alliance between liberals, feminists, neoliberals, and the far-right in defence of Euro-American values while expressing opposition to Muslims and Islam (Farris 2017)).

Similar to the far-right, the alt-bros position themselves as the resistant minority. One of my respondents, Badr, after I shared online my personal story of going through a five-year emotionally, verbally, and physically abusive marriage, comments: 'we are many to have had this kind of experiences with the female gender. This category of "oppressed" people [women] has become talented at oppression.' 'We are many' implies that there is a wave of unspoken male oppression that needs to be spoken about. They interpret oppressed people's pain as both generalized and personal attacks, turning marginalized oppressed groups into supposed oppressors by virtue of their vocalization while taking on the label of oppressed. They weaponize their boycott by mainstream Muslim institutions as proof that the world doesn't want them. From incels and betas resenting women or the wider Muslim societies for their failed journey to validation, they become alphas synonyms of self-control and control of others. If they are losing control, they need to become more controlling—one cause that unites the alt-right worldwide (Ivarsflaten 2008). For the alt-bros, feminists, LGBT Muslims, disabled Muslims, and liberals are the new immigrants foreign to their idea of *ummah*.

Haqiqatjou not only believes that Islam is the best religion; he, like others, believes that Muslims (who align with him) are better than anyone else. While numerous verses in the Qur'an affirm the existence of different ethnicities and beliefs as part of God's decree and while the Last Sermon of the Prophet states that humans are all equal except in good deeds, the alt-bros believe in an orthodox Muslim supremacy over the rest of the world. While the far-right fears the end of a white hegemony, the alt-bros imagine a clash of civilizations in a phantasmagorical, gothic narrative where collide fascination, forbidden love and death. They are romantically attached to the white conservative oppressor which they cannot love because of its Islamophobia. At the same time, they are fascinated by the figure of the liberal Muslim and its declensions: the homosexual or the trans; Haqiqatjou's critics mock his obsessive posting of pictures of drag queens. The major contention with the alt-bros, just like with racism, is therefore not prejudice but domination (Hodge et al. 1975, 11). This idea of domination is rooted in the Eurocentric idea of heroism found in cultural mythology and symbolism (Hodge et al. 1975), which hooks calls the 'dominator model' (hooks 2004, 116), understanding human relations based on power struggles. They want to become Hercules instead of prophets. By seeking liberation in Eurocentric models of masculinity instead of the Prophetic figure, they wield a double-edged sword: threatening the oppressor (the 'West') and their own community. As Paulo Freire (1993, 45–7) analyses, 'their ideal is to be men; but for them, to be men is to be oppressors... Moreover, their struggle for freedom threatens not only the oppressor, but also their own oppressed comrades who are fearful of still greater repression.'

In what becomes a Greek tragedy scenario, their love of a romanticized version of Islam paradoxically brings the destruction of the *ummah*, the same as the romanticized love of the white civilization of the far right makes them destroy their own society. They become the prophets of their own apocalypse.

3.3. Make Islam White Again

The alt-bros' social landscape is not homogenous; while many advise against sub-communities, others like Robert Dufour (not an alt-bro himself but attracting a similar audience) advocate for white-Muslim only spaces. Of French-Canadian descent, he embraced Islam in 2003 and lives in Canada where he completed a master's degree in applied social psychology. He is the main editor of the website Islam4Europeans.com. As of July 2020, the website opens on a stock picture of what seems a congregational prayer featuring only white Muslim men and women. The website features articles titled: 'White Muslims marrying each other would be good for the *Ummah*' and videos such as 'Why European Muslim sub communities are needed'.[17] However, in a podcast and in several videos, Robert Dufour claims that Islam4Europeans is not about white supremacy. On the website's manifesto, he writes: 'the White Muslim sub-community wants to be known as a group that does not support White Supremacy in any way, only the preservation of our culture and peaceful spreading of the message of Islam' (Islam4Europeans 2019a). When I interviewed him in 2024, he clarified that his intention was to fill the cultural gap between born-Muslim communities, who usually retain their culture, and white converts of European background, who often see the need to embrace South Asian or Middle Eastern culture, in his local community.

He claims that 'white Muslims are resented or alienated by pretty much everybody' because of the 'resentment from the Muslim community for white people' (Dufour in The Mad Mamluks 2019). He deplores that converts have an '80% drop-out rate' (meaning that they eventually leave Islam) partly because of cultural pressures, and his key question is therefore: 'how to keep converts in the community?' Another advocate of white Muslim solidarity is Ali al Norweji, managing the Maliki Clique accounts on multiple platforms, filming himself with a model Viking ship in the background to signal his roots. Some of the episodes are titled: 'Why I haven't left Islam', 'Males, are you ready to be men?' 'Surviving divorce: men's edition', and 'The white Muslim blame game' where he deplores white Muslims being painted as oppressors. In one of his episodes, Ali tells of his journey to Islam in prison, and how embracing Islam has been a traumatic experience both outside and within the Muslim community: 'I lost my entire family, inheritance, property . . . Born Muslims don't take us seriously . . . They see the Trump supporter, the guy who picked upon them at school . . . They don't accept us . . . Because of this, white reverts get turned off by Muslims, from Islam' (Al Norweji 2020b).

Both Al Norweji and Dufour argue that, for new white Muslims, to avoid experiencing inadequacy and rejection from non-white Muslims, there is a need for white

Muslims to establish their own support communities—what Dufour terms 'third spaces' (Islam4Europeans 2020b). Having embraced Islam myself, and having faced the rejection from my family on the one hand, and more painful rejections from the British Muslim community (for jobs and marriage) on the other, having faced scrutiny in activist spaces because of my whiteness, I can empathize with their grievances. Research shows that embracing Islam can be a traumatic experience because of various forms of abuse and life changes (Suleiman and Anderson 2013, 2016; Van Nieuwkerk 2018).

Consequently, Dufour roots his vision in two main arguments: cultural congruence (inter-white marriages) and white responsibility (presenting Islam to white non-Muslim peers). With the example of marriage, he argues: 'most marriages to born Muslim families do not end well [no proof cited]. We don't understand their culture and vice versa. Especially for the new convert who is already confused, now they have to assimilate even more while they are trying to learn the Deen?' (Islam4Europeans 2019b). He argues that 'it is better to marry another convert on the same level . . . Instead of marrying your teacher, it's better to marry your classmate' and that families will be more likely to get along. He assumes that new Muslims need to culturally assimilate in families and that inter-white marriages are easier which are not always the case. On the other end, he proposes that it is not the duty of non-white people to solve the issue of racism in white communities, paraphrasing Malcolm X: 'white people should work at ending racism in their own communities' (Islam4Europeans 2019a). 'It is our duty as white Muslims to give *dawah* [present Islam] to our own group. If anyone can try to change their opinion on Islam, it's us' (Islam4Europeans 2019b).

Dufour thinks white Muslims are in the best position to appease the far-right since there are people 'on the fence': 'the alt right and Neo Nazis would not be able to say that Islam is a threat to the white race' (Islam4Europeans 2019b). This rhetoric is similar to American scholar Hamza Yusuf or British Islamic scholar Abdal Hakim Murad's, preconizing engagement with the current political anti-Muslim discourse. He urges Muslims to acknowledge the 'suffering' of secularized Europe: 'Muslims communities need to understand the pain which many European feel in their spiritual and cultural exile' (Murad 2020, 51). Europe is constructed as a Christ-like figure which, through the sacrifice of its borders, offers Muslims a promised land of peace. However, he ignores the reliving of trauma that non-white Muslims engaging with racists would face. He critiques British mosques as 'race temples' (Murad 2020, 49) created as 'enclosures' for single ethnicities, without considering that mosques function as a barrier against racism and a safe haven for people not fluent in English. For these reasons, Murad's take has been described as 'hostile' towards Muslim migrants (Birt 2022) and compared to victim-blaming discourse, saying that the rise of the far-right, racism, and Islamophobia results from the failure of immigrants to integrate[18] (see chapter 2). Dufour displays more empathy towards ethnically minoritized Muslims, as he understands the need for solidarity hubs and the unfair emotional labour they would face engaging with Islamophobes, and is perhaps more sensible than other white-Muslims-only initiatives emerging online, this time using religious jurisprudence to justify the 'superiority' of certain ethnicities, like the #WhiteShariah[19] project, using a pyramid to illustrate their ideaHowever, Dufour's approach seems to omits that no matter the amount of work, the far-right will always see white Muslims as traitors—and that far-right converts have no power in either Muslim communities and mainstream politics (Birt 2022), a viewpoint he has nuanced in his conversation with me, saying that he's not advocating for an alliance with nationalist politics and that the best way is to 'lead by example'.

Dufour's white-solidarity stances denote a feeling of resentment towards wider Muslim communities, and 'SJWs' specifically, hinting that social movements can sometimes be exclusionary; it is echoing the alt-bros' narrative, a cry of pain and powerlessness. As sites where people process their pain, activist spaces can become places where trauma is projected on fellow activists (see section 3.5). White Islamic scholar Abdal Hakim Murad criticizes this 'grievance culture' (2020), but ignores that activist spaces have been set up for people to collectively heal, and that healing is not possible if people don't process their grief (see chapter 4). When people outside of activist circles take these expressions of pain personally instead of understanding that they are directed at systems of domination, DiAngelo (2011) terms it 'white fragility'. However, I argue that this fragility is exclusive not to whiteness but to various forms of privilege—as shown by my male interlocutors in this chapter.

Being rejected by other Muslims, being questioned for their skin colour, and for some having experienced challenging socio-economic conditions, the perspective of marginality is not alien to Robert Dufour or Ali al Norweji, which allows them to consider their position as a trust to be used in the benefit of others. Al Norweji acknowledges that 'our Black and Hispanic sisters they get it the worst' (Al Norweji 2020b). In several articles and podcasts, Dufour states: 'we understand that we have more privileges', 'Black Muslim Americans don't get the credit they deserve' (The Mad Mamluks. 2019). He acknowledges that Black Muslims struggle to get married and advocates the 'economic and spiritual' support of mixed background Muslims (Islam4European 2019): 'the last thing we want is for Black, White and Latino/a Muslims to be divided'. He even writes an 'Open letter in support of the Black American Muslim Conference', followed by a donation link to the conference, openly critiquing some Muslims, who argue against groups of solidarity based on ethnicity: 'some voices in the Muslim *ummah* might say that this conference only creates division. We believe a get-together like this is not only beneficial but absolutely necessary for any group of Muslims' (Islam4Europeans 2020a). His statements express therefore an active disengagement from white supremacy and furthermore using his privilege to promote Black Muslims.

While many white people embracing Islam live a traumatic experience, they are not at the bottom of the scale of oppression but rather at the bottom of the pyramid of white supremacy: white children develop a feeling of superiority as early as preschool (Derman-Sparks and Ramsey 2006) and for new white Muslims, embracing Islam doesn't automatically get rid of racial biases and sometimes white nationalism (Piela and Krotofil 2023). It is therefore difficult for grown adults to distance themselves from whiteness and understand the complexity of non-white experiences. In these regards, Robert Dufour is very different from some white Muslims that I have observed, using their whiteness to gain power both in Muslim and non-Muslim spaces—especially combined with class privileges.

While white new Muslims coming from working-class backgrounds are usually discriminated against, wealthier and more connected middle-class ones (such as biker Rosie Gabrielle, ex-far-right figure Joram Van Klaveren, or Andrew Tate) usually enjoy popularity amongst Muslims, often seen as valuable assets and bridges between 'Islam' and 'the West', being given a de facto role of ambassador of Islam, taking effect immediately after their *shahada* (declaration of faith). Their whiteness, held as trophies, would open more doors than for born Muslims: even relatively small social media figures in Islamicate countries such as Egypt, Saudi Arabia, Pakistan, or Turkey would receive privileges such as meeting heads of states, travelling under military escort and accessing sites forbidden to ordinary citizens.[20] One of my respondents calls them 'career Muslims' where the 'conversion' to Islam is perceived as a career-advancing exercise, a term echoing Al-Arian and Kanjwal's 'professional Muslims' (see chapter 2), making a career out of their Muslimness. They would be the preferred options on TV panels, conferences, overshadowing the participation, visibility, or social mobility of ethnically minoritized Muslims with more skills, knowledge, experience, or expertise. This lack of preparation and de facto propulsion into fame of some white Muslims is what led Dufour explicitly to refuse being treated as a 'white saviour': 'we will reject these stations unless we advocate that Black Muslims should be given the same types of positions at the masjid' (Islam4Europeans 2019a). Since things like socioeconomic status, gender, education or political opinions can be divisive factors even between white people, is creating white-Muslim-only spaces a guarantee of support and cohesion?

These positions are, however, filled with paradoxes: they reject feminism but 'will make sure that our sisters, no matter their skin colour, will have full participation and voice in our talks and meetings'. They oppose 'SJWs' but acknowledge structural oppression, support mobilization of marginalized Muslims, and take on duties of allyship. The major contention with Dufour's and Al-Norweji's narratives is the wording of their content such as 'the preservation of our culture' and the imagery they use, which can entertain confusion—which Dufour acknowledges[21] could make believe the reader that they are actually opposed to the rights of non-white people and women—and Dufour has acknowledged to me that since he has reflected on this point, these early narratives were not representative of his thoughts. These stances set them apart from the wider alt-bro movement which is centred around exclusionary narratives, to the point of self-fragmentation.

3.4. When Muslim Men Want to Be Western Boys

In 2022, the Badr Club (renamed Brothers Club[22]) was launched with a video promising for 'boys to become men' through coaching on themes such as 'Operation six-figures' or 'Operation second-wife' for £313 a membership. The highly polished video featured a Victoria's Secret shop, views of Dubai, a character driving a Bentley, and jet-skis, conflating Islam, masculinity and luxurious material possessions. Reflecting on myself as a Muslim man doing activities viewed as stereotypically masculine (practising outdoor sports, servicing my own car, fixing things at home), when watching Instagram, I never feel like a valid man. Not because I can't afford designer clothes, holidays to Dubai, or a lease for a luxury car but because I don't feel attracted to these things—while the prophets of Muslim masculinity like Andrew Tate, the Badr Club, and others would tell me that I should.

Although the transition to adulthood is socially characterized by autonomy and self-reliance, nothing in the advert suggested any activities around character development, financial strategies, conflict resolution, overcoming mental health issues, or skills related to autonomy such as cooking and repairing things. The alt-bro rhetoric peddles a hard-line personality, but without offering the skills to match it. Many of the supporters of the alt-bro movement amongst my respondents rely on their mums to prepare and serve them meals and do not practise any sports (although they watch every single possible football match). If something breaks, they will order a new one instead of fixing it. While the alt-bros want to see men at the service of Islam, they end up being those being served. I call this phenomenon 'passive pashas', slaves to materialism and popular culture trends, throwing money at any problem, with the aspiration of becoming a tough leader while factually making zero steps towards it.

Offering a Halal twist to neoliberal theology of liberation through the display material possessions, instead of offering boys pathways to 'become men', it offers men ways of living their delayed adolescent dreams. While Islam is supposed to free Muslims from the *dunya* (material world), the alt-bros sell thicker chains to it. Being a valid man is erected an exclusive status symbol which means being part of a 'club': it is not enough to be male; one has to tick the right boxes, the right markers of power and success.

Many of the popular alt-bros come from the early 2010s 'da'wah' scene, featuring confrontational debates at London's speaker corner on themes such as 'Muslim vs Atheist' 'Sunni destroys Shi'a' and other antagonistic jousts. While these debates were aiming at presenting Islam to young audiences as fun, intellectual wrestling matches instead of a boring set of rules—as many parents would paint it—the alt-bros have turned a means to an end: being Muslim is about defeating opponents. A website titled 'Haqiqatjou vs the world' caricatures the alt-bros' engagement in never-ending battles against everybody:

> Daniel is on a mission. He doesn't know the Arabic language, he has no formal Islamic education in a Western or Traditional institution. But he's furious at the World and 1000% sure that he's the only man qualified to fix it! What can possibly go wrong?[23]

Because the alt-bros and the far-right seem to share opponents in common (feminists, activists, the establishment, 'leftists', and the LGBTQ) in addition to political marginality and belligerent language, the far-right's hatred for Muslims and Islam doesn't prevent intellectual flirtations between the two, with some trying to unite over common battlefronts, or in order to satiate a morbid curiosity for the political extremes—similar to the one underpinning the production of documentaries on serial killers. Platforms targeting young and religiously conservative audiences such as 5Pillars are thus caught in a risky gamble: while trying to deflect the far-right's focus on Muslims and immigrants by giving platform and engaging in courteous debates with figures like Britain First founder Jim Dowson, former leader of the British Nationalist Party (BNP) Nick Griffin, or neo-Nazi Mark Collett, they risk dignifying exclusionary narratives, and reducing racism and Islamophobia to these marginal figures while they are propagated by more mainstream discourses (see chapter 2).

The Muslim manosphere is, however, not a space for solidarity. Azeez writes in his blog about Haqiqatjou: 'Daniel is overweight, lives a sedentary lifestyle and spends way too much time sitting . . . As his brothers in Islam and his fans, it's obligatory on us to fat-shame him into getting jacked and tan' (Azeez 2023). When Daniel Haqiqatjou criticized publicly a young woman in hijab for posting a selfie of her graduation day,[24] the popular orthodox debater Ali Dawah raised his own criticism: 'to attack her over a petty thing like that is the reason why our sisters feel suffocated!' (Dawah 2020).

The alt-bros, just like elitist clubs (see chapter 2.3), differentiate their own 'good' and 'bad' Muslims, blacklisting those with a divergent opinion as 'intellectual apostates' (Haqiqatjou 2020b). In their discursive universe, redemption or the concept of Umar Ibn Khattab (once the greatest opponent of Islam and later one of its greatest supporters) doesn't exist. Instead of potential allies, they only see potential enemies to be defeated; there is no room for mistakes, education, or even the prophetic quality of compassion. Nabeel Azeez states: 'Without Strength, Mercy Is Weakness'[25]—a similar statement can be found on Gabriel Al-Romaani's Muslim Alpha website. Andrew Tate, even after embracing Islam, would say that 'Reading books is for losers [. . .] Education is For Cowards' (Tate 2022)—are their fellow Muslims losers because they read the Qur'an and the Prophet Muhammad a coward for inciting believers to seek knowledge? Hamja, an internationally recognized artist experiencing Asperger's, left Islam after experiencing bullying at the age of 11 from fellow Muslims:

> Sometimes I wonder if Islam just fully respects, appreciate or cultivate biodiversity of people's. Or is it a predominantly machopak religion for people who de facto love up corporate America culture whatever shade that comes in . . . Machopaks and their families played a big part in damaging me and made me feel suicidal and worthless.

However, the mention in the *sirah* (biography) that the Prophet used to cry led Hamja to find a religious validation of his vision of masculinity. I have respondents commenting they 'don't care about people leaving Islam' and that cases like Hamja's are 'natural selection'. While the alt-bros oppose Darwinism, they create their own social Darwinism: the *ummah* has become gangs (see chapter 6). Their vision of Islam is totalitarian, paraphrasing former US president George W. Bush when he launched the war on terror: 'either you are with us, or against us'.[26] They use the same strategies of divide and conquer, and create the same zones of being and non-being as in colonial times: the 'West' and the 'non-West'; the 'valid Muslim' and the 'non-Muslim'. The *da'ees* of yesterday (inviting people to the faith) become today's *takfiris* (excommunicating other Muslims). They display what community historian Yahya Birt calls 'negative masculinity', a 'selfish' form of masculinity 'about showing off, about trying to be "hard", and about using physical strength to humiliate others' (Birt 2014). Hegemonic masculinity has various declensions and its own hierarchies as it is exclusionary by nature of masculinities which do not abide by its standards (Connell 1987, 1995; Connel and Messerschmidt 2005). Just like elitist clubs, their totalitarianism and lack of empathy, focus on power, individualism, and lack of collaboration are hallmarks of extrinsic goals and values (Kasser and Ryan 1996), which are correlated to a tendency to support right-wing voices (Sheldon and Nichols 2009). In fact, it is a story of pain, insecurity, melancholia, and powerlessness. They parade as protectors but throw punches at the same people they claim to protect. While ridiculing women's pain, they are burying their voices; by denying the right for Black people to protest, they put their own brothers and sisters back in the chains of *jahiliya* (pagan age of ignorance). As one of my respondents observe: 'are we replacing one oppression with the other, saying ours is better?' They echo the words of Obi-Wan Kenobi to Anakin Skywalker in *Star Wars Episode III* (2005): 'you have become the very thing you swore to destroy'.

How is it possible to break the cycle of domination? Asim Qureshi (2017, 56) reminds the reader that 'the oppressor is a brother that needs to be stopped'. What if every alt-bro had the ability to turn around the narrative? Have Muslim communities and their extreme poles failed at recognizing their brethren? This is what bell hooks argues with her concept of men as 'comrades in struggle' (2004, 25).

3.5. Comrades in Struggle?

Painted as villains in mainstream Muslim communities, some respondents suggested that perhaps these alt-bros are a form of satire or performance art for us to reflect on what not to become; monsters in the Latin sense of *monstrum*: a warning, a sign of the gods, for us to reflect. However, what if Daniel Haqiqatjou or Nabeel Azeez were just community champions turned sour? Writing about Muslim gangs in Bradford, Qasim (2018) argues that violence comes not only from the structural production of harm but also from a lack of support structures in the society, echoing the words of the African proverb quoted in the epigraph of this chapter. The alt-bros express pain. What if, before their online activism, Nabeel Azeez or Daniel Haqiqatjou were deemed inadequate, bullied and abandoned by community?

Some of my respondents have had their legitimacy or their Islam questioned because of their looks or clothing choices, receiving abuse that made them distance from other Muslims (see chapters 1, 4, and 6.2). Even activist spaces can become spaces of harm, where people use the oppressors' tools against their peers, enacting their own kinds of 'supremacies'. bell hooks observes in Black activist spaces, 'feminists to whom liberation was more about getting their piece of the pie' (2004, 110), and men vocal on racial justice who would be 'as sexist as their conservative cohorts' (2004, 109). Activist Frances Lee expands in their blog articles 'Why I've started to fear my fellow social justice activists'[27] how self-righteousness alienates activists and turns away potential allies, ultimately quelling activism in a self-destructive pattern (Lee [no date]). 'Competing oppressions' makes anti-racist struggles counterproductive: Aouragh (2019, 12) observes in the Netherlands that when Turks or Moroccans are criticized, white 'allies' remain unchallenged and 'white supremacy remains untouched'.

Among *Star Wars* fans, there is a theory about how one of the main protagonists, Anakin Skywalker, could have avoided becoming the saga's most iconic villain, Darth Vader.[28] The theory posits that young Anakin lacked support from the other Jedis, while grieving the loss of his mother, and fearing the inevitable death of his wife. His frustrations with the Jedi order coupled with the feeling of loss and powerlessness led him in anger to accept the deal offered by the dark side of the force. Is it possible to see the alt-bros as Anakin Skywalkers in search of the support of the Muslim *ummah*?

I have been myself in a similar position where, new to Islam, I would face rejection from women and organizations, and I would see my whiteness questioned. It would have been easy for me and become bitter, blaming women for my rejections, and the whole community for not accepting me. However, I had to understand that my pain was inflicted not so much by certain organizations and individuals but more by wider, global systems of production of harm. My oppressors were victims as much as perpetrators. As the Spanish proverb says, 'when a dog wants to bite you, instead of trying to control the dog, head to its owner'.

The main issue for bell hooks is that 'society doesn't provide any channels for men to process their pain and frustrations: the reality is that men are hurting and that the whole culture responds to them by saying, "Please do not tell us what you feel"' (hooks 2004, 6). hooks argues, therefore, that patriarchal men are deaf to the suffering of others because men who hurt need to heal their own pain and manage their own vulnerabilities first. To heal, men must speak their pain and should be allowed a hearing (hooks 2004, 134).

I led an experiment with a video aimed at young Muslim men (The Muslim Vibe 2020). Based on hooks' argument that feminism should consider men as 'comrades in struggle' (hooks 2004, 25), I took a more empathetic approach by starting from the perspective of male crisis. This exercise was rooted in a conscious shift in my grammar of human relations: did I want to face the other, or sit with the other (Chanial 2011, 271)?

The feedback given to me by young men is that they were seeking support from a healthy brotherhood; from brothers, fathers, and uncles who can become models of a healthy masculinity—confirming my initial assumption that most Muslim men in the UK don't enjoy a strong support network. hooks also posits that men 'become more real through the act of connecting with others, through building community' (hooks 2004, 121) so they can become men who 'respond' rather than 'react', and become 'strong, autonomous and connected, responsible to self, to family and friends, and to society' (hooks 2004, 118). Some initiatives such as Mansheds,[29] founded by Razwan Faraz in the Midlands in 2018, facilitate novel ways for men to bond and explore life challenges (from mental health to parenthood) together through outdoor activities, discussions, and workshops.

In the same spirit as the *Anti-Racism Guide for White Muslims* (Muslim Anti-Racism Collaborative 2019), it is necessary for Muslims who hold a privileged position in communities to engage in deep introspection. How is it possible for them to become stewards for their community? It is a work that starts with reading, learning, and taking the examples of other anti-racists or men supporting women's rights, joining collective activities and events. It is believing and listening to marginalized people when they share their experiences. It is holding to account people with more power, including themselves: do they consider their resources and privileges an *amana* (trust), how do they redistribute their knowledge, visibility, wealth, or networks as a form of social *zakat* (alms tax) to communities? Are they 'passing the mic'? Do they decline to being put on a pedestal, or being given undue privileges? Do they recommend more qualified, skilled, and experienced people before sitting on panels?

In Euro-American Muslim communities, the ripples of Me Too and Black Lives Matter have led the mainstream to acknowledge the existence of collective pain, that issues like racism and misogyny are not isolated acts but symptoms of greater, global forces at play. From alt-bros distorting Islamic jurisprudence to justify it to people being exposed and 'cancelled', each time everyone apologizes and swears it would 'never happen again'. It's been the same for decades. Everybody hurts but no one takes the first steps to healing. The 2010s have witnessed a boom of Muslim grass-roots mental health organizations implementing a culture- and faith-sensitive approach for tackling these very issues. They are the focus of the following chapter.

Notes

1. Becoming the Alpha Muslim. Accessed 1 February 2024. https://web.archive.org/web/20201109042140/https://becomingthealphamuslim.com
2. 'Who are the alt-right, really? (Special guest—@Ali)', Becoming the Alpha Muslim [YouTube] 7 September 2017. https://archive.org/details/who-are-the-alt-right-really-special-guest-ali-you-tube-720p
3. 'Trump: year 1—the alt-bro perspective (feat. surprise guest)', Becoming the Alpha Muslim [YouTube] 19 January 2018. https://archive.org/details/trump-year-1-the-alt-bro-perspective-feat.-surprise-guest-you-tube-720p
4. Shanti Das, 'Inside the violent, misogynistic world of TikTok's new star, Andrew Tate', *The Guardian*, 6 August 2022. https://web.archive.org/web/20220806165410/https://www.theguardian.com/technology/2022/aug/06/andrew-tate-violent-misogynistic-world-of-tiktok-new-star
5. Islam4Europeans. Accessed 1 February 2024. https://web.archive.org/web/20200822034346/http://islam4europeans.com
6. Al Norwejy, Ali. Maliki Clique YouTube Channel. Accessed 1 February 2024. https://web.archive.org/web/20230717043108/https://www.youtube.com/channel/UCeyJagbJqyiKT1SN4Bu-syg
7. 'About', Zara Faris. Accessed 1 February 2024. https://web.archive.org/web/20201101084207/https://zarafaris.com/about
8. Dave Mech, 'Wolf News and Information', davemech.org, 2013. https://web.archive.org/web/20180922024513/https://davemech.org/wolf-news-and-information
9. 'U.S. Muslim cleric Hamza Yusuf calls Trump "a servant of God" during racist rant against Black Lives Matter', *Rabhaw Times*, 25 December 2016. https://web.archive.org/web/20161225192150/https://www.rabwah.net/muslim-hamza-yusuf-racist-rant. Original audio (at 39:15): https://archive.org/details/hamza-yusuf-ris-drama-tube-ripper.com
10. 'Protector' (Abdullah Yusuf Ali), 'take full care' (Muhammad Asad), 'in charge' (Pickthall), 'take good care' (M. A. S. Abdel Haleem), 'upholders and maintainers' (Study Qur'an).
11. 'Daniel Haqiqatjou: authentic Islam is facing extinction in the United States', *5Pillars*, 7 November 2018. https://web.archive.org/web/20200804140737/https://5pillarsuk.com/2018/11/07/daniel-haqiqatjou-authentic-islam-is-facing-extinction-in-the-united-states
12. Emma Green, 'Muslim Americans are united by Trump—and divided by race', *The Atlantic*, 11 March 2017. https://web.archive.org/web/20170311210703/https://www.theatlantic.com/politics/archive/2017/03/muslim-americans-race/519282. Original audio (15:52–17:36): https://archive.org/details/hamza-yusuf-ris-drama-tube-ripper.com
13. Abu-Dharr … narrates: 'Once I was conversing with Bilal. Our conversation gave way to a dispute. Angry with him, the following insult burst from my mouth: "You cannot comprehend this, O son of a black woman!" As Islam expressly forbade all kinds of racial, tribal and colour discrimination, Bilal was both upset and greatly angered. [The Messenger of Allah] said to me: 'I have been informed that you addressed Bilal as the son of a black woman … This means you still retain the standards and judgments of the pre-Islamic days of ignorance. Islam has eradicated all those false standards or measures judging people by blood, fame, color or wealth. It has established that the best and most honorable of men is he who is the most pious and upright in conduct. Is it right to defame a believer just because he is black?' Abu Dharr felt profound remorse.

He went straight to Bilal's house and, putting his head on the threshold, said: 'This head will not rise from here until the blessed feet of Bilal tread on the face of foolish, impolite Abu Dharr.' Bilal responded: 'That face deserves to be kissed, not trodden upon, and forgave Abu Dharr.' Sahih al-Bukhari, USC-MSA web reference: Vol. 1, Book 2, Hadith 30. In Raj Bhala, *Understanding Islamic Law* (London: LexisNexis 2011).

14. Danny Boyle, 'Monday morning news briefing: "We can't photoshop our history"', *The Telegraph*, 15 June 2020. https://web.archive.org/web/20200617113921/https://www.telegraph.co.uk/news/2020/06/15/monday-morning-news-briefing-cant-photoshop-history
15. 'How Islam abolished pre-Islamic and Western colonial chattel slavery', Muslim Debate Initiative [YouTube], 19 July 2017. https://archive.org/details/how-islam-abolished-pre-islamic-western-colonial-chattel-slavery-abdullah-al-andalusi-you-tube-1080p
16. Brajesh Upadhyay, 'Meet the Muslims, Sikhs and Hindus supporting Trump', *BBC*, 10 March 2016. https://web.archive.org/web/20160311233052/https://www.bbc.co.uk/news/amp/election-us-2016-35758156; Chris Fuchs, 'For American Muslims for Trump's founder, the inauguration is a "new beginning"', *NBC News*, 20 January 2017. https://web.archive.org/web/20170120233402/https://www.nbcnews.com/storyline/inauguration-2017/amp/american-muslims-trump-s-founder-inauguration-new-beginning-n709466; Khushbu Shah and Martin Savidge. 'These Muslim Americans approve of the travel ban', *CNN*, 10 March 2017. https://web.archive.org/web/20170311105404/https://amp.cnn.com/cnn/2017/03/10/politics/muslims-support-travel-ban-and-trump/index.html; Yana Paskova, 'Meet three Muslims voting for Donald Trump', *Time*, 15 March 2016. https://web.archive.org/web/20160315220434/https://time.com/4259372/donald-trump-muslim-supporters
17. Islam 4 Europeans [YouTube]. Accessed 1 February 2024. https://web.archive.org/web/20210211071846/https://www.youtube.com/channel/UCWzvqZYgIeFhFMzl4CL1GBA
18. Niamh Harris, 'Tony Blair: we must force migrants to integrate to combat rise of far right', *Newspunch*, 21 April 2019. https://web.archive.org/web/20190501025811/https://newspunch.com/tony-blair-we-must-force-migrants-to-integrate-to-combat-rise-of-far-right
19. '#WhiteShariah' [Facebook]. Accessed 19 December 2024. https://archive.org/details/www.facebook.comstory.phpstory_fbid3519797378324562id100008830035853rdidu5r9hu5jhl4cphiz
20. Samira Shackle, 'How western travel influencers got tangled up in Pakistan's politics', *The Guardian*, 12 November 2020. https://web.archive.org/web/20201112112334/https://www.theguardian.com/news/2020/nov/12/western-travel-influencers-social-media-pakistan-politics
21. 'Why white Muslim women aren't watching I 4 E an appeal to my fellow Euro sisters in Islam', Islam4Europeans [YouTube], 11 July 2022. https://archive.org/details/why-white-muslim-women-arent-watching-i-4-e-an-appeal-to-my-fellow-euro-sisters-in-islam-240p
22. The Brothers Club. Accessed 1 February 2024. https://www.thebrothersclub.com. Original Video: 'The Badr Club: GUNS, FAST CARS, JET SKI'S & MARRIAGE!' Naseeha Sessions [YouTube], 22 August 2022. https://archive.org/details/the-badr-club-guns-fast-cars-jet-ski-s-marriage-720p
23. 'Haqiqatjou vs. the world.' Accessed 1 February 2024. https://web.archive.org/web/20200317195337/https://www.haqiqatjouvstheworld.com
24. Haqiqatjou, Daniel. [Twitter], 17 June 2020. https://web.archive.org/web/20200617010616/https://twitter.com/Haqiqatjou/status/1273036702853017600
25. Becoming the Alpha Muslim. Accessed 1 February 2024. https://web.archive.org/web/20201109042140/https://becomingthealphamuslim.com
26. 'President Bush addresses the nation', *The Washington Post*, 20 September 2001. https://web.archive.org/web/20010921064520/https://www.washingtonpost.com/wp-srv/nation/specials/attacked/transcripts/bushaddress_092001.html
27. Frances Lee, 'Why I've started to fear my fellow social justice activists', *Yes! Magazine*, 13 October 2017. https://web.archive.org/web/20171013220227/http://www.yesmagazine.org/people-power/why-ive-started-to-fear-my-fellow-social-justice-activists-20171013
28. Andrew Dyce, 'Star Wars confirms Qui-Gon would have saved Anakin', *Screen Rant*, 12 December 2018. https://web.archive.org/web/20181212155124/https://screenrant.com/star-wars-jedi-qui-gon-comic; Shaun Kitchener, 'Star Wars: THIS is the ONLY character who could have "saved Anakin Skywalker"', *Express*, 2 June 2019. https://web.archive.org/web/20190602234216/https://www.express.co.uk/entertainment/films/1135193/Star-Wars-Anakin-Skywalker-saved-prequels-Qui-Gon-Jinn-Darth-Vader-fan-theory
29. Man Sheds Facebook page. Accessed 1 February 2024. https://archive.is/dYfbo

References

5Pillars. 2020. 'Daniel Haqiqatjou | Beef with Yaqeen Institute | Blood Brothers #39.' [YouTube] 28 June. https://archive.org/details/daniel-haqiqatjou-beef-with-yaqeen-institute-blood-brothers-39-you-tube-1080p

Abdul Khabeer, Su'ad. 2016. *Muslim Cool: Race, Religion and Hip Hop in the United States*. New York: New York University Press.

Al Norweji, Ali. 2019. 'Ep. 9 Alpha's vs. beta's. An ancient struggle.' Maliki Clique Podcast, 3 November. https://archive.org/details/maliki-9

Al Norweji, Ali. 2020a. 'The men vs. women epidemic. Have we gone too far?' Maliki Clique Podcast, 8 March. https://archive.org/details/Malikimenwomen

Al Norweji, Ali. 2020b. 'Are white reverts part of the problem?' Maliki Clique Podcast, 5 June. https://archive.org/details/maliki-reverts-problem

Aouragh, Miriyam 2019. '"White privilege" and shortcuts to anti-racism.' *Race & Class* 61(2), 3–26.

Azeez, Nabeel. No Date. 'A Muslim's guide to the manosphere.' *Becoming The Alpha Muslim*. https://web.archive.org/web/20201108115954/https://becomingthealphamuslim.com/muslim-guide-to-manosphere

Azeez, Nabeel. 2017. 'Black America: canary in the coal mine.' *Becoming The Alpha Muslim*. https://web.archive.org/web/20201108090204/https://becomingthealphamuslim.com/uncle-hotep-demond-handy

Azeez, Nabeel. 2020. 'Why Muslim men should stop getting married.' [YouTube] 24 September. https://archive.org/details/why-muslim-men-should-stop-getting-married-nabeel-azeez-becoming-the-alpha-muslim-you-tube-1080p

Azeez, Nabeel. 2023. 'Haqiqatjou's health hazards and baseline standards for religious leaders.' *Muslim Man*. https://web.archive.org/web/20230603222334/https://muslimman.com/daniel-haqiqatjou-health-problems

Becoming the Alpha Muslim. 2018. 'Twitter drama, emotional muzzies, Muslim IQ, judges, and more with Murtaza Siddiqui.' [YouTube] 30 September. https://archive.org/details/twitter-drama-emotional-muzzies-muslim-iq-judges-and-more-with-murtaza-siddiqui-you-tube-720p

Birt, Yahya. 2014. 'Being a real man in Islam: drugs, criminality and the problem of masculinity.' Masud blog. https://web.archive.org/web/20150905145519/http://masud.co.uk/being-a-real-man-in-islam-drugs-criminality-and-the-problem-of-masculinity

Birt, Yahya. 2022. 'The unbearable whiteness of being: convert leaders in the West and the new ethno-nationalism.' *The Long View* 4(3), 14 July. https://web.archive.org/web/20220717100051/https://www.ihrc.org.uk/the-unbearable-whiteness-of-being-convert-leaders-in-the-west-and-the-new-ethno-nationalism

Chanial, Philippe. 2011. *La sociologie comme philosophie politique et réciproquement*. Paris: La Découverte.

Connell, Raewyn. 1987. *Gender and Power*. Sydney: Allen and Unwin.

Connell, Raewyn. 1995. *Masculinities*. Cambridge: Polity Press.

Connell, Raewyn and James W. Messerschmidt. 2005. 'Hegemonic masculinity: rethinking the concept.' *Gender & Society* 19, 829–59.

Dawah, Ali 2020. [Twitter] 17 June. https://web.archive.org/web/20200617031912/https://twitter.com/AliDawow/status/1273091095367487489

Derman-Sparks, Louise and Patricia G. Ramsey. 2006. *What If All the Kids Are White? Anti-bias Multicultural Education with Young Children and Families*. New York: Teachers College Press.

DiAngelo, Robin. 2011. 'White fragility.' *International Journal of Critical Pedagogy* 3(3), 54–70.

Faris, Zara. 2014. 'The Muslim "feminist" (who isn't really a "feminist").' Zara Faris, 12 June. https://web.archive.org/web/20140910002719/https://zarafaris.com/2014/06/12/the-muslim-feminist-who-isnt-really-a-feminist

Farris, Sara. 2017. *In the Name of Women's Rights: The Rise of Femonationalism*. Durham: Duke University Press.

Freire, Paulo. 1993 [1968]. *The Pedagogy of the Oppressed*. New York: Continuum.
Ghumkhor, Sahar and Hizer Mir. 2022. 'A "crisis of masculinity"? The West's cultural wars in the emerging Muslim manosphere.' *ReOrient* 7(2), 135–57.
Göpffarth, Julian and Esra Özyürek. 2020. 'Spiritualizing reason, rationalizing spirit: Muslim public intellectuals in the German far right.' *Ethnicities* 21(3), 498–520.
Haqiqatjou, Daniel. 2017a. 'The reality of BlackLivesMatter.' The Muslim Skeptic, 9 June. https://web.archive.org/web/20190422014304/https://muslimskeptic.com/2017/06/09/1116
Haqiqatjou, Daniel. 2017b. 'Why do Muslims have a problem with #BlackLivesMatter?' The Muslim Skeptic, 8 June. https://web.archive.org/web/20210506011336/https://muslimskeptic.com/2017/06/08/927
Haqiqatjou, Daniel. 2018a. [Facebook] 12 November. https://web.archive.org/web/20200708142815/https://www.facebook.com/haqiqatjou/posts/2316681948550514
Haqiqatjou, Daniel. 2018b. 'The research is in: women prefer patriarchy.' *The Muslim Skeptic*, 31 December. https://web.archive.org/web/20200708130148/https://muslimskeptic.com/2018/12/31/women-prefer-patriarchy
Haqiqatjou, Daniel. 2019a. [Facebook] 5 February. https://web.archive.org/web/20200708142815/https://www.facebook.com/haqiqatjou/posts/2316681948550514
Haqiqatjou, Daniel. 2019b. [Twitter] 30 October. https://web.archive.org/web/20191030205655/https://twitter.com/Haqiqatjou/status/1189642068974620673
Haqiqatjou, Daniel. 2020a. [Facebook] 27 April. https://web.archive.org/web/20200708141618/https://www.facebook.com/haqiqatjou/posts/2776013299284041
Haqiqatjou, Daniel. 2020b. [Facebook] 25 June. https://archive.is/pS1XX
Haqiqatjou, Daniel. 2020c. [Facebook] 26 June. https://archive.is/aqV2B
Heikkilä, Niko 2017. 'Online antagonism of the alt-right in the 2016 election.' *European Journal of American Studies* 12(2), 1–21.
Hidayat, Rachmad. 2015. 'Muslim masculinities in Australia: negotiating manhood and Muslim identity in contemporary Australia.' PhD thesis, Monash University.
Hodapp, Christa. 2017. *Men's Rights, Gender, and Social Media*. Lanham: Lexington Books.
ImanWire Podcast. 2017. 'Ep. 13: Muslim masculinity: challenging the Alt-Bro—Muhammad Mendes.' Al Madina Institute, 24 April. https://archive.org/details/Imanwire
Islam4Europeans. 2019a. 'Our points for Black and white American Muslim's dialogue.' 6 October. https://web.archive.org/web/20191018191111/http://islam4europeans.com/2019/10/06/our-points-for-black-and-white-american-muslims-dialogue
Islam4Europeans. 2019b. 'White Muslims marrying each other would be good for the ummah.' 14 September. https://web.archive.org/web/20190919231728/http://islam4europeans.com/2019/09/14/white-muslims-marrying-each-other-would-be-good-for-the-ummah
Islam4Europeans. 2020a. 'An open letter in support of the Black American Muslim Conference.' 18 February. https://web.archive.org/web/20200223003808/http://islam4europeans.com/2020/02/18/an-open-letter-in-support-of-the-black-american-muslim-conference
Islam4Europeans. 2020b. 'Why European Muslim sub communities are needed #1 Evidence from Quran, Sunnah and Early Islam.' 29 June. https://archive.org/details/why-european-muslim-sub-communities-are-needed-1-evidence-from-quran-sunnah-and-early-islam-360p
Hodge, John L., Donald K. Struckmann, and Lynn Dorland Trost. 1975. *Cultural Bases of Racism and Group Oppression: An Examination of Traditional 'Western' Concepts, Values and Institutional Structures which Support Racism, Sexism and Elitism*. Berkeley: Two Riders.
hooks, bell. 2004. *The Will to Change: Men, Masculinity and Love*. Washington: Washington Square Press.
Ivarsflaten, Elisabeth. 2008. 'What unites right-wing populists in Western Europe? Re-examining grievance mobilization models in seven successful cases.' *Comparative Political Studies* 41(1), 3–23.
Kashani, Maryam. 2023. *Medina by the Bay*. Durham: Duke University Press.
Kasser, Tim and Richard Ryan. 1996. 'Further examining the American dream: differential correlates of intrinsic and extrinsic goals.' *Personality and Social Psychology Bulletin* 22(3), 280–7.
Kesvani, Hussein. 2019. *Follow Me, Akhi: The Online World of British Muslims*. London: Hurst.

Lambton, Ann. 1981. *State and Government in Medieval Islam: An Introduction to the Study of Islamic Political Theory: The Jurists*. New York: Oxford University Press.

Lee, Frances. [no date]. 'Kin aesthetics // Excommunicate me from the church of social justice.' Catalyst Wedding co. https://web.archive.org/web/20170714155441/http://www.catalystwedco.com/blog/2017/7/10/kin-aesthetics-excommunicate-me-from-the-church-of-social-justice

Lumsden, Karen. 2019. '"I want to kill you in front of your children" is not a threat. It's an expression of a desire": discourses of online abuse, trolling, and violence on r/mensrights.' In *Online Othering: Exploring Digital Violence and Discrimination on the Web*, edited by Karen Lumsden and Emily Harmer. Cham: Palgrave Macmillan, 91–115.

Marwick, Alice and Rebecca Lewis. 2017. *Media Manipulation and Disinformation Online*. New York: Data & Society Research Institute.

Muhammad, Shareef. 2019. 'Muslim and critical race theory: a response to Abdullah Andalusi's poor sequel.' Black Dawah Network, July. https://web.archive.org/web/20191106212204/https://blackdawahnetwork.com/2019/07/muslims-definitely-need-critical-race-theory-a-response-to-abdullah-andalusis-poor-sequel

Muhammad, Shareef. 2020. 'A critical look at Zaytuna Professor Dr. Abdullah bin Hamid Ali's denial of systemic racism!' Black Dawah Network. https://web.archive.org/web/20200811025507/https://blackdawahnetwork.com/2020/07/a-critical-look-at-zaytuna-professor-dr-abdullah-bin-hamid-alis-denial-of-systemic-racism

Muslim Anti-Racism Collaborative. 2019. *Anti-Racism Guide for White Muslims*. https://web.archive.org/web/20240130182923/https://drive.google.com/file/d/1iQayeY3hShBbAuP02cqacT5fozX6Ts-u/view

Murad, Abdal Hakim. 2020. *Travelling Home: Essays on Islam in Europe*. Cambridge: The Quilliam Press.

Piela, Anna and Joanna Krotofil. 2023. 'White habitus among Polish white female converts to Islam.' *Sociology of Religion* 84(1), 72–94.

Qasim, Mohammed. 2018. *Young, Muslim and Criminal: Experiences, Identities and Pathways into Crime*. Bristol: Policy Press.

Qureshi, Asim. 2017. *A Virtue of Disobedience*. London: Byline Books.

Sheldon, Kennon and Charles Nichols. 2009. 'Comparing Democrats and Republicans on intrinsic and extrinsic values.' *Journal of Applied Social Psychology* 39(1), 589–623.

Star Wars Episode III—Revenge of the Sith. 2005. [Film]. George Lucas (dir.). San Francisco: Lucasfilm Ltd.

Suleiman, Yassir and Paul Anderson. 2013. *Narratives of Conversion to Islam in Britain: Female Perspectives*. Cambridge: Prince AlWaleed Bin Talal Centre of Islamic Studies.

Suleiman, Yassir and Paul Anderson. 2016. *Narratives of Conversion to Islam in Britain: Male Perspectives*. Cambridge: Prince AlWaleed Bin Talal Centre of Islamic Studies.

Tate, Andrew. 2022. [Twitter] 13 December. https://web.archive.org/web/20221213172344/https://twitter.com/cobratate/status/1602702007181185028

The Mad Mamluks. 2019. 'EP 171: Pretty hate machine: White Muslims | Robert Dufour.' [YouTube] 22 December. https://archive.org/details/ep-171-pretty-hate-machine-white-muslims-robert-dufour-you-tube-1080p

The Muslim Skeptic. 2019. '"YASS QUEEN!" My response to a lesbian hijabi Muslim.' [YouTube] 30 July. https://archive.org/details/yass-queen-my-response-to-a-lesbian-hijabi-muslim-you-tube-1080p

The Muslim Vibe. 2020. 'Men and masculinity: what does it REALLY mean to "be a man"?' [YouTube] 17 April. https://archive.org/details/men-masculinity-what-does-it-really-mean-to-be-a-man-you-tube-1080p

Van Nieuwkerk, Karin (ed.). 2018. *Moving In and Out of Islam*. Austin: University of Texas Press.

Wheeler, Renée. 2020. 'On centering Black Muslim women in critical race theory.' Sapelo Square, 5 February. https://web.archive.org/web/20230926222358/https://sapelosquare.com/2020/02/05/on-centering-black-muslim-women-in-critical-race-theory

4
Wounds and Helplines

In August 2016, Halima, a journalist in her twenties in London, at the time wearing the hijab, relates in a Facebook post a series of incidents that happened to her.

> I went to Whitechapel today to do a bit of filming on Islamophobia at East London Mosque and to do some hijab shopping! I'm sitting in Altab Ali park talking to a TV channel about rising islamophobic attacks, when these two older white guys come over, sit right next to us and keep muttering aggressive comments . . . 'We don't have sharia law in the UK yet, I've got freedom of speech.'

Later that day, another incident happened to her:

> As I'm crossing the road, a middle-aged Asian man on a motorbike shouted at me 'COVER YOUR LEGS!' . . . I really was/am in disbelief at how on two ends of the spectrum, right-wing Islamophobe and conservative Muslim uncle, these grown men had felt the need to shout abuse at a young girl . . . Sometimes as Muslim women we are just targeted from every side; racists, misogynists . . . both inside and outside our community.

Her words echo many of my respondents', expressing their exhaustion from being attacked 'from every side': by state-sanctioned systems of oppression on the one hand, and the animosity of various groups within the 'Muslim community' on the other, a space supposed to shelter them from attacks from the outside. Halima acknowledges feeling 'drained' and 'emotionally worn down'. Organizations like MEND in the UK, CAIR in the US, and the CCIF in France have been producing statistics of racist attacks which boomed after 9/11 and 7/7 and which still have not faded almost two decades. Fayma, living in Wales at the time, was hospitalized when she received a letter informing her that a national TV channel has decided to produce a documentary presenting her as an extremist:

> I often get suicidal thoughts. I was devastated, I ended up in hospital for two days, I was fainting, vomiting . . . A mainstream media was portraying me as an extremist, and I'm nothing of all what they say . . . We need to focus on community

organising ... It's not about the money, it the power, it's about building a network of support. We've been bad at it.

For most of my respondents, being a target has become accepted as part and parcel of being Muslim in Euro-America. Halima expressed the wish to be invisible, a feeling that pushes Muslims to adopt uncritically various dominant norms in order to blend in, often as a survival mechanism (see chapter 1). For many however, what starts with self-censorship eventually ends up with self-sabotage and in some cases self-harm. Fayma related how lucky she is to have a strong support network; however, she knows that most people don't and find themselves in precarious situations. Societal pressures are the main reason why 32% of young Muslims aged 16–30 have suffered suicidal thoughts at some point (MYH 2019). The most concerning fact is perhaps that most, according to the same report, didn't feel they had an opportunity to talk about their feelings to anyone. Besides glass ceilings, surveillance, and criminalization, one of metacolonization's most powerful weapons is psychological warfare, making people feel inadequate, weak, and trapped. In order to cope, many would engage in various excesses (see chapter 7), but also many would try to heal since no resistance or progress is possible without this crucial first step.

Muslim communities in Euro-America are faced with the inadequacy of mainstream mental health care for minorities. Observing the issue of Eurocentric mental health care models in Sudan is precisely what led Hussein Bulhan (2015) to coin the term 'metacolonialism'. In the early 2000s, grass-roots initiatives started to address the issue by creating their own mental health support groups, later followed by Muslim qualified psychotherapists who developed their own initiatives or professional counselling services. These efforts are also paralleled with various researchers in the Europe and in the US working at implementing faith- and culture-sensitive mental health care models in mainstream institutions such as the British NHS. Through a research-action initiative titled 'I Am Not What Is Broken',[1] I have collected written, audio, and visual testimonies about some Muslims' challenges and journeys to healing. Since social isolation is an aggravating factor in people's struggles, the initiative brought people together with non-white culture- and faith-sensitive therapists to share strategies and a sense of collective hope through an event organized at SOAS. The online public platform and collection of stories serves as a library for other people to potentially relate to the participants' journey and come to overcome perhaps one of the main barriers to healing: the realization that no, the problem is not them. I analyse the mental health journey of my respondents, their attempts at coping, surviving, healing, and ultimately flourishing where community, mentoring, and the spiritual interpretation of their own challenges are used to reframe harmful narratives. From internalized labels projected on them such as 'victims', 'patients', 'failures', and 'problem', they redefine themselves and re-appropriate the role of protagonist of their own stories.

4.1. The State Is an Abuser

Javayria highlights how she was simultaneously fed two contradictory narratives in Britain:

> Do they want us or do they not want us? You want a relationship, but you cannot have it . . . We were told a different story at school. You're one of us, and then *snap* you're not . . . Tony Blair said welcome, let's create a new Britain, multiculturalism. Then, they said multiculturalism has failed. The society, the institutions are gaslighting you. They are racist but they tell you racism doesn't exist . . . They tell you your feelings are not true, that you're imagining it, you're too sensitive. It makes you doubt your own sanity.

When at school, she was part of a wider 'us'; in her professional life or watching the news, she was not. Javayria compares it to a manipulative relationship where one partner is led into doubting their own sanity. However, she explains that if there is pain, it's because there was love in the first place. Actor Riz Ahmed similarly compares the situation to a failed relationship: 'Britain has broken up with me.'[2] In the first chapter, Javayria and Mehdi acknowledged their struggles with self-esteem because of 'code switching'. However, Javayria wonders why some of her relatives and friends born in Pakistan don't feel the same pain and need to be validated by English people.

> When I talk to Shabnam [her sister in law, born and raised in Pakistan], she says she doesn't mind, she doesn't expect anything from here. She says it's not her country. Same for Farah [a friend of hers who grew up in Pakistan], I find her much more confident. Maybe it's because when you're born here [in the UK], you're sold that if you go to school, to university, get a degree, get a job, you will be treated like everyone else. This is not true, and this disappointment hurts.

Her friends, like many others born abroad, don't share the same feeling of 'belonging' to the UK and never expected to be treated well either. Contrary to Javayria, they have a psychological 'safety net' in the sense that they can always leave and go somewhere else where they feel they belong. What about those who cannot leave and are trapped?

I have myself been in an abusive marriage where my ex-wife would gaslight me. On the one hand, she would force me to take annual leave, claiming that I was working too much and not spending enough time with her, saying that I didn't love her. On the other hand, when I would take said annual leave, she would blame me for being lazy, saying similarly that this was because I didn't love her. Whatever I was doing to please her, I was at fault; all of my words and silences would be weaponized against me. She could never be wrong. If I would argue back that 'this is what you told me to do', she would say I misinterpreted her words. I felt powerless. When her punches were bruising my face to the point of blackout, I would pray to God to keep me alive. After it had continued for a few years, I was praying God to take me back to Him. Many European states similarly entertain a gaslighting relationship with the non-white other: on the one hand, telling people they are wanted and needed as a workforce in critical sectors, on the other hand, policies such as PREVENT (see chapter 2) restrict their rights and tell people they need to assimilate. Valluvan (2019) argues that these dynamics are at core of twenty-first-century nationalism, where having a designated 'other' is central to reassert political boundaries of the nation-state. When state institutions and the media together state that the victims should be blamed for their fate, protests and social media become spaces of acknowledgement and holding. Mass protests and online sharing of content as seen in the wake of Me Too, Black Lives Matter or the human rights violations committed against Palestinians can therefore be understood as collective resistance to structural gaslighting. They are a collective effort not only at resisting structures of oppression, but for people to reassure and remind each other by metaphorically saying: 'you're not imagining things, you're not alone in this'. From a spiritual perspective, not only from their collective dimension and ritual or repetitive aspects but also from a perspective of standing for justice, protesting and demonstrations are a form of *zikr* (remembrance).

Beyond direct experiences, witnessing violence bears consequences too. On the night of 13 June 2017, during Ramadan, the Grenfell Tower in London burnt, taking the lives of seventy-two people because of a chain of negligence resulting from Conservative policies, leading to councils putting profits over people's lives. For non-white and working-class people in Britain, the message was clear: they were literally consumables. Two of my respondents, residents of Ladbroke Grove, witnessed the fire. They still experience anxiety and flashes when physically in the area. Muslim community organizer and rapper Lowkey,[3] also living next to the tower; saw it as the last nail in the coffin of British multiculturalism. Since the catastrophe happened as the result of the negligence of scaffolding companies, the landlords association and the local authority, it soon became a symbol for the treatment of minorities in Britain: through segregation, generational dispossession, over-policing, and disposability (El-Enany 2017). On 16 June 2017, a few days after the fire, on a Facebook post, community organizer and cultural producer Farzana Khan wrote: 'this is why we have always said and known that for women, for migrants, for poor and disabled people, our first abuser is the state' (Khan 2020). Life seems like an endless series of painful reminder that things won't change.

People from the Black, South Asian, and Muslim diasporas are three times more likely to suffer from mental health issues compared to the average population. Research shows how racism and Islamophobia increase feelings of depression and anxiety for Muslims worldwide (Kunst et al. 2013). There is an over-representation of people from South Asian and African backgrounds amongst mental health patients. In 2010, 23% of mental health patients in England and Wales were from 'Black and minority ethnic groups' (National Mental Health Development Unit 2011), but this group accounts for only 14% of the population in England and Wales (ONS 2012). Racism and discrimination are key triggers for mental health issues. Research finds that those who had experience verbal abuse or attacks are between three and five times more likely to suffer from depression or psychosis (Chakraborty and McKenzie 2002). Muslims living in Europe and North America have experienced intensified psychological distress since 9/11 (Amer 2005; Rippy and Newman 2006; Ahluwalia and Zaman 2010; Amer and Hovey 2012). Returning to what Mehdi mentioned in chapter 1, racial prejudice has damaging effects on people's self-esteem (Mehmood 2015). The politics of counter-terrorism are furthermore creating a loop where people with mental health issues are wrongly identified as at risk of extremism,[4] and in turn, undergo further trauma from their referral (Younis 2020). Racism doesn't have to be overt or explicit; subtle acts of exclusion or covert acts of racism (racist attacks passed as a joke, for example; Russell 1998; Alleyne 2005a) contribute to 89% of reported race-based trauma (Johnson et al. 2018).

Racism puts an extra burden on people by subjecting them to self-elimination, impostor syndrome (the feeling of not belonging or not deserving), added to the 'insecurities' of not having an economic safety net, the extra labour if one doesn't have a mentor/sponsor, and the 'lingering anxiety that stems from failing to convincingly mimic dominant behavioural norms—to "crack the code"' (Friedman and Laurison 2019, 216). Unemployment and precarious working conditions are additional factors contributing to poor mental health (Marmot et al. 2010; McManus et al. 2016). Racism can be a determinant of physiological health: aside from anxiety and depression, Paradies et al. (2013) list effects such as cardiovascular disease, decreased birth weights, increased blood pressure, premature ageing, and death. In the wake of the Coronavirus pandemic, Britain grappled with the fact that most fatalities occurred among minoritized ethnic backgrounds. While genetics and co-morbidities such as diabetes and blood pressure were ruled out, social factors gave a partial answer, but eventually, research pointed at the allostatic load of the demographics. Allostatic load is 'the wear and tear on the body' which accumulates as an individual is exposed to repeated or chronic stress (McEwen and Stellar 1993). The chronic stress resulting from exposure to racism therefore would weaken the immune system and make populations that were victims of racism more vulnerable to infections (Duru et al. 2012). All these factors led some doctors to define racism as 'the state-sanctioned and/or extra-legal production and exploitation of group-differentiated vulnerability to premature death' (Wilson Gilmore 2006, 28). However, some may argue that the state is also exhibiting toxic traits because of structural cognitive issues: why do Europe and the US struggle at examining and addressing their past? Why are they feeling threatened by inquiries into their history? Why are they obsessed with public order? What if then, in addition to the state, communities replicate the same patterns of ostracization?

4.2. Spiritual Abuse and Unsafe Spaces

Muneera relates her experience with born-Muslims shortly after she embraced Islam. Facing body shaming in the name of modesty, she recalls how her mental health was dismissed as 'a sign of lack of faith and ingratitude': 'first up in that realm of Muslim womanhood, there was no space for depression or sadness for you are now supposed to be the happiest woman in the world ... because you are [a] wife ... because you are a mother ... because your parents gave you Islam' (Williams 2017).

In chapter 1, because of social pressures, Farrah couldn't recognize herself in a mirror and Muneera was drawn to self-harm. Various studies demonstrate how certain body shapes, when mass broadcasted to preadolescent girls, affect their body dissatisfaction and their perception of what body is 'beautiful' or 'ugly', and can trigger eating disorders, depression, low self-esteem, and other psychopathologies (Anschutz et al. 2011; Boothroyd et al. 2020). Paraphrasing bell hooks (2004), the first lesson of the metacolonial matrix of domination is learning to wear a mask, as it hijacks people's true self. In the face of trauma, the modification of the body and, if not possible, its harming, are therefore escape strategies trying to find refuge, either by blending into the dominant society or by removing oneself from its toxicity. Embracing coloniality is a form of escapism. Ruqaiya Haris writes about how Muslim women undergo plastic modifications, acknowledging they are submitting to Eurocentric beauty standards because of the pressure of social media.[5] People who abide by extrinsic values, trying to reach fame or power for the sake of acceptance at the expense of others do not fare better, suffering from anxiety, stress, anger, dissatisfaction, and more (see chapter 2.4 and 7.4). Farrah comments how after her divorce, social norms led her to choose harmful partners: 'every time I fall for these men, I get hurt ... Girls like to go for those who are a bit rough, the bad boy stereotype, but don't have what it takes to make a strong marriage.' Through a journey of self-work and therapy, she learnt to say 'no' and be more careful with her choices.

Modern society is largely unhappy; in Britain, 18% of 16–25-year-olds disagree with the statement that 'life is really worth living' (Booth 2019). Although social media fulfil the need for connection, overall, image-focused platforms, because of their consumptive design and their limitation for creating meaningful engagement, are estimated to undermine well-being by making people feel 'sad and lonely' (Kross et al. 2013; Royal Society for Public Health 2017). Social media offers an addictive (Turel et al. 2014) environment of comparison and therefore competition (Chou and Edge 2012). Users are engaged in self-promotional behaviours which produce an envy spiral (Krasnova et al. 2013), contributing not only to feelings of loneliness but also to resentment (Burke et al. 2011), jealousy, and surveillance behaviour (Anderson et al. 2012).

In the neoliberal era, competitive individualism has led people to perfectionism, becoming more demanding of others and of themselves (Curran and Hill 2019) in an endless loop where people improve themselves to death.[6] Analysing job-related suicides, office-induced paranoia, and fear of relaxation, Fleming (2015) demonstrates how the ritual of work (and the fear of joblessness) has come to colonize lives and become a psychological tool to maintain class hierarchies. Furthermore, Foucault's Orwellian *Discipline and Punish* (1977) has turned into a Huxleyian happy worker culture (Cabanas and Illouz 2017): working the nine-to-five with a smile has become an implicit command. Consequently, dictates like the Forbes '30 Under 30'[7] make people break down in questions such as 'what are you doing with your life?'[8] when they hit the feared 30-year-old mark. Even though, in reality, the lists hides privileges and access that made it possible for young people to 'make it': almost no one on the list is 'self-made'.[9] Metacolonialism imprisons people through space and mind but also time—through information overload, nine-to-five work culture, attention economy on social media, police arrests, the time wasted being rejected from marriage or jobs, time in prison, and, as Asim Qureshi (2017) points out, through the time people need to recover from traumas (2017, 16). Stealing time is a tool of control, and as he observed how children of people unjustly arrested in the wake of the war on terror are affected, 'trauma and time have a cyclical nature, and trauma can potentially manifest itself continually throughout generations' (Qureshi 2017, 21).

Studying the transgenerational transmission of trauma in Black families, DeGruy (2005) coined the term 'Post-Traumatic Slave Syndrome'. Alleyne (1992) analyses it as a 'cycle of events' where parents and grandparents pass on a legacy of pain to the younger generations who internalize whiteness as a 'superego' thus building false 'self-structures' in a 'paranoid-schizoid' process and adopting traits of the oppressor. She describes the syndrome of the 'preoccupation with the white other': over generations, the legacy of Black people's painful ancestral baggage has contributed to an unconscious preoccupation with the white other which has led to complex attachment and relationship patterns through the generations and continues to exist between Black and white people today (Alleyne 2005a). Eventually, people impacted by transgenerational trauma adopt a split personality comprising an 'internal oppressor' (Alleyne 2005b). This internal oppressor is the part of the self which perpetuates internalized oppression, 'which is the process of absorbing the values and beliefs of the oppressor and coming to believe that the stereotypes and misinformation about one's group is true (or partly true)' (Alleyne 2005b, 12) as described by Lipsky (1987), Lorde (1984), and hooks (1995). While Alleyne and DeGruy refer to internalized oppression resulting from slavery, here I argue that racism and Islamophobia have similarly caused Muslims to adopt an oppressor self resulting from the hijacking, imprisonment, and holding as hostages of people's space, time, minds, epistemology, and identity. Since mimicry and the adoption of dominant norms can result from psychological violence, under metacolonialism, it also creates unsafe spaces in communities at the margins. Muneera related how Islam was used as a tool to shame her about her appearance and to dismiss her pain.

Alaa, when reconnecting with her faith in her twenties, encountered abusive behaviours in various organizations and charities: 'I started researching about religion, but I would meet scholars, TV presenters, personalities who would seduce women, get what they want and leave. The same guys who would tell me that if I pluck my eyebrows, I will not smell the perfume of paradise.' Many of my respondents experienced issues which many in Euro-America started vocalizing under the term of 'spiritual abuse'. The term emerged following scandals in the wake of the Me Too movement, when celebrity preacher Nouman Ali Khan[10] in 2017, then scholar Tariq Ramadan[11] in 2018, and later Usama Canon, were accused of sexual misconduct. Despite Khan and Ramadan admitting to un-Islamic behaviour, the internet was in disbelief: 'let's find him 70 excuses', 'we should hide the sins of our brothers', 'did anyone had four male witnesses?', 'Are you a qualified scholar to criticise him?', 'He is just human, it was a mistake', and even elaborate theories, 'it was secret *nikkahs* [Islamic marriages]', 'he was forced to lie to the judges to escape prison'. For Muslims, abuses of power by religious leaders are unique as people 'invest faith, hope, vulnerability' in what is 'a sacred trust' (Shaikh 2019, 6).

A website was created to provide guidance surrounding the phenomenon: *In Shaykh's Clothing*.[12] The website defines spiritual abuse by 'using religious authority for personal gain, ulterior purpose, to bully, harass or control others' (Qasim 2018). Similar to cults, spiritual abuse can manifest as financial misappropriation, bullying, sexual assault, molestation, exploitation, manipulation facilitated by religious arguments. Furthermore, the definition also covers 'manipulations that damage a person's relationship to God or to his/her core self' (Qasim 2018). Writer Sana Saeed (2019) asks: 'how are you supposed to keep reconciling what you experience and see, time and time again, with your faith when the men who teach you the faith keep failing you?' While movements like Me Too helped people to speak out against abuse, in marginalized communities, one factor that prevents people from holding abusers to account is the fear of the public opinion. Fauzia Ahmad (2006) writes how, for example, marginal issues such as arranged marriages can be sensationalized and generalized in the press to create narratives such as 'forced marriages'. In her works, she notes how parents rather play an instrumental role encouraging their daughters to succeed both academically and professionally (Ahmad 2001, 2012) and despite that, how the media generalizes forced marriage as a global Muslim issue.

Some of my respondents, like Beata, an Eastern European coach in London in her fifties who had embraced Islam thirty years ago, locate the cause of these social pressures and abuses of power in a lack of support structures equipping people with the tools to live healthy lives and holding abusers to account:

> [People] are too scared of naming emotions so they hold onto something that is not real, for the sake of looking good and status ... Compassion, spirituality are not taught at home. At school, the priority is to fit in ... Children pick up labels from parents and teachers. Many clients tell me: 'I don't know who I am anymore.' In society and family, we produce impoverished souls, so they compensate with ego in the workplace ... They have two lives, one in public, one in the family. I was once coaching a famous Muslim scholar who was addicted to pornography. I had clients at powerful positions, but in face to face they are like little boys.

Javayria sums up: 'in every case of a sheikh, there's always a structure that enabled it'. These patterns are also seen in the various scandals in the Muslim humanitarian charity sector (see chapter 7.3). Independently funded organization such as Facing Abuse in Community Environments[13] (FACE) in the US provide legal support for people victim of abuse by Muslim religious figures, and attempt a private mediation process before a case is submitted to the authorities. However, beyond structures of accountability, victims also need spaces for healing.

4.3. Community Healing Initiatives

Because seeking help in formal mental health services is seen as shameful (Abu Ras 2003; Khan 2006), the issues are rarely spoken about in families or addressed inadequately: 'my parents say that mental health is a white construct because they argue that there's no word for that in Urdu or Punjabi' says Javayria. However, similar narratives become rare with the younger generations. Movements such as Black Lives Matter or Me Too allowed the trauma of racism and sexual abuse to be more openly spoken about in Muslim communities. People would start sharing their struggles publicly on social media and students' societies would organize public events around the topics.

In the UK, although state and mainstream mental health care services have started to offer culture-sensitive services since the 2000s like Rethink (circa 2005)[14] or faith-sensitive services like MIND (2014),[15] their Muslim counterparts have been around for much longer: Black Womens Health & Family Support (1982), the Muslim Youth Helpline (2001), Muslim Womens Helpline (2001), or Sakoon Islamic Counselling (2006). Although grass-roots mental health initiatives provide basic support, very little work had been done around adapting Eurocentric therapeutic frameworks for specific cultures and faiths. One of my respondents recalls how, dealing with PTSD, eating disorders, and online addictions, the hospital only prescribed him Prozac and beta-blockers. His experience echoes similar ones amongst ethnically minoritized people who feel pathologized as opposed to considered as patients: 'I, as a Black woman, I am more likely to be prescribed psychotropic medication than to be offered therapy' (Kinouani 2015). Adila, who is a worker for the British National Health Service (NHS) has experienced bereavement several times. Her insights into the health system made her rather critical of the institution:

> I have questions about whether service industries manage to sustain themselves ethically in a world where so much spin exists to engineer a constant demand for pharmacopeia and cosmetics on the back of people's insecurities & vulnerabilities... I have questions about the exploitative methods used in marketing which generate perpetual feelings of failure, failure of not achieving, not having, failing to succeed or be enough. (Ahmed 2017)

Adila criticizes the 'abnormalization' of mental health issues. While events such as death are part of the life's journey, she points at the pathologization of grief as something people shouldn't feel or experience too much or for too long. Facing a mental health 'issue' is synonymous with failure. Muslim social media celebrities seem always happy, smiling, in a sunny place, sharing copy-pasted simplistic recipes for happiness such as 'good vibes only' or 'don't take life too seriously'. Since neoliberalism is a culture of individual responsibility, feeling resentment, frustration, or anger means that something must be wrong in one's brain. Just like in multicultural Britain, since racism 'doesn't exist', Muslims must be the problem. Therefore, as a Muslim, looking for mainstream therapy or counselling services as well as looking for solutions within the community can be challenging.

Various works found how Islam provides a meaning to mental illnesses and a purpose, favouring acceptance (Abu-Raiya and Pargament 2010), provides comfort, identity, spirituality and community (Ahmed and Amer 2012; Utz 2012). Other works have shaped the field of 'Islamic counselling', setting up guidelines that therapists should appreciate, coping strategies Muslims patients have utilized (Ali and Aboul-Foutouh 2012), consider the role of imams (Ali, Milstein and Marzuk 2005), adapting cognitive-behavioural and humanistic-experiential models (Amer and Jalal 2012) and rational emotive behavioural models (Ali 2007), undertaking culturally informed interviews and acculturative stress assessments, or taking into account subjective explanatory models, collective dimension, interdependence, and the distrust of dominant culture (Rahiem and Hamid 2012). Religious scholar and psychotherapist Abdallah Rothman (2022) has built a model for Islamic psychology and psychotherapy, writing frameworks almost from scratch using the concepts of *nafs* (ego), refinement of character (*Tahdib al Ahlaq*) and detachment from the material world. Other researchers have been experimenting and assessing new therapy models, such as Ghazala Mir (Mir et al. 2019). Muslim psychotherapist Rabia Malik has opened the Marlborough Centre for Islamic-based interventions (Dharamsi and Maynard 2012). Some businesses such as Sakoon Islamic Counselling offer to link patients with professional and qualified Muslim psychotherapists from various cultural backgrounds. Javayria chose Sakoon because her therapist would 'understand the spiritual and cultural complexities attached to [her] struggles'. Laila, a counselling psychologist specializing in complex developmental trauma and PTSD (whom I met as a patient) is an example of practitioners who address these gaps by going beyond simply establishing culture- and faith-appropriate interventions (Hammad et al. 2020). In addition to practising different therapies (eye movement desensitization and reprocessing (EMDR), narrative exposure therapy (NET), and trauma-focused cognitive behavioural therapy (tf-CBT), Laila's approach integrates faith and spirituality into therapy if requested by the client. She also tries to break the clinical practitioner-patient hierarchy into a more human-to-human interaction, while maintaining the obligatory boundaries. When appropriate, she would be sharing parts of her own journey as relatable experiences to accompany—rather than fix—patients in their healing process, in the vein of clinical psychologist Kay Redfield Jamison (1995), the latter embodying the concept of the 'wounded healer'—or healing and therapies themselves as a co-productive process between patients and practitioners.

Established in 2001, the Muslim Youth Helpline employs around twenty-five volunteers and eight regular paid staff members as of the end of 2018. It positions itself as 'faith and culturally sensitive organisation' rather than a structure providing religious guidance.[16] The volunteers occupy various positions, from answering calls on the hotline to administrative functions. Volunteers are selected through a skills- and character-based interview plus administrative checks (DBS), and when successful, are trained by external professional psychotherapists and faith-sensitive organizations such as Sakoon through a tailored 4-day programme. The hotline receives on average 130 contacts a month, mostly from male support seekers. Email threads and conversations are systematically quality-checked. Although volunteers are multi-lingual, the MYH provides services only in English, mainly for quality-check purposes.

MYH works not only as a mental health support service. The company has proven to be a pivotal community hub for its alumni volunteers (Barylo 2019), which provides skills, community, and inspiration. Soraya's experiences with intersectionality as a Muslim bisexual woman have already informed her choice to choose a career in mental health care: 'MYH was a step, I think, in the greater journey. I hide [my bisexuality] to my family; I don't know if I will end up with a man or a woman, and how my family would react . . . [MYH] was a space where it was fine to be Muslim and bisexual, and hearing people who experience similar things and just need to talk.' Sakeenah decided to undertake studies to become a psychotherapist during her time in the charity: 'MYH was an eye-opener. My friends and I often talk about their university counselling services [which] don't understand what does it mean to be Muslim or South Asian.' '[I]t gave me skills that followed me all my life until now,' says Hasaan, 'active listening, a sense of empathy, listening to others' problems, trying to explore options together, being an emotional shoulder, emotional intelligence ... This was a pivotal experience in my life which took me to where I am now.' Miriam has met Hasaan while volunteering and later decided to join him in his new organization: 'I've learnt through MYH the importance of selflessness and honesty; if you make mistakes, don't try to hide it ... My experience at MYH gave me a good network of friends and has strengthen[ed] the good relations.'

Their experience at MYH shed light on various extra- and intra-community issues which, for Sadeeya, led her to set up her own initiative: '[at MYH,] I got really affected by the issue of domestic violence, especially towards children. I have nieces and nephews, and I can't imagine these things happening to them.' Similar realizations led Hasaan to setting up his own charity against islamophobia and for opening conversations within the community: 'there were lots of calls related to islamophobia. People who've been abused, bullied ... also, back in the days, I found MYH was for a very South-Asian, middle-class type of Muslim; some people would not understand things like anti-Blackness in the Muslim community, while Black Muslims are already targeted by islamophobia. I felt that we need to address these issues in our community.' '[I]t's already difficult to talk about gender issues, let alone LGBT issues in the mainstream,' says Soraya, 'it's almost impossible in the Muslim community; even if you have groups like the Inclusive Mosque Initiative; and it makes people suffer a lot because they can't talk about it.' Sakeenah felt that she could relate to some beneficiaries, which was pivotal in her journey: 'it speaks to you more when it hits home, when you hear people who've been through sexual abuse, who attempted suicide, who live in London, who are your age. It's different from volunteering abroad or in big charities. I feel big charities are very corporate, they have a very capitalist perspective. Here you feel you are more in touch with people.' Faiz, struggling with depression himself, felt a sense of responsibility after being in contact with beneficiaries at MYH: 'I want, through my art, to say that it's okay, that there's hope ... if someone listens to me, to my story, and regains hope, that's the purpose.'

Whether it is islamophobia in the mainstream, or anti-Blackness or anti-LGBTQ sentiments, volunteering at MYH enabled them to realize the complexity of intersectional contexts and how forms of exclusions present in the mainstream affect to various degrees Muslim communities. However, these realizations play different roles in the volunteers' journeys. They can be pivotal as for Hasaan, Faiz, or Sakeenah, or already existing like for Sadeeya, Miriam, or Soraya, for whom the MYH was just a 'natural' step along the development of their journey or an opportunity. For Faiz or Soraya, the MYH allowed a space for articulating personal trauma or issues and potentially a better understanding of these and an opportunity to breathe if not grow. Whether it is skills, work ethics, network of friends, inspirations, or ideas, they all feel that MYH gave them more than what they visibly received. For some like Miriam, who feels her work at MYH was also a way to get 'closer to God', the dimensions of self, community (beneficiaries) and the divine are interwoven in a virtuous cycle of gift where those who give help are also receiving on the other end. For many, their experience at MYH shaped their vision of society and self in conjunction with their religious beliefs and an 'active' or proactive sense of citizenship oriented towards vulnerability and critically engaged with contemporary social debates on race, religion, and gender (Barylo 2019)—MYH confirms previous observations as local grass roots being catalysts (Barylo 2017) in the development of intrinsic values (see chapter 2).

However, one major contention with modern Muslim mental health services is, although they either try to indigenize knowledge and establish therapies rooted in Islamic psychology, or elaborate a unique framework entirely based on classic Islamic traditions, only few try to redress the failures of Eurocentric frameworks (Long 2014; Younis 2022). Psychologist Tarek Younis (2022) criticizes that many models still responsibilize individuals rather than political, economic, and social structures. However, unlike corporate initiatives using mental health as a business model, the Muslim Youth Helpline is free to use, and constitutes a bridge between people seeking help and qualified professionals.

Because of the lack of structures, grass-roots initiatives are used as mental health support by visitors, even if they were not exclusively designed for this purpose. One example is Rumi's Cave in London (see chapter 8). Ömer, who has been one of the managers of the Cave for some time, describes his experience:

> It's like a mental health hospital. You have homeless people, businessmen, divorced women . . . You listen to stories, real stories, it can be overwhelming . . . People come here to comfort their heart, it's a kind of therapy for them. But the problem is that we can't offer help. We're not trained for that.

Some other, sometimes more informal initiatives are found in the form of support groups like Rabiah Mali's Black Muslim Women Healing Collective:

> spaces for women to restore their own skills and capacities in trauma release and healing in their communities, families and within themselves. It is a hub that will create multiple online and in person safe spaces with access to the needed heart-centred therapeutic practices and teachings rooted in a rich Islamic spiritual heritage. This will be done in a compassionate, non-judgemental and non-directive environment that can meet the specific needs and experiences of the Black Muslim identity . . . A space to voice fears, difficulties and needs . . . A space of deep listening, breath work, holding space, collective *dhikr* [remembrance] and prayer.

Farzana Khan has been a community organizer for more than a decade. Through the initiative she co-founded, Healing Justice London, she builds arts and culture programmes for young marginalized people, aiming at 'undo[ing] harms, repair, vision and sustain futures possible free from intimate, interpersonal and structural violence'. She doesn't consider herself as a leader but rather sees her role as a 'relay', guiding people and then stepping back. When the 2020 pandemic happened and the government ordered the lockdown, she posted a few tips on her social media channels:

> Sickness is not a failure or something that should be punished... We are living in the consequences of hundreds of years of chronic unsustainability via systems of oppression such as colonialism and capitalism that brutalised our bodies as well as the emerging sickness due to climate degradation—this is a global and public health matter... the British Neoliberal Common Sense has made it so relationships are based on individualisation—making our wellness and health a personal responsibility, when real health and healing happens in community. (Khan 2020)

These spaces, although not counselling services, allow the holding of space for marginalized people. They show, through the use of arts and traditional methods (such as herbal medicine, tea, meditation, frankincense, prayer, and yoga), that healing doesn't have to be contingent on Eurocentric models of therapy or scientifically peer-reviewed methods. They are pivotal in the sense that, they are re-framing the pain and traumas in specific spiritual, social, and political contexts. Some respondents would find similarities between the Sufi traditions of using *zikr* (remembrance of God), using left-right body movements, tapping, and bilateral stimuli of percussion instruments and proven trauma therapies such as EMDR. Spaces like Rumi's Cave, Healing Justice London, and the Black Muslim Women Healing Collective highlight a demand for creative non-conventional methods based on community, creativity and spirituality where people can find themselves in trusted spaces. Trusted spaces are not necessarily safe spaces (can any space be truly 'safe'?) but spaces in which people identify common psychological meanings, motivations, reasons, intentions, and attitudes but also rules, values, symbols, norms, and, above all, solidarity (Sztompka 1999). While these trusted spaces provide a haven for dealing with the pain, the road to recovery can often be a long, lonely journey of trials and errors, and different for each person. However, many of my respondents share a similar overall journey from a state of hopelessness and powerlessness to a state where they have regained not necessarily control, but better self-esteem and confidence, and instead of considering mental health as something to fight against, they are focusing on the flourishing of their self. These are spaces for a restorative approach where people flourish beyond and despite trauma.

4.4. Reframing Narratives from Pain to Power

Muneera, through art, spirituality, and community, was able to use storytelling to shift her internal narrative, crafting herself as a 'Hip-Hop soldier':

> I fell in love with music and radio and become a DJ... Slowly I started to form this independent identity and crafted this personality that I was really proud of... A spiritual Hip-Hop soldier, able to roll with the Rastas and the Buddhists, the road men and those from the hills... Depression and anxiety have never really left me, I still get bouts of both, the difference is, however, I am familiar with my triggers, and I have devised strategies for dealing with them when they come round. Probably the three most helpful things have been practising a spiritual path within Islam, counselling, and a mini network of loved ones. (Williams 2017)

She eventually realized that she is 'valuable', retracing bell hooks' journey 'from pain to power' (hooks in The New School 2015). It involves for Maryam 'flipping the narrative:' on the day of her thirtieth birthday, pressured to feel a failure by standards like the Forbes 30 Under 30, she decided to count her blessings, grateful God had allowed her to reach this age. Muneera shared posts reframing neurodiverse conditions from the perspective of 'super powers':

ADHD: Extraordinarily creative, resourceful, adaptive, tenacious and resilient. Super power: hyperfocus.
Autism: methodical, sophisticated, analytical skills, attention to detail.
Super power: the brain is a steel trap for information.
Trauma survivor: strong survival instincts, grit, thrive in uncertainty, adaptable, empathetic. Super power: powerful neuroception.

Like Muneera, for many of my respondents, creative practice has been at the heart of their recovery journey because of the reframing it allows. Haseeb, suffering from PTSD following deaths in his family and events in his life, has been using the arts as a form of psychotherapy:

> [T]he goal is to keep the conversation you had with the therapist going automatically even after the therapy is finished... Carving had the biggest impact on... It became a metaphor for how my life has unravelled because at this stage. I wasn't living life according to a plan, I was just living free hand... It became okay not to know exactly what I'm meant to be doing, not to have a set plan.

Reframing negative labels by voicing positive elements for those at the margins is a form of resistance against dominating narratives. For that purpose, Tara Yosso

(2005) suggests a (still capitalist) model of cultural wealth, highlighting elements not valued by the metacolonial matrix of power:

> Aspirational capital: the capability to dream and imagine stories and nurture a culture of possibility.
> Linguistic capital: not only language and communication skills such as translating, storytelling, memorization, the ability to express oneself in verses and rhymes, but also intellectual and social skills attained through communication experiences.
> Familial and social capitals: a broader understanding of kinship not limited to blood relations, (Muslims calling each other 'brothers' and 'sisters'), the ability to feel empathy towards an extended social circle.
> Navigational capital: skills of manoeuvring through institutions not created with ethnically minoritized communities in mind such as university campuses.
> Resistance capital: the knowledge and skills fostered through the challenge of inequalities, the ability to resist, collaborate, and organize, which include the social justice heritage left by elders' generations.

Echoing Yosso's aspirational capital, Cloke et al. (2013) argue that faith-based organizations embody a particular form of resistance to neoliberalism through their 'prophetic' rationale: their ability to offer comfort and hope in times of hardship. However, Dinham (2012) argues that rather than the restrictive concept of 'capital', other concepts should be preferred such as community, reach, networks, and solidarities instead of 'social capital', etc. Baker and Skinner (2006, 12) posit that faith-based groups provide 'religious capital' as 'the practical contribution to local and national life made by faith groups' and 'spiritual capital' as something 'providing a theological identity and worshipping tradition, but also a value system, moral vision and a basis of faith'. They furthermore argue that they provide regenerative environments which are 'transforming people personally and spiritually, as well as improving their area physically' (Baker and Skinner 2006, 7). Spiritual narratives have been a major factor for healing with many of my respondents like Soraya:

> Understanding Allah, His vision for His creation, and Islam as a whole, has given me such an increased level of understanding, which has undoubtedly saved me... Your journey could help someone else, the trials can unlock something in you, a strength or talent or it can all come to light in the hereafter.

Adila expands on the sacred dimension she confers to pain and healing:

> There is a line in the book of *Physicians of the Heart* that states, '*ar-Rauf* [the infinitely compassionate, one of God's names] is the one who genuinely says, 'I can be

with you in the unbearableness that you feel' ... When I read [Rumi's Mathnavi], I found it was like a how-to-survive guide for the faithful activist. (Ahmed 2017)

The metaphysical explanations they found for the narratives in their lives allow my respondents to deal with their pain and accept what cannot be changed. In conjunction with community healing initiatives, they remind my respondents that despite living in the middle of the matrix of domination, they still have control over their lives and that from discomfort comes growth. Volunteers who have experienced the most traumatic experiences often end up being the most involved and dedicated in their work (Barylo 2017). Kraus et al. (2012) notice that when people live a life defined by chronic social threats, they develop an enhanced perception of emotions, attend more to others, and promote cooperation. They echo Carl Gustav Jung's (1954) statement that there cannot be birth of consciousness without pain. Javayria recounts her observations, following school friends who have grown up and taken very different paths: 'privilege is a curse. The most attractive people I know are in the less stable relationships. The more privileged they are, the less empathy they have. There's this friend of mine, she was very materialistic, only when her husband was randomly harmed by someone on the street, she started reflecting on her life and changed her lifestyle.'

The emergence of community mental health initiatives shows that Muslims are becoming more vocal about these issues and transparent about weaknesses of 'the community. Through the reframing of narratives, they embody Alleyne's (2005b) fifth stage of repairing and healing through the emergence of a true self in a state of grace. They are able collectively to build psychological suits of armour to navigate institutions they have accepted as racist. However, although people have found ways to heal and survive in a hostile environment, it doesn't replace effective structural changes. In the meantime, some Muslims like Rabiah Mali, founder of the Black Muslim Women Healing Collective mentioned earlier, root healing and the flourishing of the community in another sacred element in Islam: the natural environment.

Notes

1. I Am Not What Is Broken. Accessed 1 February 2024. https://web.archive.org/save/http://iamnotbroken.williambarylo.com
2. Ian Youngs, 'Riz Ahmed on the long goodbye: why he says "Britain's broken up with me"', *BBC News*, 6 March 2020. https://web.archive.org/web/20200306044242/https://www.bbc.co.uk/news/entertainment-arts-51697553
3. 'LOWKEY ft. MAI KHALIL—GHOSTS OF GRENFELL (OFFICIAL MUSIC VIDEO)' VoiceOver [YouTube] 8 August 2017. https://archive.org/details/lowkey-ft.-mai-khalil-ghosts-of-grenfell-official-music-video
4. Jamie Grierson, 'Mental health may be "significant factor" in NHS referrals to Prevent', *The Guardian*, 2 July 2020. https://web.archive.org/web/20200702010856/https://www.theguardian.com/uk-news/2020/jul/02/mental-health-may-be-significant-factor-in-nhs-referrals-to-prevent

5. Ruqaiya Haris, 'Why cosmetic surgery can be complex when you're Muslim', *Dazed Digital*, 17 October 2018. https://web.archive.org/web/20181022025722/https://www.dazeddigital.com/beauty/head/article/41850/1/cosmetic-surgery-muslim-beauty-modesty
6. Alexandra Schwartz, 'Improving ourselves to death', *The New Yorker*, 8 January 2018. https://web.archive.org/web/20180108101910/https://www.newyorker.com/magazine/2018/01/15/improving-ourselves-to-death
7. Heather Schwedel, 'Why it's so hard to watch people your age do better than you', *Slate*, 16 November 2018. https://web.archive.org/web/20181117035849/https://slate.com/human-interest/2018/11/30-under-30-millennials-in-congress-envy.html
8. Priyanka Mattoo, 'Fighting the scourge of the "30 Under 30" list', *Vulture*, 20 March 2019. https://web.archive.org/web/20190320201504/https://www.vulture.com/2019/03/fighting-the-scourge-of-the-30-under-30-list.html
9. Aditi Juneja, 'I was on a Forbes 30 under 30 list. Here are the hidden privileges that made me a "success"', *Vox*, 13 November 2018. https://web.archive.org/web/20181114014119/https://www.vox.com/first-person/2018/7/14/17569650/forbes-30-under-30-list-2019-kylie-jenner
10. Hannah Allam, 'Payoffs, threats, and secret marriages: how an accused preacher is fighting to save his empire', *Buzzfeed News*, 21 December 2017. https://web.archive.org/web/20180727055757/https://www.buzzfeednews.com/article/hannahallam/payoffs-threats-and-sham-marriages-women-say-a-celebrity
11. Angelique Chrisafis, 'Tariq Ramadan admission sparks fresh row over rape claims', *The Guardian*, 31 October 2018. https://web.archive.org/web/20181101005030/https://www.theguardian.com/world/2018/oct/31/tariq-ramadan-admission-sparks-fresh-row-over-claims
12. In Shayjh's Clothing. Accessed 1 February 2024. https://web.archive.org/web/20170629120802/https://inshaykhsclothing.com
13. Facing Abuse in Community Environments. Accessed 1 February 2024. https://web.archive.org/web/20180831024156/https://www.facetogether.org
14. 'Rethink Sahayak Asian mental health helpline', Rethink. Accessed 1 February 2024. https://web.archive.org/web/20200716144345/https://www.rethink.org/help-in-your-area/services/advice-and-helplines/rethink-sahayak-asian-mental-health-helpline
15. 'The Qur'an and emotional health', MIND. Accessed 1 February 2024. https://web.archive.org/web/20190217221655/https://www.mind.org.uk/about-us/our-policy-work/equality-human-rights/our-work-with-muslim-communities
16. 'FAQs', Muslim Youth Helpline. Accessed 1 February 2024. https://web.archive.org/web/20200809024209/https://www.myh.org.uk/faqs All the subsequent data was obtained through direct interviews of the MYH managers in October 2018.

References

Abu-Raiya, Hisham and Kenneth Pargament. 2010. 'Empirically based psychology of Islam: summary and critique of the literature.' *Mental Health, Religion and Culture* 14(2), 93–115.

Abu-Ras, Wahiba. 2003. 'Barriers to services for Arab immigrant battered women in a Detroit suburb.' *Social Work Research and Evaluation* 3(4), 49–66.

Ahluwalia, Muninder and Noreen Zaman. 2010. 'Counseling Muslims and Sikhs in a post 9/11 world.' In *Handbook of Multicultural Counselling*, edited by J. G. Ponterotto, J. M. Casas, L. A. Suzuki, et al. Thousand Oaks: Sage, 467–78.

Ahmad, Fauzia. 2001. 'Modern traditions? British Muslim women and academic achievement.' *Gender and Education* 13(2), 137–52.

Ahmad, Fauzia. 2006. 'The scandal of "arranged marriages" and the pathologisation of BrAsian families.' In *A Postcolonial People: South Asians in Britain*, edited by Nasreen Ali, Virinder Kalra, and Salman Sayyid. London: Hurst, 272–89.

Ahmad, Fauzia. 2012. 'Graduating towards marriage? Attitudes towards marriage and relationships among university-educated British Muslim women.' *Culture and Religion* 13(2), 193–210.

Ahmed, Adila. 2017. 'Love's unfolding.' I Am Not What Is Broken. https://web.archive.org/web/20240129223422/https://iamnotbroken.williambarylo.com/?p=292

Ahmed, Sameera, and Mona Amer (eds). 2012. *Counselling Muslims: Handbook of Mental Health Issues and Interventions*. New York: Routledge.

Ali, Osman, Glen Milstein, and Peter Marzuk. 2005. 'The imam's role in meeting the counseling needs of Muslim communities in the United States.' *Psychiatric Services* 56(2), 202–5.

Ali, Osman and Frieda Aboul-Foutouh. 2012. 'Traditional health coping and help-seeking.' In *Counselling Muslims: Handbook of Mental Health Issues and Interventions*, edited by Sameera Ahmed and Mona Amer. New York: Routledge, 33–51.

Ali, Rameez. 2007. 'Application of REBT with Muslim clients.' *Rational Emotive Behaviour Therapist* 12(1), 3–8.

Alleyne, Aileen. 1992. *Cycle of Events*. MA dissertation, University of Hertfordshire.

Alleyne, Aileen. 2005a. 'Invisible injuries and silent witnesses: the shadow of racial oppression in workplace contexts.' *Psychodynamic Practice* 11(3), 283–99.

Alleyne, Aileen. 2005b. 'The internal oppressor—the veiled companion of external racial oppression.' *The Psychotherapist* 26, 10–13.

Amer, Mona. 2005. 'Arab American mental health in the post September 11 era: acculturation, stress, and coping.' *Dissertation Abstracts International: Section B: The Sciences and Engineering* 66(4-B), 1974.

Amer, Mona and Blaand Jalal. 2012. 'Individual psychotherapy/counseling: psychodynamic, cognitive-behavioural, and humanistic-experiential models.' In *Counselling Muslims: Handbook of Mental Health Issues and Interventions*, edited by Sameera Ahmed and Mona Amer. New York: Routledge, 87–119.

Amer, Mona and Joseph Hovey. 2012. 'Anxiety and depression in a post-September 11 sample of Arabs in the United States.' *Social Psychiatry and Psychiatric Epidemiology* 47(3), 409–18.

Anderson, Beth, Patrick Fagan, Tom Woodnutt, et al. 2012. 'Facebook psychology: popular questions answered by research.' *Psychology of Popular Media Culture* 1(1), 23–37.

Anschutz, Doeschka, Donna Spruijt-Metz, Tatjana Van Strien, et al. 2011. 'The direct effect of thin ideal focused adult television on young girls' ideal body figure.' *Body Image* 8(1), 26–33.

Baker, Chris and Hannah Skinner. 2006. *Faith in Action: The Dynamic Connection between Religious and Spiritual Capital*. Manchester: William Temple Foundation.

Barylo, William. 2017. *Young Muslim Change-makers: Grassroots Charities Rethinking Modern Societies*. London: Routledge.

Barylo, William. 2019. 'When trauma and citizenship intersect: British Muslims volunteering for mental health services.' In *Muslim Volunteering in the West between Islamic Ethos and Citizenship*, edited by Mario Peucker and M. Reyhan Kayikci. Basingstoke: Palgrave Macmillan, 161–78.

Booth, Robert. 2019. 'Anxiety on rise among the young in social media age.' *The Guardian*, 5 February. https://web.archive.org/web/20190205050626/https://www.theguardian.com/society/2019/feb/05/youth-unhappiness-uk-doubles-in-past-10-years

Boothroyd, Lynda, Jean-Luc Jucker, Tracey Thornbarrow, et al. 2020. 'Television consumption drives perceptions of female body attractiveness in a population undergoing technological transition.' *Journal of Personality and Social Psychology* 119(4), 839–60.

Bulhan, Hussein A. 2015. 'Stages of colonialism in Africa: from occupation of land to occupation of being.' *Journal of Social and Political Psychology* 3(1), 239–56.

Burke, Moira, Robert Kraut, and Cameron Marlow. 2011. 'Social capital on Facebook: differentiating uses and users.' In *Proceedings of the SIGCHI Conference on Human Factors in Computing Systems (CHI '11)*. New York: Association for Computing Machinery, 571–80.

Cabanas, Edgar and Eva Illouz. 2017. 'The making of a "happy worker": positive psychology in neoliberal organizations.' In *Beyond the Cubicle: Insecurity Culture and the Flexible Self*, edited by A. Pugh. New York: Oxford University Press, 25–50.

Chakraborty, Apu and Kwame McKenzie. 2002. 'Does racial discrimination cause mental illness?' *The British Journal of Psychiatry* 180(6), 475–7.

Chou, Hui-Tzu Grace and Nicholas Edge. 2012. '"They are happier and having better lives than I am": the impact of using Facebook on perceptions of others' lives.' *Cyberpsychology, Behavior and Social Networking* 15(2), 117–21.

Cloke, Paul, Justin Beaumont, and Andrew Williams. 2013. *Working Faith: Faith-based Organisations and Urban Social Justice*. Milton-Keynes: Paternoster.

Curran, Thomas and Andrew Hill. 2019. 'Perfectionism is increasing over time: a meta-analysis of birth cohort differences from 1989 to 2016.' *Psychological Bulletin* 145(4), 410–29.

DeGruy, Joy. 2005. *Post Traumatic Slave Syndrome: America's Legacy of Enduring Injury and Healing*. Milwaukie: Uptone Press.

Dharamsi, Sabnum, and Abdullah Maynard. 2012. 'Islamic-based interventions.' In *Counselling Muslims: Handbook of Mental Health Issues and Interventions*, edited by Sameera Ahmed and Mona Amer. New York: Routledge, 135–61.

Dinham, Adam. 2012. *Faith and Social Capital after the Debt Crisis*. London: Palgrave MacMillan.

Duru, Kenrik, Nina Harawa, Dulcie Kermah, et al. 2012. 'Allostatic load burden and racial disparities in mortality.' *Journal of the National Medical Association* 104(1–2), 89–95.

El-Enany, Nadine, 2017. 'The colonial logic of Grenfell.' Verso Books Blog, 3 July. https://web.archive.org/web/20180613222434/https://www.versobooks.com/blogs/3306-the-colonial-logic-of-grenfell

Fleming, Peter. 2015. *The Mythology of Work: How Capitalism Persists Despite Itself*. London: Pluto Press.

Foucault, Michel. 1977 [1975]. *Discipline and Punish*. New York: Pantheon Books.

Friedman, Sam, and Daniel Laurison. 2019. *The Class Ceiling: Why It Pays to Be Privileged*. Bristol: Policy Press.

Hammad, Jeyda, Amell El-Guenuni, Imane Bouzir, et al. 2020. 'The hand of hope: a co-produced culturally appropriate therapeutic intervention for Muslim communities affected by the Grenfell Tower fire.' *Journal of Muslim Mental Health* 14(2), 15–62.

hooks, bell. 1995. *Killing Rage: Ending Racism*. New York: Penguin.

hooks, bell. 2004. *The Will to Change: Men, Masculinity and Love*. Washington: Washington Square Press.

Johnson, Rae, Lucia Leighton, and Christine Caldwell. 2018. 'The embodied experience of microaggressions: implications for clinical practice.' *Journal of Multicultural Counseling and Development* 46(3), 156–70.

Jung, Carl Gustav. 1954 [1925]. *Collected Works*, Volume 17, paragraph 331. Princeton: Princeton University Press.

Khan, Zeenat. 2006. 'Attitudes toward counseling and alternative support among Muslims in Toledo, Ohio.' *Journal of Muslim Mental Health* 1(1), 21–42.

Khan, Farzana. 2020. '#Loveinatimeofcorona/#covid-19—practical tips/support.' https://web.archive.org/web/20200919022740/https://farzanakhan.net/loveinatimeofcorona-covid-19-practical-tips-support

Kinouani, Guilaine. 2015. 'The language of distress: Black women's mental health and invisibility.' *Media Diversified*, 6 May. https://web.archive.org/web/20150514050209/https://mediadiversified.org/2015/05/06/the-language-of-distress-black-womens-mental-health-and-invisibility

Krasnova, Hanna, Helena Wenninger, Thomas Widjaja, et al. 2013. 'Envy on Facebook: a hidden threat to users' life satisfaction?' In *Wirtschaftsinformatik Proceedings* 92.

Kraus, Michael, Paul Piff, Rodolfo Mendoza-Denton, et al. 2012. 'Social class, solipsism, and contextualism: how the rich are different from the poor.' *Psychological Review* 119(3), 546–72.

Kross Ethan, Philippe Verduyn, Emre Demiralp, et al. 2013. 'Facebook use predicts declines in subjective well-being in young adults.' *PLoS ONE* 8(8), e69841.

Kunst, Jonas, David Sam, and Pål Ulleberg. 2013. 'Perceived Islamophobia: scale development and validation.' *International Journal of Intercultural Relations* 37(2), 225–37.

Lipsky, Suzanne. 1987. *Internalised Racism*. Seattle: Rational Island Publishers.

Long, Wahbie. 2014. 'Critical reflections on the Islamicisation of psychology.' *Revelation and Science* 4(1), 14–19.

Lorde, Audre. 1984. *Sister Outsider*. Trumansburg: Crossing Press.

Marmot, M., J. Allen, P. Goldblatt, et al. 2010. *Fair Society, Healthy Lives: Strategic Review of Health Inequalities in England post 2010*. London: Institute of Health Equity. https://web.archive.org/web/20111221102217/http://www.instituteofhealthequity.org/Content/FileManager/pdf/fairsocietyhealthylives.pdf

McEwen, Bruce and Eliot Stellar. 1993. 'Stress and the individual. Mechanisms leading to disease.' *Archives of Internal Medicine* 153(18), 2093–101.

McManus, Sally, Paul Bebbington, Rachel Jenkins, et al. (eds). 2016. 'Common mental disorders.' In *Mental Health and Wellbeing in England: Adult Psychiatric Morbidity Survey 2014*, edited by S. McManus, P. Bebbington, R. Jenkins, and T. Brugha. Leeds: NHS Digital, 37–68.

Mehmood, Maryyum. 2015. 'The role of self-esteem in understanding prejudice.' In *Muslims in the UK and Europe vol. 1*, edited by Yasir Suleiman. Cambridge: Prince AlWaleed Bin Talal Centre of Islamic Studies, 150–8.

Mir, Ghazala, Ruqayyah Ghani, Shaista Meer, et al. 2019. 'Delivering a culturally adapted therapy for Muslim clients with depression.' *The Cognitive Behaviour Therapist*,12, e26.

MYH. 2019. *Muslim Youth: What's The Issue?* London: Muslim Youth Helpline. https://web.archive.org/save/https://myh.org.uk/wp-content/uploads/2021/03/MYH-Research-Report-Muslim-Youth-Whats-the-Issue-1-2.pdf

National Mental Health Development Unit. 2011. *Count Me In Census 2010*. London: Care Quality Commission.

ONS. 2012. 'Religion in England and Wales 2011.' 11 December. https://web.archive.org/web/20160309021427/http://www.ons.gov.uk/peoplepopulationandcommunity/culturalidentity/religion/articles/religioninenglandandwales2011/2012-12-11

Paradies, Yin, Jehonathan Ben, Naomi Priest, et al. 2013. 'Racism as a determinant of health: a protocol for conducting a systematic review and meta-analysis.' *Systematic Reviews* 2, article 85.

Qasim, Danish. 2018. 'Defining spiritual abuse: how and why we use the term.' In Shaykh's Clothing, 10 July. https://web.archive.org/web/20220120200504/https://inshaykhsclothing.com/home/intro/defining-spiritual-abuse-how-and-why-we-use-the-term

Qureshi, Asim. 2017. *A Virtue of Disobedience*. London: Byline Books.

Rahiem, Farah Tasleema and Hamada Hamid. 2012. 'Mental health interview and cultural formulation.' In *Counselling Muslims: Handbook of Mental Health Issues and Interventions*, edited by Sameera Ahmed and Mona Amer. New York: Routledge, 51–71.

Redfield Jamison, Kay. 1995. *An Unquiet Mind: A Memoir of Moods and Madness*. New York: Knopf.

Rippy, Alyssa and Elana Newman. 2006. 'Perceived religious discrimination and its relationship to anxiety and paranoia amongst Muslim Americans.' *Journal of Muslim Mental Health* 1(5), 5–20.

Rothman, Abdallah. 2022. *Developing a Model of Islamic Psychology and Psychotherapy: Islamic Theology and Contemporary Understandings of Psychology*. London: Routledge.

Royal Society for Public Health. 2017. *Status of Mind: Social Media and Young People's Mental Health*. London: Royal Society for Public Health.

Russell-Brown, Katheryn. 1998. *The Color of Crime*. New York: New York University Press.

Saeed, Sana. 2019. 'Our faith and the men who break it.' *Medium*, 8 November. https://web.archive.org/web/20191213195956/https://medium.com/@SanaSaeed/our-faith-the-men-who-break-it-b087afc6d76f

Shaikh, Sa'diyya. 2019. 'Spiritual abuse—the violation of an Amanah: rethinking Muslim gender ethics.' *Muslim Views* 33(5), 6.

Sztompka, Piotr. 1999. *Trust: A Sociological Theory*. Cambridge: Cambridge University Press.

The New School. 2015. 'bell hooks: moving from pain to power I the new school.' [YouTube] 12 October. https://archive.org/details/bell-hooks-moving-from-pain-to-power-i-the-new-school-240p

Turel, Ofir, Qinghua He, Gui Xue, et al. 2014. 'Examination of neural systems sub-serving Facebook "addiction".' *Psychological Reports* 115(3), 675–95.

Utz, Aisha. 2012. 'Conceptualizations of mental health, illness and healing.' In *Counselling Muslims: Handbook of Mental Health Issues and Interventions*, edited by Sameera Ahmed and Mona M. Amer. New York: Routledge, 15–33.

Valluvan, Sivamohan. 2019. *The Clamour of Nationalism: Race and Nation in Twenty-first-century Britain*. Manchester: Manchester University Press.

Williams, Tanya Muneera. 2017. 'We are valuable.' I Am Not What Is Broken. https://web.archive.org/save/https://iamnotbroken.williambarylo.com/?p=41

Wilson Gilmore, Ruth. 2006. *Golden Gulag: Prisons, Surplus, Crisis, and Opposition in Globalizing California*. Berkeley: University of California Press.

Yosso Tara J. 2005. 'Whose culture has capital? A critical race theory discussion of community cultural wealth.' *Race Ethnicity and Education* 8(1), 69–91.

Younis, Tarek. 2020. 'The psychologisation of counter-extremism: unpacking PREVENT.' *Race & Class* 62(3), 37–60.

Younis, Tarek. 2022. *The Muslim, State and Mind: Psychology in Times of Islamophobia*. London: Sage.

5
Green Deen and Stewardship

When, in 2014, Elon Musk declared 'fuck Earth', encouraging the colonization of Mars, Rabiah Mali was making tea. This is how I met Rabiah for the first time. In her workshop, she was teaching her small audience about everything from leaves, water temperatures, scents, herbal infusions, and tasting. In January 2017, Rabiah organized a talk at Rumi's Cave in London around the theme of 'spiritual ecology'. Most people know Rabiah as the second half of the duo Pearls of Islam. Whenever they perform, events are sold-out and entire halls are packed. At the time, Rabiah's events around the environment would gather no more than ten people. Since everyone at Rumi's usually is offered a cup of tea, everyone had a warm cup in their hands. This would be her starting point:

> Acknowledge the warmth in your hands. Guess what flavours are in the tea . . . You can experience Nature anywhere at any time. You can even experience Nature in the city. There is Nature around you . . . You can even experience Nature in the tube during rush hour. Close your eyes, focus on your breath. This is Nature. You don't need to be 'in' Nature to experience it . . . Because we are Nature. We need to 'be' Nature . . . There is no dominance of humans. When human beings are called *khalifa* in the Qur'an, it means we are stewards. We were given a trust.

Rabiah, now in her thirties, born from Muslim Jamaican and Guyanese parents, graduated from the University of Westminster in 2008 in Western herbal science. She then travelled to Ghana to study Islamic herbal medicine where she observed herbalists reading prayers acknowledging that the healing power of the tree comes from God and thanking a tree before cutting its bark. This encounter made her realize that 'everything in the creation is in conversation, everything is praising the divine', as also mentioned in the Qur'an (22:18). Back in London in 2010, she co-founded with other women the Rabbani Project, a community collective around 'creativity, nature and spirituality', and later the Green Deen Tribe, the Herbal Blessing Clinic, and the Black Muslim Women Healing Collective (BMWHC). The Green Deen Tribe, whose goal is 'reconnecting souls with nature & their purpose of tending to the Earth', aims at re-establishing a dialogue between humans and nature, synonym with a conversation between humans and the divine: 'one thing . . . we realise is very powerful, is to take people out of the city and let them be in Nature. And let Nature speak, let Nature reveal itself and let Allah speak to us through Nature.'

British Muslims in the Neoliberal Empire. William Barylo, Oxford University Press. © William Barylo 2025.
DOI: 10.1093/9780198924975.003.0006

The retreats, so far for women only, are opened and closed with acknowledging people's feelings, where participants can let go of their emotions. Respondents I interviewed afterwards share how the retreats relieved them from the weight of their wounds, in a space where they finally feel safe and held. Centred around developing face-to-face and face-to-nature interactions, the days are rhythmed with prayers, lectures, cooking sessions, songs, workshops such as knitting, and silent walks in nature. Rabiah's views, backed with scriptural evidence, are that human beings, God, and the natural environment are part of the same ecosystem. These views echo the observations of Rosemary Hancock (2017) around other Muslim environmental charities where the boundaries 'Islamic' and 'environmental' or the 'religious' and the 'political' are not clearly demarcated. As some of my respondents would state, 'Islam is environmentalism': every action and word has an impact in the material world but also in the spiritual universe. The absence of distinction between nature and the products of human existence (culture) has also been advocated as an analytic framework in the Social Sciences. Anthropologists such as Lévi-Strauss (1962), Mauss (2007), or Descola (2005, 15) invite researchers to consider that 'borders of humanity never stopped at the human species'. In his idea of culture as an ensemble of complex systems, French sociologist Edgar Morin writes about how culture and nature make a same substance in 'permanent movement' that 'modifies and transforms itself always' (Morin 1986, 296), and how 'it is not only mankind that is a by-product of the cosmic destiny, it's also the cosmos that is a by-product of an anthropo-social destiny' (Morin 1977, 92).

Since the late twentieth century, Muslims from Europe have created abodes of greenery like in the Alqueria de Rosales in Andalusia (established in 1998) or Zaytuna farm in Australia, founded by British-born Geoff Lawton in 1997. In urban spaces, initiatives like An-Nisa Society in North-West London started around the same time programmes to raise awareness about the environment. For decades, the Nation of Islam in the United States has been prescribing healthy diets and the protection of the environment has been interwoven in many hip-hop lyrics (Abdul Khabeer 2016, 68–70). The Nation promoted the concept of *tayyib* (excellence), alluding to food grown in an organic manner, and praised vegetarian and vegan diets. In 2002, a couple founded the first British *tayyib* farm, Willowbrook Farm, offering halal organic meat. The concept of *tayyib* is a strict application of the Islamic rules of breeding and slaughter which include that the animal should not be held captive or distressed and treated all life-long with kindness because slaughtering an animal is not a right but a derogation in Islam. While the festival of Eid AlAdha is traditionally associated with the slaughter of animals (remembering Abraham's sacrifice), some Muslims in Europe and America decided to follow early Islamic traditions of sacrificing part of one's finances for a charitable cause[1] instead of an animal. The 2010s saw Muslims joining protests around the globe such as Extinction Rebellion, the establishment of numerous charities such as Muslim Action for Development and Environment (MADE), encouraging mosques to implement eco-friendly measures (Pettinato 2016), the inauguration of the first purpose-built eco-mosque in the UK—in Cambridge, the first *khutba* (Friday sermon) about climate change delivered in 2019 at the East London Mosque, the largest mosque in London.

Hancock (2017) notes that while Muslim environmentalists rely on Islamic narratives and concepts to bring values and commitments into their activism, many actors also bring their experience from mainstream secular grassroots environment activism. They can be either goal-oriented (transforming mosques) or focused on implementing environmental values in their own lives and community (upcycling clothes). Through the 2010s, I have observed that Muslim environmentalism has increasingly become vocalized in concert with issues of social, economic, and racial justice. In the era of metacolonial hegemonies, the natural environment has been colonized, exploited, and relegated to the margins—thus, the fight against hegemonies, whether racial, socio-economic or gendered, and therefore justice, is linked to the protection of the environment, the first victim of the human ego (Meziane Amer 2021). I argue that Muslim environmentalism in the UK could not have survived without the struggle for decolonization and specifically Black liberation. In this chapter, I explore Muslim environmentalist spaces, where people not only pray, talk, and play music, but also walk in the mud and climb on rocks. I analyse the different strategies they implement, their impact, and their effectiveness at mobilizing people. I also analyse how the month of Ramadan has turned into a month for decolonization, how the Eurocentric idea of 'leadership' has been replaced by *khilafa* (stewardship) and how it influences modes of governance.

5.1. The Disease of Leadership: Modernity and Its Disconnections

Freshly arrived to the UK in 2013, I spent my first British Ramadan alone. Although working in a Muslim organization and knowing Muslim Londoners prior to my move, nobody invited me for *iftaar* (breaking of the fast). When I tried to find out why, most people would mention work or studies. This situation contrasted with the usual emphasis on 'solidarity' and 'togetherness' of Ramadan. In France, I usually had to decline politely the avalanche of invitations for *iftaar* that I would receive every single day. Furthermore, in the UK, when it came to casual socializing, every time I would try to secure a catch-up meeting around tea with people I considered as friends, I would often be met by people searching in their diary for the next five-minute slot which at the earliest occurrence fell in . . . two months' time. None of this would happen even with the busiest of my friends in France. This is perhaps one of the key observations that led me to ask myself the question: why is that in London, most people are so absorbed by their studies or career to the point of leaving fellow believers isolated during Ramadan?

In the middle of the 2010s, amongst my respondents, people increasingly started to express a specific problem: the work environment. After the 2008 financial crisis, boosted by the worship of economic growth, the 2010s erected productivity as an idol. This concept has been inscribed in the collective mind amongst Muslims in 2014 through Omid Safi's widely shared piece 'The disease of being busy', where the author realizes how much time has been stolen from him by emails and other professional commitments:

> What happened to a world in which we can sit with the people we love so much and have slow conversations about the state of our heart and soul? ... Tell me you remember you are still a human being, not just a human doing. (Safi 2014)

His thoughts echo those of Ahuvia (2002), linking unhappiness in materialistic societies to individualism, self-interest, and social competition as opposed to social responsibility and solidarity. In the *Mythology of Work*, Peter Fleming (2015) paints a psychological landscape of workplaces where workers are in majority disengaged because of routines making their life appear as a journey between the two hells of home and work. In the same work, he observes how the question 'what do you do' signifies how people have assimilated professional activity to a primary identifying marker: people have become the work they do. The modern office is the space of many disconnections. The problem lies not only in the nine-to-five routine and the consequent commute in traffic jams or public transports, but also in its social dynamics—specifically classist, gendered, and racial ones, as seen with white professionalism (see chapter 1). There is an ongoing battle for our time and attention. In attempts to reclaim time, the 2010s saw the rise of Muslim personal productivity coaches offering people 'acceleration workshops and new success strategies' and 'powerful self-development evening shows', selling the 'law of attraction concept' backed by questionably interpreted religious texts. Some of my respondents saw in this trend a hijacking of Islam by an 'explosion of the self'. Whitewashed yoga exercises or micro-planning trainings soon were ironically falling in the same pitfalls they were supposed to fix: under the pretext of offering a pathway to liberty, they were simply preying on people's time and money through predatorily marketing, selling financial enslavement in the guise of financial freedom.

In the same wave, countless organizations in Euro-America wanted to see young Muslims as 'leaders': the Muslim Leadership Initiative, the Oxford Centre for Islamic Studies's 'Young Muslim Leadership Programme', the Cardiff University's Muslim Young Leaders Award, CAIR's Muslim Youth Leadership Programme, the Australian Multicultural Foundation's Australian Muslim Youth Leadership Program, or the Muslim American Leadership Alliance in the US. Most of these programmes have three things in common: they allow participants to gain skills (public speaking, campaigning), expand their networks, and learn about legislative processes. Their terminology is crafted around the theme of power: 'skills', 'officials', 'training', 'institutional', 'challenges', and 'changing the world'. In France, some Muslim organizations use the term 'elite' (Barylo 2017), selling the French dream: that anyone from any background can find themselves part of the ruling class. The term, implying a form of oligarchic domination of the whole society by a few (Arendt 1963, 409).

'Leader' belongs to the semantics of war, politics, and business: the commander, the president, the CEO, a single person in command of others, who rules and inspires their followers,[2] an authority figure at the top of a hierarchy. The modern idea of leader find its roots in the archetypal heroes of Greek mythology (Hodge et al. 1975), an individual solving alone problems quickly through their strength or intelligence rather than with the help of others. The modern leader hold his strength in their qualification and socioeconomic rank obtained through exams and ruled-out contestants, crushed opponents and competitors, a machine producing results and thinking in terms of problems and solutions and acting through authority and control—it is bell hooks' idea of the dominator model (2004) (see chapter 3). Humanity has entered the era of the *Homo Oeconomicus*, when the human being becomes a machine that earns, produces, and consumes. In the infinite quest for growth, the leader is always in a quest for things to control and conquer: enemies, nature, disease, mortality, feelings, and bodily limitations, although there is no such thing in nature as infinite growth; 'growth for the sake of growth is the ideology of the cancer cell' (Abbey 1977, 183). The reliance on mythological European heroism and its perdurance through popular culture, as in superhero blockbusters, has made the leader, in the collective imaginary, synonymous with the powerful white male. Popular culture has therefore carved in stone whiteness as a brand.[3] Faithful to the idea of modernity as a culture of separation (Touraine 1992), in the business world, Lovric and Chamorro-Premuzic (2018) and Keltner (2016) analyse how the idea of 'leader' embodies many of the characteristics found in personality disorders, from narcissism, psychopathy, histrionicity, and Machiavellianism,[4] taking the examples of Steve Jobs or Richard Branson. In the Muslim charity industry, my own experiences and numbers of my respondents pointed at how most jobs are given to internal candidates, acquaintances, or to the loudest, most arrogant, and overconfident, regardless of experience or qualifications. When mistaken for leadership,[5] these qualities, because inversely related to talent and team building, increase the risk of mismanagement (see chapter 7.3) (Chamorro-Premuzic 2013). Beata, having coached some of the executives in the largest Muslim charities in the UK, testifies: 'these charities do not hire the best qualified person but people from the 'same tribe'; they mistake arrogance and ego for leadership. Loud people are magnetic, they get what they want, but concretely they're not brilliant. Some I don't know how they get positions.'

The modern leader divides, displaces the balance to his advantage and ultimately disconnects. Syed Mustafa Ali (2019) argues that this Promethean quest for control, which led to the development of artificial intelligence and transhumanism, is the translation of a fear of a civilizational (white) apocalypse, where the white civilizational project falls into becoming a self-fulfilling prophecy and thus ironically, a suicide cult.[6] In the context of Muslim diasporas, it leads to de-diasporization (see chapter 1), when the nostalgia for the ancestral culture disappears, thus becoming uprooted.

Some Euro-American academics have attempted at shifting away from the idea of leadership with works such as the Convivialist Manifesto (Convivialist International 2020), initiated by French sociologist Alain Caillé. Caillé and others compare the neoliberal project to the Greek notion of *hubris*, the desire for omnipotence, control, possession of wealth and power (Convivialist International 2020, 7) and states that the only possible response could be found in conviviality, from the Spanish *convivir* (living together), as per the works of Ivan Illich (1973). Other theories specific to business management have emerged such as Servant Leadership (Greenleaf 1970; Van Dierendonck 2011; Eva et al. 2019) or stewardship (Block 2013), relying on Eurocentric narratives such as Herman Hesse's Journey to the East. They advocate for observation, reflection, long-term thinking, consultation, or contemplation. However, these concepts lack some of the values and dynamics found in grass-roots organizations such as resistance, navigation, healing, community, mentorship, inter-generational dynamics, reconciliation, or speaking truth to power.

In a podcast where the host suggest Rabiah Mali is an 'example of spiritual leadership', she replies: 'I don't think the term sits comfortably with me. Leadership is a dictatorship, do what I say not what I do. It feels very egoistical . . . I prefer the idea of invitation and stewardship' (The Future Is Beautiful 2020). Similarly, Salih Whelbourne manager of Mu'allif, a rhizomic community for new Muslims in Nottingham, thinks: 'the quest for leadership ruin things. There's nothing wrong with scaling down ambitions, otherwise you miss issues in front of your nose.' Consequently, as an alternative to leadership, some Muslim organizations propose the Qur'anic (6:165) concept of *khilafa* (stewardship).

5.2. Hikers and Healers: From Leadership to Stewardship

Since my high school years, I have been into hiking. I enjoy the silence, the majesty of the mountains, and the feeling of being insignificant compared to the landscapes. I met Fozia in 2014, then in her early forties, when she organized a hike in the Lake District. At the hostel, I met with a group of around thirty people, all Muslims, mostly of South Asian descent, from various social, economic, professional, and religious backgrounds, but largely working class or lower middle class. Some of them had never hiked before. There were people of all ages, men, women, and children. Some of them joined for the experience, others to have a break, others just to follow their friends. These walks were not framed by a religious perspective, there were no *du'as* (supplications) at the beginning or the end, and people would individually accommodate their prayers. During the walk, people were chatting, joking, checking on each other, and, for some, subtly getting to know each other for the purpose of marriage. People brought samosas, masala chai, and kebabs, which were shared with everyone during the breaks. However, Fozia would stop, looking at waterfalls or valleys from the top of mountains and say: 'look at all of this, how can you say that there is no creator?' When I caught up with her in 2020, I asked her how it all started:

> In 2001–2002 I was doing a graphics design degree in London. We used to go out with friends, I just followed them. On the very first hike we did, it was pouring rain but I somehow enjoyed it ... What I like the most is the silence, when you're walking and when you're on the top of the mountain, you realise how all your problems are so small, it gives you a different perspective ... In Yorkshire, I was doing days out with the kids at work [she was managing a youth centre], and their parents were always like 'can we come with you?' Then in 2014, I organised the walk in Blencathra. I was really surprised. forty people came. Because it's not really in our [South Asian] culture ... Also, the hiking community is extremely white-dominated. When I spoke to kids during the days out, they're always like we don't feel we belong here, we don't fit in. No one speaks to them. Even myself, when I'm amongst these guys with expensive North Face or Berghaus gear and I'm with cheap JD Sports, you don't feel you belong.

Fozia is not the only one organizing hikes catering for a Muslim South Asian audience, but similar initiatives are still rare. Amongst 1,972 qualified Mountain Leaders as of 2021, only six are of Muslim background.[7] Javayria, highlights the paradox and recalls how in her family, people kept a bond with nature:

> When Asian parents say: 'you're hiking, you're so white', it doesn't make sense. My granddad knew the name of more than fifty species of tree. Our ancestors were all connected to the land. Our society has stripped this connection. When my great granddad came to the UK in 1924, he didn't like Whitechapel because it was too urban. He asked around when could he find fields, and someone told him to take the train South from Victoria. He stopped at Redhill and chose to settle there because he said, it reminded him of Punjab.

South Asian women, even at the heart of London, would grow plants, spices, and vegetables from the subcontinent, just like Javayria's mum grows her own in the garden of their suburban house. Many Muslims growing up in urban centres do not have easy access to wilderness. What was part of daily life in the villages, like seeing cows, comes as a fascinating surprise when we brought some friends' children on a walk across the fields. Fozia highlights that traditionally, outdoor activities in South Asian culture were associated with work and not leisure: 'this is why it feels strange to [the elders]'.

Only a few Muslims that I've encountered would make parallels between immersion in the natural environment and Islam. When I went walking across Iceland with Baber in 2015[8] (who has been organizing a few nature walks with Rumi's Cave), his approach was much more spiritual. First, instead of a hotel, we decided to stay at the main mosque of Reykjavik to learn more about Muslims who have settled in Iceland. During the trek, Baber would hold his *tasbih* (chaplet) and recite *zikr* (remembrance). The walking, the contemplation, the effort, were all tightly linked to his relationship with God, about 'taming the ego' and observing nature as 'the mirror of the Qur'an'. I found that trekking mirrored the journey of life: sometimes, the trail is straight, flat, and wide, and the weather is agreeable. At other times, the paths will become narrow, the slopes steep and slippery, and I have to walk in the pouring rain. Still, I have to carry on, no matter the conditions, in order to reach the next camping spot. These analogies served me both as guidance and reassurance. To quote Rabiah Mali, herself quoting George Washington Carver, 'I love to think of nature as an unlimited broadcasting station, through which God speaks to us every hour, if we only will tune in.' Recent research in psychology shows that contemplative practices in the vastness of nature such as awe (a feeling in the presence of vast things not immediately understood) reduces self-focus, promotes social connection, and fosters prosocial actions by encouraging a 'small self' (Sturm et al. 2020), and are therefore a gateway to compassion (Porges 2017). Some other initiatives like the Urban Equestrian Academy in Leicester, founded in 2015 by Freedom Tariq Zampaladus, aim at introducing horse riding to 'inner city' young people. When Javayria went on a hack with them, some of the staff described how horse riding is also about the care of the equines, how much it provides a sense of humility in the face of such powerful animals, and how it is also connected to the Prophetic tradition.

Another theory regarding why people haven't been going into the wilderness is that in a majority urban demographic in survival mode, wilderness doesn't serve a practical use—unless it is used for entertainment or for-profit purposes. In the neoliberal market, nature has become a consumable, another battlefield for amassing money and attention. Is the commercialization of nature necessary to get people *out there*? After the 2020 pandemic, various groups of Muslim hikers mushroomed in the UK. However, they have been criticized, notably for transforming people's relationship with the outdoors into a branding exercise. Many of my respondents called these groups a 'gimmick', saying they 'charge too much' and deploring the fact that any hike needs a brand partnership, a fundraiser, media coverage, marketing, and professional video documenting. Fozia comments: 'I feel annoyed when charities organise these climbs to raise funds, people just walk, there is no training, no preparation, no guidance. At some point an accident will happen.' Less than two years after our interview, a Muslim charity brought people hiking with heavy backpacks to the K2 base camp, but didn't schedule time for people to acclimatize. Two people ended up on intravenous drips.

Others organize ascents abroad and market them with hashtags like 'conquer Kilimanjaro'. The belligerent vocabulary suggests a hierarchy, that humans are better than nature, that we can dominate it, that we are, ultimately, against nature. However, if we consider ourselves part of nature, this means being at war with our own selves. Have we become impostors of our own humanity? The modern relationship with nature as a separate entity to conquer *ad eternam* is a symptom of the modern neoliberal mindset and the white dominator model. Islamic scholar Dustin Craun considers the Darwinian quest for the domination of others first an ego problem: building his reflections on decolonial scholars and Du Bois concept of 'religion of whiteness' (DuBois 1999, 18), Craun (2013, 105) argues that the white man has positioned himself as a creator, rival to God, constructing other humans only in relation to his whiteness and Eurocentric epistemologies. Therefore, organizations like the Green Deen Tribe, Rumi's Cave, or Fozia's informal hikes are overshadowed by these recent groups thirsty for recognition and monetary profits.

During the hikes, Baber or Fozia never led the crowd for long period of times. They would often stay at the back, supporting the slowest walkers. Rabiah too, walks behind during the nature walks she organizes with Muslim women in the English countryside. The Green Deen Tribe's work is very different from that of other Muslim environmental initiatives—which exist on a spectrum of different strategies and modes of engagement with the public. Organizations like MADE, as observed by Hancock (2017), rely on an Islamic framing of the environmental crisis: Islam is used as a motivation for other Muslims to get involved or adopt environmentally friendly behaviours—and thus integrated in pre-existing forms of activism such as protests. The Tribe doesn't demonstrate in front of Parliament like MADE or take part in protest movements; it builds an environmental-conscious Islam and an Islam-conscious environmentalism through healing. While they oppose big corporations or fossil fuels, their work is not antagonistic but first a work of service. Rabiah's compass is *rahma* (mercy): 'the Prophet was sent as a mercy for everyone, all the creation. So if the Sunnah is to follow the Prophet, we should be a mercy as well. For everything I do, I ask myself: am I being a mercy?' She doesn't take a problem-solution approach but rather a theocentric, holistic interweavement of spirituality and healing through nature. These differences, between antagonizing and building on the one hand, fixing and healing on the other, are the main differences between the western archetypal leader and *khilafa*. The term itself has various meanings (successor, deputy, vicegerent, etc.) (Kadi and Shahin 2013)—and many other narratives of 'leadership' exist such as *imara* (governance), *siyada* (sovereignty), and *tarbiya* (training to lead). Central to Islamic environmental narratives (Hancock 2017, 152), *khilafa*, as stewards of the Earth, gained popularity in Euro-America with the book *Green Deen* (Abdul-Matin 2010). Since then, the term has taken on a wider meaning of service and care.

English Islamic scholars such as Abdal Hakim Murad would characterize this form of 'prophetic leadership' not as ruling but serving: '[he] spoke of how he would sweep the floor, stitch his clothes, serve his family and wouldn't allow for a single coin to stay under his roof overnight; finding someone needy deserved of it ... Prophetic leadership thinks laterally' (Murad 2015).

In the context of the Tribe, *khilafa* connotes collectivity instead of individuality, and consultation (*shura*). While the modern leader would cultivate strength and power, the prophets and caliphs would acknowledge that they have none. Rabiah always humbly (from the Latin *humus*, meaning ground) refuses to acknowledge her merits when complimented: 'this has nothing to do with me ... the space has allowed it to happen'. Rabiah often recalls that in Islamic traditions, Adam was created from earth and that 'the Earth is your *masjid*' (the Earth is your mosque), meaning that not only any places can be spaces of prayer but at the same time, the whole Earth is sacred and thus one need to take care of. While elitist organizations (see chapter 2) attempt at reaching the divine spheres of power and control, the Green Deen Tribe literally drags people along the muddy tracks of West Sussex to converse with God. While the Western leader shifts the balance, the caliph works towards restoring it. The caliph is a facilitator of skills and energies to achieve a common goal; it is not an actor of change but rather its medium.

After years of hardship due to lack of funding and running out of staff members, MADE closed down in 2020. In her analysis, Hancock (2017) points out that campaigns like 'Green Up My Community' (aiming at mosques to implement eco-friendly measures like solar panels) failed mainly because most volunteers did not have a direct connection with the mosques. While the charity was a symbolic pillar on the Muslim environmental scene, the lack of social capital more than the lack of interest from Muslims led to its demise. At the same time, Rabiah's initiatives such as the Rabbani's Project 2019 vegan *iftaar* (breaking of the fast) at Rumi's Cave packed the main hall with more than 300 people. The Green Deen Tribe's retreats are sold out months in advance, with attendees coming from all over Europe. Why has MADE closed down, despite starting with solid funding, advertisements, and support, while smaller initiatives with no resources are successful?

Comparing MADE, the Rabbani Project and the Green Deen Tribe allows us to shed some more light on the differences between styles of leadership and stewardship. MADE as a campaigning organization has decided to adopt a utilitarian strategy, expecting direct outcomes: campaigns and the participation to demonstrations were performed hoping for changes in government policies and mosques' attitudes towards the environment. MADE thus has been equipping people with tools (campaigning skills, knowledge, visual materials) and expecting to influence the current situation similar to the dominator-leadership model employed by many players in the NGO sector. MADE gave, hoping for results. The Green Deen Tribe retreats, however, are spaces of receiving. They are times and spaces free from professional formalities where social performance is a norm. Similarly,

Rabiah's Herbal Blessing Clinic is not a clinic where people leave with a fix—she offers a space and time for people to express their concerns, and holds a mirror for people to look at. Whoever comes to the clinic or the retreats embarks on a journey of discovery of self. Rabiah doesn't try to provoke change, but shepherds elements of their ecosystem (space, time, collective, faith, and arts) as a medium.

Some respondents from large charities criticize similar approaches as they don't yield measurable impact and stretches over a long time. However, assessing the impact of Rabiah's work over the long term, the building of long-lasting and strong social bonds, and it being considered as a point of reference in the field (Rabiah was invited to a series of filmed interviews at Cambridge Muslim College) are proof that her recipe works and seems replicable. Her other initiative, the BMWHC, once crowdfunded nearly £10,000 in a month. The dimension of stewardship and service, at the heart of this not-so-new wave of Muslim environmentalists and nature enthusiasts, takes a particular dimension during the month of Ramadan. The month when people harness their desires and distance themselves from food is increasingly rebranded as a month for detoxification of the body. However, in recent years, more community organizers, artists, and thinkers have also highlighted its role in the detoxification, if not decolonization, of the mind.

5.3. Ramadan as a Decolonial Month

The month of Ramadan is associated in popular culture with fasting from food, drinks, and sexual intercourse from dawn to sunset. For many Muslims, fasting is supposed to remove worldly distractions from the remembrance of God. For some more privileged and less religious Muslim fitness gurus, Ramadan is a trendy lifestyle choice, an opportunity for a 'detox' backed by scientific evidence. Since it is the month when the Qur'an was revealed while the Prophet was on a meditative retreat in cave Hira, some spend the ten last days in *ithikaf* (retreat), usually at home or at their local mosque, distancing themselves from worldly activities. However, Ramadan has increasingly become associated with excessive consumerism. Some Muslims have grown wary of the copious amounts of meat and fried food consumed and wasted during the month, and the consequent impacts on health and the environment. They argue that meat-heavy *iftaars* (breaking of the fast), a relatively recent sign of wealth and status linked to newly acquired economic prosperity, are in direct opposition with the Prophet's humble dinner composed of milk and dates.

The Rabbani Project organizes each month of Ramadan a Green Iftaar without meat, plastic, or food waste. Their events include talks and artistic performances, using faith, scriptures, spirituality, storytelling, and friendship building for talking about the protection of the environment. Outside of Ramadan, the Rabbani Project has already been active at promoting upcycling and bartering as alternative forms of making oneself fashionable like with their Ethical Swap.[9] At the 2019 Green Iftaar at Rumi's Cave, between 250 and 300 people gathered. Clinical psychotherapist and storyteller Jumana Moon imagines in her performance what archaeologists of the next centuries will say when stumbling upon the buried landfills people have left in the twentieth and twenty-first centuries 'what will they think about us?' Another young woman tells her personal story about adopting reusable cotton handkerchiefs and Japanese reusable ear picks (*mimikaki*)—both of which I immediately adopted. The supper includes Rabiah's own signature nettle soup, dishes of pasta or rice and lentils with a good amount of spices and deserts. The remaining food is given to the homeless or taken home by the attendees. People attending these *iftaars* are from various social and cultural backgrounds. Many come more for the feeling of togetherness and catching up with friends, for whom the talks, the cause, and the food are side priorities. Some others come out of curiosity and others because they live in the local area. Although everyone agrees with the cause, it is however difficult to count or assess how many people actually implement changes after these events. Nevertheless, Rabiah is only 'planting seeds', her actions only show people that doing things differently is possible.

Like many other Muslim grass-roots charities, the Rabbani Project or Rumi's Cave disenfranchise themselves from rules and restrictions imposed by the norms of standardization and formalization attached to western 'professionalism' (see chapter 1). People eat on the floor, sometimes with their hands (an Islamic tradition) and the food is home-made (while earning a five-star hygiene rating from the Food Standards Agency). In a very un-British fashion, strangers talk to each other. The philosophy of these spaces is to offer a home-like and family-like atmosphere. The sensory and social experience is at the polar opposite of the asepticized European dining table where each dish has its plate and cutlery. It is an anti-professional space: people are not bonded any more by occupational identities and work culture (Evetts 2014). This is the kind of event that would immediately panic *Daily Mail* readers and BBC watchers, as the broadcasting service produced an inquiry on informal food trades, showing predominantly South Asian aunties selling home-made food on Facebook Marketplace.[10] The construction of professionalism around Eurocentric rules and regulation assumed universal (Cruess and Cruess 2016) becomes another barrier between the white valid and the other. Rumi's Cave's and the Rabbani Project's vision of conviviality and hospitality is therefore decolonial in many declensions: socially, sensorially, environmentally, through its use of time and space, spirituality, and non-European traditions. While fasting is seemingly a disconnection from food and other worldly material pleasures, the Rabbani Project and Rumi's Cave make it an act of reconnection with the spiritual and humanity.

Some Muslims go further. Over the years, an increasing amount of online religious opinions and personal stories advocate veganism for Muslims, backing their claims with scriptural sources and scientific facts. One popular piece is *The Halal Bubble and the Sunnah Imperative to Go Vegan* by Mohamed Ghilan (2016).

Although the Prophet used to eat meat occasionally, the author reflects on how the *halal* label has imprisoned believers into consumerist bubble made by an 'undeserved inflated sense of moral high ground ... religion is not a ticket to become somnambulant as one mindlessly applies a rulebook. It is a call to waking up and being conscious of how one engages with the world.'

Similar thoughts around Ramadan have prompted Muslims to reflect critically on their consumerist habits beyond food. Shemiza Rashid, a community radio presenter, has been for years advocate of ethical fashion and vocal about the discrepancy between 'modest fashion' promoted by Muslim designers in Euro-America and the production of cheap items by exploited workers in South Asian countries (see chapter 7.2)—what she refers to as 'fast fashion', the fashion equivalent of fast foods (such as Pretty Little Thing owned by British Muslims Umar and Adem Kamani). One of the wake-up calls were the Rana Plaza disaster in 2013, in Bangladesh, where 1,134 people died, mostly low-paid workers producing clothes for high street brands. While many Muslim social media personalities fight to get sponsored by brands like Nike, many condone the brand's use of Muslim forced labour in China.[11] Many compare these paradoxes to the *ummah* 'drinking its own blood'. Shemiza gave a speech at the Ramadan Tent project (an initiative which offer short talks from celebrities before *iftaar*), titled 'Fasting from fast fashion'.

> [I]t's not about me criminalising fashion it's about more consumer conscience. I stopped purchasing [South-] Asian [cultural] garments because I found them very unethical ... and how cheaply it was being made and the difficulty it is to upcycle it ... That is clearly not Islamic if workers have not been provided a fair living wage.

She believes that a movement is emerging and that designers just need educating. In her family, 'taken over by mass culture', she recalls that the addiction to material goods as a way to 'measure up' against other people. Her taste for fashion initially started with her intention to preserve her cultural classical heritage for her children but realized that she also wanted this culture to be rooted in Islamic principles of fairness and justice. For this purpose, as she highlights it, she uses her wide network and popularity to influence Muslim designers.

During Ramadan, I saw people sharing content not related to fasting, such as invitations to reflect on limiting how much their children use technology. Ali Harfouch paints Ramadan as 'radical revolt against the *Homo Oeconomicus* and consequently, the modern condition':

> There is something to be seen in fasting as a communal and global practice in an epoch characterised by the 'god of Capital' and liberal hegemony; it is an expression of mass dissensus ... the relevance of Muslims will depend on our ability to reclaim Islām as a counter-narrative ... that posits a formidable challenge to liberal theology and the excesses of the modern condition. (Harfouch 2018)

In light of global events such as the Black Lives Matter protests and seeing global figures of the Muslim elite falling into the pitfalls of power and fame, for some, Ramadan has also started to become a month for contestation and resistance to dynamics of power. For many of my respondents, there is power in saying 'no'. Boundaries are resistance, as Qureshi and others argue in the book *I Refuse To Condemn* (Qureshi 2020): when ethnically minoritized people are pressured to condemn, as if responsible because sharing the same skin colour, every single terror attack; if they say yes, they would accept the racial premise of the question. Many would share thoughts of the Black American community organizer, artist, and theologian Tricia Hersey, founder of the Nap Ministry[12] advocating 'rest, as recovery, is resistance and reparations'. Asim Qureshi, researcher for the organization CAGE and one of the most popular British figures of resistance against policies targeting Muslims, wrote in Ramadan 2019 in a widely shared post: 'it's much about starving the body and soul from the excesses of life: . . . seeking leadership, righteousness without sincerity, denigration and arrogance, sitting with the rich' (Qureshi 2019).

His post understands Ramadan not only as an opportunity to starve the body but also the soul from one's character and inclinations. In 2014, American Palestinian decolonial academic Hatem Bazian wrote a piece in his blog interpreting Ramadan as a month of resistance to oppression, *From Fast to Feast*:

> Ramadan today must be about severing our relationship to products produced by corporation in sweatshops at a far distant lands using the poverty of people to maximizes profit while treating them as modern wage slaves, including Muslim countries . . . Finding alternative to the destructive media that uses hate, racism, objectification of women, crude sexuality and fear to distance people from one another and help foment wars near and far. (Bazian 2014)

British Islamic scholar Abdal Hakim Murad similarly paints resistance as a prophetic quality: 'to be Prophetic is to be counter-cultural, to be a dissident; you simply can't be Prophetic if you're driving around in the Sultan's Bentley. To be Prophetic you must be, by definition, difficult for those in power' (Murad 2015).

Since social media literally uses 'feeds' as a term to describe the flow of content that people consume and ingurgitate, Bazian urges people to reconsider their media consumption, which similarly to junk food, inoculates people with 'hate, racism, objectification of women' and other ways to 'distance people from one another'. While Bazian's post is about unplugging and severing ties with mass media and oppression, this act of fasting is ultimately, for a greater reconnection, with humanity, with one another, with the vulnerable, and, in that sense, essentially decolonial:

A de-colonial Ramadan involves committing oneself to a process of first cataloguing the existing modern and material mental inventory that originates in the colonial epistemic and is centered on capitalism, secularism and distorted rationality. A de-colonial inventory insists on making a distinction between Islamic ethics and economic principles and capitalism ... A de-colonial Ramadan involves a commitment to navigate out of the racism deeply embedded in modern Muslims that are in an endless search to affirm its worthiness by means of physical and mental proximity to the superior whiteness. (Bazian 2016)

Over the years, in the community circles that I have been navigating, the month of Ramadan has become about much more than fasting from food. In the global matrix of power, because food is linked to consumer habits and therefore to the subsequent exploitation of humans and natural resources, it is ultimately linked to the relationship between consumer-citizens and the structures of power ruling over them. Philosopher Mohammed Meziane Amer asserts in one of his talks: 'Blackness, the feminine, the earth on one hand, Whiteness, maleness, industrial exploitation on the other [...], the climate crisis is eco-racial as much as it is eco-spiritual.' However, Ramadan is not only 'saying no'. For these actors, is not an uprising but a time of withdrawal and critical examination of all the things the body and the mind are served, a re-definition and re-building with the aim of reconnecting with God and each other. Therefore, Ramadan has become for many a decolonial exercise in healing and self-determination, redefining a Muslim identity as standing for justice.

5.4. Rabiah Mali: The Hijra of Muslim Liberation

The Green Deen project and other of Rabiah's initiatives such as the Black Muslim Women Healing Collective (BMWHC, see chapter 4) stem from the inadequacy of white-dominated environmental activism spaces and the necessity to have conversations around healing in her own terms: 'can a Black Muslim woman ever feel held and grounded in the heart of the Empire?' Rabiah has been participating in interfaith programmes like those offered by St Ethelburga's Centre in London—however, her experiences with various organizations wasn't always smooth, as organizers and participants often have little awareness of class and race dynamics. Rabiah argues that healing the wounds of colonialism and displacement starts with reconnecting with the land:

> How many plants do you know? None. How much of the land have you actually explored? Do you feel safe? Do you feel held? Do you feel earthed and grounded in this land? Is this land your masjid? ... Colonialism has disconnected people

from their land... I was born and raised in East London but there is still a sense of not belonging to this land, my parents come from the Caribbean, and my ancestors were taken from their land in Africa... What we have to do now, is just really recreate and redefine our connection to the earth. (The Future Is Beautiful 2020)

One of the ideas behind the BMWHC and the Green Deen is to be a 'tribe', since as she argues, 'collective trauma requires collective healing': 'the idea of being of a tribe and family is dear to us because the city encourages this idea of isolation.' For Rabiah, however, the boundaries of her tribe don't stop at the realm of the living. Rabiah roots herself in a Muslim lineage of love, faith, but also resistance borrowed from the vocabulary of Black liberation. In one of their Facebook posts, the Pearls explain the cover of their latest album, *Love is My Foundation*, depicting an embroidered anatomic human heart surrounded by plants and African patterns:

We chose an anatomical heart as there is wisdom and perfection in the design of Allah. We wanted to reclaim it from its 'medicalisation'. This heart is more than a blood pumping organ. It is the seat of the mind, the leader of your body's dhikr. It keeps us in rhythm with nature... The African inspired border around the heart is in honour of our ancestors, who were taken from their lands, their roots. But we are forever surrounded by their love and the beat of dhikr that was once in their hearts—now beats in mine. Alhamdulillah. It is their love that is part of the foundation of our songs.

Rabiah's identity is informed by her roots and lineage. Her Islam, her existence, her community work around the environment, are at the opposite of a liberal, binary, and ahistorical vision of the future; they all are at the crossroads of the tangible and the invisible, they are a social contract between the dead, the living, and the to-be-born. In our conversations, I asked Rabiah about how Muslims, like myself, who come from a cultural lineage very distant from Islam, can find strength in their ancestry? Rabiah replied to me that 'the same way trauma can be passed on through generations, Mercy can be passed on through generations', and that, because we all share the same spiritual lineage, at some point, someone who was pious (even if not Muslim), perhaps prayed God for pious descendants, and this is the reason why some of us 'come back'.

Rabiah's existence is the sum of the knowledge and culture of resilience of the geographic places where her roots are located, and ultimately in the ecosystem of Islam. There are many parallels between Rabiah's work and the prophetic *Hijra*: a forced physical and intellectual exile, leaving everything behind, for affirming one's existence. Rabiah, similarly, is on a *Hijra*, in order for others to find a place of acceptance, healing, and flourishing. Because exile to the margins and the condition of marginality puts people in a situation where they have nothing to lose, margins create in turn a universe of infinite possibilities (hooks 1989). Similar to what bell hooks names a journey 'from pain to power' (hooks in The New School 2015).

> I am the answer of the *dua* [supplications] of my ancestors who set the foundation for us to sing songs from our hearts. Who taught us to continue with resilience and are the perfect example of the long-lasting reality of love ... We are here because they loved and had trust in Allah.

Her work is a self-definition, a self-wording of her beauty. The celebration of roots simultaneously as an exercise of grounding, healing, and flourishing echoes the therapeutic spoken-to-self poetry of Muneera (see chapter 4). Her own existence, and her staying faithful to her own identity, is resistance to colonialism and therefore a sacred duty. She acknowledges the challenges of her situation but she refuses to compromise, as she explains:

> One of the things we are working on at the moment is our language, because we're trying to get funding. And the language that we are using is not funder-friendly ... What I will do is, I will hand over to somebody else, and then let them translate it into a language that the funders will understand ... But in the circle, we will use our own language.

Her approach is not a carefully crafted one and does not follow any precise plan. Like for plants, it reflects a rhizomic growth, taking different paths from the soil in the search for the nourishing light. Through the informal conversations I had with Rabiah, her initiatives are the organic results of her journey and the sum of her encounters, trials and errors, from Ghana to East London, her readings, her challenges and struggles, the music she listens to and performs, friends, contemplation, spiritual events and activities, the dialogue she has with God, and, also important, her ancestors' journey. She argues that activism hasn't got to be perfect since 'perfectionism is white supremacy, but perfection is only to God'.

While she may argue the contrary, Muslim environmentalism in the UK could not have survived and flourished without her and others. Echoing the research of Su'ad Abdul Khabeer (2016), I would even argue that practical Muslim environmental consciousness in the UK and the US is what it is today because of movements for Black liberation and their legacy. The Green Deen Tribe itself has been inspired by the work of other Black Muslim environmentalists such as Ibrahim Abdul Matin, Kori Majeed, Rhamis Kent, and others. While environmentalist organizations take a problem-solution approach, Black Muslim liberation had to find holistic and practical answers at the root of all challenges experienced by Black people under white supremacy: how to cope, heal, and flourish while getting closer to God?

Retreats and Ramadan are a *hijra*: a marronage, a departure from the worldly oppressive constructs. Departing is acknowledging that one cannot bear a situation anymore, it is about acknowledging vulnerability. Beyond tea-tasting, prayers, songs and walks in the English countryside, the activities organized by the Green Deen Tribe teach people through sensorial and spiritual experiences how to be attune with their own vulnerabilities and accept them, in a world where vulnerability has become a sign of weakness. People enter the only space out of everywhere else where, for the first and only time, they can cry without being judged. Vulnerability, along with mercy and kindness as qualities of stewardship, is the antithesis of competition.

As such, in the modern neoliberal world, kindness, mercy, and vulnerability are deviances (Lewellyn Jones 1998). These initiatives navigate upstream of the main societal injunctions: in a world of para-social interactions and weak or secondary trust (Granovetter 1973; Dogan 1994; Listhaug 1995; Misztal 1996), they create new primary social circles characterized by deep trust (Williams 1988; Newton 1999; Barylo 2017). In a volatile society governed by impulses and stimuli, they create opportunities for grounding. In a world governed by rationality deaf to people's pain, they cultivate emotional intelligence. They create new imaginaries of what 'home' looks, sounds, and feel like. They facilitate the creation of new points of Saidian (1984) anchorage. The tribe is a multi-layer work of dignity: it is not the duty of the plants and the animals to prove their right to exist; it is for us humans to recognize their existence as part of ours. Similarly, it is not the duty of Muslims to justify and prove their humanity.

If ownership is supremacist, is anything truly ours? What initiatives such as the Rabbani Project answer is that we only own the power of making our own choices. The Green Deen project is an example of how small initiatives with no budget and little publicity can inspire underprivileged demographics to transform their daily lives. It demands the difficult departure and distancing from any form of man-made supremacy and trusting that the work will not go unnoticed, even if nothing happens over the course of a whole decade. Decoloniality is not only a work of the present; it is building a bridge from the past to a more hopeful future; it is planting seeds which fruits may not be seen in one's lifetime, just like the initiatives around history in the next chapter.

Notes

1. Kat Smith, 'Vegan Muslims created an animal-free sacrifice for the Eid Al-Adha tradition', *Live Kindly*, 20 August 2018. https://web.archive.org/web/20190212093722/https://www.livekindly. co/vegan-muslims-create-new-qurbani-sacrifice-tradition; Evelyn Lau, 'How vegans in the UAE celebrate Eid Al Adha', *The National*, 22 August 2018. https://web.archive.org/web/20180822160 311/https://www.thenational.ae/lifestyle/food/how-vegans-in-the-uae-celebrate-eid-al-adha-1.762727; Nina Ahmedow, 'Make your Eid al-Adha vegan: the most important reasons', *Lemons And Luggage*, 7 August 2020. https://web.archive.org/web/20200805160233/https://www.lemon sandluggage.com/make-your-eid-al-adha-vegan

2. 'Influencer', Collins English Dictionary 2014.
3. Claudia Rankine, 'The fire this time: Claudia Rankine on whiteness as a brand', *The New Yorker*, 12 October 2015. https://web.archive.org/web/20201204083133/https://www.newyorker.com/video/watch/the-new-yorker-festival-the-fire-this-time-part-2
4. Darko Lovric and Tomas Chamorro-Premuzic, 'Why great success can bring out the worst parts of our personalities', *Harvard Business Review*, 9 August 2018. https://web.archive.org/web/20180809125713/https://hbr.org/2018/08/why-great-success-can-bring-out-the-worst-parts-of-our-personalities; Dacher Keltner, 'Don't let power corrupt you', *Harvard Business Review*, October 2016. https://web.archive.org/web/20161006191341/https://hbr.org/2016/10/dont-let-power-corrupt-you
5. Tomas Chamorro-Premuzic, 'Why do so many incompetent men become leaders?', *Harvard Business Review*, 22 August 2013. https://web.archive.org/web/20150629093728/https://hbr.org/2013/08/why-do-so-many-incompetent-men
6. Pankaj Mishra, 'The religion of whiteness becomes a suicide cult', *The New York Times*, 30 August 2018. https://web.archive.org/web/20180830205856/https://www.nytimes.com/2018/08/30/opinion/race-politics-whiteness.html
7. Find A Leader. Mountain Training. Accessed 1 February 2024. https://web.archive.org/web/20210724124203/https://www.mountain-training.org/find-a-leader
8. 'Nature and spirituality—hiking in Iceland', William Barylo [YouTube] 8 May 2017. https://archive.org/details/iceland-1080p
9. 'Ethical swap', The Rabbani Project. Accessed 1 February 2024. https://web.archive.org/web/20200918084223/http://therabbaniproject.co.uk/the-ethical-swap
10. 'Facebook Marketplace: the unlicensed food trade', *BBC News*, 24 February 2020. https://web.archive.org/web/20200224232936/https://www.bbc.co.uk/news/av/uk-51492975/facebook-marketplace-the-unlicensed-food-trade
11. Vicky Xiuzhong Xu, Danielle Cave, James Leibold, et al., *Uyghurs for Sale* (Canberra: Australian Strategic Policy Institute, 2020). https://web.archive.org/web/20200301160438/https://www.aspi.org.au/report/uyghurs-sale
12. The Nap Ministry. Accessed 1 February 2024. https://web.archive.org/web/20200702072730/https://thenapministry.wordpress.com/about

References

Abbey, Edward. 1977. *The Journey Home: Some Words in Defense of the American West*. New York: Dutton.
Abdul Khabeer, Su'ad. 2016. *Muslim Cool: Race, Religion and Hip Hop in the United States*. New York, New York University Press.
Abdul-Matin, Ibrahim. 2010. *Green Deen: What Islam Teaches about Protecting the Planet*. San Francisco: Berrett-Koehler.
Ahuvia, Aaron. 2002. 'Individualism/collectivism and cultures of happiness: a theoretical conjecture on the relationship between consumption, culture and subjective well-being at the national level.' *Journal of Happiness Studies* 3, 23–36.
Ali, Syed Mustafa. 2019. 'White crisis and/as existential risk, or the entangled apocalypticism of artificial intelligence.' *Zygon* 54, 207–24.
Arendt, Hannah. 1963. *On Revolution*. New York: Viking Press.
Barylo, William. 2017. *Young Muslim Change-Makers*. London: Routledge.
Bazian, Hatem. 2014. 'From fast to feast: meaning of Ramadan and the global poverty crisis.' Hatembazian.com, 6 July. https://web.archive.org/web/20200925152959/http://www.hatembazian.com/content/from-fast-to-feast-meaning-of-ramadan-and-the-global-poverty-crisis
Bazian, Hatem. 2016. 'Ramadan: a de-colonial centering moment.' Hatembazian.com, 2 June. https://web.archive.org/web/20160602205339/http://www.hatembazian.com/content/ramadan-a-de-colonial-centering-moment
Block, Peter. 2013. *Stewardship: Choosing Service over Self-Interest*. San Francisco: Berrett-Koehler.

Chamorro-Premuzic, Tomas. 2013. *Why Do So Many Incompetent Men Become Leaders?* Brighton: Harvard Business Review.
Convivialist International. 2020. 'The second Convivialist Manifesto: towards a post-neoliberal world.' *Civic Sociology* 1(1), 12721.
Craun, Dustin. 2013. 'Exploring pluriversal paths toward transmodernity: from the mind-centered egolatry of colonial modernity to Islam's epistemic decolonization through the heart.' *Human Architecture: Journal of the Sociology of Self-Knowledge* 11(1), 91–113.
Cruess, Sylvia and Richard Cruess. 2016. 'Professionalism as a social construct: the evolution of a concept.' *Journal of Graduate Medical Education* 8(2), 265–7.
Descola, Philippe. 2005. *Par-delà nature et culture*. Paris: Gallimard.
Dogan, Mattei. 1994. 'The pendulum between theory and substance: testing the concepts of legitimacy and trust.' In *Comparing Nations: Concepts, Strategies, Substance*, edited by D. Dogan and A Kazancigil. Oxford: Blackwell, 297–313.
Dubois, William E.B. 1999. *Darkwater: Voices from Within the Veil*. New York: Schocken.
Eva, Nathan, Mulyadi Robin, Sen Sendjaya, et al. 2019. 'Servant leadership: a systematic review and call for future research.' *The Leadership Quarterly* 30(1), 111–32.
Evetts, Julia. 2014. 'The concept of professionalism: professional work, professional practice and learning.' In *International Handbook of Research in Professional and Practice-based Learning*, edited by Stephen Billett, Christian Harteis, and Hans Gruber. New York: Springer, 29–56.
Fleming, Peter. 2015. *The Mythology of Work: How Capitalism Persists Despite Itself*. London: Pluto Press.
Ghilan, Mohamed. 2016. 'The Halal bubble and the Sunnah imperative to go vegan.' Al Madina Institute. https://web.archive.org/web/20160521044135/http://almadinainstitute.org/blog/vegan-sunnah
Granovetter, Mark S. 1973. 'The strength of weak ties.' *American Journal of Sociology* 78(60), 1360–80.
Greenleaf, Robert K. 1970. *The Servant as Leader*. Cambridge: Center for Applied Studies.
Hancock, Rosemary. 2017. *Islamic Environmentalism: Activism in the United States and Great Britain*. Oxon: Routledge.
Harfouch, Ali S. 2018. 'Fasting: a revolt against the modern condition.' *Islam21c*, 7 June. https://web.archive.org/web/20200924165742/https://www.islam21c.com/islamic-thought/fasting-a-revolt-against-the-modern-condition
Hodge, John L., Donald K. Struckmann, and Lynn Dorland Trost. 1975. *Cultural Bases of Racism and Group Oppression: An Examination of Traditional 'Western' Concepts, Values and Institutional Structures Which Support Racism, Sexism and Elitism*. Berkeley: Two Riders.
hooks, bell. 1989. 'Choosing the margin as a space of radical openness.' *Framework* 36, 15–23.
hooks, bell. 2004. *The Will to Change: Men, Masculinity and Love*. Washington: Washington Square Press.
Illitch, Ivan. 1973. *Tools for Conviviality*. New York: Harper & Row.
Kadi, Wadad and Aram Shahin. 2013. 'Caliph, caliphate.' In *The Princeton Encyclopedia of Islamic Political Thought*, edited by Gerhard Bowering, Patricia Crone, Wadad Kadi et al. Princeton: Princeton University Press, 81–6.
Keltner, Dacher. 2016. *Don't Let Power Corrupt You*. Brighton: Harvard Business Review.
Lévi-Strauss, Claude. 1962. *La pensée sauvage*. Paris: Plon.
Lewellyn Jones, Angela. 1998. 'Random acts of kindness: a teaching tool for positive deviance.' *Teaching Sociology* 26(3), 179–89.
Listhaug, Ola. 1995. 'The dynamics of trust in politicians.' In *Citizens and the State*, edited by H.-D. Klingemann and D. Fuchs. Oxford: Oxford University Press, 261–97.
Lovric, Darko and Tomas Chamorro-Premuzic. 2018. *Why Great Success Can Bring Out the Worst Parts of Our Personalities*. Brighton: Harvard Business Review.
Mauss, Marcel. 2007 [1924]. *Essai sur le don*. Paris: Presses Universitaires France.
Meziane Amer, Mohammed. 2021. *Des empires sous la terre: Histoire écologique et raciale de la secularisation*. Paris: La Découverte.

Misztal, Barbara. 1996. *Trust in Modern Societies: The Search for the Bases of Social Order.* Oxford: Blackwell.
Morin, Edgar. 1977. *La Méthode: La nature de la Nature.* Paris: Seuil.
Morin, Edgar. 1986. *La Méthode: La vie de la Vie.* Paris: Seuil.
Murad, Abdal Hakim. 2015. 'Prophetic Leadership.' On The Path To Knowledge blog, 23 April. https://web.archive.org/web/20150528221441/https://otpok.com/2015/04/23/prophetic-leadership
Newton, Kenneth. 1999. 'Social capital and democracy in modern Europe.' In *Social Capital and European Democracy*, edited by J. W. Van Deth, M. Maraffi, K. Newton, et al. London: Routledge, 3–24.
Pettinato, Davide. 2016. '"MADE a difference?"—British Muslim youth and faith-inspired activism between "post-conventional politics", "post-secularity", and "post-immigration difference".' In *Muslims in the UK and Europe II*, edited by Yasir Suleiman and Paul Anderson. Cambridge: Centre of Islamic Studies, 100–13.
Porges, Stephen W. 2017. 'Vagal pathways: portals to compassion.' In *The Oxford Handbook of Compassion Science*, edited by Emma M Seppälä, Emiliana Simon-Thomas, Stephanie L. Brown, et al. Oxford: Oxford University Press, 189–202.
Qureshi, Asim. 2019. [Facebook] 11 May. https://archive.is/a9mwc
Qureshi, Asim (ed.). 2020. *I Refuse to Condemn: Resisting Racism in Times of National Security.* Manchester: Manchester University Press.
Safi, Omid. 2014. 'The disease of being busy.' *On Being*, 6 November. https://web.archive.org/web/20190118094826/https://onbeing.org/blog/the-disease-of-being-busy
Said, Edward. 1984. *The World, the Text and the Critic.* Cambridge: Harvard University Press.
Sturm, Virginia, Samir Datta, Ashlin Roy, et al. 2020. 'Big smile, small self: awe walks promote prosocial positive emotions in older adults.' *Emotion* 22(5), 1044–58.
The Future Is Beautiful. 2020. 'E96—Rabiah Abdullah ON EARTH MEDICINE, RECIPROCITY AND IHSAN/EXCELLENCE.' 23 July. https://archive.org/details/rabiah-abdullah-on-earth-medicine-reciprocity-and-ihsan-excellence
The New School. 2015. 'bell hooks: moving from pain to power I the new school.' [YouTube] 12 October. https://archive.org/details/bell-hooks-moving-from-pain-to-power-i-the-new-school-240p
Touraine, Alain. 1992. *Critique de la Modernité.* Paris: Fayard.
Van Dierendonck, Dirk. 2011. 'Servant leadership: a review and synthesis.' *Journal of Management* 37(4), 1228–61.
Williams, Bernard. 1988. 'Formal structures and social reality.' In *Trust: Making and Breaking Cooperative Relations*, edited by D. Gambetta. Oxford: Blackwell, 3–13.

6
Praying Alone
Collapse and Revival of the Muslim Community

On Friday 19 January 2018, for the first time in History, the *adhan* (call to prayer) echoed within Tate Modern. *Jumu'ah*, the Friday mid-day prayer and its sermon, would be performed in one of most the famous modern art galleries in Euro-America, one of these spaces which traditionally excluded ethnically minoritized people in general and specifically Muslims. The idea of a traditional Muslim prayer at the Tate was blasphemous in the modern art world: how could one dare pronounce the name of God, the ultimate *persona non grata* in curatorial spaces, the church of secularism? However, history was made possible by Abbas Zahedi, London-based conceptual artist in his thirties: 'Studio Jum'ah was a re-imagining of the muslim Friday prayer, as a site of contemporary art and knowledge production ... Furthermore, this intervention interrogated the idea of a studio and gallery as sanctified spaces of post-enlightenment modernity' (Zahedi 2018).

The event, open to the public, like any Friday prayer, started with a 'Sermon of the Technical Image', adapted from the writings of Vilém Flusser read by Lara Orawski, and stories by Jumana Moon, before the prayer, led by a celebrity imam. The event attracted more than fifty people, a crowd made up of artists, curators, Tate visitors, and staff from nearby offices. However, the event was a temporary interruption: after the event, the local community asked Tate Modern whether it would be possible to facilitate regular Friday prayers in the building—a request met by an outright rejection.

Having grown up around Ladbroke Grove, Abbas Zahedi graduated from Central Saint Martins in 2019. His work was included in the Diaspora Pavilion at the 57th Venice Biennale, and he then obtained a residency at the South London Gallery before one of his works was acquired by the Tate—one of the greatest achievements possible for a British artist. Although a professional artist, Abbas is also known for his community work, as one of the former managers of Rumi's Cave, who animated the space with various art events and discussions (see chapter 8). Studio Jum'ah (imagined by noticing how Tate Modern shares similar features to a mosque) is at the same time a religious performance in an arts space and an arts performance in a religious space. I personally don't understand modern conceptual art; however, Abbas was always keen on explaining the meanings and symbols behind his choices, the literary sources of his reflections and inspirations.

> By choosing to host a Friday prayer I am making a statement which raises a number of questions ... Could a mosque host an artist's studio? ... How contemporary galleries and arts institutions can become more accessible to diasporic bodies [?] ... It's fair to say that Muslims are seen as a primary category of Other in Europe today and maybe that's why it doesn't feel like a public gallery is a relevant space in which to pray. (Zahedi in Khan, Lamisa 2018)

Despite his diasporic identity, Abbas has gained recognition only thanks to white-dominated secular institutions. Reflecting on his journey alone, he questions how much unconventionality the so-called 'Muslim community' can accept and how much support it can give to fellow Muslims:

> Activists and community figures often ... appropriate my existence wholly to ... further their entitlement to positions, capital and physical/virtual space in society. Hipsters on the other hand may appropriate my recipes and cultural practices, but they are still the only ones to have given me a fair wage that is paid on time and with which I can feed my family. And because they run businesses I usually know where I stand with them as they don't claim to be my saviour—probably because they're busy saving some endangered species of kale or wheat.

This chapter focuses on others who, like Abbas, disrupt institutions from the margins. Since metacolonization creates glass ceilings and ahistorical societies, it highlights those who, for more than a decade, have resisted the erasure of Muslims in the public sphere, quietly working at archiving, researching, and showcasing Muslim heritage in Britain and the exceptional stories that have been being similarly ignored, for future generations to remember. It also poses the question of solidarity: is there a 'British *ummah*' (community) or even a 'British Islam'?

6.1. Can the Muslim Speak?

Abbas Zahedi's performance at Tate Modern is not the only Muslim disruption of British Art institutions. In 2018, artist, curator, and community organizer Hassan Vawda arranged an Eid celebration in the gardens of his workplace, Tate Britain. The event, in collaboration with the local Eritrean mosque, featured food, art workshops, activities for children, speeches by Tate officials, a sermon from a local imam and a guided tour of Tate by a Muslim tour guide for seventy attendees—the largest group ever seen in the gallery's history. Hassan responded to Putnam's call for 'new ways to use the arts as a vehicle for convening diverse groups of fellow citizens' (Putnam 2001, 411). However, Hassan received mixed reactions from managers and directors:

> Despite the event being praised by directors at Tate, referenced positively in formal and particularly informal channels, and in channels where Tate did not have a presence in (i.e. Muslim Council of Britain tweeting about it) and the verbal/written feedback from visitors and staff, there seemed to be no possibility for this happening again... I was met with phrases such as 'if we do it again, we are going to have to do it with all faiths', 'there is no resources whatsoever'.

Hassan locates this event in a longer series of hard times at Tate Britain:

> When they hear a white person being loud, they say, 'oh you know, he's just a bit stressed.' When it's me, they tell me to calm down... it's so emotionally draining and damaging... But I stayed, and I saw I was able to have an impact... I was the first person in the history of the Tate to connect and build a relationship with the local Eritrean mosque which is one of the closest mosques to Tate—been their neighbour for 30 years. Why is this?

Hassan mentions how, after obtaining PhD funding, the directors' attitude changed towards him—'as if suddenly [he] was taken seriously'. Similar stories are rife in other industries, even for famous people, whether it is for Nadiya Hussain's (winner of *The Great British Bake-Off*, and who made a cake for the Queen's birthday) rejection from a modelling agency with the comment 'Black hands don't sell jewellery'[1] or Riz Ahmed, a renowned actor, who was prevented from attending an awards ceremony when he got stopped and searched[2] after a flight. In 2020, musician Ballake Sissoko found his kora smashed after it went through the American Transportation Security Administration. He draws parallels between white-dominated structures and terrorists who, in his native Mali, destroy musical instruments and 'cut' musicians' tongues; the white world also doesn't care about non-white musicians.[3] A meme on Freeze Magazine's Instagram, shared by Abbas, expresses the collective sentiment about how 'White Art' is considered as 'Conceptual, Traditional, Historic' and 'Brown Art' is just 'Artefacts'.[4] Farah Soobhan, a professional artist wearing the hijab, evoked her experience of participating in art fairs, exhibitions, and workshops and being excluded from 'videos and communication materials': 'when religion becomes visible, it becomes a problem'. Nargess has similarly tried to promote a documentary on the murder of Mohammad Saleem in 2013 by a neo-Nazi, when it was blocked by YouTube: 'YouTube won't let the video be promoted. In an email it said there is "no chance" the video can be promoted with an ad because "the content is too religious..." [and YouTube and Google] "don't want to be partisan" on the issue of Islamophobia' (Moballeghi 2019).

Sometimes, even a PhD, a university position, and a £300,000 grant are not enough. When my university pitched my documentary project to mainstream media outlets and digital platforms, despite me having produced commercially acquired documentaries and fiction on streaming platforms and TV channels, the reply from commissioning editors was always: 'we want to see Muslims only if it's entertainment: reality TV shows or comedies'. Muslims cannot be taken seriously, just like issues cannot be 'political'. No matter how high you get, there are still glass ceilings. For those who make it, they remain in precarious work conditions like Hassan, with little support, which can lead some to eventually conform and submit (chapter 2). Thus, those who attain high positions despite not ticking the right boxes are the exception. Laila, who just obtained her PhD, shared with me her struggles of being a North African Muslim woman in higher education in France. Using 'we', she included me in her thoughts, sharing how she often wants to give up, and what keeps her afloat: 'we weren't supposed to get to a PhD, we are a few out of a thousand. It is normal we feel we don't belong; we are statistical anomalies ... Nobody can take my PhD away from me ... my students tell me: "I'm glad we have someone like you as a teacher."'

Laila reframes the unworthiness narrative dictated by her impostor syndrome: being a female Muslim academic in the 2020s, is being an exceptional feat, given the forces working against minorities. Academia still follows Foucault's (1977) *Discipline and Punish*—positing that structures of power do not need intelligent people, they need people who do not question the structure. As Hatem Bazian puts it, universities produce 'replacement parts'[5] for the transmitting and maintaining of systemic, structural, epistemic, and symbolic violence (Sian 2019). Universities are 'the new plantation' (Abdul Khabeer 2016). Laila stresses how this anomaly is, however, of vital importance for the students whom she taught. Exceptions like her are allow people to visualize the concretization of their dreams and reinforce the conviction that a better future is possible. One of these exceptional academics is Sadia Habib, working at the time at the University of Manchester and co-author of the Riz Test (a Bechdel test for Muslim representation (Habib 2019)). She uses her position as an academic for experimenting through action-research, like encouraging critical pedagogy when bringing children to museums, and not shunning difficult conversations around British history (Habib 2021). The existence of these glass ceilings illustrates the paradoxes and conditionality of 'diversity and inclusion', which in metacolonial language means 'not just any kind of people'. 'Diversity' means not including the local Eritrean mosque—only lawyers and people over a certain salary threshold and above a certain social status. 'Diversity' doesn't mean change of the structures, but change of the other, of the subaltern, or its silencing, to answer the long unanswered question '*Can the subaltern speak?*' (Spivak 1988). What is left, if not to protest?

On 12 March 2019, the Goldsmiths Anti-Racist Action (GARA), a Muslim-led group of students at the Goldsmiths College (University of London) started the occupation of the Deptford Town Hall. Their occupation would last 137 days, the second longest student occupation of a university building in the UK to date.[6] This move was the result of several racially motivated events including graffiti, the scrapping of the scholarship for two Palestinian students, in a climate already worsen by racial aggressions towards students and security and cleaning staff. In their manifesto,[7] their demands included for the cleaners and security staff to be sourced in-house, for statues of colonizers and slave-owners to be removed, for the Palestinian students' scholarships to be reinstated, a complete overhaul of the curricula, mandatory anti-racist training for teaching staff, a racism audit by an independent body, and the employment of culturally competent staff for well-being and counselling services, amongst others. On 31 July 2019, the College Management came to agree with GARA and the occupation ended,[8] though not without some backtracking and unexpected turns afterwards. The group became a national symbol of resistance and the proof that even if structures can't easily change, disruption and contestation of a small but united group can make some waves.

However, these dreams are often interrupted by nightmares such as the fire of Grenfell Tower in 2017, which directly affected some of my respondents (see chapter 4). The event bore a strong symbolic power for local Muslims as it happened during Ramadan, and as one of the victims was Khadija Saye, a promising artist on her way to international recognition, whose work was exhibited at the Venice Biennale at the very same time. Khadija used to work in one of the tower's small council flats that she turned into her studio. Mainstream media almost never mentioned anything about Khadija's faith or her work as a volunteer with a Muslim grass-roots organization called Jawaab, empowering young Muslims against systemic Islamophobia through creative and soft skills. Her existence was only brought to light to the mainstream after her death, by her friend MP David Lammy. However, the astounding silence of Muslim media outlets sparked debates: at times when there are more Muslim millionaires in the UK than ever before, and people give tens of thousands of pounds to charities, how was a talented figure like Khadija completely ignored and not supported? Is it because she was a Black female living in a council flat? Khadija's situation echoes those of many Muslims, who like her, are ignored by mainstream and Muslim media outlets because they are too remote from symbols of power or too 'uncool' to be marketable. Where was the *ummah* when Khadija needed it? Similarly, Hamja Ahsan, one of the very few British Muslim artists selected for Documenta (a festival so important it is nicknamed the Olympics of Arts), never received any support from British Muslims, even when attacked for opposing Islamophobia in the art world and supporting the Palestinian cause. In a nod to Putnam's *Bowling Alone* (2001), Muslims are feeling isolated not only from mainstream institutions but also from their own imagined 'community': being Muslim in modern Euro-America is being surrounded by a *jamat* (congregation) but ultimately *Praying Alone*.

6.2. 'The *Ummah* Is People's Gangs'

Ömer, born and raised in Turkey, was shocked by the British Muslims he met when he came to London for his studies: 'they live in a country where they can practice their faith, study, work better than in any other country ... Why do they want to become like those who have colonised and murdered their ancestors? Where is their dignity?'

Colourism and anti-Black racism within Muslim communities led many to feel that they don't belong to a community (see chapter 1). Although initiatives such as Black Muslim in Britain[9] (set up in 2017) assert that Black Muslims lives matter, the widespread replication of harm led some like British Islamic scholar Momodou Taal to distance himself completely:

> Everyday, I'm reminded why I actively choose to disassociate myself from 'the muslim community' ... Best decision I've ever made to date ... I quickly realised, many Muslims, including scholars were far more content with reproducing harmful systems of oppression and dominance than actually seeking to dismantle them ... So yes, I will never be in community with such people. (Taal 2021)

Kasia, a Polish new Muslim working in an 'Islamic' charity, recounts how her employer stole her portfolio and got someone from the 'Muslim mainstream community' to claim her achievements: 'I stopped believing in a concept of modern *ummah* because of exclusion of many, starting from poverty to marginalisation of "reverts" in the mainstream Muslim communities.' Some others deplore the disconnection between religious scholars and people, urging believers to be friends with their parents: 'they don't know what having abusive parents are ... Children have rights too.' British Islamic scholar Mohammed Nizami, vocal on the distortion of Islam by social norms, describes the *ummah* as a 'nebulous body of people I can't recognise in real life and expect deep fraternal bonds with this mythological group'. Sadiya from Everyday Muslim (see next section) mentions how Muslims would offer deals to non-Muslims because 'they are more popular', but also how her more privileged position made people distance themselves without question:

> Some of the most difficult challenges I've faced was working on a project about Black Muslim heritage ... in a non-paid capacity, ... led by people from Black Muslim background, ... Yet, someone wrote an email to the community to boycott the project because I wasn't Black ... How are we supposed to be one community if we don't support one another? I often felt like giving up.

Whether it is because of the reproduction of systems of oppression, the numbness to the suffering of others and their subsequent marginalization, exploitation, and abuse, like Hamja bullied in childhood (chapter 3), Javayria's brother bullied by other Muslims for going to the mosque (chapter 1), Halima being shouted at by elders, and Muneera being made to feel inadequate (chapter 4), many—myself included after my misadventures (chapter 1)—don't believe in the existence of an *ummah* any more.

In almost every mosque, Muslim student society or association, madrassa, and charity, one can hear the narrative that 'Muslims are brothers and sisters', or 'the *ummah* is like one body, when one limb hurts, the whole body hurts'. The narrative implies that Muslims are one community of solidarity where no one is left alone. The main contention my respondents express is that they were sold a lie, as this solidarity is nowhere to be found. Sultanah, a community organizer who grew up in East London, summarizes: 'it's not what we signed for!' While I have covered how, between the most and less privileged Muslims, despite sharing the same religion and the same struggles, there is little support, redistribution of resources, or solidarity (chapter 2), the same dynamics are present across class and ethnicity and regardless of religiosity. The absence of support is a cause for some, especially 'reverts' like Kasia, to leave Islam (Alyedreessy 2018), or leave the UK to go to other countries where their contribution will be valued. Sultanah points out: 'what is the point of Islam if there's no solidarity with Muslims, and it's just you alone with God?'

Community historian Yahya Birt (2022, 8) argues that the *ummah* at the time of the Prophet was multi-religious and based on values as 'a framework of mutual peace, security, and consultation' whereas its modern usage has been colonized by the Western political imagination and nationalism to mean 'a people' or a form of 'passive identity'. The concept of *ummah* was helpful for Muslims in the immediate post-9/11 era to feel a sense of belonging to an imagined community (Anderson 1983), experiencing shared suffering, solidarity, and compassion for each other (Bayat 2005; Paterson et al. 2018). *Ummah* meant belonging to a two-billion-strong family saying: 'we are in this together'. The *ummah* sometimes appears in protests or on social media: it is the generalizing 'we' that appears when people march for the end of occupation in Palestine in slogans such as 'we exist, we resist'—around which rally Muslims from the whole political spectrum from alt-right supporters, some influencers, and even some Muslims supporting counter-extremist policies. The Muslim 'we' is a rhetorical device, which through uniformization and generalization speaks to the collective imaginary, notably through nostalgia: 'we were here from 711 . . . we left a mark'. It is similar to the use of essentializing terms such as 'Islamic countries', 'Muslim countries' or 'Muslim world', implying that any Islamicate country is a safe haven for any Muslim, that people and governments in these places follow Islam perfectly. It is as absurd as calling the UK a 'Christian country': while the state has an official religion, religion has little effect on the way the country is governed. Cemil Aydin (2017) argues that the idea of a 'Muslim World' is a colonial concept that emerged in the nineteenth century Eurocentric discourses on Muslim inferiority and theories of decline, now both used by 'pan-Islamists' and Islamophobes alike, the latter as an othering lexical device. Muslims, including those amongst my respondents, are increasingly weary of branding exercises such as Saudi Arabia's image of 'Custodian of the Two Holy Mosques'. The assassination of journalist Jamal Khashoggi, the starvation of Yemeni people, the erasure of historical landmarks, the violations of human rights, and the normalization of the occupation of Palestine by Saudi Arabia have led some Muslims to call for a boycott of the country, some, including amongst my respondents, renouncing the performance of one of the most important rituals, the pilgrimage of *Hajj*.[10]

However, Sultanah recalls her childhood in a Bengali neighbourhood in east London and the solidarity between people:

> People would live with the families in the same flat. The men would work in the same factory and the women would stay home. The whole building would cook for someone's wedding. People would march together in the streets against racism. People would send together money back home. They would create these spaces of resistance where people existed being themselves.

Another of my respondents, Tayyibah, from an Afghan background, in Manchester, relates how the system of committees (interpersonal loans without interest, what is called now 'peer-to-peer'): 'committees were the backbone of the community, committees got people houses, university tuition fees, this is how we paid our walima [Islamic wedding reception]'. Sadiya and Javayria recall how their parents' generation had an open-house policy where anyone could visit and be welcomed. However, it seems that the newer generations have become much more individualistic.

Although Muslims are becoming wealthier, money and other resources are not equally shared. My respondents share stories from their work or family, where they noticed people giving £10,000 of zakat to charity works abroad instead of to vulnerable Muslims in the UK, a relative buying a £100,000 Rolls Royce in cash, or another one completely refitting their kitchen every year for around £70,000. If there's so much wealth within the 'community', why don't people reinvest their wealth into the 'community'? Some respondents deplore this: 'while we give abroad, we become refugees at home'. Sultanah analyses how things have changed since her childhood:

> Since austerity our borough is going down the pan. Homelessness, drugs, prostitution, you name it. It wasn't like this even 10 years back but cuts are now visible ... The Muslims albeit practising are absolutely ... disengaged ... And this is why the whole aspiration to 'make it' and follow some capitalist Islam-esque model I believe has bore the fruits of depoliticising our communities to the

point of dangerous. The *ummah* has become a whitewashed term, which means people's gangs.

Mohammed Qasim (2018) argue that, especially amongst those coming from the most challenged backgrounds, there is no participatory culture (as defined by Jenkins et al. 2005), a strong support for creating and innovating where people from underprivileged social status enjoy a degree of social connection and support with the most privileged ones and are even able to receive informal mentorship from the latter. The few groups where I have observed strong support for each other were Ismailis in Canada and the Shi'a in North London, who are more willing to invest in non-tangible assets such as social and cultural capital, encouraging people to reach decision-making positions in politics, the media, or the fields of the arts and heritage.

In my fieldwork, I come across four different theories as why there is no more solidarity.

- The atomization of Muslims by wider power structures.
- Younger generations living at their parents' for longer, increasing living costs which pushes people to work more and make less room and time for face-to-face interactions outside of immediate family.
- A rise in the self-interested pursuit of egoistical aspirations and material comfort.
- Islam being reduced to an ethno-cultural identity.

Following 9/11 and 7/7, the climate of economic austerity, the 'hostile environment' policy, and assimilationist narratives divided Muslims depending on whether they would abide by governments' dichotomy of good and bad Muslims (see chapter 2). Sultanah deplores the aggressive language that kids hear at school, in the labour force, or on social media, and how popular culture depoliticized Muslims who understood that 'we have no village'. Imad, commenting on British Bangladeshis, insists that this dynamic is not exclusive to Muslims: 'this breakdown of community is a collective experience for all groups in the UK facing the ill effects of atomisation that comes from hypercapitalisation'.

Birt (2022) argues that self-interested individuals are to blame for the building of a gatekeeping culture more interested in short-term financial profits. One example is the initiative Imam Connect,[11] set up by Concordia Forum fellows (see chapter 2), marketed as an 'Uber' for imams.[12] The website turns imams into freelancing professionals competing against each other in exchange of 25% of their rates. If Imam Connect is supposed to be a community service, why not embrace the model of a digital *waqf* (charitable entrustment) where wages of religious facilitators are guaranteed by the collective or people's *zakat* (alms tax)? There is an irony when while Euro-American think tanks invest millions in the media and academia to feed Islamophobic narratives (see chapter 2), despite the millions available amongst British Muslims, MEND's volunteers (an advocacy charity monitoring racist and islamophobic abuses) have to take side jobs to survive. Abdullah, a community organizer, comments on what kept Bengalis seemingly together:

> The Bengalis in [Tower Hamlets] identified as Muslims yes but as Bengalis. They did not see themselves the same as Arabs, or say Pakistanis with whom they were at war with in 1971 . . . I think talk of a Muslim community is helpful as there are shared interests and alignments (for example Eid dates . . .) but there is no real sense of UK Muslim community genuinely that I am aware of—just lots of sub groups and grand claims.

Nizami suggests that 'Islam never came to Britain' but instead 'ethno-linguistic cultural communities' demarcated themselves on the basis of ethnicity, language, and politics but not theology. 'Community', he argues, is about family clusters or *a maxima*, people of a same caste living in the same neighbourhood and acquainted with common elders. For the elders, community wasn't necessarily defined by religion: Javayria's parents would visit and drop food to their Sikh friends and invite them to family weddings. Despite being of different faiths, they shared the same language, the same roots (from Jalandhar, pre-partition) and their grandparents knew each other. Conversely, they would have derogatory views on Bangladeshis or other Pakistanis from lower castes and tribes, despite them being South Asian Muslims too. Even amongst younger generations, community can be delimited by social status, wealth, occupation, and also British-vedic remnants of caste: Darzis (tailors) may find it hard to marry Mochis (shoemakers, of lower status), or, no matter how rich or educated, they may not be accepted by Rajputs (of higher status) as I observed in Britain, including in my family-in-law. For these reasons, many of those among my respondents born in Pakistan have negative views of British Pakistanis, whom they find 'corrupt, flashy, arrogant, losing their values' and 'stuck in the 1970s'. The British *ummah* has become an inward-looking impenetrable block to newcomers, making it almost impossible for cultural outsiders to find jobs, marriage, networks, support, or resources—an antithesis of its original meaning. Paraphrasing Simon and Garfunkel's *Sounds of Silence*, the *ummah* has become people prostrating without praying.

These ethno-cultural boundaries have been useful in the early days and the elders' generation to find support within mosques, make new connections for business, marriage, and committee, which allowed families to finance studies, cars, and properties. These boundaries were also a form of protection from the hostile environment of racism and Islamophobia. However, this protectionism has created in-group favouritism and outgroup derogation (Taijfel 1970), which has been passed onto younger generations. The situation is very different to that of French

Muslims, for whom community is less confined to culture or ethnicity and focused more around similar socio-religious practices (mosque attendance, charity works, etc. (Barylo 2017a)): newcomers to Islam in France can more easily find themselves embedded in a family outside their blood family, despite the structural adversity against Islam. My observations since 2009 amongst French Muslims make me theorize that the uncompromisingly antagonistic narratives against Muslims since the 1980s has led people to develop cross-cultural solidarity. While in the UK, greeting random Muslims on the streets with *Salaam 'Alaykum* (peace be upon you) is as offensive as greeting strangers on the London Tube, in France, Muslims still greet each other to show support—some compared it to the silent nod between members in *Fight Club*.

If, as per the Islamic traditions, the whole Earth is a mosque (where people can worship God) and no one owns the Earth, why not simply distance oneself physically from the centres of oppression? Some Muslims from Great Britain, the US or France have settled in Andalusia, in the village of Órgiva, or to a remote area in Tunisia, trying to build a village from scratch, or to Jordan in a permaculture community. Some acknowledge that this lifestyle has its rewards such as financial and food autonomy, like Medina who grows vegetables in her garden, and works from home as a writer: 'people want to disengage from the system and create their own *jannah* [paradise], but it can create a bubble'. A couple who moved to Pakistan was satisfied with the quality of material life; housing and food are cheaper; but on the other end concerned by the cost of education and healthcare. While moving abroad is a dream for some, others resign because of technical challenges like Fozia: 'there's nowhere better. I can't imagine living somewhere else. America is worse. You would need to get a new job, learn a new system ... England is home. Racism is here and you have to accept it. If I react to it, I will be victimised.' She instead moved to Scotland, where she says that 'people are more friendly'.

Some others voice the moral responsibility to support those who are still 'on the frontline': 'if God has allowed me to go to university and learn about these things [racism and inequalities], don't I have a duty to use this knowledge for helping those at home? I think it's [moving abroad] is fair for those who want to retire, but moving to a farm in my twenties and act as if nothing bad was happening, it's a bit negligent'. Asim Qureshi backs this approach with the following reasoning: 'I am someone who has been given specific privileges by Allah, and I owe it to the privileges I have been given to use them to the maximum effect' (Qureshi 2017, 197), as an argument that his skills and expertise are more effectively used in the context of the UK.

> We were thrown unwillingly and unknowingly into an insidious battlefield where we are on the frontline without knowing the codes, strategies and tactics of the enemy and taking blow after blow until we surrender or retreat without being able to shift the line. Or burnout ... But we are witnessing more organised forms

of resistance, care, healing, and are able to respond at a more or less equal level … We know how to spot the attacks, dodge them, take rest, heal, preserve ourselves, prepare, plan, respond and impact. (Harfouch 2018)

'Even if they hold the whole *dunya* [material world] in their hand, the *dunya* doesn't penetrate their heart' one of my respondents told me, referring to the concept of the *zahid*: the ascetic is not necessarily the one who flees from the centres of power and disengage from the system, but the one who, in the middle of the system, is able to say 'no' to it. Like the example of the London community hub Rumi's Cave or Root25 (see chapter 8), a few other initiatives are building communities based on values and solidarity such as Mu'allif in Nottingham, a rhizomic support network for new Muslims led by Salih Whelbourne advocating the idea of a Three-Tone *ummah* (Black-Brown-White), and the Cambridge Crescent circle led by Nabila Winter. In the atomized modern society, they are able to build community not as clusters but constellations, as Sultanah comments: 'if you have friends cling to them. Appreciate them … Appreciate the village wherever you can find it.'

6.3. Muslim History Tours and Archives: The Ecosystem of the Past and Present

It was for her kids to 'find traces of the community's legacy' that Sadiya Ahmed set up in 2014 the Everyday Muslim Project and Archive Initiative.[13] The project describes itself as a 'long-term project to create a central archive of Muslim lives, arts, education, and cultures from across the UK'. It aims at 'creating tangible connections between their Muslim heritage and the representation of their identity in the wider society' and taking 'ownership of experiences and memories for the purpose of preserving our history in Britain'.

She realized that Muslim narratives were absent from the British Archives, museums, and history books. Although not having any business, museum management, or archival skills, she began to record interviews and collect photographs, documents, letters, films, artefacts, and ephemera to document stories about people's everyday lives: childhood, education, migration, food, celebrations, prayer, and more. The collections are partially catalogued and archived in archival institutes across the UK such as the Bishopsgate Institute, Vestry House Museum, George Padmore Institute, Surrey History Centre, the Shah Jahan Mosque and Library, and Brent Museums and Archives. Their projects include '"We weren't expecting to stay", documenting the lives of British South Asian Muslim from 1940 to the present day, 'Exploring the diversity of Black British Muslim heritage in London', and the Muslim Heritage Trails, a set of waypoints around the Woking including, Britain's first Muslim cemetery (1884), Britain's first purpose-built mosque (1889), and the first Muslim military cemetery (1915), accompanied by printed leaflets including biographies, maps, a chronology, and facts. She recalls how it all started:

> [In 2009], I started considering how and where our children would learn about being 'Muslim' outside of the usual Qur'an classes. It was on a trip to the Roald Dahl Museum where my then very young children spent their time drawing, attended storytelling session and dressing up... I noticed they learnt so much and how the museum setting could be used for self-directed learning... This, coupled with my parents' stories of their child and early adulthood I began to realise that these recollections of their lives wasn't just storytelling but an important transmission of culture, heritage and a snapshot of a space and time we could not understand in our context... Without knowing these,... each generation has to start from the beginning.

Although not very popular at the time of writing and struggling to obtain funding (she is careful for the project to remain independent), Sadiya sees her work as planting seeds that may grow and bear fruits perhaps after her lifetime. The Everyday Muslim Heritage project looks at the past through the present; viewers and participants are able to compare items from older times to their present lives. Another initiative looks at the present through the lens of the past, and this on red double-decker buses: the Muslim History Tours.

AbdulMaalik Tailor is Britain's first professionally qualified Muslim tour guide, and the only one in London wearing a red fez. He offers guided tours through London's landmarks and museums (and other places outside the capital such as Windsor, Brighton, Woking, etc.), showing people the traces of Muslim heritage in the capital. Taking participants on buses or on cruises along the Thames, themes include 'North Africans in London' or 'Ottomans in Britain'. AbdulMaalik takes participants to see Ottoman cannons, paintings, and places such as the location of the earliest Friday prayers in London, or the location of the first publicly known Eid prayers (which have been decorated with a blue plaque thanks to his efforts), between 'Moroccan "pirates"', 'north African Tudors', and 'Shakespeare's Muslim friend'. Just like Sadiya, AbdulMaalik has done all the training and the research by himself:

> I started... in 1999... as a hobby... instead of choosing engineering or IT, I wanted something which brings me job satisfaction, not just for the money... I get the buzz when I find out about a place I never heard of before. When I was trying to find the first mosque in London, I spent weeks with volumes big like that table... When I found it,... I went there, I asked can I use one of your meeting rooms to pray, and explained I wanted to perform the prayer of gratitude... they let me do it... It takes 3 months to organise a tour, 6 months in a place I don't

know, there's all the research work in the archives, sometimes I can spend days trying to find a location in the archives, and there's no trace.

The tours show how, in the heart of the Empire, people have stolen and appropriated Muslim cultural elements but also how power has opened its doors to the Other. Talking about Muslims invited to the kings' court, mingling with poets, got their portrait done and now shown in the National Portrait Gallery, Tate Britain and other places, it allows the Muslim collective imaginary to say: 'once, we were there', 'once, we were respected'. This collective self-esteem exercise finds its illustration in the celebration of the victories of MMA fighter Khabib Nurmagomedov or the Turkish drama *Ertugrul*: just like the nostalgia for the 'Golden Age' of Islam, they have become collectively appropriated symbols of power and respectability—at times when Muslims, after colonization and 9/11, have been systematically pushed to the margins of society.

Sadiya and AbdulMaalik are doing the equivalent work of university researchers, spending months excavating decades of work and archives, but earn no recognition and no compensation for their investment. Historically, Muslims were always 'subjects' of research; only the white man did research *on* Muslims (Said 1978). The colonial narrative has embedded in the collective mind that non-white people cannot be producers or facilitators of knowledge and scholarship. When 43% of people polled by the *Guardian* feel proud of the colonization,[14] how can British subjects expect to voice counter-narratives?

On the other side of the Atlantic, Su'ad Abdul Khabeer's project Umi's Archive[15] explores, through the life of her late mother, the meanings of being Black in the world. According to her, the power of memory, even learning from one single person, has the ability to collectively educate and elevate people. The archive is a 'dreamspace', a space where people can imagine that justice and liberation are possible. She argues, along with Satya Mohanty's (2000) research, that through personal experiences of trauma, memories of resistance, and emotions, ethnically minoritized people, and specifically Black women, are 'repositories' of knowledge who can provide people 'with a view of the past that differs from the traditional mainstream one' (Mohanty 2000, 33). Grass-roots initiatives show that institutions don't have a monopoly on knowledge and non-canonical ways of producing and dissemination knowledge are not only valid but necessary in marginal spaces. History and memory also rely on individuals outside any organization, like community historian Yahya Birt. Witnessing and documenting the changes in various communities for decades, and despite not holding a formal university position, his contributions are found in various forms from blog to research pieces, reports, events and social media posts, weaved in the production of the British Muslim socio-cultural fabric.

However, AbdulMaalik expresses his frustration about the institutional barriers he faces, from museums, and even Muslims: 'when I write to museums, I'm sure they have this box ticking policy, no one gets back to me. Even in the community, people are not interested. I contacted mosques, no one got back to me. Islam Channel don't want to talk about it, they like to hear me about domestic violence, my story of conversion, but they're not interested in heritage.'

Sadiya has encountered similar struggles. Their work is nothing 'cool' or marketable in an ahistorical neoliberal society of instant gratification—AbdulMaalik mentions how offering 'selfie tours' would be much more lucrative, but refuses because 'there's no meaning behind it'. He says his audience is often a majority of South East Asian tourists, sometimes American Muslims but curiously, British Muslims don't seem interested.

6.4. Sacred Footsteps and Film Clubs

While British Muslims share a fascination with an imagined common cultural heritage in distant countries, why are Sadiya's or AbdulMaalik's initiatives not under the spotlight in Britain? Is Britain not distant enough for melancholia to operate? When, in 2019, the Cambridge Eco mosque was inaugurated, a Bangladeshi community organizer noticed a paradox when everyone started calling it 'the Cambridge Mosque': Cambridge already had mosques which have been running for decades. In a sarcastic post advertising for the original 'Cambridge Mosque', the oldest mosque in the city, also known as the Abubakr Siddiq Islamic Centre at 1A, Mawson road, he argues that it is much more British than the new Eco Mosque funded by foreign governments: 'everyone is talking about the mosque in Cambridge so I went to visit it this evening ... This is a truly "British" mosque, as it was built by Bengali migrants to Britain—and Bengalis have been British subjects and paying taxes for more than 300 years. The local British community have selected their imam, with no foreign non-British interference.'

The disappearance of community heritage in the collective mind is symptomatic of how the dynamics of class and race have shaped and metacolonized the Muslim collective thought; what is British is labelled 'modern', 'eco-friendly', 'matching the local area', what comes from the elders' generation is de facto perceived as 'backwards', 'dirty' and 'wasting resources', 'not integrated', 'disorganized', and thus not truly belonging to here and now—a past that the collective mind wants to selectively hide and forget.

People are not interested in culture if it doesn't come from dominant structures. Javayria recalls, when studying History, 'I had a British Pakistani girl say to me, ... I was weird because I was "obsessed with Indo-Pak history," "Why didn't I want to study Islamic history?"' Abbas Zahedi puts forward a theory he calls the Jamie Oliver paradox: 'if an uncle would talk on TV about tajine, nobody would listen. They are not Jamie Oliver. But when Jamie Oliver talks about tajine, everyone listens.' People cheer for Mohammed Salah leading his football team to victory,

Nadiya Hussein winning *The Great British Bake-Off*, or Riz Ahmed starring in Hollywood blockbusters while unique performances done in the past such as the 'Punjab Road Runners', a group of taxi drivers taking their Ford Transit Mk2 on a 6,000-mile journey from Bradford to Lahore,[16] are forgotten.

It was common for many of the elders' generation of various diasporas to achieve similar journeys by road to the homeland. In France, the UK, and Germany, many of my respondents born in the 1980s and the 1990s still remember the yearly days-long road trips to North Africa or Turkey, to see extended family. These trips were bridges through which communities kept in touch with the social, financial, and political realities of relatives but also how they would emotionally and psychologically strengthen each other. I remember when my dad would load his Mercedes 190E every summer and drive us to Poland from Paris. We would reach the country after two days of driving, sleeping in the car at night while our parents kept driving, and eventually wait countless hours at the Polish border (which was not in the European Union at that time). Looking back, these trips mirror the infinite possibilities that my parents could imagine through their do-it-yourself mindset. Although miles away from Poland, I would realize that I have family that would open their doors to me and my sister, on whom we could rely. They too, knew that, somewhere in France, they had family. In the French Muslim diaspora, these experiences have been immortalized by the 1999 title *Tonton du Bled* (Uncle From Back Home) by French rap collective 113.[17]

The same dynamics are found with tourism: people travel to Islamicate countries for the food, the beaches, and the resorts more than for the heritage. Sacred Footsteps,[18] an organic travel blog and global community focusing on locations of spiritual interest across the globe from a Muslim perspective. Focusing on sustainable, ethical, and responsible travel practices, the blog is a slow-paced not-for profit, volunteer- and community-led initiative aiming at decentring travels away from a tourist-consumerist or orientalist relationship to places; and finding genuine connection to lands through history, language, and faith.

When it comes to the mainstream, does it mean a few generations need to pass before Sadiya's or Abdulmaalik's work are valued? In 2019, for the first time since the 1970s, artist and curator Hassan Vawda organized in Walthamstow the screening of the 1957 Indian film *Pyasaa* by Guru Dutt. Hassan chose the film for its story, a metaphor for our current times. In the film, the main character, Vijay, a talented poet, faces rejection from publishers because his writings are not 'trendy', rejection from his own family and rejection for marriage because of his profession. Only when he is believed dead after an accident do people from all over the country idolize Vijay for his writings; his publishers fight for the rights to his texts and Vijay's own brothers try to get money out of their brother's posthumous fame.

The screening took place in a church. The room at the basement contains space for maybe thirty people, but was packed with well over fifty people, elders, parents, children, and teenagers, and with South Asians as well as white local residents.

Attendees were offered free chai and home-made samosas. The free screening was part of Hassan's project to revive the Apne Film Society (Our Films society), in the spirit of desi film clubs in Walthamstow 'in a way that the old Asian cinema clubs of the 60's and 70's use to be [AbdulMaalik managed to locate the original address]. In community centres, church halls and other cinemas—a place for the community and to come together.' More than for watching films such as *Kabhi Kabie*, *Noorie*, *Pakeeza*, and many more, cinema clubs were community hubs that brought people together, families, elders and the young, 'in a space that felt like home'. Hassan compares how the event contrasts with when the BFI [British Film Institute] screened *Pyaasa* three times over the last five years, to 'largely half-empty screenings with mainly white middle class people who laugh at the wrong times, all with wine and no chai'.

The printed programme handed over to viewers contains a short synopsis of the film, a description of the initiative, a contribution from AbdulMaalik about the history of the club, one archive picture of a film screening at a local cinema and the injunction 'PLEASE TALK THROUGH THE MOVIE' written in capital letters—bringing back the spirit of conviviality (people didn't talk but shed tears). The programme also contains a two-pages piece entirely in Urdu, without any translation, written by Hassan's mum, which Hassan encourages people to find someone next to them to translate it.

In the closing remarks after the screening, Hassan relates his struggles trying to make the screening happen: 'we tried four years ago, it didn't work, we tried three years ago, it didn't work . . . Let's consider the Vijays and Gulabs [the other main character] of this world and not be fooled by fame, egos and money.' Hassan explains to be how he managed to get the Barbican Centre to fund the initiative and how aunty Hafsah got Barbican funding for her samosas: 'this sector is dominated by individual relationships and partnerships . . . rather than through strict measurement and application process. This way of distributing resources based on trust is usually just locked to the elite dominant culture, but sometimes it materialises in lower down.'

The past, as used by Hassan, Sadiya, and AbdulMaalik, has a similar function to the environment for the Green Deen Tribe (chapter 5): the past is a way of grounding the collective psyche and make it feel at 'home' in a land where they were always made to feel like undesirable; or actors in a film where they were made extras. They are forms of *zikr*, a remembrance with a spiritual dimension.

6.5. Is There a British Islam?

In the town of Surrey where I live, there are three different mosques. Each year, each one celebrates Eid on a different day. Imad Ahmed has been trying since 2018 to unite British Muslims for celebrating Eid on the same day through New Crescent

Society, a pioneering attempt to make every mosque in the UK agree on one unified Islamic calendar based on moonsighting. Until now, a considerable number of mosques have relied on Eid dates released by Saudi Arabia, which uses a calendar disconnected from physical sightings of the moon. Imad managed to partner with the Royal Observatory at Greenwich, holding its first ever live moonsighting streamed on Facebook to mark the beginning of Ramadan in 2018:

> Saudi Arabia has even claimed the moon has been sighted when it was in fact below the horizon. We know that's not possible from our data and this is a cause for alarm . . . For many Muslims living in the UK—the penny has dropped. It is now irrefutable that Saudi Arabia's moonsightings are not credible . . . Saudi Arabia, Bangladesh, Pakistan, South Africa and Morocco all do their own moonsightings—so it's time we did too! (Ahmed in Wan 2019)

While the initiative has become popular, Imad has been facing difficulties at changing decades-old habits. While religious scholars and politicians alike have been advocating the advent of a 'British Islam', if Muslims across the country cannot agree on a unified religious calendar, what does a national Islam mean?

Within communities, 'British Islam' has first been about cultural accommodation of symbolic 'British' practices within the frame of religious orthodoxy—like Christmas celebrations or Valentine's day. Some of my respondents buy a Christmas tree 'because the kids wanted one' or had a Christmas dinner because it was an 'opportunity to have a family meal'. Some other respondents organized a Christmas dinner with a roast Halal turkey. 'I don't worship anyone else for Christmas, it's fine, it's just a commercial celebration', others would justify. An online discussion emerged on my feed about Valentine's, and Muslim companies offering 'Valentine's deal' or matchmaking events. Some people opposed the idea, some others defended it:

HUSSEIN: 'When Islam spread throughout the world, it embraced and enhanced the indigenous cultures it came into contact with . . . Despite its Zoroastrian roots, Nowruz for example, the celebration of the Persian New Year, remains a prominent festival amongst many Muslims around the world.

ALAA: These Muslim organisations are just copying others and following them blindly . . . It is like Islamising Rihanna's and Drake's songs to make them sound like *nasheeds* [acapella devotional music] lol. Add to that the commercialism of religion, leveraging on the consumer's mind and naivety of Muslims is sickening and shortsighted.

JESSICA: Did Muslims in India adopt Diwali? Did we adopt Easter in Europe? No, because these holidays are inherently tied to un-Islamic beliefs . . . it seems the most generous opinion is that it's opportunistic consumerism, the more stringent that it borders on shirk. Neither are things we should be happy about imo.

ALAA: I don't find it a problem if you send a letter or give a present to a neighbour or friend who celebrates these occasions as an act of kindness but I find it a problem when Muslim organisations and institutions are adopting such occasions for shortsighted visions.

HUSSEIN: Our uniqueness is our ability as Muslims to deeply connect with different cultures. This is how Islam spread. There are some here that would prefer there was no unique Turkish architecture or calligraphy. *Bidaa* [unlawful religious innovation]. Ertugurul with their non Arab names. *Bidaa*. Morrocan style *jalabiya* [long garments]. *Bidaa*. Malaysian style *dhikr* [rememberance]. *Bidaa*. They would cut the head of Islamic civilisation before it grows.

Further on in the same conversations, Hussein shared two documents: *Islam and the Cultural Imperative* by Umar Faruq Abd-Allah (2004) and *Towards the Greater Integration of Islam in Britain* by Abdalhaqq Bewley (2017). Very similar to the thought of Abdal Hakim Murad (2020), the books draw parallels between Islamic values and 'old-fashioned toryism' (Bewley 2017, 9), warn from 'predatory Islamist ideologies from abroad', illustrate the lack of Islamic education amongst Muslims, and paint 'brides' from abroad as primarily a 'linguistic problem'. Hussein's comments denote bitterness about religious stringency which impose the cutting of ties with anything not part of an imagined Islamic canon (see chapter 3). While they argue about whether celebrating Christmas and Valentine's are cultural enrichment or worshipping Plutus, the god of money and consumerism, governments had different visions.

For politicians, like French president Nicolas Sarkozy wanting to see a 'French Islam',[19] national forms of Islam oppose the 'Islam from abroad', considered a problem to social harmony. French president Macron publicly stated his will to 'liberate' Islam in France from foreign influences.[20] It bears an assimilationist perspective: to be valid, Islam and therefore Muslims somehow have to adapt to the local context. These are arguments found in works of ex-Muslims such as Ayaan Hirsi Ali (2010) or in Sara Khan's *Battle for British Islam* (2016). British Islam hints the issue of official representation: if there's a national Islam, it assumes that there is someone—or a small select group—to speak on behalf of it (such as the government-engineered *Conseil Français du Culte Musulman* or CFCM, French Council for the Muslim Faith). It is a wish rooted in colonial history, as in the 1958 campaigns in Algeria encouraging women to remove their hijabs, which comprised mass 'unveiling' public ceremonies[21] or, in 1806, French Emperor Napoléon attempting at 'regenerating' Judaism and making it 'compatible' with the Empire.

While between Muslims, the debate around festivals revolves around the question of what is in line with the worship of God, when it comes to Islam as a nationalized banner, it is about possession. Putting Islam under a banner submits it to a hierarchy of power and therefore control. Creating a spontaneously indigenous form of 'Islam' means a homogeneous insular identity disconnected from the rest of the world—while British Muslims (see 6.2), are a mix of various heterogeneous and balkanized groups. Further, I argue that there is a difference between Islam as a faith, texts, beliefs, principles, etc. and Islam as a social phenomenon practised by people, tinted with culture, political opinions, and personal preferences (Barylo 2017b): if there are four million Muslims in Britain, an external observer would see four million different forms of British Islam.

There is a British Islam of neoliberals thirsty for money and power and a British Islam which believes in reciting the Qur'an in ancient Latin to the rhythm of military marches and Gregorian chants. There is a British Islam of charities with repeated scandals of misconduct, abuse and mismanagement, a British Islam of egoistic marketing geniuses who would turn any aspect of the religion or cultures into a money-making scheme and a British Islam of white supremacist, anti-Blacks, and misogynists who bend the Qur'an to justify their agenda. There is a British Islam of people wanting to strip non-white people of their Nationality but then, at the same time . . . a British Islam of people who silently prepare the next generation to navigate racism, neoliberalism and patriarchy in a white supremacist world. There is a British Islam of healers, artists, and storytellers who design, imagine, and do the collective work of resistance, healing, and flourishing, a British Islam of academics and organizers holding to account harmful behaviours, and a British Islam of White, Brown, and Black Muslims standing for the Uyghurs, the Rohingyas, Palestine, Kashmir, Yemen, and Black lives. When people appropriate and attach Islam to human-made labels (which is different from contextualizing it), it can be bent to people's subjective values while for those who believe, God has established a universal framework independent of human existence—Islam, as a framework, is different from what people make of it.

Notes

1. Sabrina Barr, 'Nadiya Hussain recalls being told "Black hands don't sell jewellery" during modelling interview', *The Independent*, 15 June 2020. https://web.archive.org/web/20200701074646/https://www.independent.co.uk/life-style/nadiya-hussain-hands-modelling-black-lives-matter-a9566641.html
2. Zack Sharf, 'Riz Ahmed missed Star Wars celebration because Homeland Security stopped him at airport', *Indie Wire*, 28 June 2019. https://web.archive.org/web/20190701003250/https://www.indiewire.com/2019/06/riz-ahmed-missed-star-wars-celebration-homeland-security-blocked-flying-1202154028
3. Maria Cramer, 'A noted musician's instrument was ruined. Not by us, Says T.S.A.', *The New York Times*, 6 February 2020. https://web.archive.org/web/20200207002003/https://www.nytimes.com/2020/02/06/arts/music/ballake-sissoko-kora-tsa-customs.html
4. freeze_magazine. Accessed 1 February 2024. https://archive.is/LOU0V
5. Speech of Hatem Bazian, at the launch of his book *Palestine It's Something Colonial*, P21 Gallery, London, UK. 7 December 2016.
6. Second after the 2011 Hetherington House Occupation, from 1 February 2011 to 31 August 2011 (211 days).
7. 'Occupation Manifesto', Goldsmiths Anti-Racist Action. 2019. https://web.archive.org/web/20190425215837/https://docs.google.com/document/d/1l6Jn-q8TLqnZtEGiEjEt0d_egF70q2ENcOmwJyk5ulM/edit

8. 'GARA protest in Deptford Town Hall: College response (July 2019)', Goldsmiths College. 2019. https://web.archive.org/web/20200924111307/https://www.gold.ac.uk/racial-justice/committments/dth-protest-college-response
9. Black and Muslim in Britain. Accessed 1 February 2024. https://web.archive.org/web/20200615142237/https://www.facebook.com/blackandmusliminbritain
10. Adela Suliman, 'Politics v pilgrimage: some Muslims call for Saudi haj boycott', *Reuters*, 9 August 2019. https://web.archive.org/web/20190809082545/https://www.reuters.com/article/us-saudi-haj-boycott-idUSKCN1UZ01R
11. Imam Connect. Accessed 1 February 2024. https://web.archive.org/web/20200920103412/https://www.imamconnect.com
12. 'ImamConnect—the 'Uber for Imams' BBC Asian Network [Facebook] 16 September 2020. https://archive.org/details/imam-connect
13. EveryDay Muslim Heritage Project and Archive. Accessed 1 February 2024. https://web.archive.org/web/20200809073439/https://www.everydaymuslim.org
14. 'Empire state of mind—why do so many people think colonialism was a good thing?', *Guardian*, 20 January 2016. https://web.archive.org/web/20160120182950/https://www.theguardian.com/politics/shortcuts/2016/jan/20/empire-state-of-mind-why-do-so-many-people-think-colonialism-was-a-good-thing
15. Su'ad Abdul Kabeer, *Umi's Archive*. Accessed 1 February 2024. https://web.archive.org/web/20210620184416/https://www.umisarchive.com
16. 'The Punjab Road Runners Bradford to Pakistan in Ford Transit Mk2', Davy [YouTube] 28 January 2013. https://archive.org/details/the-punjab-road-runners-bradford-to-pakistan-in-ford-transit-mk-2-you-tube-480p
17. '113—Tonton Du Bled Clip HQ', NiggazRepresent [YouTube] 18 August 2009 [1999]. https://archive.org/details/113-tonton-du-bled-clip-hq-you-tube-360p
18. Sacred Footsteps. Accessed 1 February 2024. https://web.archive.org/web/20221214111248/https://sacredfootsteps.com
19. Alain Auffray, 'Non, Nicolas Sarkozy n'a pas «inventé» l'islam de France', *Libération*, 8 Avril 2016. https://web.archive.org/web/20160411031141/https://www.liberation.fr/france/2016/04/08/non-nicolas-sarkozy-n-a-pas-invente-l-islam-de-france_1444895
20. 'France's Macron says Islam 'in crisis all over the world today', *Middle East Eye*, 2 October 2020. https://web.archive.org/web/20201005051653/https://www.middleeasteye.net/news/france-macron-says-islam-crisis-today
21. Katarzyna Falecka, 'From colonial Algeria to modern day Europe, the Muslim veil remains an ideological battleground', *The Conversation*, 24 January 2017. https://web.archive.org/web/20170127015156/https://theconversation.com/from-colonial-algeria-to-modern-day-europe-the-muslim-veil-remains-an-ideological-battleground-70242; Neil McMaster, *Burning the Veil: The Algerian War and the 'Emancipation' of Muslim Women, 1954–62* (Manchester: Manchester University Press, 2012).

References

Abd-Allah, Umar Faruq. 2004. 'Islam and the cultural imperative.' Crosscurrents blog. https://web.archive.org/web/20060927235228/https://crosscurrents.org/abdallahfall2006.pdf

Abdul Khabeer, Su'ad. 2016. *Muslim Cool: Race, Religion and Hip Hop in the United States*. New York: New York University Press.

Alyedreessy, Mona. 2018. 'British Muslim converts: comparing conversion and deconversion processes to and from Islam.' In *Moving In and Out of Islam*, edited by Karin van Nieuwkerk. Austin: Texas University Press, 257–80.

Anderson, Benedict. 1983. *Imagined Communities: Reflections on the Origin and Spread of Nationalism*. London: Verso.

Aydin, Cemil. 2017. *The Idea of the Muslim World*. Cambridge: Harvard University Press.

Barylo, William. 2017a. *Young Muslim Change-Makers*. London: Routledge.

Barylo, William. 2017b. 'Islam as a matrix: young Muslim volunteers blurring the lines between mundane and sacred.' *Method and Theory in the Study of Religion* 29(2), 181–204.

Bayat, Asef. 2005. 'Islamism and social movement theory.' *Third World Quarterly* 26(6), 891–908.
Bewley, Abdalhaqq. 2017. 'Towards the greater integration of Islam in Britain.' wynnechambers. co.uk. https://web.archive.org/web/20180902154618/http://www.wynnechambers.co.uk/pdf/SAH%20Article%20-%20October%202017.pdf
Birt, Yahya. 2022. *Ummah at the Margins: The Past, Present and Future of Muslim Minorities.* London: Ayaan Centre.
Foucault, Michel. 1977 [1975]. *Discipline and Punish.* New York: Pantheon Books.
Habib, Sadia. 2019. 'The Riz Test.' *Media Magazine*, 67.
Habib, Sadia. 2021. 'Horrible British histories: young people in museums interrogating national identity through principles and practices of critical pedagogy.' *PRISM* 3(2), 34–47.
Harfouch, Ali S. 2018. 'Fasting: a revolt against the modern condition.' *Islam21c*, 7 June. https://web.archive.org/web/20200924165742/https://www.islam21c.com/islamic-thought/fasting-a-revolt-against-the-modern-condition
Hirsi Ali, Ayaan. 2010. *Nomad: From Islam to America: A Personal Journey through the Clash of Civilizations.* New York: Free Press.
Jenkins, Henry, Ravi Puroshotma, Katherine Clinton, et al. 2005. 'Confronting the challenges of participatory culture: media education for the 21st century.' New Media Literacies. https://web.archive.org/web/20130902103144/https://www.newmedialiteracies.org/wp-content/uploads/pdfs/NMLWhitePaper.pdf
Khan, Lamisa. 2018. 'Jum'ah at the Tate: interview with Artist Abbas Zahedi.' *Amaliah*, 18 January. https://web.archive.org/web/20190112230714/https://www.amaliah.com/post/39422/jumah-tate-interview-artist-abbas-zahedi
Khan, Sara and Tony McMahon. 2016. *The Battle for British Islam: Reclaiming Muslim Identity from Extremism.* Self-published.
Moballeghi, Nargess. 2019. [Facebook] 6 July. https://archive.is/NCsfr
Mohanty, Satya. 2000. 'The epistemic status of cultural identity. On beloved and the postcolonial condition.' In *Reclaiming Identity: Realist Theory and the Predicament of Postmodernism*, edited by Paula Moya and M. Hames-Gracía. Berkeley: University of California Press, 33–9.
Murad, Abdal Hakim. 2020. *Travelling Home: Essays on Islam in Europe.* Cambridge: The Quilliam Press.
Paterson, Jenny, Mark Walters, Rupert Brown, et al. 2018. *The Sussex Hate Crime Project: Final Report.* Brighton: University of Sussex.
Putnam, Robert D. 2001. *Bowling Alone: The Collapse and Revival of American Community.* New York: Simon & Schuster.
Qasim, Mohammed. 2018. *Young, Muslim and Criminal: Experiences, Identities and Pathways into Crime.* Bristol: Policy Press.
Qureshi, Asim. 2017. *A Virtue of Disobedience.* London: Byline Books.
Said, Edward. 1978. *Orientalism.* New York: Pantheon Books.
Sian, Katy P. 2019. *Navigating Institutional Racism in British Universities.* London: Palgrave Macmillan.
Spivak, Gayatri C. 1988. 'Can the subaltern speak?' In *Marxism and the Interpretation of Culture* edited by C. Nelson and L Grossberg. Basingstoke: Macmillan Education, 271–313.
Taal, Momodou. 2021. [Instagram] 10 April. https://archive.is/rXDIg
Taijfel, Henri. 1970. 'Experiments in intergroup discrimination.' *Scientific American* 223(5): 96–102.
Wan, Taufiq. 2019. 'Is Saudi Arabia getting Eid wrong? Meet the British Muslim on a moon mission.' *The New Arab*, 8 August. https://web.archive.org/web/20200930232336/https://english.alaraby.co.uk/english/indepth/2019/8/10/moon-wars-exposing-saudi-arabias-fake-lunar-sightings
Zahedi, Abbas. 2018. 'Studio Jum'ah.' abbzah.com, 19 January. https://web.archive.org/web/20200811040111/https://abbzah.com/2018/01/19/studiojumah

7
I Was Just Following the Trend
Art of the Oppressed or Oppressive Culture?

> 'Fair&Lovely never worked on the skin but only penetrates the minds'
> (Unknown source)

WILLIAM: Why is there no Black people in your videos?
AYAZ: I want to be relevant to my audience so I produce content relevant to what they want and what they respond to ...
WILLIAM: What is your aim, how it all started?
AYAZ: I found that hijab tutorials and pranks [allusion to popular Muslim influencers at that time] were antithetic of what I saw every day. British Muslim TV or Islam Channel are a sterilised, perfect vision of what Islam is. The only cool stuff in our minds was the Fresh Prince of Bel Air.
WILLIAM: What do you mean by 'cool'?
AYAZ: Cool is something people wish to embody or copy.
WILLIAM: So, who is your work for?
AYAZ: My narrow target audience are creativity-inclined diaspora urban crowd. I want it non-Islam-centric or Muslim-focused. I want it a convergence for different communities. We need a time and space for diversity.
WILLIAM: What's the purpose of your work, then?
AYAZ: The vlogs were for the purpose of showing the process of building the company.

In 2017, Ayaz, enjoying several dozens of thousands of followers, launched his own brand in the form of a multi-platform media where he posts 'vlogs', excerpts of his travels across the world and conversations with 'cool' Muslims. However, his launch video has upset number of my respondents. The video aimed at depicting Muslims' diversity but only showed rich, trendy, creative, slim and fashionable people doing sports, walking in front of Harrods or driving expensive cars, and only three Black people out of more than forty different personalities. Using 'our' and 'we', the video presents him as an ambassador for Muslims.

Javayria comments: 'this is not me. I am not rich or slim. These are the kind of images that made me want to kill myself when I was younger. How does that affect someone with depression and low self-esteem?' Emir bounces: 'it's all about looking good, appear happy, while they're unhappy in reality.... They are 24/7 PR.' Ayesha, working for a reputable marketing agency, which produces Christmas adverts for high street brands comments from her expertise: 'they are commodifying us, tapping in the Muslim pound. We're just exploited... I'm so frustrated because it becomes the narrative, flashy cars, success . . . "I'm flying the world, flocking people around me..." We need stories for healing with love, not this.'

However, contentions didn't stop there. Outrage happened when Ayaz decided to sell online *tasbih* (prayer beads) as a fashion accessory and when he took part in an influencer programme funded by a counter-extremism think tank. He later became an ambassador for a high-street brand which was found to manufacture their products in forced labour camps in China, and was paid £3,000 a month after tax for this partnership, while not redistributing wages fairly. Interviewed by a TV channel about his newly founded sports club, he spoke about how Muslims get health problems because they don't exercise, which sparked another burst of furore:

> He doesn't see people going to the gym? He doesn't see the growing interest in martial arts? . . . you're perpetuating the idea that Black and Brown people are lazy and don't exercise . . . you're doing the work of white people for white people, you're being their diversity donkey.

In 2023, during the Israeli offensive on Gaza, Ayaz was called a 'narcissist' and a 'grifter' for commodifying people's pain after posting a picture of himself on holiday in a luxury Marrakech riad with a caption about the plight of Palestinians. In 2020, he tried to use Black Lives Matter to advance his brand image, as related by Hassan, an ex-staff member, sharing the story along with screenshots of his WhatsApp exchanges:

> I joined [the club] ultimately because it looked cool. . . . In February this year, we all learnt of the violent racially-driven murder of Ahmaud Arbery . . . the founder messaged: . . . 'we need to do something with it' . . . Still grieving myself, I expressed the dangers of performativity and that it lacked genuine allyship to the cause. There was a complete lack of empathy shown to me as the only Black person in the team. . . . The founder stated that the death of Ahmaud Arbery should be used as a marketing opportunity for [the club] . . . He used his work with a well-known intergovernmental organisation as evidence to suggest that he had more experience than me, a Black man, in this field.

Ayaz's family and friends tried to reason with him multiple times, to no effect. Consequently, a group of six Muslims with connections to Ayaz's sponsors demanded action. Shortly after, his title of brand ambassador disappeared from his profile.

One of the challenges of the production of culture while Muslim in the Wild White West in a context of power, visibility and financial deprivation is how ethical poverty enables people to break moral boundaries and amplify global systems of oppression such as anti-Blackness for the sake of representation or rewards. A relative justifies Ayaz's choices, which echo a global feeling of deprivation (see chapter 2): 'he's been hurt by the Muslim community when [one of his videos] came out [alluding to criticisms by ultra-orthodox Muslims]. His parents are in financial difficulty and his intention was to use YouTube and these sponsorships to buy them a house' (an intention that Ayaz admitted to in one of his videos). 'I was just following the trend' becomes the new 'I was just following orders', a reference to the infamous Nuremberg defence.

This chapter presents an overview of the Muslim 'influencer' scene and testimonies from insiders, about how they've put God for sale to fit in an ecosystem of mutual consumption, how neoliberalism has hijacked Muslim's quest for liberation by turning two billion believers into two billion consumers, and how profit-seeking 'humanitarian charities' have become colonial agents. At times when social media celebrities have the power to influence millions, commodifying Muslims or Islam is seen as being as serious as religious scholars abusing their power (see chapter 4). However, 'the community doesn't want the fall of [people like] Ayaz; people want his racism and harmful behaviours to stop', says Hassan. I thus analyse these celebrities from the perspective of 'comrades in struggle' trapped in the gears of wider systems of domination. Some others use culture as a medium for disrupting the hegemonic normalized production of culture, making community and renewing a collective sense of cultural strength. The hybridations of these productions and their ethical boundaries pose the question: what is the difference, if it exists, between Muslim culture and Islamic culture?

7.1. Allah for Sale

Combined with the aspirational aesthetics of social media, the climate of deprivation gave birth to the first Muslim 'influencers' (human marketing devices), in a new neoliberal theology of liberation. Figures like Dina Tokio and Amena Khan among others were the first Muslim women to become famous online for wearing the hijab. Male figures such as Adam Saleh or Sham Idrees's business included prank videos and showing off luxurious lifestyles. Never seen working, always smiling, earning from brand deals, they belonged to a universe of fashion, cosmetics, gyms, fast cars, and luxury holidays in Dubai, which for many became the new Makkah. These figures were at first welcomed by audiences finally seeing the 'representation' that mainstream media never gave Muslims. Many respondents recalled how seeing *hijabis* (women in hijab) ascending to fame boosted their self-esteem. Although many identify as Muslim or use religious terms—'*inshaAllah*' (God willing) and '*Alhamdulillah*' (thank God)—quote the Qur'an, and vlog their pilgrimages, one can find some of them drinking, revealing their body in transparent clothing, and having multiple partners outside of marriage, while on their profile, there's often a link to their page on the adult website OnlyFans.[1] Social media users have developed increasingly effective methods to bypass censorship and advertise for sexualized labour[2] (Drenten et al. 2020), sometimes framing objectification as empowerment, and Muslims are not exempt. Some present themselves in bikinis posting advice about how to prepare for Ramadan. Others post selfies in front of the Kaaba next to portraits in lingerie. Others, like one of my respondents, would acknowledge singing *nasheeds* (acapella devotional music), although it is a style that they 'don't like', in order to 'become famous amongst a Muslim audience'; once he obtained what he felt was a satisfactory status, he would then switch to music with instruments and explicit lyrics. Since the early 2000s, researchers have pointed at how Islam has been reduced to a brand, a marketing ploy, a tool for entertainment void of any religious sentiment or meaning but the quest for profit (Boubekeur 2005; Haenni 2005; Shirazi 2016). British Muslim social media is populated by adverts for items such as halal pet food or metal bracelets with engraved verses of the Qur'an promising that the wearer will experience 'the protection of God', while brands fabricate new diseases such as 'hijabi alopecia' to sell supplements. Many online conversations echo a feeling of dissonance between the presented Muslim or Islamic self of influencers and their actions:

> 'Have you guys seen Lord Aleems [a Muslim celebrity] recent posts? Going to refugee camps, asking people for donations and the posting with diamonds Rolex on a boat? Can someone be more hypocrite?'
>
> 'Why do Asian girls in particular try and make themselves look lighter? I thought we had got past that.'
>
> 'Modest Street is using the Qur'an as a prop to promote Daniel Wellington watches... have these people got no shame?'
>
> 'I can't believe people actually comment "Masha'Allah" under the pictures of Amaira when she's standing there half naked.'
>
> 'They're basically part-time Muslims. They'll post Eid photos for likes... They probably won't eat pork but are happy to share photos of then drinking alcohol—seeing the pattern?'

They sense a conflict between their understanding of Islam and those other Muslims revealing their bodies and consuming drugs—and frustrated when they see that they are being rewarded for it—while they try to stay within moral boundaries.

Social media 'influencers' originate in a strategy shift by companies replacing expensive celebrity product placements or sponsored events with a cheaper form of advertising closer to the end customer. In the era of gig economy, social media sold the idea to users that anyone with a smartphone can become an advertising support, and to brands that the average user can influence purchase decisions. They are the digital equivalent of sandwich men, whose two cumbersome panels have been replaced by the subtler mention 'paid partnership with'. Their main currency is viewers' attention, measured in engagement rates: the more views, followers, likes, comments, shares, the more potential reach they can achieve, and therefore the more valuable. Since social media is mainly visual, users need to provide sensorial stimuli: buzzwords, colours, images, terms such as 'make money online'. 'Productivity guru' Ali Abdaal admits publicly, his business 'is about seeking attention' (Abdaal 2020). The attention economy is a supremacist endeavour, a colonial expedition into audiences' minds. Consequently, businesses adapt their décor, lighting, and food presentation to become 'instagrammable': becoming more visually stimulating for the sake of engagement rates.[3] Consequently, people too present an 'edited self':

> a set of practices and a mindset, a way of thinking about the self as a salable commodity that can tempt a potential employer. . . . a self-conscious persona . . . using tools drawn from commercial advertising . . . The edited self is an entrepreneur whose product is a neatly packaged, performed identity. (Marwick 2013, 166–7)

The neoliberal influencer paradigm commodifies, overhypes, markets, and monetizes every aspect of existence. Eating has been transformed into an aesthetic: food becomes bought for pictures; '75% goes in the trash' (Mull 2017). Someone taking part in their first panel at a conference abroad becomes an 'international expert'; a prize in a local competition makes someone them 'award winning'. The lexicon employed around influencer culture is a similar exercise: people label themselves 'content creator' instead of 'marketer', 'explorer' instead of tourist, showing off wealth is justified as 'inspiring others', 'third culture kids' instead of 'children of immigrants'. Some fabricate achievements: 'this British Pakistani has solved sogging skin!' Some parents create social media accounts for their new-borns in return for brand deals in a novel form of child exploitation. A famous Canadian Muslim vlogger admits about himself and his wife, trying to deflect people intruding their privacy: influencers are not 'real people' but commodified beings which existence is to be consumed; 'Sham Idrees and Froggy, they're brands' (Sham Idrees VLOGS 2018).

Influencers become impostors in the sense of French psychopathologist Roland Gori (2013), social chameleons using Bourdieu's *illusio* (1979), competing for desirability in a world that chooses leaders according to appearance and reputation rather than 'work and probity' or 'merit'—similar to cultural matching (see chapter 1). Gori describes impostors as opportunists, conformists or 'living sponges' absorbing rituals, opinions, values, trends, and appearances, who move through society by calibrating their behaviours, looks, and discourses so they end up 'looking like' the society. Social media thus are 'technologies that encourage people to regulate their own behavior along business ideals... teaching their users to be good corporate citizens' (Marwick 2013, 12), inviting 'a normalization of surveillance that threatens individual agency' (Marwick 2013, 277). However, not everyone is an impostor. Frenzo Harami (whose stage name translates as Frenzo the bastard), born and bred in Walthamstow, of Pakistani Punjabi descent, openly raps about his life as a heroin and cocaine dealer, going to prison eight times, being a pimp, having done every possible *haraam* (non-permissible) thing except eating pork, with lyrics sparkled with Punjabi words and Islamic references:

> I ain't prayed in a long time brudda trust me
> I remember days I was gripping on *tasbih* [prayer beads]
> Nowadays I'm on the roads looking for some *masti* [fun]
> Money went low so I went and got a *gashti* [prostitute]
>
> (Harami 2019)

He is aware that he is producing harm and 'wasting' his life (5Pillars 2020), doesn't parade as a saint, a role model, or even an ambassador of Islam, but remains an exception in the British Muslim landscape.

In her art project *Excellences and Perfections*, Amalia Ulman demonstrates that the more someone performs according to prescribed behaviours, the more engagement they will receive.[4] She created Instagram accounts of fake personalities according to various stereotypes that she would embody. The most popular personalities were those replicating the more mainstream normative narratives: social media doesn't reward original visions and novel ideas with purpose and meaning but those who write to be read and film to be watched. It values the annihilation of the authentic self.

Farrah Azam, a henna artist and designer who set up her own business, had more than 80,000 followers on her professional Instagram account at the time of our conversations. Thanks to Instagram, she managed to secure commissions by high street brands which have allowed her to survive in her North London flat, despite being a single mother of two.

> Everything is distorted on social media.... I distort my photos all the time, I slap on filters, I choose specific photos which don't have certain people in it to remember the best form of that moment.... I take pictures of my food and don't finish it, I take pictures of what I do every day... If I don't do it, I lose followers. I can lose like 100 followers a day. People keep on messaging me are you alright? Where are you?... Every time you get out of the house, you have to dress well, put

makeup... I wish I didn't have to do it... but these figures give me some credibility for people who could work with me. Everything is fake... I am also aware that the way I look gave me some opportunities for work which I wouldn't have had otherwise.

Media professional Mehreen, although not earning her main income through social media, reflects on her edited self-presentation:

We shamelessly bare our private moments (and for some, our private parts) for complete strangers to give us approval. We buy into this fake happiness, fake popularity and this fake world. What does it help us achieve? Nothing.... it's all bullshit. We all put up these photos to impress old enemies and ex boyfriends or potential new enemies and new boyfriends. None of us are happy. In fact, the more photos we upload, the unhappier we are.... My bio says I'm an actress, model, teacher, scientist, doctor and some other stuff. But I'm not even up to the detox tea level in my career yet. And I didn't go to Waitrose to buy the bread with my mum. We don't shop at Waitrose; it's too expensive.... But that goes to show, the internet can make you believe anything. (Baig 2015)

Mehreen and Farrah described social media as a tool for social engineering which aims at inducing specific feelings or to be perceived as legitimate in the eyes of potential brand partners. While they consume items, products, and food, their audiences consume their image in turn in a loop of consumption from which they can hardly break away—it would mean for Farrah losing her income. However, for their curated display on social media doesn't always serve a business purpose, as Farrah mentions in chapter 1; in a climate of deprivation and pessimism, it is because users' self-esteem is contingent on engagement rates, perceived as a measure of one's worthiness as a human being. Sometimes, luxury goods are not for showing off. I was intrigued by one person wearing designer underwear costing hundreds of pounds (which no one can see), which made him 'feel good', especially before business meetings. Brands are worn as talismans, objects which supernatural powers are supposed to attract luck in a form of superstition; brands' success depends less on their quality than on the theology people build around them, along with their places of worships (malls, Dubai, and so on), rituals, and prophets (Robinson 2013; Kasser et al. 2014; Liu and Wang 2020).

The calibrating of discourses, looks, and behaviours are not only about financial stability or visibility; they act as an armour (see chapter 4), and attempt to reclaim validity by entertaining the illusion of success. Influencers follow a *materialistic value orientation*, the belief that life is about pursuing culturally sanctioned goals of financial success, fame, power, luxury possessions, and high social status (Kasser et al. 2004, 13). However, validity is conditional on the respect of dominant norms, which means the content produced online is dictated by neoliberalism and consumer culture (Marwick 2013, 5 and 166) and whiteness (see chapter 1). Muslim men and women would use plastic surgery and injections, and display hypersexualized images of themselves in settings signalling an abundance of money (see chapters 1 and 4). Influencer culture has birthed a whole industry focused on the creation of 'fake wealth'[5] and responsible for the rise in counterfeit goods (Shepherd et al. 2023). Neoliberalism becomes pseudoliberalism, a culture where illusions matter more than actions. Many criticize influencers for being egoistical, while in reality, they are closer to mythomaniacs.

Because neoliberal culture is about competition, 'you can only be cool if you are more desirable than someone else. The logic of envy or social competition is a logic of scarcity, it reframes the world as a zero-sum game', comments Abbas Zahedi, resulting in the creation of 'ego-related lifestyles' (Beck and Beck-Gernsheim 2001, 4). Social media thus becomes another battlefield for social Darwinism where visual performance creates a hierarchy between the valid, the 'cool' ones, in the sense of Ayaz's desirability, and the others. While originally social media was a haven for Muslims to create their own spaces in an increasingly hostile environment (Kesvani 2019), it is now about escaping the white gaze by adopting white aesthetic norms and values, a hybridation in an attempt to 'adjust-to-fit' (Nilan 2017) where trends such as 'ghetto fabulous' and similar performance of individual success reproduce race and class hierarchies (Abdul Khabeer 2016)—just like Ayaz was conditioned not to feature Black people in his videos. This 'cool' is not Black Cool (Abdul Khabeer 2016), which comes from a perspective of marginality and self-determination and which is about anti-conformism rooted in Black self-love, without attaching importance to what others have to say about it. 'Black cool is an embodied form of resistance to a host of dehumanizing social norms and it offers a redemption of Blackness through the creation of separate sets of social standards' (Abdul Khabeer 2016, 142). Coolness as power and privilege is wearing Fanon's white masks in hope of liberation.

Although these edited-selves are built upon illusions, they yield power—images affect people (chapters 1, 2, and 4). Nishat, who I have been in touch with for a few years, doesn't follow the norms, has barely a few hundred followers (most known to her), posts about art and 'sunscapes', and uses her social media as a personal archive. When she changed her hijab style, someone she didn't know wrote her a private message: 'why did you remove your hijab? [sad face emoji]'. A simple change in her appearance caused someone's distress. Nishat conceded to me: 'I don't want to be harsh or cruel to someone I don't know and who may be struggling with something that is very difficult for women but I just wanted to tell her to get offline! This kind of weakness is very sad and not just a personal flaw but something the whole community really needs to address.' Celebrities (and now regular people we see online) are a proxy for existence (Ferris 2007); they bridge the gap between the harsh reality of life and an imaginary, idealized 'successful' self, and provide 'a sense of transcendence' (Rojek 2012, 185).

Social media, because of its interactive nature, allows strangers to grab power at unprecedented scale, able to build a level of trust as strong as between friends[6] with para-social interactions (Horton and Wohl 1956). When million-follower-worth Amena starts a pre-recorded video, she begins with:

> Hi Lovelies! ... I just wanted to sit and have a chat with you guys ... It was just about me having this connection with you guys and sharing things with you as you do with friends ... I've shared so much with you guys because you've let me into your lives, you've let my family, my kids, my husband, you guys have opened your hearts and your homes ...' (Amena 2020)

Her introduction conveys the illusion of proximity and two-way communication and exchange of trust. Para-social interactions create an 'illusion of intimacy between strangers' (Rojek 2012, 123), aiming at getting the audience emotionally attached to the performer. To one end of the spectrum, some women, wearing hijab or not, would caption their pictures with 'you're my favourite thought to wake up to', 'come a little closer', or 'craving you', addressed to a male audience in the aim of creating an imaginary relationship with what would be an ideal girlfriend. It is no surprise that in the wake of the fall of the ever-inaccessible celebrity scholars, people started asking influencers like Dina or Amena them for religious rulings: 'is non-waterproof polish halal?', 'Is it permissible to date before marriage?', etc.

The repetition of norms in the form of social media's wall of images materialize a world which 'boundary, fixity and surface' are produced (Butler 1993, 9): algorithms become the culture and since culture shapes human cognition (Oyserman and Lee 2008), people cannot see or imagine themselves except through the algorithm and the faces it feeds us. According to Facebook's own ex-president, features such as the 'like' button were engineered to 'exploit a vulnerability in human psychology' because it gives users 'a little dopamine hit', so they would spend as much time on the social network as possible.[7] Through their interactive interface, the consumer is consistently to believe that they are an actor, while they are only a chooser. Because no one understands how social media algorithms work, and given their power to cancel or validate certain people as per the expression 'blessed by the algorithm' (Singler 2020), the algorithm becomes God, as per Abbas Zahedi's 'Allahgorithm',[8] a metaphysical entity able to judge and sort people between those who deserve to be loved and those not (Ahmed, Sara 2014)—taking over Islam as a main defining cosmography: liberation and paradise are sought in the white supremacist neoliberal market.

7.2. Oppression Sold as Resistance

In December 2017, Nike released a sports *hijab*. Although several Muslim-women-led businesses started to produce sports *hijabs* as early as 2004,[9] Muslim consumers celebrated the move as a sign of validation and some influencers aspired at becoming Nike's 'brand ambassadors'. However, many had contentions. First, with the company only using Muslim women as a niche market in a tick-box exercise: 'stop using Muslim women as props!' 'this really isn't about "empowerment".... It's about money.... The one thing possibly more harmful than invisibility is simplistic or tokenistic representation' (Malik 2018), people commented. Second, Nike was listed as one of the companies producing items using Muslims in Chinese forced labour camps.[10] People across the UK, the US, and France[11] (including European Parliament Member Raphaël Glucksmann[12]) called for action against the sports company. 'Our representation stops at the cash registers. And fighting for inclusion in the very systems that require exploitation and even violence against our own communities is not a step forward, but a step back', writes American community organizer and fashion entrepreneur Hoda Katebi (2019). In a situation of economic deprivation (see chapter 2), the crossing of moral or ethical boundaries has become commonplace: it is fine to profit from people's death as long as there's a *halal* stamp or a Muslim on the poster.

These phenomena have been observed for decades since the advent of racial capitalism (Robinson 1983), 'the economic and social value derived from an individual's racial identity, whether by that individual, by other individuals, or by institutions' Leong (2013, 2190). Writer Aisha Hasan argues that the commodification of the *hijab* mimics neoliberal feminism, where the argument of 'free will' is used as a marketing argument for encouraging women to buy breasts implants or engage in porn and thus ironically conform to patriarchal expectations[13] as she highlights the appearance of '*hijabi* porn' as a sign of a new form of Orientalism:

> Go to any Muslim fashion website. Are the artistic shots of women in fitted dresses and loosely wrapped hijabs, elegantly (and suggestively) poised on a sofa or ledge, not the 21st century's Ingre? It is ironic that the very piece of clothing that was ordained in Islam to protect women from being sexually objectified by society has turned into a weapon with which to do just that.... I would argue that the Orientalists of today have found a way to possess Muslim women, whilst keeping her veil on. (Hasan 2017)

Islam came to free people from slavery, yet modern society has found a way to use Islam as a tool for putting back people in chains, turning the hijab 'into everything it stands against':

> [The *hijab*] represents liberation; a stand against objectification and sexualisation.... a way to free oneself from societies that tell women that their worth is determined by their appearance.... It seems as though we have now submitted to society's beauty demands that we had been resisting since the beginning of Islam. We are now following all the latest trends and styles; the only difference is that we have a scarf wrapped around our heads. (Begum 2018)

Is there a conspiracy from tech companies, influencers and the cosmetic industry to colonize the minds of Muslims in order to make them produce government- and corporate-vetted 'edited selves'? This is the theory we submitted to the public in the form of an experimental dystopic video co-created between friends titled *Muslim Fashion Sexy Make Up Tutorial Robot Influencer*.[14] With myself playing a scientist and my friend Jayde an executive for Google, we both presented our product, Huda 3.5, a robot equipped with Artificial Intelligence for Muslims to conform to governments' assimilationist wishes in the fashion of an Apple commercial. The idea was to show how materialistic values orientation dismisses environmental impacts, political agency, and solidarity (Ku and Zaroff 2014). As of 2020, the video had accumulated more than 224,000 views and was shared more than 2,400 times after being uploaded by *The Muslim Vibe*.[15] A lot of people loved it, some hated it, and conservative men misinterpreted it (they thought it was about wearing the *hijab* correctly). Amena Khan herself was furious about it. Some felt it was an attempt at policing the behaviour of Muslim women. Overall, most understood the underlying critique of consumerism and Eurocentric beauty standards, and felt the video was a catharsis, vocalizing what they had been thinking for a long time. I assume that its popularity lies in its ambiguity: the familiarity of its content, and its subversion of symbols (Muslim influencers), explored from a not-so-absurd perspective made it relatable on the one hand, but disturbing on the other. Because, ultimately, Muslim celebrities are divisive symbols.

However, influencers still have agency. In the era of metacolonialism, the margins can also appropriate other cultures for commercial purposes. Lina Bhatti criticizes two famous content creators, Subhi Taha and Nadir Nahdi of *Self-Orientalism* (Bhatti 2020), making appear as rare, endangered and therefore desirable a vest which is still available in Pakistan, sourcing their products in China and Nahdi for being sponsored by Nike while the brand disregards the plea of the Uyghurs: 'being Muslim does not equate to one being able to partake in the culture of any Muslim in the world—being a victim of orientalism does not allow you to steal from other victims of orientalism'.

The 2010s saw a cultural revival sweeping British South Asians and specifically British Muslims. Diaspora-focused zines mushroomed such as Burnt Roti (South Asian women-focused) or the Khidr Collective (Muslim-focused). People in their early twenties would attend *Qawwali* (South Asian devotional music) events in London, and the open-mic scene was booming with spoken word artists and poets (such as the critically acclaimed Warsan Shire or Saraiya Bah) writing about their longing for a romanticized version of their ancestral homelands (see chapter 1):

> Somewhere, in that direction, East, there is a missing piece of me. It doesn't have eyes or ears or flesh or blood. It has only memories of a life that never played out, a version of me that never became. (Yalina Q 2018)

However, many criticized influencers for heavily using plural pronouns like 'we' and 'our', assuming positions of ambassadors or spokespersons for the diaspora, blurring the boundaries of 'individual' and 'collective trauma', leading to the 'exploitation and commodification of those who experience said trauma' (Giovanni 2017). Javayria, in a conversation about Rupi Kaur, comments:

> Let's give Rupi Kaur a fucking goat and put her in a village in Punjab and let's see if she misses the 'motherland'. I understand when my mother says she misses the grass, the village and sleeping on the roof under the stars when it was too hot, but when someone from my generation who's never been to India or Pakistan says they miss India or they miss Pakistan, it doesn't make sense. When the packaging my pain is used to inflate their ego, their quest for liberation is a process of domination.

Since celebrity gives de facto the power of having a platform, it gives at the same time the power of eclipsing others. Shazia comments on the sudden rise to fame of a Muslim poet:

> She's falling into that trap becoming a brand, doing a book tour, being at every single event, doing panel discussions. She's taking up space of Black and Brown women in East London who've been doing the work for more than 40 years, doing youth work, fighting air pollution, building of high rise, fighting the council, fighting austerity. She's Oxbridge educated, she's middle class, she talks with long words.

In some extreme cases, the commodification of pain has been translated in 'safe spaces dinners' or 'anti-racist supper clubs' inviting ethnically minoritized people to attend a 'masterclass' for a budget way above a normal restaurant dinner: 'Omg its £225!! They've made anti-racism a money-making venture!! I've never seen anything like this before', 'from the images its very lavish and the way it's being pushed its like fine dining experience but with BAME people there who make you feel "woke"'.

Cultural appropriation is about how culture can be used to assert power (Lena 2019); as Lewis and Hamid observe about Nadir Nahdi, it is still about performing an image of Muslimness palatable to the white gaze which stems from a sense of insecurity (Lewis and Hamid 2018, 192–3). Social media professionals have the luxury of being able to choose what and how to feel, and how to present emotions: they are flexible Muslims with many identities to choose from, but at the same time none. Voluntary homeless with a house, nomads with a bank account. Heirs of multiple cultures but at the same time disconnected from their roots, faith, past, future, nature, and being. Distinct from the crowd but at the same time obeying the crowds. Modernity has created malleable ghosts and empty shells.

Reacting to various social media professionals, people comment: 'kinda tired of privileged western raised Brown girls participating in the same level of exoticism that white people do with India'. 'Ya can't just brush off casteism, colorism, and "other-ness" because you're from the same race of people.' 'It has robbed people of dignity and privacy so why are brown artists replicating this shit and exploiting their own people.' 'Can we please have this social media guide to taking ethical pictures abroad already! "Art" like this has fetishized people in the past.' In a dig to mainly South Asian perpetrators, the comment about Fair&Lovely at the beginning of this chapter caricatures similar behaviours through an allusion to the popular skin-whitening cream Fair&Lovely, which for decades has been used by South Asian parents willing to whiten their children's skin. The cream is notoriously ineffective, and the author suggests that, alluding to those who joined the ranks of the empire, perhaps the cream was never designed for the skin but rather for the mind. In an attempt to showcase or appreciate the culture of their 'homelands', social media professionals fall into the same pitfalls as long-ago missionaries and colonial officers, taking pictures of themselves amongst groups of villagers or children abroad, a trend that has spread to another multi-million-pound industry heavily relying on influencer marketing (sometimes paying them more than luxury brands), the Muslim charity sector.

7.3. Colonial Charities

> The photos of them holding up Black babies on social media gave me serious white saviour complex vibes. They rarely seem to liaise with Gambians on their projects and taking advantage of their position is truly perverted.... The fetishisation of Black bodies and in this instance of kids is truly sickening. And the lack of widespread condemnation from the wider muslim 'community' speaks volumes. Gambia is 96% Muslim. To think other Muslims will take advantage when they position themselves as aid workers is beyond sickening.

These comments of Momodou Taal, a rising scholar of Gambian roots, followed the shutting down in 2020 of the British charity Penny Appeal in Gambia, following the local government's inquiry which found that the organization was operating illegally and let a case child sexual abuse to happen in their orphanages.[16] These events happened a few weeks after the worldwide Black Lives Matter protests. However, it was just the tip of the iceberg, the last in a series of many red flags. Many who volunteered with them in the Gambia raised the alarm, in vain.

> The language they use is very colonial. You see Muslims but there's nothing about Islam. When you're a charity it's important to think about budget, but these were just like companies, like white Christian missionaries. Lots are about becoming

rich, powerful. They are becoming the *shouyoukhs* [religious authorities] of our time, but there's no one to teach them.

My curiosity was sparked in the early 2010s having freshly left France, where, in my fieldwork, most charity volunteers were working pro bono (*fi sabilillah*). When I arrived in the UK, I was surprised by a very different culture. Ömer, in charge of a small community hub in London, explained to me: 'in Turkey, people have jobs and get involved in charitable activities for free. Here people go to charities for adding lines on their CV'. On social media, a celebrity strikes suggestive poses in front of an aid convoy for Gaza for promoting a specific charity. One user asks: 'are you paid for this?' The celebrity replies: 'I'm not an influencer, I'm a business woman'. Habib, once managing a small venue in London, recalls his interaction with a famous scholar visiting from the US, and later a large charity:

[A celebrity scholar] wanted to do a talk . . . but they asked us £1,000. I said we don't have £1,000, so he said 'make entry tickets for £20 and if we get 50 people it makes 1,000', but I declined because [the local area] is an area with support families who can't afford such things. . . . Then, these [Muslim TV station] came. . . . They're too much into this thing: If you pay, you will have a house in Paradise, etc . . . I didn't like it. But they went further. And they turned [the community centre] into something that produces content for [the TV station].

Another volunteer in charge of soup kitchens relate her experience: '[a charity] wanted to fund the kitchen. I said "ok". When they came, they put orange T-shirts while we don't put uniforms—we don't want any difference between us and the guests. They started to take pictures with the homeless, I felt very upset'. As my interviews went, comments from staff, volunteers, donors, and beneficiaries became more alarming:

The 'last straw' for me is the way so many emotionally manipulate you to donate, including the public displays of donation. People getting hounded, harassed, even abused and bullied in public to make donations. . . . All the Arabic spiritual words and slogans, just lip service.

Farrah, the famous henna artist, observes the dissonance between the 'Islamic' face of charities and their internal strategies when approached to be a fundraising speaker:

Once, this guy put me in touch with this lady, . . . she told me I could get the most luxurious hotel in Mayfair, organise it as I want, there's no budget limit, and of course I will get a cut of the amount raised. . . . They all have mistresses, they're all cheating on their wife. The head of this charity drives a Porsche. You look at Edhi

[Pakistani charitable figure who lived in poverty], and his wife dressed with rags. Charity should be all about humility. What are you doing you're supposed to be Muslim! You're literally selling your soul.

Shazia, a long-time volunteer, expands on her personal experiences of patriarchy at play:

Charities offer you jobs if you're the loudest, you don't have to have the skills. It's all about ego. A friend of mine was unemployed for a long time, and he got offered a job by one of these charities, because he's got this vibe of confident imposing man.... Is it normal when I see a poster for a religious event with faces of scholars, the first thing I think is 'I know what you've done'?

Adam, a famous British chaplain, relates his personal experience:

Over the years, staff from a charity ... have approached me and tried to buy me out with offers like: 'Whatever you earn now, we'll double it.' 'You can choose your own job title, description and salary.' Each time, I refused ... It was clear that they wanted to use my face and my reputation to distract from many of the terrible things that were going on behind the scenes. (Kelwick 2020)

I have encountered similar experiences too when a charity director offered to pay all of my expenses for a trek in the Himalayas (more than £3,000) from donations. I declined, mentioning this money could be better used for actual charity work.

Raising hundreds of millions of pounds yearly, the Muslim 'humanitarian' 'not-for-profit' charity sector has become an industry ruled by neoliberal ideas and using Islam as an excuse for racing for profit (Barylo 2016), birthing 'charity magnates': people who have become rich by running charities. Mainstream and Muslim media are rife with stories of financial concerns, misconduct and irregularities, harassment, suspension of directors, conflicts of interest, obscene sums spent on 'consultants', donor money used in vanity projects, competition, threats, aggressive fundraising tactics, and public relations firms hired to shut down negative reports.[17] More than individual influencers, they enjoy financial and social resources comparable to multi-national businesses. However, unlike sole individuals, they explicitly market themselves as 'Muslim' or 'Islamic', giving them an aura of legitimacy. They are examples of metacolonial culture gone into overdrive. Some would use the cover of Islam to steal the *zakat* (alms tax) money of thousands of people, as in the case of Mohammed Hasnath and Ruksana Ali (Charity Commission 2020).

Amongst my respondents' parents, charity had a different meaning. People would give directly to poor people in the UK or in the villages abroad through relatives. In my previous publications (Barylo 2016, 2017), I trace the roots of this phenomena to US Christian megachurches and voluntourism culture, copied and pasted in desperate hope to make it. In defence of the absurd amounts spent on marketing, influencers, and selfies abroad, many invoke the ethical poverty dilemma: 'but how do we get recognition?' 'How do we get funding?' 'How do we get people to donate?' 'How do we pay the bills?'—as if growing bigger was the only possible answer; however, many viable alternatives exist (Barylo 2016, 2017). Organizations trying to win by being popular, paradoxically exhibiting profound deficiencies in leadership, self-knowledge, and human potential: they are fit for attracting people but not so much for inducing change or even recognizing their members' talent, skills, and knowledge (Riesman et al. 1950). Effectively, they end up being Muslims replicating the same fetishization, commodification, and exploitation of Islamicate lands and people as colonial officers and missionaries in the nineteenth century—in a presentation at Zaytuna College,[18] I compared side by side twenty-first-century charity selfies and nineteenth-century pictures of officers posing with 'natives', showing striking resemblances. Azadeh, a prominent voice in the charity sector and a pillar amongst grass roots, raises her voice on this harmful culture:

> Let's stop following colonialistic examples of charity and corporations. Lets stop taking selfies with poor people and thinking we are saving them (in our 1 week travels). They need long term, committed sustainable solutions and not hand outs.... Why is our *qiblah* [direction of the prayer] faced towards western economic ideals of "happiness." Modest fashion wear designer labels that fuels probably Muslim loathing corporations, selfie culture, materialism...

Like Azadeh, other prominent voices urge charities at being more accountable with 'the *amanah* [trust] they have of OUR MONEY' (Younas 2020), where Shahzad Younas, CEO of Muzz (formerly Muzmatch) and some organizations like the National Zakat Foundation (NZF) focus on using zakat money for local Muslims living in precarious conditions. A community regulator exists, the Muslim Charities Forum (MCF), which has published a guide, *Ethical Considerations for Muslim Charities*,[19] including guidance on marketing materials, competition, transparency, fundraising, and other ethical issues such as the use of beneficiaries' pictures for advertising purposes. But what is the power of a grass-roots initiative like the MCF which doesn't have access to millions in funding? History shows that more often than not, empires do not fall because of external pressures, but cracks form on the inside.

7.4. Twilight of the Idols

In June 2020, the 1-million-follower-worth Amena Khan surprised her fans by removing her *hijab*, two years after the equally famous Dina Tokio did the same.

The overwhelming majority of negative comments focused on the supposed hypocritical nature of the move, motivated by business priorities and the performative nature of online 'influencing': 'I made my money now bye', 'they make it on these platforms to make a living', 'they wear it to make business deals', 'she's modelling, she's acting'. However, the event came after a long series of disillusions with Muslim social media celebrities. The first scandals arose when Amena ended her contract with l'Oreal because of her tweets in support of Palestine, swiftly removed, which triggered a wave of criticism:

> You sold yourself to L'Oréal and also simultaneously turned your back on your genuine supporters after retracting your tweets. Her apology was towards L'Oréal and she alienated her own community. . . . She deserves the backlash she got because if she can't stand up for her own community she should not be hired and isn't fit to represent that community. (Anonymous)

Dina Tokio provoked outrage when comparing the '*hijabi* community' to a 'toxic cult', using language similar to Islamophobic rhetoric.

> This lady thought it acceptable to say the *hijabi* community is like a 'toxic cult'. You don't do this at a time that tens of thousands of the far-right are on the street calling Islam a cult . . . It is appalling to hide behind the privilege you've now been afforded of using the individualistic, secular, selfish, consumerist concept of 'my right to be me and chose'—seeped in [white western] feminist ideals that too often demonise alternative feminist critiques of what you are doing. (Moballeghi 2018)

By removing their *hijabs*, antagonizing the community that made them famous and remaining politically silent, Dina Tokio and Amena Khan broke the unspoken social contract of para-social interactions: for many Muslim women, they were not relatable any more. The era of all-powerful '*hijabi* influencers' was over. Influencers' content evolves and adapts, and audiences shifted their attention to the 'next big thing'. As of 2020, it was Muslim doctors. Not doctors of social sciences (the wrong kind of doctor, remember?). In 2024, it is *hijabis* at the gym. Although some like Ali Abdaal talk about preparing for medical exams in his videos, there's always a consumerist hook: it's always doctors and lifestyle, doctors and fashion, doctors and modelling, doctors and travels, tech reviews, productivity, etc.

For insiders, with time comes fatigue from evolving in a precarious and harmful scene. I spoke to the personal manager of a famous British female influencer who has around 500,000 followers: 'there is so much backstabbing in the modest fashion industry. I saw franchises being stolen. Where is Islam?' Farrah relates: 'I went to events with some of these famous influencers, it's very utilitarian. They're not interested in you except when they can use you. I once did a collaboration with [a famous influencer], her post was with no effort, just tagging me, not saying thank you. I didn't even get one follower.' Sara, a fashion designer and entrepreneur who has bathed in the world of influencers, has similar comments: 'they lie, cheat, ignorant wanting followers and no ethics or morals. They don't want to work hard but find the easiest way to get what they want, as a result, they are willing to lie to their followers/customers. It's all about fame, status, power and money... . For girls, look is number one. People are taught that way.' These experiences led my respondents to distance themselves, change industries, switch to conventional jobs, or take a step back because of the extra labour.

The fast pace of changing market trends and audiences' expectations lead social media professionals to mental health issues and burn out. 'Fake it until you make it' culture has been demonstrated to have negative psychological effects (Lisjak et al. 2015; Bahl and Ouimet 2022). British Muslim celebrity NabiilaBee concedes that her struggles with her appearances stemmed from comparisons with other people on the platform:

> If I keep on looking the Instagram models, you feel really insecure not wearing makeup or even less makeup on social media. . . . I have been suffering with acne for almost ten years . . . I hated my nose so much, my nose is so big . . . I struggle with this so much, I'm like I have to put eyelashes on because I don't look Instagram ready . . . All the Youtubers they are like I have to be a Instawhore. (Nabiilabee 2017)

In 2018, *the Guardian* published insights from British influencers talking about their burnout where many conceded feeling 'depressed', 'stressed', 'lonely', and 'exhausted':[20] the frequency of content creation and interaction with fans, the anxiety, information overload, lack of time, abuse, and the emotional labour (Marwick 2013) (forcing a behaviour for a desired emotional affect) can lead to PTSD—while the industry doesn't have any unions, and there is no paid overtime and no job security. Those following materialistic values experience more frustration, dissatisfaction, stress, anxiety, anger, and compulsive behaviour, and are overall more dissatisfied (Kasser et al. 2014). As I have observed, the cost of 'success' in a neoliberal world is the devaluation of the non-numerable such as emotions and well-being. Success is driving an expensive car but arguing with your partner, then mending things thanks to a Louis Vuitton bag. Consumerism becomes a love language where peace is bought instead of built. Love becomes in the collective psyche a consumable and conflict resolution a household expense. Influencers voluntary submit themselves to a kind of modern 'serfdom' (Rojek 2012, 185). They can also be cursed by 'fame attack', the psychopathologies associated with sudden celebrity (Rojek 2012): bipolarity, borderline, and narcissistic personality disorders, sense of entitlement, delusions of success and sense of importance, paranoia, ruthless self-interest and lack of empathy, readiness to exploit others by manipulation and bullying, and, in some cases, the Icarus complex (Rojek 2012, 142), when over-ambition and tunnel effect lead to their own downfall.

Brands are switching strategies too. Poor engagement rates of multi-million-follower influencers led brands to focus on micro- or nano-influencers (those with fewer than 5,000 followers).[21] In a world of illusion, brands have realized that influencers can easily buy followers, likes and even customized comments to fake engagement—it is estimated that more than 65% of social media users fraudulently inflate their engagement rates.[22] Modern money-for-likes websites keeping up with Instagram's algorithms keep the process relatively untraceable, despite the existence of audience-analysis tools such as Hype Auditor. Smaller influencers would fake brand deals, posting a picture of a product they have paid with their own money—or borrowed—and advertising it as a 'paid partnership'. All of these have led towards the early 2020s being a time for a 'devaluation of the influencer':[23] brands have increased background checks and deals have become harder to secure for those who cannot prove organic engagement. With the rise of AI, faking anything from holidays to material possessions has become easier; however, will people lose interest in influencers? Will real-life achievements become more important? Only the future will tell.

In 2020, in coincidence with the pandemic, some community figures emerged to warn aspiring influencers about the social and mental health damages that can experience both audiences and Muslim celebrities.[24] Omar Shahid, founder of the Muslim Influencer Network, in what seemed like a complete U-turn, posed publicly on his Facebook feed a piece titled: 'DO NOT BECOME AN INFLUENCER':

> I've seen first-hand how the pursuit of popularity can destroy lives, literally.... I've seen how this can screw with the heads of married men who don't quite understand how to handle all the female attention. I've witnessed people I've worked with or have been following deteriorate, have break downs, and suffer deep mental health issues as a result of their popularity. This week news emerged of a 16-year-old social media star in India who killed herself, allegedly due to non-stop hate and abuse. (DaCosta-Shahid 2020)

Influencers, however, do change. In 2020, model Halima Aden decides to abandon fashion as a career, realizing all the boundaries she had broken:

> I was just so desperate back then for any 'representation' that I lost touch with who I was ... the minute I got comfortable ... well let's just say I got too carried away ... I remember wanting to be the 'hot *hijabi*' as if that didn't just defeat the whole purpose. A hot mess is what it was truthfully ... Looking back now I did what I said I would never do. Which is to compromise who I am in order to fit in.[25]

Are influencers solely responsible? Would they hold power if there was no ecosystem for them to thrive? Nargess Moballeghi questions collective responsibility:

> Perhaps the biggest lesson of all, is the critique of celebrity and the creation of idols... It is ultimately all of us that buy in to it, give it worth and give it fuel. We create the exaggerated worth of an individual who shouldn't have that influence. (Moballeghi 2018)

In a scarcity mindset, people associate 'scaling down' or 'ethical choices' with risk and failure. However, a few initiatives show that decolonizing cultural production in the way of justice doesn't mean self-sabotage; it is about putting intentionality and meaning at the forefront in a new ecosystem of support which merges social, spiritual dimensions, and more.

7.5. Muslim Culture or Islamic Culture?

Abbas Zahedi's healing journey is an experimental process through conceptual art, shaped by his subjective interpretation of his roots, his own family, his travels to Iran, his upbringing in West London, and mourning. From the disconnection from his parents' ancestral land, to the loss of his parents, his grandmother, his own brother, his friend Khadija Saye, Abbas interweaves his journey of survival with the chants mourning the martyrdom of Imam Hussain, a core part of the tradition of those following the *Ahlul Bayt*, the family of the Prophet. He acknowledges the disconnection between children of the various diasporas in the UK and their roots: 'after years of organising around the theme of identity, I realised that I have spent 99% of my life living in the UK ... so that begs the question—am I "self-appropriating" my own imaginary culture?'

His art installation for his graduation show at Central Saint Martins, titled *Dwelling: In This Space We Grieve* (Zahedi 2019) features a transparent fridge, lit with green lights from the inside, continuously playing *latmiya*, lamentations chanted on Ashura, mourning the murder of imam Hussain and his family. As a coincidence, the colour green, identifying Hussain's supporters at Karbala, is also the colour representing the plight of those who were killed in the Grenfell catastrophe. Abbas was standing in front of the tower when he lost her friend and mentor Khadija Saye in the fire, only a few days after both exhibited their work at the Venice Biennale. Abbas's installation was dedicated to her.

> It may not be clear why I have chosen to install an empty bottle fridge, filled with the sounds of grief... The premise of this work is to offer a libation, within a space where the serving and spilling of drinks is forbidden. For I am mourning the death of my neighbour, friend and colleague Khadija Saye; because I cannot be

in this space without thinking of her. She was the one who brought me here two years ago, to see a previous version of this degree show and made me promise that I would join her as a prospective student; so that we could both graduate together in the summer of 2019. Yet I stand here alone today, because a few weeks after that fateful encounter, Khadija was killed in the fire of Grenfell Tower. A blaze that was apparently caused by the faultiness of an immigrant's fridge. (Zahedi 2019)

Abbas doesn't assume the role of ambassador or spokesperson for Muslims, Islam or Ladbroke Grove, doesn't define his work as 'Muslim' or 'Islamic', doesn't perform for a particular audience or expect to produce a specific impact. His art is a commentary, an experimentation, an archive, the visualization of the multiple subjective universes and ecosystems he has lived in, in a combination of loss, liquids and lemons; a spiritual and cognitive contract (see chapter 5) between the absent and the present, both of which cannot exist without the other (see chapter 4). When I discuss secular art spaces and influencer culture, he argues that 'there can be no art if the illusions are not broken; art comes from a place of sensitivity'.

> I'm a singer who happens to be a Muslim, I'm a Muslim who happens to be a singer, I don't really see what is Islamic and what is not Islamic music ... All of it is God given, so I don't see what of it is not Islamic. What is 'Islamic Music'? What is a Muslim Artist? Shouldn't all music performed by Muslims essentially be Islamic? Or does Islamic Music only consist of traditional *nasheeds* and poetry?

Fatiha is a singer and guitarist familiar with Rumi's Cave, a community hub in North West London (see chapter 8). She sings about love and her personal struggles in a fashion inspired by Lauryn Hill. While she argues that the intersection of the labels 'Muslim' and 'singer' are coincidental, she argues that whatever she produces is Islamic. Hamza, a traditional multi-disciplinary artist from Morocco, specializing in book binding, leather works, wood carving, and brass works, comments: 'art is secular, Moroccan art doesn't have any sacred components as seen by Western orientalists. The "breath of the compassionate" [a geometric motif] is a term made up by orientalists. The term has no grounding in Moroccan or Islamic traditions.' If art is not Islamic in itself, what makes it sacred? Intention? Purpose? Positioning? How viewers want to see it? Or a bit of everything?

'Islamic' art was a label reserved for traditional crafts emanating from Islamicate countries such as geometric patterns, calligraphy, or *nasheed* (acapella devotional songs). Conservative opinions would make music unlawful (see chapter 1) and forbid the representation of living beings. Contemporary opinions would give the green light to forms of art which, even if not devotional, inspire the audience to aspire to do good and remember the divine.

Because of these different opinions, Muslim artists face barriers. Josue, from France, has been exhibited in renowned art galleries, but concedes: 'I would leave [France] to anywhere [else in the world]. People don't get my work. . . . Your work is not important. You can't find places [in white-dominated art spaces] where to connect with like-minded people. And for Muslims, you still can't be a Muslim artist who does representation of living beings.' Nuria, another of my respondents, relates how her friend changed after arts school: 'a convert friend of mine, a talented artist who went to art school, is now doing sculptures with poop. I asked her: "what have you become? Your previous art was much deeper. It's like you've been colonised!"' Another of my respondent recalls the reason why she gave up arts: 'I wanted to do arts school at Goldsmiths, but I couldn't take it further, you have to do nudity, etc...'. However, throughout history, art performed by Muslims did not necessarily follow the various jurisprudences and schools of thoughts; art has always been the mirror for the artists' persona, their time, space and social, economic, or political context.

Su'ad Abdul Khabeer (2016) paints the ecosystem of hip hop as a performance of *khilafa* (see chapter 5) through its dimensions of healing, education, and self-determination. She locates the artistic practice of hip hop 'in a history of Muslim artistic production as the work of liberation—art as activism' (Abdul Khabeer 2016, 183). At times when the dominant society tells people 'seek halal products but ignore the plea of the poor and the vulnerable', hip hop is an 'extension of the proper Islamic tradition: 'Hip Hop is Islam and Islam is Hip Hop' (Abdul Khabeer 2016, 48).

The 2010s have seen the emergence of Muslim arts collectives such as The Cave Collective (music, spoken words, storytelling, and poetry specifically), Oomk and Khidr Collective (poetry, writing, and illustrations). While in France the collective Umm'Artists has been short-lived, the US has seen collectives taking deep roots, such as the IMAN network (Chicago and Atlanta), Performing Arts Mosaic (New York), Muslim Writers Collective, or the GAMA (Gathering All Muslim Artists) collective (Oakland, CA). GAMA's activities include open mics, social evenings, grant writing workshops, and discussions around 'art for social change' or titled 'What does liberation look like?'. Is GAMA more or less Muslim than politically apathetic influencers? I argue that the debate Muslim art versus Islamic art is a question built on flawed premises.

I posit that Islam, as a sociological phenomenon, is an ecosystem made of various, different and sometimes divergent opinions, beliefs, and praxis (see introduction). It is thus difficult to assess an objective and normative 'proximity' or 'distance' to Islam. With phenomenology, labels cannot be imposed; it is for people to define themselves subjectively: if Frenzo Harami considers himself Muslim, I will identify him as such—although he doesn't represent all Muslims or Islam. What matters here is the way these initiatives are received by their audiences, and the mission they confer upon themselves, which places them on a spectrum of positionality towards dominant powers: what is their relation to white supremacy? Neoliberalism? Patriarchy? Do they work from the perspective of prosperity, power, and domination? Or the perspective of support, healing, and nurturing? What moral compass do they follow?

The ways my respondents enjoy, produce, and perform arts are guided by ethical and spiritual considerations. Salahuddin collect clothes from his travels as memories of the connections he established with people and the land. Of mixed Pakistani and Syrian heritage, he would wear at times an Uzbek Chapan or a Malaysian Songkok for formal occasions. He expands on the intentions behind his blog 'Adventures in Fashionistan':

> Fashion is part of the journey, not the purpose.... Fashion is a platform to discuss deeper things. We have to be people of meaning, kick-start conversations about identity. Those fashion vloggers have a responsibility. They need to avoid falling in the trap of the capitalist modern monster that lives on the lives of other people who labour in sweatshops.

Maaida Noor is a calligrapher, painter, and illumination specialist. She posts mainly pictures of her work around which her social media platform is centred. She opposes the idea of teaching calligraphy online for money:

> I don't want to commercialise it and make money out of it. Although yes I can, I prefer not to just because aesthetic and ethical reasons. I'm doing Arabic Calligraphy so I can learn and help others.... you need that personal relationship and also that connection, that bond with your teacher. It has to be live, you have to be there, it has to be face to face, it cannot be online.

Farah Soobhan specializes in Islamic pop art. She merges Islamicate symbols, Arabic, English writings, and bright colours as a commentary on current affairs or an expression of her connection with the divine. Her works don't display faces, to be in accordance with rulings regarding the representation of living beings.

> I draw no faces to make it more accessible for the Ummah.... Most people at the Living Islam festival said about my work it's nice but ended buying some calligraphy. Only the younger ones like 15 years old were fascinated by my work. My art is bright and loud, people say Islam should be classy and respectful. I'm away from being a commercial artist, I want to change people's thinking, get people talking, it's a kind of da'wa. To be creative is to be the way you are, for me it was not calligraphy, it is being true to yourself.

Sakinah, Rabiah's sister and half of the duo Pearls of Islam, evokes the importance of her connection to drumming, specifically during the 2020 pandemic:

> Creative expression is so essential when it comes to healing and to be involved in an artistic expression which is strongly rooted in my ancestry just humbles me. The beat of the drum and the sound of the song ran through the blood and

DNA of my mother, my grandmother, my great grandmother. As women, as Black women, as Muslim women the drum and song is our history. Don't let anyone else tell you otherwise. (Le Noir 2020)

Maaida, Sakinah, Farah, and Salahuddin all use art as a medium for a dialogue with audiences, with God, with their lineage or their craft itself—as if the art was an interlocutor. Since my first interview with Farah in 2017, her journey in various Muslim and mainstream arts spaces has profoundly shaped her discourse and refined her aim. Invited to the Women of Colour Reading Group at the South London Gallery in 2019, she expands:

> My art work is a major form of activism for me, it's a visual representation of my fight against stagnation of the Muslim arts scene, against misogyny in the Muslim community and in the mainstream as well. . . . I find it ironic and interesting to merge an art movement founded by the privileged of the West based primarily on consumerism and capitalism with one of the most ancient religions . . . I want my work to be more than just decorative; I take it upon myself to challenge the mentality of the Muslim community as well as the main western ideology.

Machine-learning tools such as Midjourney have enabled Muslims without skills in graphics design to depict futuristic mosques and hijab styles, creating their own dreamscapes. However, artists do not always stick with Islamicate symbolism. Salahuddin sometimes wear Eurocentric clothes, with an Islamicate tweak—there would often be a *tasbih* (chaplet) hanging from somewhere. Dawuud Loka, a full-time clothes designer, offers through his brand, Meezant LMT, streetwear with a symbolic aesthetic built upon layers of meaning inspired from Eurocentric and Eastern philosophy, current affairs and more, which he describes at length in his blog posts. Of Congolese descent, he evokes his inspiration by the Congolese lineage of *Sape*, a fashion movement. They echo 'Black dandyism' which, despite the use of Edwardian and Victorian clothing, is a form of subversive mimicry used to 'disarm Whiteness through the use of its own signs' (Su'ad Abdul Khabeer 2016, 143).

In his video essay, Sikh artist Narvir Singh, invited to Rumi's Cave for a discussion with other Sikh and Muslim creatives, reflects on the meaning of 'Sikh art': is it art produced by Sikhs, or art in line with the teachings of the Sikh gurus?[26] As a mirror to the debate between Muslim art and Islamic art, attendees, whether Muslim or Sikh, agree that only when used in the divine way, the way of justice and beauty, does art take a sacred dimension, when it takes audiences on an introspective journey, or as a way to care for the most vulnerable in society. Fais Hussain uses arts as a form of contestation, summarizing volumes of research and decades of lived experiences in the shape of a cupcake as a metaphor for the PREVENT strategy: 'Prevent Cakes are a seemingly generous offer (. . .)

but whose presentation disguises an inedible acrid taste.'[27] Poet Nouri Sardar[28] would write: 'Hussain never died': there will be no silence as long as the oppressed shed tears. On YouTube, Zeeshan Ali creates on his channel, Smile 2 Jannah,[29] entertaining videos as a vehicle to equip young Muslims with nuance, critical thinking, and a few psychological and sociological concepts for them to read through the complexity of contemporary debates. The collective Muslim Sisterhood[30] purposely features pictures of Muslim 'women who are not fashionistas, bloggers or stereotype breakers', posing in corner shops or chicken shops. Hamja Ahsan, a multi-talented artist having exhibited at some of the most prestigious art festivals in the world (including Documenta), wrote *Shy Radicals* (Ahsan 2017) a fictional manifesto for introvert people in a quest of a land, Aspergistan, where they could live in peace. Their initiative, featuring pictures that mirror real life, is an ode to self-love but far away from self-aggrandizement. Alaa Alsaraji's exhibition, Mapping Sanctuaries,[31] illustrates 'the sanctuaries that have been created for and by Muslim communities, in light of the profound effects of state surveillance, Islamophobia and racism in Britain'. The exhibition includes Rumi's Cave, formal places of worship like the East London Mosque or improvised ones such as local import shops or family kitchen tables. She defines 'sanctuary' as a place where one can 'feel safe to exist fully ... without having to explain or defend [oneself]'.

However, staying faithful to one's ethics as a creative freelancer is a difficult journey. The same goes for conveying complex messages to audiences avid for entertainment, leading creatives to either dilute or abandon their message and obey the crowd's desires. YouTuber Mohammed Hijab, having risen to fame amongst younger audiences thirsty for antagonistic religious debates, has explored Ngũgĩ wa Thiong'o's concept of colonization of the mind in his drama *Burning Hands*. However, he is more an exception than the norm; the success of his film wouldn't have been possible without the million followers he gathered over the course of a decade. For those amongst my respondents who have no access to resources or a large following, they use spiritual narratives to retain hope. Farrah, the henna artist, was once offered a deal worth thousands of pounds from a company selling alcohol. Despite being a single mother raising two kids, she declined, remaining faithful to her beliefs. It was a hard decision but ultimately rewarded: a few days later, another deal came, from a different company, in line with her ethics, and even more profitable. In our conversations, she says how she found in *tawwakul* (trust in God's plan), the strength to say 'no'. Dawuud interpret hardships as safety barriers preventing him from diverting from the path of righteousness:

> I remind myself that we are not alone [God is with us]. . . . When I'm feeling down, I look at the greater picture, the greater purpose, the long term. Hardship

is temporary, there will always be times with ease.... There is a verse about hardships: 'if I would have given you your sustenance at once, you would have gone astray'.

Similarly, struggling with the lack of recognition and support, Rabiah and Sakinah would say that 'maybe it's a blessing we didn't have all these things', after observing how money and power corrupted other public figures. IMAN argues that arts, activism and spiritually are indissociable:

> [A]rt becomes a creative endeavour and a vehicle for 'powerfully, radically reimagining the world'.... This spiritual identity is one that invokes the Prophetic model that mobilised the marginalised and oppressed in a social justice movement.... IMAN members are engaged in creative selfmaking and placemaking; [they] and cultivate the arts not for entertainment but to inspire people to radically reimagine the world through social justice work. (Ali 2017, 368)

IMAN echoes Abbas Zahedi's intent: 'it's not about creating songs or pictures; we are creating worlds'. Art helps imagining alternative universes where Muslims are not oppressed and be whoever they want to be. It is an exercise in re-building selfworth. Artists allow others to stay alive: some respondents related how the Pearls' music 'prevented [them] from committing suicide'. Javayria, in a conversation with friends, comments on what gives her hope when Instagram makes her feel depressed:

> Metacolonisation has won if you cannot imagine a happy future. What gives me hope is that for every Nadir [Nahdi], there is a Rabiah Mali. Can any Instagrammer or any YouTube video make people feel the way Rabiah makes people feel? This is heart work. We listened to some recitation in Bengali. We only understood one word: Muhammad, but people were crying. How can we explain that?

Beyond labels and belief, perhaps sacred art is what encourages human dignity and flourishing, as in nurturing spaces in the next chapter.

Notes

1. Adam Cailler, 'I make adult content in my hijab—I'm fuming after 300 photos of me were removed', *Daily Star*, 21 May 2023. https://archive.is/VF19w
2. 'The rise of Instagram prostitution', *Evie*, 9 February 2019. https://web.archive.org/web/20190615073643/https://www.eviemagazine.com/post/the-rise-of-instagram-prostitution; J.S. von Dacre. 'Instagram's prostitution secret', *Inside Over*, 1 August 2019. https://web.archive.org/web/20200919180805/https://www.insideover.com/society/instagrams-prostitution-secret.html/amp

3. Rachel Hosie, '"Instagrammability": most important factor for millennials on choosing holiday destination', *The Independent*, 24 March 2017. https://web.archive.org/web/20170324203723/http://independent.co.uk/travel/instagrammability-holiday-factor-millenials-holiday-destination-choosing-travel-social-media-photos-a7648706.html
4. Amalia Ulman, *Excellences & Perfections*. Accessed 1 February 2024. https://web.archive.org/web/20150519225511/https://webenact.rhizome.org/excellences-and-perfections; 'Amalia Ulman: excellences and perfections', New Exhibitions Museum. Accessed 1 February 2024. https://web.archive.org/web/20141024150431/https://www.newmuseum.org/exhibitions/view/amalia-ulman-excellences-perfections
5. Nana Baah, 'The "fake wealth" industry making influencers look rich', *Vice*, 17 December 2020. https://web.archive.org/web/20201217094842/https://www.vice.com/en/article/k7a7mw/the-fake-wealth-industry-making-influencers-look-rich
6. David Kirkpatrick, 'Twitter says influencers are almost as trusted as friends', *Marketing Dive*, 12 May 2016. https://web.archive.org/web/20160518031918/https://www.marketingdive.com/news/twitter-says-influencers-are-almost-as-trusted-as-friends/419076
7. Olivia Solon, 'Ex-Facebook president Sean Parker: site made to exploit human "vulnerability"', *The Guardian*, 9 November 2017. https://web.archive.org/web/20171109230800/https://www.theguardian.com/technology/2017/nov/09/facebook-sean-parker-vulnerability-brain-psychology
8. Abbas Zahedi, 'MANNA form below (transcript)', *Issuu*, 11 September 2019. https://web.archive.org/web/20200715165510/https://issuu.com/abbzah/docs/manna_from_below_-_abbas_zahedi_-_printed_edition_
9. '6 Muslim companies that created sports hijabs way before Nike', Raqtive. Accessed 1 February 2024. https://web.archive.org/web/20200908081253/https://www.raqtive.com/blog/6-muslim-companies-that-created-sports-hijabs
10. Vicky Xiuzhong Xu, Danielle Cave, James Leibold et al., *Uyghurs for sale* (Canberra: Australian Strategic Policy Institute 2020). https://web.archive.org/web/20200301160438/https://www.aspi.org.au/report/uyghurs-sale
11. Al-Kanz [Facebook], 10 July 2020. https://archive.is/HNu4U
12. Raphael Glucksmann [Instagram], 9 July 2020. https://archive.is/9pvaf
13. Yomi Adegoke, 'Feminism is now used to sell almost everything—even breast implants', *The Guardian*, 13 November 2019. https://web.archive.org/web/20191113184802/https://www.theguardian.com/commentisfree/2019/nov/13/feminism-is-now-used-to-sell-almost-everything-even-breast-implants
14. 'Muslim fashion sexy make up tutorial robot influencer', BBC—Big Badmash Channel [YouTube], 23 December 2017. https://archive.org/details/muslim-fashion-sexy-robot-you-tube-1080p
15. The Muslim Vibe [Facebook], 8 September 2017. https://archive.is/TEFcq
16. 'Gambian government close Penny Appeal orphanage after child sex abuse allegations', 5Pillars, 15 August 2020. https://web.archive.org/web/20200818173045/https://5pillarsuk.com/2020/08/15/gambian-government-close-penny-appeal-orphanage-after-child-sex-abuse-allegations; Adama Makasuba 'Penny Appeal-Gambia closed over illegal operation', *The Voice Gambia*, 13 August 2020. https://web.archive.org/web/20210113210045/https://www.voicegambia.com/2020/08/13/penny-appeal-gambia-closed-over-illegal-operation; 'Amir Khan slams Penny Appeal after child sexual allegations at Gambian orphanage', 5Pillars, 15 August 2020. https://web.archive.org/web/20200818163916/https://5pillarsuk.com/2020/08/15/amir-khan-slams-penny-appeal-after-child-sexual-allegations-at-gambian-orphanage
17. Rebecca Cooney, 'Regulator begins statutory inquiry into Human Appeal', *Third Sector*, 18 May 2018. https://web.archive.org/web/20180518154611/https://www.thirdsector.co.uk/regulator-begins-statutory-inquiry-human-appeal/governance/article/1465155; 'Muslim Aid launches investigation after CEO Jehangir Malik no-confidence letter', 5Pillars, 03 January 2020. https://web.archive.org/web/20200501142044/https://5pillarsuk.com/2020/01/03/muslim-aid-launches-investigation-after-ceo-jehangir-malik-no-confidence-letter; Murtaza Ali Shah. 'UK-based charity Muslim Aid launches probe after CEO no-confidence letter', *The News*, 4 January 2020. https://web.archive.org/web/20200104170750/https://www.thenews.com.pk/latest/593505-letter-of-no-confidence-against-ceo-forces-muslim-aid-to-launch-investigation; Nick Frame, 'Chief executive of troubled Wakefield charity steps down', *Wakefield Express*, 20 December 2019. https://web.archive.org/web/20191220180734/https://www.wakefieldexpress.co.uk/news/people/chief-executive-of-troubled-wakefield-charity-steps-down-1-10164965; Murtaza Ali Shah, 'Adeem Younis suspended in Penny Appeal war', *The News*, 15 October 2019. https://web.archive.org/web/20191015032707/https://www.thenews.com.pk/latest/541481-adeem-younis-suspended-in-penny-appeal-war; Nick Frame, '"Financial concerns" raised at Wakefield charity Penny

Appeal', *Wakefield Express*, 11 October 2019. https://web.archive.org/web/20191011195248/ https://www.wakefieldexpress.co.uk/news/people/financial-concerns-raised-at-wakefield-charity-penny-appeal-1-10047021 'Penny Appeal spent 27% of its income on charity in 2014', *5pillars*, 14 January 2016. https://web.archive.org/web/20160119085222/https://5pillarsuk.com/2016/01/14/penny-appeal-spent-27-of-its-income-on-charity-in-2014; 'SKT Welfare denies malpractice allegations', *5Pillars*, 24 February 2018. https://web.archive.org/web/20210804063920/https://5pillarsuk.com/2018/02/24/skt-welfare-denies-malpractice-allegations; Rebecca Cooney, 'Regulator says former trustees of Muslim Aid seriously mismanaged the charity', *Third Sector*, 7 December 2018. https://web.archive.org/web/20210804063920/https://5pillarsuk.com/2018/02/24/skt-welfare-denies-malpractice-allegations; Hannah Somerville, 'Muslim charity lashes back at regulator after cash seized at border', *The Docklands and East London Advertiser*, 18 October 2019. https://web.archive.org/web/20191019053908/https://www.eastlondonadvertiser.co.uk/news/human-aid-uk-responds-to-charity-commission-1-6328351Saeed Niazi, 'Penny Appeal CEO Aamer Naeem embroilled in controversy', *The News*, 18 October 2019. https://web.archive.org/web/20191019060452/https://www.thenews.com.pk/latest/542879-penny-appeal-ceo-aamer-naeem-embroilled-in-controversy Nick Craven, 'Rich list landlord's threat to bankrupt rent arrears tenants: multi-millionaire Asif Aziz sends out final demands threatening to wind up firms who are as little as one day late settling their bills despite coronavirus crisis', *The Mail Online*, 5 April 2020. https://web.archive.org/web/20220902163933/https://www.dailymail.co.uk/news/article-8188251/Rich-list-landlords-threat-bankrupt-rent-arrears-tenants.html
18. 'Muslims in the West: embodying the change | Dr. William Barylo', Zaytuna College [YouTube], 2 November 2017. https://archive.org/details/muslims-in-the-west-embodying-the-change-dr.-william-barylo-360p, at 09:00.
19. 'Ethical considerations for Muslim charities', Muslim Charities Forum. 2020. https://web.archive.org/web/20201205081416/https://www.muslimcharitiesforum.org.uk/wp-content/uploads/2020/05/Ethical-Considerations-Guide-Version-2.pdf
20. Simon Parkin, 'The YouTube stars heading for burnout: "The most fun job imaginable became deeply bleak"', *The Guardian*, 8 September 2018. https://web.archive.org/web/20180908100257/https://www.theguardian.com/technology/2018/sep/08/youtube-stars-burnout-fun-bleak-stressed
21. Ryan Kucey, 'Nano-influencers: who they are and why they matter', *Medium*, 31 May 2019. https://web.archive.org/web/20190620122156/https://medium.com/swlh/nano-influencers-who-they-are-and-why-they-matter-c4278cc95d8f
22. 'Share of Instagram influencers involved in fraud worldwide in 2019 and 2020, by number of followers', Statista Research Department, 17 August 2021. https://web.archive.org/web/20220118002349/https://www.statista.com/statistics/1250681/share-of-instagram-influencers-involved-in-fraud-worldwide
23. Taylor Lorenz, 'Rising Instagram stars are posting fake sponsored content', *The Atlantic*, 18 December 2018. https://www.theatlantic.com/technology/archive/2018/12/influencers-are-faking-brand-deals/578401
24. Omar Shahid, 'Keeping in check: maintaining spirituality in the influencer space', The Muslim Vibe Podcast, 28 June 2020. https://archive.org/details/Omarshaheed
25. '"I went wrong": fashion model Halima Aden opens up about reconnecting to hijab on social media', *The Muslim Vibe*, 24 November 2020. https://web.archive.org/web/20201124160245/https://themuslimvibe.com/western-muslim-culture/i-went-wrong-fashion-model-halima-aden-opens-up-about-reconnecting-to-hijab-on-social-media
26. 'Sikhs and culture: a video essay', Narvision [YouTube], 27 July 2020. https://archive.org/details/sikhs-and-culture-a-video-essay-you-tube-1080p
27. 'PREVENT CAKES', Hussain, Faisal [Instagram], 8 July 2017. https://archive.is/ZzdTl
28. Nouri Sardar. Accessed 1 February 2024. https://web.archive.org/web/20200803173319/https://nourisardar.com
29. 'Smile 2 Jannah', YouTube channel. Accessed 1 February 2024. https://web.archive.org/web/20200315173758/https://www.youtube.com/channel/UCeccrNGLzk6d0M_vaomD3LQ
30. Salma Haidrani, 'Capturing the spirit of London's young Muslim women', *Huck Magazine*, 11 January 2018. https://web.archive.org/web/20200924153513/https://www.huckmag.com/art-and-culture/photography-2/portraits-capture-spirit-londons-muslim-women; Muslim Sisterhood Instagram Page. Accessed 1 February 2024. https://web.archive.org/web/20200223173242/https://www.instagram.com/muslimsisterhood
31. 'Mapping sanctuaries', P21 Gallery. Accessed 1 February 2024. https://web.archive.org/web/20200920210435/https://p21.gallery/react/call-out-mapping-sanctuaries

References

5Pillars. 2020. 'Frenzo Harami | Lessons from a haram life | Blood Brothers #42.' [YouTube] 28 August. https://archive.org/details/frenzo-harami-lessons-from-a-haram-life-blood-brothers-42-you-tube-1080p

Abdaal, Ali. 2020. 'How to make money online—the 3 levels.' [YouTube] 19 May. https://archive.org/details/how-to-make-money-online-the-3-levels-you-tube-1080p

Abdul Khabeer, Suad. 2016. *Muslim Cool: Race, Religion and Hip Hop in the United States.* New York, New York University Press.

Ahmed, Sara. 2014. *The Cultural Politics of Emotion.* Edinburgh: Edinburgh University Press.

Ahsan, Hamja. 2017. *Shy Radicals: The Antisystemic Politics of the Militant Introvert.* London: Book Works.

Ali, Muna. 2017. '"Art is not just about entertainment": the social activism and cultural production of Chicago's Inner-City Muslim Action Network (IMAN).' *Culture and Religion* 18(4), 353–70.

Amena. 2020. 'Change…' [YouTube] 3 June. https://archive.org/details/change...-you-tube-1080p

Bahl, Nancy and Allison J. Ouimet. 2022. 'Smiling won't make you feel better, but it might make people like you more: interpersonal and intrapersonal consequences of response-focused emotion regulation strategies.' *Journal of Social and Personal Relationships* 39(7), 2262–84.

Baig, Mehreen. 2015. 'InstaFake.' Mehreenbaig.com, 8 November. https://web.archive.org/web/20190830151057/http://www.mehreenbaig.com/instafake

Barylo, William. 2016. 'Neo-liberal not-for-profits: the embracing of corporate culture in European Muslim charities.' *Journal of Muslim Minority Affairs* 36(3), 383–98.

Barylo, William. 2017. *Young Muslim Change-Makers.* London: Routledge.

Bhatti, Lina. 2020. 'Self-orientalism amongst Muslim content creators'. *Medium*, 28 June. https://web.archive.org/web/20200924152417/https://medium.com/@lina.abh/self-orientalism-amongst-muslim-content-creators-7efd8a72f6bc

Beck, Ulrich and Elisabeth Beck-Gernsheim (eds). 2001. *Individualization: Institutionalized Individualism and Its Social and Political Consequences.* London: Sage.

Begum, Priya Jasmin. 2018. 'Is the hijab being turned into everything it stands against?' *The Huffington Post*, 17 March. https://web.archive.org/web/20170319101011/http://www.huffingtonpost.co.uk/priya-jasmin-begum/is-the-hijab-being-turned_b_15380682.html

Boubekeur, Amel. 2005. 'Cool competitive Muslim culture in the west.' *ISIM Review* 16, 12–13.

Bourdieu, Pierre. 1979. *La Distinction Critique sociale du jugement*, Paris: Minuit.

Butler, Judith. 1993. *Bodies that Matter: On the Discursive Limits of 'Sex'*. New York: Routledge.

Charity Commission. 2020. 'Charity Inquiry: a fund raised for the charitable purpose of the prevention and relief of poverty of Rohingya Refugees.' 15 December. https://web.archive.org/web/20201218193014/https://www.gov.uk/government/publications/charity-inquiry-funds-raised-for-the-prevention-and-relief-of-poverty-of-rohingya-refugees/charity-inquiry-a-fund-raised-for-the-charitable-purpose-of-the-prevention-and-relief-of-poverty-of-rohingya-refugees

DaCosta-Shahid, Omar. 2020. [Facebook] 26 June. https://archive.is/TxDj5

Drenten Jenna, Lauren Gurrieri, and Meagan Tyler. 2020. 'Sexualized labour in digital culture: Instagram influencers, porn chic and the monetization of attention.' *Gender, Work and Organization* 27(1), 41–66.

Ferris, Kerry O. 2007. 'The sociology of celebrity.' *Sociology Compass* 1(1), 371–84.

Giovanni, Chiara. 2017. 'The problem with Rupi Kaur's Poetry.' *Buzzfeed News*, 4 August. https://web.archive.org/web/20180805052938/https://www.buzzfeednews.com/article/chiaragiovanni/the-problem-with-rupi-kaurs-poetry

Gori, Roland. 2013. *La Fabrique des Imposteurs*. Paris: LLL

Haenni, Patrick. 2005. *L'islam de marché : l'autre révolution conservatrice.* Paris: Seuil.

Harami, Frenzo. 2019. 'Haraam life.' *Chaabian Boyz Vol. 1.* London: AC Mainz.

Hasan, Aisha. 2017. 'We need to talk about the sexualisation of Muslim women.' The Qarawiyyin Project, 27 July. https://web.archive.org/web/20200922154119/https://qarawiyyinproject.co/2017/07/27/we-need-to-talk-about-the-sexualisation-of-muslim-women

Horton, Donald and R. Richard Wohl. 1956. 'Mass communication and para-social interaction.' *Psychiatry* 19(3), 215–29.

Kasser, Tim, Richard Ryan, Charles Couchman, et al. 2004. 'Materialistic values: their causes and consequences.' In *Psychology and Consumer Culture: The Struggle for a Good Life in a Materialistic World*, edited by T. Kasser and A. D. Kanner. Worcester: American Psychological Association, 11–28.

Kasser, Tim, Katherine Rosenblum, Arnold Sameroff, et al. 2014. 'Changes in materialism, changes in psychological well-being: evidence from three longitudinal studies and an intervention experiment.' *Motivation and Emotion* 38(1), 1–22.

Katebi, Hoda. 2019. 'Muslims have more visibility than ever. But can we praise it?' *The Washington Post*, 2 June. https://web.archive.org/web/20190604011047/https://www.washingtonpost.com/opinions/2019/06/02/muslims-have-more-visibility-than-ever-can-we-praise-it

Kelwick, Adam. 2020. [Facebook] 16 August. https://archive.is/88xVT

Kesvani, Hussein. 2019. *Follow Me, Akhi, The Online World of British Muslims*. London: Hurst.

Ku, Lisbeth and Charles Zaroff. 2014. 'How far is your money from your mouth? The effects of intrinsic relative to extrinsic values on willingness to pay and protect the environment.' *Journal of Environmental Psychology* 40(1), 472–83.

Lena, Jennifer. 2019. *Entitled: Discriminating Tastes and the Expansion of the Arts*. Princeton: Princeton University Press.

Le Noir, Sakinah. 2020. [Facebook] 14 June. https://web.archive.org/web/20200929110553/https://www.facebook.com/permalink.php?story_fbid=10163561885315332&id=818860331

Leong, Nancy. 2013. 'Racial capitalism.' *Harvard Law Review* 126(8), 2151–226.

Lewis, Phillip and Sadek Hamid. 2018. *British Muslims: New Directions in Islamic Thought; Creativity and Activism*. Edinburgh: Edinburgh University Press.

Lisjak, Monika, Andrea Bonezzi, Soo Kim, et al. 2015. 'Perils of compensatory consumption: within-domain compensation undermines subsequent self-regulation.' *Journal of Consumer Research* 41(5), 1186–203.

Liu, Wei and Cheng Lu Wang. 2020. 'We have faith in Apple: brand worship among Apple fans.' In *Handbook of Research on the Impact of Fandom in Society and Consumerism*, edited by Cheng Lu Wang. Hershey, PA: IGI Global, 81–103.

Malik, Nesrine. 2018. 'Thanks, L'Oréal, but I'm growing weary of this hijab fetish.' *The Guardian*, 25 January. https://web.archive.org/web/20180125060843/https://www.theguardian.com/commentisfree/2018/jan/25/oreal-hijab-fetish-amena-khan-muslim-women

Marwick, Alice E. 2013. *Status Update: Celebrity, Publicity, and Branding in the Social Media Age*. New Haven: Yale University Press.

Moballeghi, Nargess. 2018. [Facebook] 31 October. https://archive.is/tHUco

Mull, Amanda. 2017. 'Instagram food is a sad, sparkly lie.' *Eater*, 6 July. https://web.archive.org/web/20170706154209/https://www.eater.com/2017/7/6/15925940/instagram-influencers-cronuts-milkshakes-burgers

Nabiilabee. 2017. 'Is social media driving me crazy? | NABIILABEE.' [YouTube] 27 February. https://archive.org/details/is-social-media-driving-me-crazy-nabiilabee-you-tube-1080p

Nilan, Pam. 2017. *Muslim Youth in the Diaspora: Challenging Extremism through Popular Culture*. London: Routledge.

Oyserman, Daphna and Spike Lee. 2008. 'Does culture influence what and how we think? Effects of priming individualism and collectivism.' *Psychological Bulletin* 134(2), 311–42.

Riesman, David, Nathan Glazer, and Reuel Denney. 1950. *The Lonely Crowd: A Study of the Changing American Character*. New Haven: Yale University Press.

Robinson, Cedric 1983. *Black Marxism: The Making of the Black Radical Tradition*. London: Zed Books.

Robinson, Brett T. 2013. *Appletopia*. Waco, TX: Baylor University Press.

Rojek, Chris. 2012. *Fame Attack: The Inflation of Celebrity and Its Consequences.* London: Bloomsbury.
Sham Idrees VLOGS. 2018. 'The truth.' [YouTube] 10 March. https://archive.org/details/the-truth-you-tube-1080p
Shepherd, David, Kate Whitman, Mark Button, et al. 2023. 'The impact of deviant social media influencers and consumer characteristics on purchasing counterfeit goods.' *Deviant Behavior* 44(12), 1746–60.
Shirazi, Faegheh. 2016. *Brand Islam: The Marketing and Commodification of Piety.* Austin: University of Texas Press.
Singler, Beth. 2020. '"Blessed by the algorithm": theistic conceptions of artificial intelligence in online discourse.' *AI & Society* 35, 945–55.
Yalina Q. 2018. In *Khidr Zine* 2. London: Khidr Collective.
Younas, Shahzad. 2020. [Facebook] 11 January. https://archive.is/yKXY8
Zahedi, Abbas. 2019. 'Dwelling: in this space we grieve.' Abbzah.com, 22 May. https://web.archive.org/web/20200811043341/https://abbzah.com/2019/05/22/dwelling

8
Spaces of Nurture and Resistance

> Come, come, whoever you are ... Ours is not a caravan of despair.
> Come, even if you have broken your vows a thousand times.
> (Abu Saeed Abil-Kheir)

Rumi's Cave has been, since its inception in 2011, one of the most pivotal centres for Muslims in London. The Cave initially started in a space no bigger than a barber's shop in Kilburn, Northwest London. Initiated by Sheikh Babikir, Rumi's was thought as a hub where not only people could pray and attend Friday *khutbas* (sermons), but also socialize, learn, express themselves creatively, and be at the service of the most vulnerable. Sheikh Babikir got the idea from Rumi's Café in Islamabad, where young intellectuals would offer discussions about social topics. He called it 'cave' in reference to cave Hira, where the Prophet Muhammad used to retreat in search for spiritual direction. In 2017, I sat with Sheikh Babikir to learn the story behind The Cave:

> I realised after 7/7, I was ... trying to help that generation ... who were brainwashed by these new modern groups who are confused in their understanding of faith ... I realised the majority of those people are professionals who are in good jobs, good universities, they don't regularly come to the mosque ...
>
> Noor [one of the first managers] said to me: I have a vision for it: what you want to create we can do it by inviting people who want to go out but they can't fit outside, they can't go to the pubs, the bars ... We can do poetry nights, we can do drama nights, we can do talks ... we pick up a subject that is gonna benefit the community outside ... I thought, those who come here, listen to these talks and enjoy themselves, why shouldn't they do something to show the outcome of their worship?
>
> ...
>
> If the best of people are those who help people, and I want them to help people ... who are the least helped in this city London which I love very much, it's the homeless ... [The Prophet] used to love the poor, sit with them, share their food. I want them to break their egos by sitting with those people ...
>
> ...
>
> Your prayer, your fasting, are meaningless, if it does not produce a heart that encompasses mercy, gentleness, kindness, a heart that will love, a heart that will

be loved by others. Through that, we can then build a community. Not through money or titles or positions.

Since the early days, Rumi's Cave was developed as a space for artistic expression, where people can 'enjoy themselves', but at the same time be of service. The young and less young Muslims I met at Rumi's see and use the space as a site for healing, flourishing, and self-determination. I've seen people recovering from hardships, launching their artistic careers, making lifelong friends and finding their spouses through Rumi's. A global *ummah* might be a utopia (see chapter 6) but Sheikh Babikir and all the people involved succeeded in building a 'community' which shares trust and solidarity on the level of the most tight-knit groups I have encountered in my fieldwork.

Since Rumi's started welcoming volunteers in 2012, as of 2017, the Cave has seen up to a thousand volunteers a year, between twenty and seventy that come every week and between 400 to 500 people benefiting from the soup kitchen. Winning a bid by the council to occupy a derelict school, the Cave expanded to a three-storey building around 2018—before returning back to smaller spaces. While their flagship events are the monthly open-mics and Salaam Sundays (discussions with Sheikh Babikir), the Cave offers film nights, services to the elderly and the homeless in addition to poetry, calligraphy, or photography workshops and martial arts classes. During the 2020 pandemic, the space was used as a shelter for the homeless.

Initially, the initiative was entirely funded by Sheikh Babikir, before donations came in and the Cave partnered with larger charities while remaining independent. Because of its functioning outside of modern neoliberal and supremacist frameworks, I consider Rumi's Cave as a comprehensive decolonial space (Barylo 2017). It is a space that came from the margins and stays at the margins: no media outlet would write about it, it doesn't interest celebrities, predatory businesspeople, or politicians, as they have realized they can't commodify the Cave.

Following bell hooks' concept of margins as sites of infinite possibilities, I explore here how other grass-roots organizations and informal initiatives defy the system by using alternative resources and transcend systemic borders: they show it is possible to flourish without money or power. How nurturing spaces build organic communities defined by thick trust (family-like bonds of solidarity), new political strategies, and pathways to justice—not through control and domination but rather through love and compassion. This chapter thus explores the question of the accountability of those in power, the power of protest, whistleblowing, and the question of redemption. Eventually, this chapter ends on a reflection on the core vision that unifies all the decolonial actors mentioned in this research. In our conversations and readings, I attempt to create a draft of what is 'Islamic' decoloniality, from the perspective of my respondents, and what it looks like.

8.1. Nurturing Spaces: Come Whoever You Are

Noor, one of the first managers of the Cave, finds in the space a heterotopia outside of normative social structures:

> With your shoes at the door, you leave your ego at the door, everyone sits on the floor . . . It's a space I didn't have when I converted to Islam, I felt so isolated in masjids, people make you feel you're not good enough if you don't have an abaya. At Rumi's Cave, it's come as you are, if you are outside not wearing the hijab, you don't need to be another person . . . It's a non-judgemental space and it's all fed into each other.

Community hubs are an oasis in the desert of modern individualistic societies where loneliness puts people at risk, and people are willing to pay the equivalent £30 per hour to hire a friend.[1] However, what makes them effective at building communities is the values and ethics that shape their modes of action (Barylo 2017). Noor's appreciation of the space comes from its inclusivity compared to other Muslim spaces that abide more by social norms than Islam. She relates how non-Muslims take regularly part in open-mics or art exhibitions, whether it is Rastafari, young people from the Jewish centre nearby, Sikh artists sharing their perspective on creativity, or LGBTQ people curious to have a peek. When she says 'come as you are', she is referring to a quote by Persian poet Abu Saeed Abil-Kheir, often misattributed to Jalaluddin Rumi (see introduction of this chapter), used as a symbol of the inclusivity of Sufi traditions. Breaking from us-them binaries (see chapter 3) has been an integral part of Sheikh Babikir's mission; he summarizes: 'we are all sinners we need repent and live. It's not the rituals which makes us Muslim, it's the outcome of our rituals.'

Aminah left a career with a very 'competitive' architecture firm to work at Rumi's and refuses to be labelled with any title. To be faithful to her wish, I will just say that she has been one of the main driving energies in the Cave, along with others. From an 'empty' career, she finds 'meaning' in 'being here for others'. To be there 'for others' meant rethinking the intentions of the space and meaning of service. She was horrified at how many Muslim spiritual retreats turned into business ventures, using celebrity scholars as a marketing ploy and selling individual tickets costing hundreds of pounds for vacuous events with no personal engagement with scholars. Consequently, Rumi's retreats have always been priced low and given the opportunity for attended to discuss personal matters with Sheikh Babikir. Rumi's events almost never advertise the names of the speakers on posters and at the soup kitchens, no photographs of the homeless are allowed. In the age of social media, there is no publicity or advertising about the soup kitchens: 'it's all about people discovering it'. Aminah describes the Cave as a 'shelter from this materialistic, capitalist society'; she talks about the steps the team have been taking to ensure that the purpose of the Cave takes centre stage instead of the people behind it.

> When someone comes to cave I like the fact no one knows who the manager is or how the events happen. I like to philosophise about the space interior and how it's been designed e.g not to have western desks to create barriers and is open. 'Leaving your ego at the door.' . . . We always say if you want to come to Rumi's start at the kitchen . . . Serve the homeless, let's see how you treat them . . . then perhaps let's talk about serving those whom walk through the doors.

What makes Rumi's different from other spaces is not only the humility and intentions but the responsibilization of volunteers: Rumi's is an ecosystem of activities from religious lectures to creative workshops where volunteers can either attend or be active participants—and whoever participate to a workshop as a student might end up sharing their knowledge and skills with others in turn. Sheikh Babikir never gives himself the *khutbas* at Rumi's but delegates the task to members of the team. Rumi's Cave is not a space for 'leadership' or 'empowerment', but rather humility and stewardship (see chapter 4).

Instead of formal and hierarchical decision-making processes, Rumi's follows an informal, organic process based on consultation and consensus where even occasional volunteers and visitors are asked about their opinion on important decisions—which follows the Islamic rules of *shura* (consultation and consensus (Barylo 2017)). Like many organizations using more experienced volunteers are guides and mentors (Barylo 2017), Aminah highlights how including people of different generations allows them to keep working in the right direction:

> You meet all kinds of energies: someone just died, someone is visiting the hall for his wedding, someone just got a baby . . . People get married here, people die here, people give birth here . . . It's good here we have every generation, children, elders who see things differently, who have seen different things in life. Being around so many elders is a blessing, like Nuria, I told her: 'if I go astray, tell me and bring me back.' Rakin just brings his children whenever they come to the cave. They stay in a corner, playing on their phones, but when they grow up, they know that this is a safe space.

Talking about Rumi's, Sultanah draws a parallel with the Bengali community in East London where she grew up (see chapter 6): 'these movements recreate the solidarity of the elders'. While no space is completely 'safe' (Hanhardt 2013), Rumi's and similar organizations are 'breathable spaces' (Zavos 2017) or 'convergence spaces' (Baker 2016) where people from different walks of life work together and develop affinities although holding different if not divergent theological, moral or political principles. These spaces are proven to be cradles of democracy, active citizenship, and political conscientization (Baker 2016; Barylo 2017). They are spaces for political conscientization (Baker 2016), where volunteers start 'questioning the structures that produced these experiences' (Baker 2016, 22–5; see also chapter 4). In a wounded society, they are groups formed around the ideas of collective healing. Although they do not offer formal therapy or counselling, they are spaces for listening and creating social bonds (see chapter 4)—what I call 'empathetic communities'.

Rumi's Cave is, however, not a 'progressive', 'moderate' mosque or the evolution of mosque structures (it defines itself as a 'non-defined space'); it is a radical return to the seventh-century idea of a mosque: 'it's a space of community, healing, joy and nourishment' (Rabiah Mali in Rumi's Cave 2019). The Cave and similar spaces create heterotopias (Foucault 1971); they are real and therefore are not 'utopic' but different to 'normal' spaces abiding by dominant norms; just like Rumi's is not exactly a mosque, not exactly a home, not exactly a café or a charity. They are ambiguous thirdspaces (Soja 1996), flexible and constantly moving and re-negotiating their boundaries and what includes 'an-other' (Soja 1996, 5). They are disrupting accepted borders by defining for themselves a 'zone of being' in a society that declares them in a space of 'non-being'.

Similar spaces worked as community centres long before Rumi's: the Crawley Education Institute started by offering Qur'an and extra-curricular support classes in a home in Crawley; the flats of Rakin Fetuga and Humera Khan, and Fuad Nahdi's house or auntie Nabila Elahi's were some of the first hubs in north-west London. Similar initiatives are found around the world such as the Ta'leef collective in the Bay Area, Islah LA in Los Angeles, the Sanad Collective through the Café Floraison in Montreal (now closed), Benevolence (Melbourne, Australia), or the Maison Soufie near Paris (Barylo 2018). However, all of these spaces faced difficulties of different kinds: Ta'leef collective was built around the personality of the late Usama Canon, Café Floraison didn't resist the 2020 pandemic and the Maison Soufie, although still offering events, hardly brings an audience outside of Sufi sympathizers.

These initiatives offer a comprehensive experience: they involve their participants on the various levels of action and reflection that shape individuals and communities alike: subjectivation, socialization, and interdependence (Dubet 1994): they allow people to distance themselves from their daily life so they can analyse it; to build a social identity and eventually to build new strategies. Few similar initiatives have been assessed by research. Ceasefire, founded in 1995, became known by the wider public through the work of Ameena Matthews, who featured in the 2011 documentary *Interrupters*. The organization featured local mediators working at bringing back confidence and self-esteem in young people in underprivileged areas through workshops and arts. It notably reduced the rate of shootings and killings, bringing the area to a forty-five-year low (Skogan et al. 2008). A similar initiative exists in the UK: Save Our Boys, founded by Rakin Fetuga.

However, rather than sustaining a dependence of the poor, they are breaking the cycle of dependence and building an ecosystem by giving some people jobs like at Rumi's Café. Rather than being accommodative spaces that help people to get their basic needs met, they are 'restorative spaces' (Baker 2016).

Organizations that involve their teams and volunteers in providing services to others have been the most successful at retaining audiences, acting as a de facto community hub, although they were not created for that purpose, such as Amatullah (soup kitchens in Bagnolet) and Averroès (providing exam papers corrections and meals to students) (Barylo 2017). Not any space makes community, but rather, as Imad Ahmed mentioned (see chapter 6.2), spaces of service: those which facilitate marriages and friendships, accommodate families and children, and offer spaces of shared experiences and struggles. In a conversation with Aminah, Javayria reflects on the abnormality of community hubs as a symptom of modern atomized societies and the dysfunctions of political structures:

> Rumi's Cave shouldn't exist in the first place, it is a symptom of our times. Our parents invited each other to their homes. They offered meals to their neighbours, Muslim, non-Muslim... my mum, she had Sikh friends, she offered food every Ramadan to their English neighbours. That was community. Texting each other: 'hey how are you,' this is community.

Nurturing spaces can take various forms; they can be digital media outlets like Amaliah, founded by Nafisa and Selina Bakkar, a platform for Muslim women with an abundance of tips on self-care and mental well-being which do not shy away from acknowledging dynamics of race, power, class, and gender, and aim at restoring more balance in the media scene. Another outlet is the Muslim Vibe, founded by Salim Kassam, Hasseb Rizvi, and Nouri Sardar, where Muslims from around the world who could never dream being published can have their thoughts read by almost a million readers. They can be spaces for learning just like Humera Khan's An-Nisa society and their Saturday schools. They can also be places for questioning and difficult conversations, such as the discussions about anti-Blackness set up by Sultanah Parvin. These spaces are not only important because they provide familiarity, knowledge, connection, service, and trust; they are offering social experiences where people do not have to perform and wear a mask (see chapter 1):

> We're afraid that people will reject and abandon us, that we're not good enough or we're too much, we're too Muslim or we're too poor or too Black, all of this stuff... The most important question is: How can I be who I am?... Let you choose you, because oppression doesn't let you choose you. (Khan 2018)

They make people feel at 'home' or 'ground' them, to paraphrase Rabiah Mali (see chapter 5). The main challenges, however, for these under-resourced spaces are economic sustainability, in a neoliberal society that doesn't value healing, community, and not-for-profit service.

8.2. Funding, Perseverance, *Sabr*, and Imagination

Winner of a Winston Churchill Memorial Trust fellowship, Zain Dada, co-founder of Khidr collective, travelled to the US to meet arts and community collectives, in search of alternative modes of survival, in response to the precarious situation in which grass-roots spaces in the UK find themselves in.

> Khidr Collective is an unincorporated, un-constituted organisation which has thus far relied on the support of donations, trusts, foundations and crowd-funding campaigns to produce the magazines we make, the events we produce and the animations and other digital work we are delving into. At the time of writing, Khidr Collective is made up of a team of 12 with a core team of 5 members who lead on everything from editorial responsibilities to administrative tasks including funding applications. However, the time and capacity offered by the wider collective is voluntary and unpaid ... it does mean, smaller community arts organisations run the risk of burning out. Sustainability concerns not only an organisation's health but the health of individuals involved in organisations who are often operating in difficult circumstances. (Dada 2020)

Community hubs, arts, and other grass-roots organizations are key players in democratic processes due to their power at facilitating cultural capability, their ability to express, to be heard, to experience, to make, to build, to contest, and to create (Wilson et al. 2017). Their survival is vital for social cohesion, as they make some of the strongest social fabric by developing bonds of thick trust between their members (Barylo 2017). Most organizations that I have encountered have been able to survive mainly through the organizers' pocket money, using existing familial flats and houses as venues and offices, and non-financial donations (such as friends helping with catering, audio and visual equipment, and so on). Rarely, they are able to rely on private donations, crowd-funding, or grants (such as the Wainwright Reform Trust, Joseph Rowntree, and 30Percy). Noor, one of Rumi's Cave former managers, recalls the challenges of keeping Rumi's afloat, even thirteen years after its inception:

> Every month we were minus. I am disappointed with lack of support from the community. There were times we were on the point of closure. There is no loyalty

to Rumi's, not thinking about what you can put back in. Here in the UK, relations with faith spaces are very transactional.

Despite their impact, Muslim grass-roots organizations in the UK are perceived as plasters for social problems, smokescreens used by the state which retreats from its obligations or 'moral safety valves' for liberal guilt (Baker 2016)—on top of British Muslims at large not investing much in the arts, community, culture, or heritage. This is another reason why many initiatives resort to counter-extremism funding, thus perpetuating cycles of injustice (see chapter 2). Javayria, in conversation with Aminah, deplores this:

> Now we believe it can only exist in an institutionalised way. We shouldn't be seeking partnerships with larger organisations. Artists shouldn't struggle to make a living. Back in the days, rich people would naturally commission artists to perform or do work.

Because of the struggles for obtaining funding, some organizations close down (see MADE, chapter 5.2), and some others transform into a business. The Ramadan Tent Project was started as a small student gathering for *iftaar* (breaking of the fast) in a park near SOAS in London. Convivial, informal, and relying on volunteers, the initiative would invite students, small community organizers or little-known religious figures as speakers. However, as the years went by, the project expanded in branches across the country, and put celebrities at the forefront instead of people at the grass roots. As a consequence, many ex-volunteers and attendees criticized the founder for commercializing the initiative, going into an 'ego overdrive' that has transformed inspirational evenings into entertainment shows.

The very few times I've witnessed when grass-roots projects were able to get institutional support without compromising on their values is when several likeminded people from the same community were able to get into positions of power such as in city councils, funding panels, or as commissioning editors. In the US, where Muslims have different investment priorities, I've observed rich personalities donating (without strings attached) sums as high as $10,000 for an arts collective to organize a retreat in Hawaii. Writer and storyteller Rahma Dutton asks: 'what if there's a different way? What if it's simpler than we previously thought? What if the answer lies in our tradition, in the way our great grandparents did things?' (Dutton 2020).

Dada (2020) encourages in his report a 'marriage' of 'practical support' and 'building capacity'. He notes how grass-roots initiatives, in a similar way to Rumi's Cave, run businesses (renting out space or catering for food), but also benefit from non-financial help in the form of premises, equipment, publicity, and more—while grants, because of their rarity, should be awarded to cases where financial kick-starting is the first step in a risk-proof sustainable model with a solid strategy, or for preventing organizations at critical risk of closure. Another example is Restless Beings,[2] a charity bringing help to the needy across the globe, which is funded by the profits of their Café, Root25[3] in London; their model is also notable for being a *waqf* (a perpetual trust) which cannot be bought or used outside of its aim of service. Farzana Khan argues that since 'the revolution will not be funded, the master's tools can't build our house', she advocates collective 'alternative economies and ecologies' rooted in stewardship (Khan in Akram 2019):

> The responsibility of those who have means, resources, who are privileged in our community, is making these choices available. How do you create businesses that are accessible? How to equip platforms and food spaces that are available? ... I'm moving from 'me space' to 'we space' ... I am in service. (Khan 2018)

In 2020, Farzana co-founded Resourcing Racial Justice[4] a fund offering grants ranging from £5,000 to £50,000 that enable people to pursue creative and social endeavours without asking for government funding, thanks to hedge-fund-managers-turned-philanthropists at 30Percy. Her foundation is a game-changing disruption of the system: Muslims don't have to go for counter-extremism funding. A few other initiatives rethink current models of wealth distribution such as the National Zakat Foundation (NZF), focusing on solving issues 'at home' as a priority, or the Norwich Free Market,[5] inspired by the model of the Islamic Market in Madina at the time of the early Muslims—no participation fee or charges for space are levied on traders, to help businesses starting up. It can involve diverting power and resources from the ivory towers of Oxford and Cambridge as Imad Ahmed (founder of the New Crescent Society) has organized the People's PPE[6] (philosophy, politics, and economics, a programme exclusive to Oxford University attended by a considerable number of future politicians in the UK). Initiatives such as the Rabbani Project develop alternative economies based on contemplation; what is exchanged are not money or material goods but rather emotions, feelings, and sensorial experiences. The Rabbani Project was able to survive without permanent premises or staff members, because while money facilitates transport and accommodation, the primary service provider is nature itself, an infinite gift—recognizing that not all forms of wealth are numerable (see chapter 4).

Another challenge is the difficulty to notice an impact in the short term, which wears down people's motivation. Sakinah, from Pearls of Islam, recalls: 'to expect things to change when you do something is a trick of the ego. Ultimately, [God] is the one who changes things.' Dawuud, in times of difficulties, recalls how Islam, in the early days, started at the margins of society: 'the *ummah* started small. The Prophet with the Qureish, he started small, people used to say: "we thought Islam was only with beggars," then he brought Abu Bakr, Uthman, etc.' Ibrahim, a doctoral student involved in anti-racist activism, expands:

> Giving up, or asking myself 'what's the point?', it's a recurring question for me. When we can't measure the impact, it casts doubts... [People] remind me that... everything that happens today, the rise of the far right is a response to the progress made, to more people having accepted ideas of real equality. I have little hope but I have a responsibility as a Muslim to keep hope and carry on doing the work... even if I know that justice is not to be found in this world.

Sabre has initiated M-Talks in France, a TED-like talk series offering a platform to young Muslim thinkers and practitioners who wouldn't get recognition otherwise. Although it was hugely popular, the initiative died a few years down the line because of the lack of financial support and media partners. Sabre wanted the organization to remain independent from any business or political agenda—which, he acknowledges, came at a cost. However, it wasn't enough for him to give up:

> Your brain tells you your work isn't useful for anything, and you feel like you want to give up. We have lots of expectations from the community so disappointments are rather hard... The relationship to God is really defining. I limit the number of people I'll be meeting, I have learnt to say 'no' to partnerships with big organisations, the media... It can be self-limiting... but we don't need anyone, we are not seeking validation from anyone. We need solid and sound foundations.

For many small organizations, saying 'no' to harmful but powerful partners, in times of ethical poverty (see chapter 2), can be a leap of faith, as Aminah mentions about Rumi's severing ties with predatory organizations, and a test of patience. My respondents identify this process of perseverance as *sabr*. Often translated as 'patience' or 'hope', *sabr* is about trust and work, doing one's best and trusting that the rest is in God's hands; it is 'tying one's camel' as per the popular hadith, as Aminah explains:

> When you start walking on the spiritual path, things become difficult... It's "Remember Me so I will remember you" [Qur'an (2:152)]... Focus on the work and not being distracted by small events here and there. A space, even if people are present for one hour, it can change things for them.

Sabr is a cognitive move from a state of incapacity, vulnerability, or precariousness to a stable and safe one, but at the same time, like hope, an action, 'a social practice' (Day 2016, 131). It is planting seeds, knowing that one has done their best (chapter 5), and leaving the impact to God. *Sabr*, like seeds, requires fertile spiritual soil. Just as Rabiah suggests grounding (see chapter 5), Farzana Khan suggests raícism or rootedness (from the Spanish *raíces* or roots) as a catalyst for change, a concept coined by Aurora Levins Morales (2019) as 'practice of rooting ourselves in the real, concrete histories of our people: our families, our local communities, our ethnic communities'.

> The ability to take root in our displacement and our borderland ways is something that can catalyse new ways of being and consciousness ... Utilizing our hybridity, we can start to re-imagine and reconfigure our world: create new ways of living; housing that are people- and earth-centered, economic systems that prioritize our values instead of profit ... outside of the state's criminal justice system ... It means we can step out of positions of not being enough or having enough, and into positions to getting comfortable with who we are and have been. Settling in, in our rejection of social constructs that don't serve us, deepen roots in communities instead of nations. (Khan 2015)

Referring to young ethnically minoritized people in London as 'border-crossers' (Anzaldúa's 1987), Farzana echoes bell hooks' (1989) concept of margins as a 'site of radical possibility, a space of resistance', abandon the 'scarcity mindset' to select 'what serves us', as in a fertile field where Anzaldúa's (1987) cross-pollination can be practised. Even prison becomes a university, as Asim Qureshi (2017, 28) calls the Jamiat Yusuf, the university of the prophet Joseph (who was unjustly imprisoned). While imagining a borderless world is utopic, Farzana argues instead for a 'broaderland' as a new way of 'being open': 'if we are really serious, when we say "No Borders", what we could be doing is inviting ourselves to rise to broader borderlands'.

8.3. Moses and Pharaoh: Resistance and Rehabilitation

In the aftermath of 9/11, advocacy groups such as CAGE, MEND, CAIR, or the CCIF would contest racism and Islamophobic policies and narratives from the government or think tanks such as the Quilliam Foundation, the Henry Jackson Society, or the Institute for Strategic Dialogue (see chapter 2). Their work, in the form of reports, conferences, videos, and other public interventions with the help of lawyers, academics, and religious figures, was usually praised within Muslim circles[7] and their main figures held as examples,[8] compared to famous whistleblowers such as Edward Snowden. Articles of Islamic law favour whistleblowing as long as it is done in the public interest against anyone at risk of harming others (Abd Samad and Khalid 2015; Zainudin et al. 2018), backing it with scriptural evidence. The whistleblower even has a name in Islamic jurisprudence: *muhtasib* (one who forbids the evil and commands the good) (Zainudin et al. 2018, 105), and is entitled to protection from reprisals.

Although these interpretations are widely accepted when it comes to non-Muslim racists or Islamophobics, debates arise when it comes to Islamicate countries and Muslim celebrities. Asim Qureshi recalls when he was met by opposing views through his local imam:

> Yet, when I sit in the *jumma khutba* (the Friday prayer sermon) my local Imam tells me that one day of anarchy is worse than a thousand years of injustice. He further explains that we have a duty of obedience to the leader... I'll be honest, I didn't have much problem with most of what he was saying, until he said, even if he oppresses you, you should not protest against it, as protesting leads to anarchy and disbelief. (Qureshi 2017, 7–8)

Debates got more heated when the international celebrity shaykh Hamza Yusuf first blamed the killing of Black people for 'Black on Black crime' and labelled the US the 'one of the least racist countries' in the world.[9] Later, he would label Trump 'God's servant',[10] undermine Syrians' struggle for dignity,[11] and eventually paint the UAE as 'tolerant'[12] while the regime was fuelling the war in Yemen. In 2023, talking about Palestinians, he outraged crowds by declaring that sometimes, 'it is necessary to suffer in silence'. Firmly defending rebellion against oppressive leaders, he advocated a 'Theology of Obedience which would cost him a considerable amount of trust':

> That's why our '*ulamā*' [religious scholars] traditionally were opposed to revolution. Not because they thought oppression wasn't wrong or they were trying to keep the oppressors in power. They saw it from a metaphysical perspective first and foremost... We do not accept any rebellion (*khurūj*) against our leaders or our public affairs even if they are oppressive. This is the '*aqīdah* [belief] of the Muslims. (Yusuf in Quisay and Parker 2019)

I am not sure what Moses or Abraham would have thought of his opinion. Since the multiple scandals amongst influencers, celebrity scholars, and the charity sector, community organizers have been debating about the best strategies to hold the powerful to account. Sultanah has called out publicly an organization that made her suffer spiritual abuse (see chapter 4), highlighting examples found in the Islamic tradition:

> I think enjoining good and forbidding evil would include taking a public stand even if the people disliked the manner in which they regarded it as impolite or trouble making. A woman stood up and publicly told Umar when he was caliph he was wrong. He accepted he was wrong publicly. Another time a man also corrected the Prophet publicly when he said he jabbed him too hard. What this tells us is that Islam is not to produce sheep and faint-hearted mindsets. It's to allow dissent and disagreement even if done forthrightly.

While she disregards the consequences of a harsh tone, this strategy, along with the boycotting of oppressive individuals and organizations, usually triggers defensiveness (see chapter 7) and intense counter-reactions, as seen with the alt-bros (see chapter 3), consequently leading to a dead-end. The challenge is that those in positions of power or visibility are perceived as symbols: they are proxies for aspiration and provide a sense of transcendence (see chapter 7). They speak to the Muslim imagined 'we' (see chapter 6). Speaking truth to power is perceived by an attack on those symbols and therefore the collective. Sultanah recalls the atmosphere at an event around masculinity: 'at the talk [these alt-bros] were denying the pain of the sisters. People don't want to have these conversations. If you have them, they blackball you as a liberal, a feminist.' Others, like Safia, advocate holding to account perpetrators in private first, speaking about how she raised the alarm within the charity she was volunteering with: 'I think they need to be called out privately. When we were working with them, I raised the concerns to them, but they didn't listen. It [calling out publicly] depends on the gravity, if it's harming the whole community.'

However, as she highlights, this strategy has a limited effect. Shahzad Younas speaks in broader terms, careful not to confront people, but responsibilizing them in the fight against oppressive systems:[13]

> As Muslims we must always stand with and support the oppressed. We should be right beside them protesting and amplifying their cause too. As a non Black Muslim we also have to look at ourselves too, and fix our own prejudices, however awkward they are. That said, it's crucial we maintain perspective of the wider structural issues at play here against Black people which have existed for hundreds of years. (Younas 2020)

Aminah advocates a middle-ground, using public call-outs as a last resort:

> I like the Prophetic pedagogy, when he saw someone not doing *wudu* [ablutions] properly or calling the *adhan* [call to prayer], he was like with children, he would show them the right way, not shaming, not blaming... But then, I think it's important to be provocative sometimes to get people out of their bubble, but you have to be mindful of so many sensitivities... my dad says it's ok to reply to these on the same level of arrogance. Otherwise, you will be seen as a doormat.

Farzana Khan explains how PREVENT has 'fragmented' communities through a game of 'divide and rule', which even affected community spaces (see chapter 3):

> What's the point of having decolonized, queer, de-capitalized, anti-oppression, intersectional institutions, if we are still exercising power and injustices on each

other?... [L]earn to re-member our dismembered selves and our communities... Commit to not letting go of each other, even when it's hard—especially when it's hard. Commit to finally learn that the ends do not justify the means . . . In our efforts to bring down our oppressors, we can forget to raise ourselves up. (Khan 2015)

Following the outrage that ensued after misogynistic statements uttered by a sheikh in her local community, Nafisa reflects on the use of 'cancel' culture, trying to look at the broader implications:

I get that as a community, and as a central teaching of our faith forgiveness, reverence for *ulama*, and protecting the dignity and character of others are important and necessary to facilitate fidelity and unity. When a wrong has been done, we don't cancel or vilify the person, we (correctly and comprehensively) identify the harm/sin/mistake/fault etc, we reflect on the broader consequences, we reassess our discourses, methods and epistemologies, we draw from our scriptural resources and pool of collective wisdoms—in an effort to genuinely address the issue and try to do and be better . . . We show our love and reverence for our *ulama* by holding them to higher standards of responsibility and accountability, especially when they falter (as we all do), simply because they speak of and in the divine name.

Aminah, Nafisa, and Farzana advocate for a duty of care, reframing mobilization and holding to account as a work of love for the betterment of the collective. It is giving others another chance, saying 'you can do better'. Prophetic pedagogies rooted in *tawbah* (repentance), *rahma* (mercy, compassion), and rehabilitation suggest that anyone can be rehabilitated and welcomed back if they change. In the seventh century, it was common to find some of the fiercest opponents of Islam later becoming its biggest supporters, such as Umar Ibn Khattab or Abu Sufyan, and accepted in the community even despite their earlier opposition and crimes. Communities don't want the fall and the cancellation of its most powerful figures; they want them to stop harming people (see Hassan's comments on Ayaz, chapter 7). They know that while complicit, they are also victims and, therefore, potential comrades in struggle (Chapter 3). Sara Ahmed sees in 'hardness' a 'different emotional orientation towards others' (Ahmed 2014, 4). Keri Day (2016), mirroring bell hooks' perspective on love as an action verb, erects love as 'a strategy for constructing compassionate political communities . . . which challenges neoliberal forms of projective disgust based on fear and hatred of difference' (Day 2016, 17):

'I suggest that love is not merely an ideal sentiment but a concrete revolutionary practice. Love is a movement. It is movement toward each other... love can birth new moral worlds in response to the pathologies of neoliberal societies. They do not hold love and the political as antithetical concepts or realms' (Day 2016 105).

Rather than dominate, control, discipline, punish, and using power as a driving force, can the collective follow the prophetic teleology where enemies can be turned into friends and invited to build a bigger picture? However, can colonial agents change? In my previous works (Barylo 2017), I demonstrated that such powerful changes are possible; however, they mostly only happen when people undergo disruptive and emotionally intense life events, such as displacement, illness, or the loss of relatives or employment, for them to undergo a work of critical introspection. Halima Aden (see chapter 7) shows that it is not a weakness to admit errors of the past. Transparency and accountability are symbols of strength.

However, when perpetrators apologize, it is not granted that trust will be recovered. When counter-extremism supporter Maajid Nawaz wrote a public apology for not supporting the plea of the Uyghurs in the past,[14] he was met with reservations by Asim Qureshi, one of the main figures of advocacy against counter-extremism policies:

> As Muslims, we don't love or hate anyone excessively ... If this is an honest intervention and an honest claim of change, then Maajid should be allowed to fade into obscurity ... In order for this to be sincere, Maajid would need to acknowledge the role that he has played in developing and reinforcing the narrative of the War on Terror, particularly around extremism ... As someone who considered Maajid a friend once upon a time, I won't be welcoming him back so easily, he has a very long way to go to earn any sort of trust, and a very long list of people and communities from whom he needs to gain forgiveness.

Asim highlights the missing elements of the latter's discourse which would have been necessary for him to grant forgiveness, reducing Maajid's lengthy post into a public relations exercise. However, as Nargess Moballeghi argues (see chapter 7), aren't oppressors in position of power mirrors of our collective mind? Why did people give them power and made idols out of them? This is where Islamic decolonization enters the game.

8.4. Islamic Decoloniality

Some of my respondents into Japanese culture compare the current situation of Euro-American Muslims to what happened to Japan in the Meiji period:

> Educated Japanese realized that national survival depended on careful study and emulation of the ideas and technology that gave the Western colonial powers

> their advantages ... The main slogan of the Meiji period (1868–1912) was ... Everything Western, from natural science to literary realism, was hungrily soaked up by Japanese intellectuals. (Buruma and Margalit 2004, 3–4)

History tells us that while Japanese intellectuals held meetings to reverse the trend, it was too late. Japan, victim of a 'cultural indigestion', became and remained the hyper-modern nation we know, with asepticized traditions and spirituality.

Quijano, Maldonaldo-Torres, Mignolo, Lugones, and Grosfoguel (see introduction) locate the first step of decolonization in a delinking (Mignolo 2007, 459), divestment (Tuhiwai Smith 2010, 33) and liberation from Eurocentric powers, knowledge, and epistemologies, which implies a delinking of school and university curricula from Eurocentric frameworks (Sabaratnam 2017; Bhambra et al. 2018; Moncrieffe et al. 2019), which means including non-Eurocentric elements. The challenge, however, is that the 'Global South' can still embrace colonial frameworks (Bulhan 2008). Decolonial thinkers have tried to establish the outlines of decolonial frameworks through existing concepts such as with Black Marxism (Robinson 1983). However, some counter-argue that, paraphrasing Russell Means, 'Marxism is as alien to my culture as capitalism':[15] there is a need to decolonize 'minds', as put by Ngũgĩ wa Thiong'o (1986), which book title inspired Zain Dada to set up the Decolonise Your Mind student society at SOAS.

> The first act of Muslim de-colonization is in the mind and it involves first emptying out the colonial, post-colonial and Eurocentric nationalist edifice then setting out to imagine a de-colonial Muslim world and through it shape the future. (Bazian 2014)

Decoloniality means, for Quijano (2007, 176), a work of reconstitution, reparations, and re-attribution, as poet and community organizer Suhaiymah Manzoor-Khan offers a practical example after writing her own 'decolonized' syllabus:

> What if more than updating the course we fully restructured it? What if more than adding lesser-known authors with longer names but still palatably well-written English, we questioned the idea of authorship and 'sources' themselves? What if we removed the course assessment methods and encouraged students to combine memory, poetry, visual art and creativity? ... What if we gave credence to rumour in the barbershop as much as we do to information found in libraries that require identity cards? (Manzoor-Khan 2017)

Such a vision of decolonization of knowledge echoes a rethinking of production, assessment, and validity of knowledge, as advocated by Su'ad Abdul-Khabeer in her project Umi's Archive and others (chapter 6). These commitments are rooted in a quest for justice and liberation through civil rights of oppressed demographics

(Matsuda 1991), and thus are founded on the experiential knowledge (lived experiences, storytelling, family histories, biographies, and more) of oppressed demographics, often invalidated by dominant standards of the production of knowledge. I argue that this delinking imperative has repercussions even at the heart of the empire, as the very way Euro-America looks at its past is shaped by coloniality (Bhambra 2007). How much of fields like arts, humanities, social sciences, politics, and economics has been influenced by—and perhaps lost to—modern binaries, categories, and epistemologies around culture, society, or religion? Are we understanding pre-industrial literature, Molière, or Shakespeare correctly? In that sense, at times of hyper-modern neoliberalism, when anything which cannot be quantified has no value (emotions, feelings, spirituality, friendship, forgiveness, patience, compassion . . .), I argue that works such as Alain Caillé's anti-utilitarian theory for Action (2009) or Edgar Morin's reflections around culture, nature, and ecosystems (1977, 1986) bear decolonial value: they are a response to the modern, binary, and neoliberal colonization of the methods and frameworks developed in the social sciences.

The subsequent challenge is therefore to differentiate: what is colonial and what is not? Yosso (2005) in her article about cultural capitals, writes about how critical theories (around race, gender, religion, and class) are useful for defining, mapping, and explaining the power dynamics in societies under hegemonies (Crenshaw 1989; Bell 1992; Russell 1992; Crenshaw 1993; Valdes et al. 2002). These theories challenge dominant ideologies by challenging their 'neutrality' and 'objectivity' at the expense of non-dominant epistemologies (Bell 1987; Calmore 1992; Solórzano 1997; Delgado Bernal 1998; Ladson-Billings 2000). Although critical theories are often accused of 'racializing' or 'genderifying' social debates, categories such as class, race, gender, and belief are not 'self-conscious principles of social identity', but structural explainers of societal divisions created by power inequalities (McCloud 2009): they are about observable circumstances and their effects: they help articulate the whys and hows of contemporary forms of harm. From a Muslim perspective, they do not highlight victimization but 'identify and stop injustice and *munkar* (evil), not out of a utopic and materialist vision of justice on earth, but for the sake of the *umma* and its souls' (Kashani 2023, 212).

However, Javayria is critical of how theories are becoming a cult in activist spaces:

> We look for liberation theories with no God in it. Is critical race theory your religion? University makes you feel that understanding the oppressor gives you *shifa* [healing]. This is what I believed for 11 years, it simply doesn't work. Edward Said doesn't give you *shifa*. My liberation should not be contingent of understanding the oppressor's mind but contingent on understanding myself. If I have Him [God], this white supremacist capitalist society doesn't mean anything. It [white supremacy] has no power over Him.

Islamic decolonial scholar Syed Mustafa Ali observes the same in academic circles:

> I want to disrupt the race-gender-class-sexuality mantra which is near sacrosanct to feminism and some decolonial thought. The assumption of global patriarchy, heteronormativity etc, is a means by which white supremacy travels to co-opt, subsume and colonise non-white people through alleged sameness across difference. Decolonists, and feminist-antagonistic, are not solution oriented, they are rooted in white frameworks which have become a religion.

Both, and others, argue that the absence of a 'solution' or practical steps is a major weakness of contemporary decolonial thought (Hallaq 2018). The idolization of theories and obsession with culture and othering of the dominant powers pushes Islamic decolonial scholars to advocate shifting from an ego-centric framework (Craun 2013) to a God-centric one, a theology of liberation attempting 'to reflect on the experience and meaning of the faith based on the commitment to abolish injustice and to build a new society' (Dabashi 2008, 257). Syed Mustafa Ali describes the Islamic decolonial movement as 'committed to replacing all man-made forms of supremacy with a non-system of justice based on The Qur'an', or 'a spiritual-political project aimed at resisting, undermining and eventually replacing the contemporary Eurocentric world order with a multiversal or pluriversal system informed by an Islamic perspective' (Ali 2016).

As such, the first pillar of Islamic decoloniality is a *shahada*: smashing idols, speaking truth to power, divesting from seeking validation from those in power, and starting to re-link with each other. It is humbly rejecting the desire for domination and realizing that the oppressor has no right of power over the oppressed, since this right belongs to God. It is *tawheed*: considering nature, culture, the environment, daily life, and community organizing as part of one unified ecosystem. At the same time, *tawheed* supposes plurality: the Qur'an reminds its readers that if God wanted, He would have made everyone Muslims and, therefore, He has scattered people into 'tribes and nations' so that they can get to know each other and learn from each other (Qur'an 49:13). Therefore, decoloniality transcends identity labels and aligns on values. Among the rules of one of the many online Muslim decolonial discussion groups, this supposes a 'post-madhhabist' point of view (beyond existing schools of thought): while Islam is plural and accepting of a diversity of opinions, it is about practising critical thinking (*iqra*) 'no shaykh, no scholar, no imam, no philosopher, no *'ālim* [scholar], no thinker, no writer, past or present, who is above honest critique' (anonymous Facebook Group description).

Decoloniality through an Islamic framework understands Islam beyond a 'religion, a culture, a civilization, a discursive or religio-legal tradition, a nomocratic order or a master signifier' (Ali 2016). Consequently, religious scholars have started urging Euro-American Muslims to abandon the Eurocentric understanding of Islam as a 'religion' or a social construct (Barylo 2017; Nizami 2020). While most Muslims I've encountered (including myself) were taught (as with every book for beginners) rituals first (prayer, fasting, etc), Rakin Fetuga, a teacher and community organizer in north-west London, teaches Islam as it was chronologically revealed: I hear him first talk about 'reading', 'the pursuit of knowledge', then becoming 'trustworthy', make sure you have a 'good character', that you behave with 'compassion' and 'mercy', mentioning how the Prophet Muhammad would make peace between rival tribes. Chronologically in Islam, the prescription of prayer, fasting, and zakat came indeed several years after the beginning of the revelation; the first commandments of Islam were around social justice (the freeing of slaves, support of the poor) and primarily the building of empathy, compassion, and a sense of justice. Syed Mustafa Ali advances the concept of *taqwa* (trust, reliance) on God, and the story of Musa (Moses):

> Taqwa comes from the word shield: I don't fear white supremacy. He [God] is more powerful than the Matrix. It's at the same time the colonial white neoliberal matrix reloaded—but also Muslims reloaded: what does it mean if Muslim reload their full potential given by their heritage? We [Muslims at the heart of the Empire] are living the story of Musa: not from here, schooled here, schooled outside, and came back to confront power; it's who we are.

Decolonization supposes justice and, thus, reparations. Whether state structures will make amends or not does not preclude taking the first step in escaping the metacolonial prison: the breaking of illusions and illusory theologies of liberation. Decoloniality is thus not submitting or only opposing, but taking action, navigating: 'let us not go around, but instead, courageously through' (Khan 2015). Syed Mustafa Ali evokes 'Muslims reloaded' in the same vein as Farzana Khan, Rabiah Mali, and others such as Sadiyah Ahmed and AbdulMaalik Tailor, and work on rootedness, 'an accounting of the debts and assets we have inherited, and acknowledging the precise nature of that inheritance is an act of spiritual and political integrity' (Khan 2015). Moses, born in Egypt from Hebrew parents, part of a diaspora, educated in the heart of the Pharaoh's empire, bears many similarities to the modern Muslim diaspora. He experienced another world-view outside and then came back to confront obsolete structures. Pharaoh was a supremacist in his own right, a master of ego who considered himself as God, who eventually lost his life at the hands of his own arrogance. Islamic decoloniality is being an insider to the world of oppression and at the same time an outsider, constantly in the borderlands, facing ugliness but at the same time creating beauty. Islamic decoloniality is a prayer, in the words of Khaled Abou El Fadl (2020): 'prayer is resistance, prayer is connection, prayer is love. Prayer is a rejection of any kind of supremacy.

Islam is a passion for justice, beauty and for the disempowered. Islam is Adl and Ihsaan: Justice and Beauty.'

Another pillar expressed by my respondents in the pages of this book is *khilafa* (stewardship, see chapter 5), echoing Hallaq's (2018) call for creating a new idea of the human as a steward. Earth is a passing place which is borrowed from God and to be passed on future generations. Thus, stewards have a duty to take care of this *amana* (trust). It is setting limits to our thirst of control: 'most Westerners have forgotten that in all religious traditions, including Islam, there is a concept of ... personal responsibility of the believer *vis-à-vis* God ... However, the modern individual is defined by the absence of limits in the pursuit of his or her desires', Cesari posits (2013, 125). The steward therefore questions: am I being a mercy (*rahma*)? Stewardship is not only expressing and sustaining love, compassion, and solidarity, but also setting boundaries (instead of borders), being at the service of the vulnerable. It is not so much about displacing the balance as in an arm-wrestling contest, or stealing power in a Promethean quest for control, but rather about finding ways of nurturing what needs to grow. Decoloniality is a deviance,—random acts of kindness (Lewelyne-Jones 1998) when competition and brutality are the norm. It is understanding that victory will not be achieved by crushing the opponents who are, ultimately, siblings in distress, comrades in struggle. It is therefore recognizing resources and privileges as an *amana* (entrustment) to be shared. It is equipping people with tools, a lexicon, a map to navigate societal challenges, and tools to discern and confront how we participate in systems of oppression. As my respondent Ibrahim puts it: 'power is like a house: when you enter the house, either you burn it, either you let people in from the backdoor'. He echoes the words of Toni Morrison (2019, 110): 'your real job is that if you are free, you need to free somebody else. If you have some power, then your job is to empower somebody else.' It is, for decolonial academics, diverting power from the ivory tower. While metacolonialism's strength is its pessimism, it is showing *tawwaqul* (trust, confidence) and *sabr* (patience, hope, perseverance): planting seeds and trusting the process.

The challenge with decoloniality, as with any academic word hitting the mainstream, is how not to let the concept be essentialized and appropriated by diversity-and-inclusion tick-box exercise resulting in a 'decolonisation without decolonising' (Moosavi 2020)? As Suhaiymah Manzoor-Khan predicts H&M soon selling 'Decolonise Your Mind T-shirts' manufactured in sweatshops, she also suggests pointers to recognize decoloniality: 'decolonising should unsettle, provoke, stimulate and dismantle' (Manzoor-Khan 2017). It is unsettling the order of the world which doesn't fit in: 'decolonization ... is an elsewhere' (Tuck and Wayne 2012, 35–6)—or, in other terms, it began as something strange, and will remain something strange.

Notes

1. Roc Morin, 'How to hire fake friends and family', *The Atlantic*, 7 November 2017. https://web.archive.org/web/20180328011433/https://www.theatlantic.com/family/archive/2017/11/paying-for-fake-friends-and-family/545060
2. Restless Beings. Accessed 1 February 2024. https://web.archive.org/web/20201201223338/https://www.restlessbeings.org
3. Root 25. Accessed 1 February 2024. https://archive.ph/m9ur6
4. Resourcing Racial Justice. Accessed 1 February 2024. https://web.archive.org/web/20200508221111/http://resourcingracialjustice.org
5. Norwich Free Market. Accessed 1 February 2024. https://web.archive.org/web/20201030125637/https://opentrade.org.uk/norwichfreemarket
6. 'Yanis Varoufakis speaks truth to power at Clapton economics talk', *Hackney Citizen*, 29 February 2016. https://web.archive.org/web/20160309194942/https://www.hackneycitizen.co.uk/2016/02/29/greek-finance-minister-yanis-varoufakis-peoples-ppe
7. 'The need for Muslim whistleblowers—reviving a prophetic tradition', *5 Pillars*, 25 July 2013. https://web.archive.org/web/20150411083658/https://5pillarsuk.com/2013/07/25/the-need-for-muslim-whistleblowers-reviving-a-prophetic-tradition
8. Amanpaul Dhaliwal, 'Moazzam—the way of the whistleblower', *Islam21c*, 14 March 2014. https://web.archive.org/web/20140320162750/https://www.islam21c.com/politics/moazzam-the-way-of-the-whistleblower
9. Maha Hilal, 'It's time for Muslim Americans to condemn Hamza Yusuf', *AlJazeera*, 15 July 2019. https://web.archive.org/web/20190715205738/https://www.aljazeera.com/indepth/opinion/time-muslim-americans-condemn-hamza-yusuf-190715130254222.html; original audio (15:52–17:36): https://archive.org/details/hamza-yusuf-ris-drama-tube-ripper.com
10. Thomas Parker, 'Hamza Yusuf may be the token Muslim Trump's administration needs', *TRT World*, 11 July 2019. https://web.archive.org/web/20190809034137/https://www.trtworld.com/opinion/hamza-yusuf-may-be-the-token-muslim-trump-s-administration-needs-28175; original audio (at 39:15): https://archive.org/details/hamza-yusuf-ris-drama-tube-ripper.com
11. 'Hamza Yusuf issues apology for "hurting feelings" with Syria comments', *Middle East Eye*, 13 September 2019. https://web.archive.org/web/20190917213257/https://www.middleeasteye.net/news/hamza-yusuf-issues-apology-hurting-feelings-over-syria-comments; interview excerpt: https://archive.org/details/HamzaYusufSyrians
12. Thomas Parker, 'The doublespeak of Hamza Yusuf and Abdullah Bin Bayyah', *TRT World*, 14 December 2018. https://web.archive.org/web/20181215065355/https://www.trtworld.com/opinion/the-doublespeak-of-hamza-yusuf-and-abdullah-bin-bayyah-22483
13. Shahzad Younas, 'The anti-Black racism when it comes to Muslim marriage', Muzmatch, 7 June 2020. https://web.archive.org/web/20200929103657/https://muzmatch.com/en-GB/blog/community/the-anti-black-racism-when-it-comes-to-muslim-marriage
14. Maajid Nawaz [Facebook], 6 August 2020. https://archive.is/unBWe
15. Russell Means, 'Revolution and American Indians: "Marxism is as alien to my culture as capitalism"', Films for Action, 12 November 2011. https://web.archive.org/web/20170324034646/http://www.filmsforaction.org/news/revolution-and-american-indians-marxism-is-as-alien-to-my-culture-as-capitalism

References

Abd Samad, Khairunnisa and Haniza Khalid. 2015. 'Whistle-blowing as an aspect of Amar Ma'Aruf Nahi Munkar iniInstitutional governance.' Paper, International Conference on Aqidah, Dakwah And Syariah, Kuala Lumpur, 13 October.

Abil-Kheir, Abu Saeed (d. 1048). *Nobody, Son of Nobody*. Translated by Vrage Abramian (2001). Chino Valley, AZ: Hohm Press.

Abou El Fadl, Khaled. 2020. 'When Mecca is empty, what remains?' The Usuli Institute, 17 April. https://web.archive.org/web/20200806212526/https://www.usuli.org/2020/04/17/when-mecca-is-empty-what-remains

Ahmed, Sara. 2014. *The Cultural Politics of Emotion*. Edinburgh: Edinburgh University Press.
Akram, Sophia. 2019. 'The revolution will not be funded, but that won't stop her.' *The New Arab*, 8 March. https://web.archive.org/web/20190326124432/https://www.alaraby.co.uk/english/indepth/2019/3/8/voices-that-shake-developing-creative-responses-to-social-injustice
Ali, Syed Mustafa. 2016. 'An introduction to Islamic decoloniality.' Presentation, Impact Hub Birmingham, 8 October.
Anzaldúa, Gloria. 1987. *Borderlands/La Frontera: The New Mestiza*. San Francisco: Lute Books.
Baker, Chris. 2016. 'Foucault at the foodbank: locating religious power within the bio-politics of risk and austerity.' Paper, Sociology of Religion Study Group Annual Conference, University of Lancaster, 13 July.
Barylo, William. 2017. *Young Muslim Change-Makers*. London: Routledge.
Barylo, William. 2018. 'Spaces and modes of Muslim community organisation(s) in Paris and London.' *Francosphères* 7(2), 219–32.
Bazian, Hatem. 2014. 'A discourse on the colonized Muslim subject.' HatemBazian.com, 26 December. https://web.archive.org/web/20200914170224/http://www.hatembazian.com/content/a-discourse-on-the-colonized-muslim-subject
Bell, Derrick. 1987. *And We Will Not Be Saved: The Elusive Quest for Racial Justice*. New York: Basic Books.
Bell, Derrick. 1992. *Faces at the Bottom of the Well: The Permanence of Racism*. New York: Basic Books.
Bhambra, Gurminder. 2007. *Rethinking Modernity: Postcolonialism and the Sociological Imagination*. London: Palgrave.
Bhambra, Gurminder K., Dalia Gebrial, and Kerem Nişancıoğlu (eds). 2018. *Decolonising the University*. London: Pluto Press.
Bulhan, Husein. A. 2008. *Politics of Cain—One Hundred Years of Crises in Somali Politics and Society*. Bethesda: Tayosan International Publishing.
Buruma, Ian and Avishai Margalit. 2004. *Occidentalism: The West in the Eyes of Its Enemies*. New Delhi: Penguin.
Caillé, Alain. 2009. *Théorie Anti-Utilitariste de l'Action et du Sujet*. Paris: La Découverte.
Calmore, John. 1992. 'Critical race theory, Archie Shepp and fire music: securing an authentic intellectual life in a multicultural world.' *Southern California Law Review* 65, 2129–231.
Cesari, Jocelyne. 2013. *Why the west Fears Islam: An Exploration of Muslims in Liberal Democracies*. New York: Palgrave.
Craun, Dustin. 2013. 'Exploring pluriversal paths toward transmodernity: from the mind-centered egolatry of colonial modernity to Islam's epistemic decolonization through the heart.' *Human Architecture: Journal of the Sociology of Self-Knowledge* 11(1), 91–113.
Crenshaw, Kimberle. 1989. 'Demarginalizing the intersection of race and sex: a Black feminist critique of antidiscrimination doctrine, feminist theory and antiracist politics.' *University of Chicago Legal Forum* 1989(1), 139–67.
Crenshaw, Kimberle. 1993. 'Mapping the margins: intersectionality, identity politics and the violence against women of color.' *Stanford Law Review* 43(6), 1241–99.
Dabashi, Hamid. 2008. *Islamic Liberation Theology: Resisting the Empire*. Oxon: Routledge.
Dada, Zain. 2020. *Space, Survival and Sustainability: The Future of Community Arts Organisations in the UK*. London: Winston Churchill Memorial Trust.
Day, Keri. 2016. *Religious Resistance to Neoliberalism Womanist and Black Feminist Perspectives*. Basingstoke: Palgrave Macmillan.
Delgado Bernal, Dolores. 1998. 'Using a Chicana feminist epistemology in educational research.' *Harvard Educational Review* 68(4), 555–82.
Dubet, François. 1994. *Sociologie de l'expérience*. Paris: Seuil.
Dutton, Rahma. 2020. 'The moon, money and motherhood: conversations with a new wave of Muslim leaders.' *Amaliah*, 30 July. https://web.archive.org/web/20200813181848/https://www.amaliah.com/post/59781/moon-money-motherhood-conversations-new-wave-muslim-leaders
Foucault, Michel. 1971 [1966]. *The Order of Things*. New York: Vintage Books.

Hallaq, Wael. 2018. *Restating Orientalism: A Critique of Modern Knowledge.* New York: Columbia University Press.
Hanhardt, Christina. B. 2013. *Safe Space: Gay Neighborhood History and the Politics of Violence.* Durham: Duke University Press.
hooks, bell. 1989. 'Choosing the margin as a space of radical openness.' *Framework* 36, 15–23.
Kashani, Maryam. 2023. *Medina by the Bay.* Durham: Duke University Press.
Khan, Farzana. 2015. 'Moving from "no borders" to Broaderland for the borderless.' *New Internationalist*, 17 December. https://web.archive.org/web/20151218230455/https://new int.org/features/web-exclusive/2015/12/17/solidarity-and-new-community
Khan, Farzana. 2018. 'Farzana Khan x Project Ribcage.' Project Ribcage Podcast, 29 August. https://archive.org/details/farzana-khan-x-project-ribcage
Ladson-Billings, Gloria. 2000. 'Racialized discourses and ethnic epistemologies.' In *Handbook of Qualitative Research*, edited by N. Denzin and Y. Lincoln. Thousand Oaks: Sage, 257–77.
Levins Morales, Aurora. 2019. 'Raícism: rootedness as spiritual and political practice.' In Aurora Levins Morales, *Medicine Stories: Essays for Radicals*. Durham: Duke University Press, 99–103.
Lewellyn Jones, Angela. 1998. 'Random acts of kindness: a teaching tool for positive deviance.' *Teaching Sociology* 26(3), 179–89.
Manzoor-Khan, Suhaiymah. 2017. 'The lessons I learnt from writing my own "decolonised" syllabus.' The Brown Hijabi blog, 1 November. https://web.archive.org/web/20190321121018/https://thebrownhijabi.com/2017/11/01/the-lessons-i-learnt-from-writing-my-own-decolonised-syllabus
Matsuda, Mari J. 1991. 'Voices of America: accent, antidiscrimination law, and a jurisprudence for the last reconstruction.' *Yale Law Journal* 100(5), 1329–407.
McCloud, Sean. 2009. 'The ghost of Marx and the stench of deprivation: cutting the ties that bind in the study of religion and class.' In *Religion and Class in America: Culture, History and Politics*, edited by Sean McCloud and William Mirola. Leiden: Brill, 91–107.
Mignolo, Walter D. 2007. 'DELINKING.' *Cultural Studies* 21(2–3), 449–514.
Moncrieffe, Marlon, Yaa Asare, Robin Dunford, et al. (eds). 2019. *Decolonising the Curriculum. Teaching and Learning about Race Equality* 1(1).
Moosavi, Leon. 2020. 'The decolonial bandwagon and the dangers of intellectual decolonisation.' *International Review of Sociology* 30(2), 332–54.
Morin, Edgar. 1977. *La Méthode: La nature de la Nature.* Paris: Seuil.
Morin, Edgar. 1986. *La Méthode: La vie de la Vie.* Paris: Seuil.
Morrison, Toni. 2019. *The Source of Self-Regard: Selected Essays, Speeches, and Meditations.* New York: Knopf.
Ngũgĩ wa Thiong'o. 1986. *Decolonizing the Mind: The Politics and Language of African Literature.* London: James Curry.
Nizami, Mohammed. 2020. 'What is this "Islam" that people claim to subscribe to?' Nizami. co.uk. https://web.archive.org/web/20200222025133/http://nizami.co.uk/what-is-this-islam-that-people-claim-to-subscribe-to
Quijano, Anibal. 2007. 'Coloniality and modernity/rationality.' *Cultural Studies* 21 (2–3), 168–78.
Quisay, Walaa and Thomas Parker. 2019. 'On the theology of obedience: an analysis of Shaykh Bin Bayyah and Shaykh Hamza Yusuf's political thought.' *The Maydan*, 8 January. https://web.archive.org/web/20190804170839/https://www.themaydan.com/2019/01/theology-obedience-analysis-shaykh-bin-bayyah-shaykh-hamza-yusufs-political-thought
Qureshi, Asim. 2017. *A Virtue of Disobedience.* London: Byline Books
Robinson, Cedric 1983. *Black Marxism: The Making of the Black Radical Tradition.* London: Zed Books.
Rumi's Cave. 2019. [Facebook] 11 October. https://web.archive.org/web/20201005084355/https://www.facebook.com/rumiscave/photos/a.382929208390238/2955809084435558
Russell, Margaret. 1992. 'Entering great America: reflections on race and the convergence of progressive legal theory and practice.' *Hastings Law Journal* 43(4), 749–67.

Sabaratnam, Meera 2017. 'Decolonising the curriculum: what's all the fuss about?' SOAS blog. https://web.archive.org/web/20171022041041/https://www.soas.ac.uk/blogs/study/decolonising-curriculum-whats-the-fuss

Skogan, Wesley G., Susan M. Hartnett, Natalie Bump, et al. 2008. 'Evaluation of CeaseFire-Chicago.' National Criminal Justice Reference Service. https://web.archive.org/web/20090701115026/https://www.ncjrs.gov/pdffiles1/nij/grants/227181.pdf

Soja, Edward W. 1996. *Thirdspace*. Malden: Blackwell.

Solórzano, Daniel. 1997. 'Images and words that wound: critical race theory, racial stereotyping and teacher education.' *Teacher Education Quarterly* 24(3), 5–19.

Tuck, Eve, and K. Wayne Yang. 2012. 'Decolonization is not a metaphor.' *Decolonization: Indigeneity, Education & Society* 1(1), 1–40.

Tuhiwai Smith, Linda. 2010 [1999]. *Decolonizing Methodologies*. London: Zed Books.

Valdes, Francisco, Jerome McCristal Culp, and Angela Harris (eds). 2002. *Crossroads, Directions and a New Critical Race Theory*. Philadelphia: Temple University Press.

Wilson, Nick, Jonathan Gross, and Anna Bull. 2017. *Towards Cultural Democracy: Promoting Cultural Capabilities for Everyone*. London: King's College London.

Yosso Tara J. 2005. 'Whose culture has capital? A critical race theory discussion of community cultural wealth.' *Race Ethnicity and Education* 8(1), 69–91.

Younas, Shahzad. 2020. [Facebook] 7 June. https://web.archive.org/web/20200929103544/https://www.facebook.com/shahzad.younas/posts/10156824462567142

Zainudin, Nur Hazirah, Wan Zahari, and Wan Mohd Zulhafiz. 2018. 'Whistleblowing: a Western and Shari'ah perspective.' *IIUM Law Journal* 26(1), 99–120.

Zavos, John. 2017. 'Religion and social action in a city of posts.' *Journal of Contemporary Religion* 32(1), 67–82.

Conclusion

As a Muslim born in a family contaminated by white supremacy, a French-Polish citizen in post-Brexit Britain, a white man entering a community of ethnically minoritized people, an agnostic who resigned from doubt, a homeless man now in a university job, I happened to have explored both sides of the multiple borders I grew up around before realizing there's no set place or group of people I can call home. I understand now why my parents erased my Polish identity, why like many others, they harboured a hatred towards Black people and Muslims, why I couldn't find a job or get married within British Muslim communities; people like the illusional safety of ready-made categories. 'Stepping outside of one's culture is equivalent to walking outside of the law' (Gómez Peña 1993). I tried to fit on either side before realizing you don't find your community; instead, you build it.

In the twenty-first century, not fitting anywhere flags you as a 'societal risk'. It makes one, willingly or not, a political subject at times when we are told not to be 'too political'. Since politics comes from the Greek *politikos* (civic, public, social), every social interaction by essence is political. Neutrality is a tool to decide what is acceptable by those in power. To be apolitical, neutral, or impartial as humans would suppose us to be asexual, a-racial, asocial, or, in sum, inhuman. Coloniality negates the right of minorities to be perceived as human (Maldonado-Torres 2007) and thus millions echo Fanon begging '*je voulais être homme, rien qu'homme*', 'I wanted to be human, only human' (my translation). A huge corpus of literature already analyses the dynamics all border-crossers go through. We know what causes harm, and why and how. The aim of my life journey and this research is to know: how to move forward? How do I resist, heal, and flourish so I become myself again?

This work focuses on Fanon's *damnés* (the doomed, the wretched); statistical anomalies, never meant to be here and there in the first place. They are people who do not believe in big changes but rather small acts of resistance, planting seeds even if the fruits will be ripe in a few generations. More than transforming the public sphere (Soliman 2017), these interventions work by a constant 'doing' and 'undoing' of social norms (Lewicki and O'Toole 2017), becoming citizens by dissent (O'Loughlin and Gillespie 2012). They embody Ruha Benjamin's concept of *Viral Justice* (2020): small actions and connections spreading like a virus that create complex systems, patterns, ecosystems, and societies, dismantling harmful systems and create alternatives nurturing structures. They are at the image of modern pirates in the sense of the ancient Greek *peira*, 'to attempt', 'to try', they experiment various ways of navigating the white civilizational project, taking the reins of their own narrative, in the spirit of the mutineers of the HMS *Sandwich* in 1797, who declared: 'long have we been endeavouring to find ourselves men, we now find ourselves so. We will be treated as such' (Gill 1999, 300). They are the heroes of Terrence Malick's *A Hidden Life*: 'the best advocates, are the ones we do not see' (Qureshi 2017, 113).

Before my move to the UK, I met Ibrahim, a Tuareg man from Niger. He used to come twice a year to France and Spain to sell hand-made silver jewels people would craft in his village at the borders of the Sahara, where people would eat meat perhaps once in ten years' time. Shocked by the differences between France and Niger, he told me: 'here in Europe, if a child is given a piece of cake, he will eat it. In Niger, if a child is given a piece of cake, he will eat it, but not before running into each house in the village to share it with everybody.'

Power is a cake. In our society of competition, instead of sharing it, everyone wants a piece of it. Metacolonialism tells the diaspora that anyone with hair straighteners can become Kim Kardashian (chapter 1). The white civilizational project has achieved the unthinkable: replacing God with whiteness. God was never for sale, but to paraphrase Tarantino's *Django Unchained*, white supremacy knew how to make an offer so ridiculous that Muslims would be forced to consider. The recipe for controlling minorities is simple: offer and demand. Bring some demographics to a point of deprivation and at the same time, occupy a position of monopoly on the market of liberation. Promise them visibility, financial stability, and representation in exchange of doing the job of oppressing themselves on their peers. Post signs to indicate the right direction: this way go the 'bad' Muslims, that way go the 'good' ones, and here you've got a theology of liberation that enslaves people (chapter 2) and produces depoliticized, apathetic, disconnected, and conforming citizens in a powerful Orwellian-Huxleyian double-punch. This is how one resigns from their culture, values, ethics, and identity and how neoliberalism, whiteness, and patriarchy among others have become the road to *jannah* (paradise) in modern eschatologies. Metacolonialism has made people exiles at home; it has put the diaspora in debt of their conformity while they are owed reparations.

These politics conquered and divided minds into three categories of colonial agents: self-interested hedonists, power-hungry collaborators, and hatemongering declinists. As 'engagement rates' have become a new currency for algorithmic forms of abuse, the metacolonial hedonist finds nothing wrong with selfishness, commodifying one's identity and oppression as long as there's a *halal* (permissible) stamp on it. They don't go YOLO (You Only Live Once) but live LTNA (Like There's No *Akhirah* (afterlife))—when there's nothing after death, there's no accountability. Sandwich men of the modern days, they end up being themselves sandwiched between the dictatorships of greedy corporations and relentless followers. Similarly do those collaborators who turn charities into colonial missions, embrace the role of native informants, chase selfies with politicians, medals, and 'leadership' titles following a theology of greed: to be free, one must grasp and hold onto as much power as possible. On the other end of the spectrum, some alienated by both dominant structures, and parts of what they considered once as a community, try to find liberation in a totalitarian retreat to their imagined roots using binary narratives of empowerment: you're either with us or against us (chapter 3). If the *ummah* is a family, it is a dysfunctional one. A family of estranged members who don't recognize each other.

However, more people are becoming aware that showing off or begging for recognition are not sustainable strategies. Many of these 'successful' politicians have failed at listening to people's concerns. 'Successful' influencers and religious celebrities have failed at using their platform for good. Instead of Moses, they have become the servants of pharaoh. History shows that no matter how white they try to become, how much they try to love the material world, the *dunya* (material world) won't love them back and they will remain the undesirable other. It is a matter of time before they cross a red line or lose their relevance, once people realize they only offer empty promises. My observations show that the grass roots never fail at discerning what is authentic from what is artificial; there are enough watchdogs, informal online discussion forums and trusted individuals that will always raise flags for the wider community to see. As summed up by Suhaiymah Manzoor-Khan: 'the community has eyes, voices and any attempt of colonisation will be spotted and exposed'. Maybe, as we cross the Red Sea of the borderlands, the empires will collapse under the weight of their own arrogance. Because, in the end, these organizations and people don't guard the doors of *jannah*. They don't pay people's bills. My validity and existence cannot be tied to the opinions of people. Especially since the pandemic, people are looking for people with depth, intentions, thoughts, seeking quality instead of quantity, money, or fame, those seeing them as persons rather than tools, numbers of a bank account. Success, fame, and wealth can't replace lost loved ones.

As long as there will be an irreducible core, no matter how small, of people aware and critical of their current situation and the ongoing oppression, there will be hope. Being at the margins means fighting on many frontlines at the same time, being involved in the emotional labour of grieving and healing (see chapters 4 and 5). There is no mandate after which they retire. There is no paid annual leave. The margins produce sensitive people, attune to emotions, the trauma they witnessed and experienced broke their illusions. They might be an undesirable minority, but while practising one's faith or ethical framework will become like holding a burning charcoal in one's hand, they will become part of a global tight-knit family where people separated by miles of sea and land will come to support one another in various shapes—'Islam began as a something strange and it will return to being strange, so blessed are the strangers' (Sunan Ibn Majah Vol. 5, Book 36, Hadith 3986). They are all anomalies for Britain and white supremacist, neoliberal, ego-driven systems. From a spiritual perspective, they are miracles.

Initiatives such as Everyday Muslim Project and Archive, Muslim History Tours or Apne Film Club ask: instead of being nostalgic of Golden Ages, can the diaspora's Golden Age be now? Can Rumi's Cave be the new Andalus, the new Silk Road? Thirdspaces like Rumi's, Root25 show that service can win over profits. Khidr collective show that creativity will not be silenced. 5Pillars, Amaliah, or The Muslim Vibe and other outlets show that Muslims don't need to rely on mainstream media. Sacred Footsteps show that people don't need to follow consumerist trends. Poets like Shareefa Energy and comedians like Nabil AbdulRashid show that one can be unapologetically themselves, uncensored, and stand for their values in arenas like formal events at Parliament or *Britain's Got Talent*. But what about people who can't access Oxford? Let's bring Oxford to the people, says Imad Ahmed, when he set up his People's PPE. Bolder, the New Crescent Society, posits that Muslims can even agree on an independent and unified calendar. It is possible to be a politician and not take bribes and fall into corruption, affirms Zarah Sultana. There is no alternative political strategy; they are the strategy and the politics. Even if institutions have not followed yet, Hassan Vawda affirms that yes, Tate Britain can organize an Eid day with the local Eritrean mosque and that institutions can pay for masala chai and home-made samosas. The Muslim Youth Helpline, Healing Justice London, the Rabbani Project, the Herbal Blessing Clinic, or the Black Muslim Women Healing Collective demonstrate that people can heal and redefine 'home'. No resources? No mentoring? No money? No venues? No problem. People progress, unite, and help each other. The diaspora is rich with resources that structures of power will never be able to fathom; as Farzana Khan says, the diaspora can be 'more than anything we could have even imagined' (Khan 2018). The initiatives in this research show that indeed, from an apparent 'nothing' at the margins, it is possible to nurture a new 'everything'. After almost twenty years of existence, although the French government shut it down, the CCIF (*Collectif Contre l'Islamophobie en France* [Collective Against Islamophobia in France]) in France was never appropriated by the dominant structures or corporations; furthermore, the initiative has relocated to Belgium as the CCIE and now has expanded their works to the whole of Europe. As Javayria puts it, metacolonialism wins when one cannot imagine a happy future. There are many other names that I omit and of whom I don't even have knowledge; however, they don't simply affirm, they create a new future.

In the final scenes of the movie *The Matrix*, what mattered to me the most was less Neo's powers than his level of confidence. This is perhaps this idea of self-worth that has shaped my idea of decoloniality. It is about reframing narratives and ideas. How do we collectively define success? Is it achieving one's dreams of power or stability like conquering the top of mountains? Or is it to define how to live one's life with conscious choices every day? Are we living in a world of prestige or are we breaking illusions (prestige comes from the Latin *praestigium*, illusion)? What if the winners were losers, wealthy in money, but deprived from intelligence, community, spirituality, solidarity? *In fine*, what is Islamic decoloniality? As my respondents more eloquently say, it is when faith, love, mercy, and the political are merged in the same ecosystem.

Islamic decoloniality is *tawheed*: moving from an ego-centric (Craun 2013) to a God-centric framework for liberation, which Syed Mustafa Ali refers to as Islamic decoloniality, free from man-made supremacies (Ali 2016). It is a *shahada*: smashing the idols, speaking truth to power, divesting from seeking validation and starting to re-link with each other. It is *khilafa* or stewardship, considering privileges as an *amana* (trust) to be at the service of those around us. It is *sabr* and *tawwaqul*, doing our best but leaving the results to God, writing a love letter without recipient. It is *tawbah* (repentance), knowing our weak spots, acknowledging our mistakes, healing our wounds, seeking forgiveness, and improving our ways. It is *rahma* (mercy), seeing in the oppressor potential comrades in struggle who can change their ways, as Black elder and community organizer Ruby Sales says to her oppressors: 'you can't make me hate you'. It is fasting from harmful feeds and saying 'no' to harmful decisions. It is *iqra*, reading, learning, thinking critically, and sharing the tools of our own liberation.

However, this work has limitations. Aren't these organizations the plasters that neoliberalism wants? Are they creating dependency? While I've observed some people relying on them for years, my contention is that there are no other structures for people to go to and few are those with the resources to create specialize in more than one field. There is simply no ecosystem for these initiatives to be a stepping stone among others—yet. In addition, can everyone attain liberation or transcend the barriers of race and socio-economic status? Some of the people who 'made it' or are still active are exceptions. Not all of it is patience, hard work, and perseverance. Some of them were lucky to find gatekeepers who opened the door to some unique funding, grant, networking opportunities, had the luxury of living at their parents', or having a spouse providing for the household to have the time and the means to undertake community work. The grass roots are not always success stories. For every Rumi's Cave, perhaps more than ten similar initiatives have failed. Marginal spaces are subject to 'activist fatigue': after years of struggle, people don't have the energy to organize things anymore. People are hard to mobilize and in the absence of momentum, people give up and prioritize their own existence, or survival. Initiatives created around charismatic individuals are more often than not short lived. Communities are collectively traumatized and while people don't overcome and process and heal trauma, they can remain a minefield. The functioning of these organizations cannot be replicated and standardized as they are too specific to their local context. However, they can provide ideas for bigger organizations with concepts such as stewardship.

Is this work even decolonial? It's written in English and there are too many references to Greek mythology and ancient Latin words. Isn't that enough to corrupt and falsify the voices and the writings of those at the forefront of decoloniality? Perhaps, it is just an imperfect work from the frontline (since perfection only belongs to God—see chapter 5.4), written by a metacolonial writer at the heart of the empire, trying to make sense of decades of chaos, between London and Paris, born from whatever mud of epistemologies it found itself plunged into. Being between borders is messy. To paraphrase Gómez Peña (1993), border culture is to be fluid in English, Arabic, Urdu, Hinglish, and Angrezi... 'it also means to question and transgress border culture'. Echoing the questions of Suhaiymah Manzoor-Khan, does this work unsettle? Does this work provoke? Stimulate? Dismantle? And I would add: is this work a mercy? Only the readers of this book have the power to say.

In my life, I've experienced that anything dear to one's heart can vanish in the blink of an eye. Similarly, a multitude of even better things can appear. How many other people and initiatives are living Malick's *A Hidden Life*? It's not about fighting the empire, but rather about showing that another way is possible. The empire is powerful, but the diaspora will strike back.

References

Ali, Syed Mustafa. 2016. 'An introduction to Islamic decoloniality.' Presentation, Impact Hub, Birmingham, UK, 8 October.
Benjamin, Ruha. 2020. *Viral Justice: How We Grow the World We Want*. Princeton: Princeton University Press.
Craun, Dustin. 2013. 'Exploring pluriversal paths toward transmodernity: from the mind-centered egolatry of colonial modernity to Islam's epistemic decolonization through the heart.' *Human Architecture: Journal of the Sociology of Self-Knowledge* 11(1), 91–113.
Gill, Conrad. 1913 [1999]. *The Naval Mutinies of 1797*. Manchester: Manchester University Press.
Gómez Peña, Guillermo. 1993. *Warriors of Gringostroika*. St Paul: Graywolf Press.
Khan, Farzana. 2018. 'Settling in our skins: gestures towards the frontiers of human spirit.' Farzanakhan.net. https://web.archive.org/web/20200919025411/https://farzanakhan.net/settling-in-our-skin-gestures-towards-the-frontiers-of-human-spirit
Lewicki, Aleksandra and Therese O'Toole. 2017. 'Acts and practices of citizenship: Muslim women's activism in the UK.' *Ethnic And Racial Studies* 40(1), 152–71.
Maldonado-Torres, Nelson. 2007. 'On the coloniality of being: contributions to the development of a concept.' *Cultural Studies* 21(2–3), 240–70.
O'Loughlin, Ben, and Marie Gillespie. 2012. 'Dissenting citizenship? Young people and political participation in the media-security nexus.' *Parliamentary Affairs* 65(1), 115–37.
Qureshi, Asim. 2017. *A Virtue of Disobedience*. London: Byline Books
Sunan Ibn Majah. Edited by Muhammad Bin Yazeed Ibn Majah Al-Qazwînî (2007). English translation by Nasiruddin al-Khattab. Riyadh: Dar-Us-Salam.
Soliman, Asmaa. 2017. *European Muslims Transforming the Public Sphere: Religious Participation in the Arts, Media and Civil Society*. London: Routledge.

Index

For the benefit of digital users, indexed terms that span two pages (e.g., 52–53) may, on occasion, appear on only one of those pages.

abuse 2, 12, 29, 39, 70, 79–80, 86, 93, 96–97, 104, 141–42, 155, 171, 175–76, 214–15
   racial 144–45
   sexual 71, 72, 73–74, 101, 170
   spiritual 100–1, 200
acceptance 14–15, 34–35, 39, 40, 46, 57–58, 60, 98, 102–3, 130–31
activism 2, 4, 6, 54, 71–72, 86, 117, 123–24, 129, 131, 179, 181, 183, 197
   activist 10, 12–13, 30–31, 32, 49, 52, 57–59, 71, 76, 79–86, 108–9, 137, 205, 217
Africa 6–7, 26, 35, 49, 96–97, 129–30
alienation 12, 39, 51, 79, 86, 174, 214–15
alternative 2–3, 5, 6–7, 53, 58, 120, 125–26, 128, 172–73, 174, 183, 190, 195, 196–97, 213–14, 216
alt-bro 70–88, 201
alt-right *see* far-right
America 6–7, 8–9, 32, 47, 49, 57–58, 71, 74–75, 85, 146
   American Muslim 9, 31–32, 33, 50, 55, 58–59, 61, 71, 75, 80–81, 96–97, 116–17, 118–19, 128, 150, 167
   Black Americans 30–31, 76, 81, 128
   USA 1–2, 9, 13, 36–38, 47–55, 57–58, 59–60, 72–73, 74–75, 76, 85, 93, 97–98, 101, 107, 118–19, 131, 146, 166–67, 171, 172–73, 179, 195, 196, 200
anti-utilitarian *see* utilitarian
appropriation 5, 26, 27–28, 29, 77, 94, 100, 137, 149, 155, 168, 169, 177, 208, 216
art 15–16, 33, 34, 86, 104, 107, 136–40, 163, 165, 170, 177–83, 191, 204
   arts 3–4, 15–16, 33, 106, 107, 124–25, 136–38, 140, 144, 147, 178–80, 181–83, 190, 193–94, 195–96, 204–5
assimilation 3–4, 14, 26–27, 28, 30–31, 33, 49, 53, 80, 95–96, 118, 144, 154, 168
astroturfing 53–54, 58–59
authority 3–4, 40, 49, 73, 74–75, 96, 101, 119
   authoritarian 8–9
   religious 52–53, 100, 170–71

background
   ethnicity 6–7, 40, 45, 58, 79, 81, 96–98, 102–3, 125–26, 141, 143
   religious 55
   socio-economic 6–7, 10, 24, 31, 40, 57, 82, 118–19, 120–21, 125–26, 144
Bangladesh *see* South Asia
belief *see* faith
belonging 12, 26–27, 28, 32–33, 34–35, 37–38, 95, 97–98, 121, 129–30, 139, 141, 142–43, 150
Black 2, 14, 76, 86, 96–97, 99–100, 101–2, 105, 115, 117, 129–31, 140, 141, 147, 149, 165, 169, 170, 180–81, 201, 204
   American *see* America
   anti-Blackness 10, 15–16, 26, 37–39, 40, 46, 57–58, 59–60, 70–72, 76, 77, 104–5, 138, 141, 155, 158–60, 194, 200, 213
   Black Lives Matter 2, 50, 70, 74–75, 76, 85, 101, 128, 129, 170
   Muslims 29, 34–35, 37–38, 56–57, 81–82, 147–48
   women 14, 29, 101–2, 105–6, 129–32, 149, 180–81
Britain 1, 3–4, 26, 31, 47, 58, 84, 95, 96–99, 102, 137, 145, 146–48, 150, 154–55, 181–82, 213, 215
   British 1, 2–3, 8–9, 24, 26–27, 31, 34–35, 37, 40, 45, 47, 48–49, 55, 60, 94, 96, 106, 116–17, 137–38, 139, 147–48, 149, 175–76
   British Islam 137, 152–55
   British Muslims 1–2, 4–5, 15–16, 26, 30–32, 33, 37–38, 58–59, 79–81, 127, 128, 136–37, 140–41, 144–45, 147–48, 149, 150–51, 160–61, 162, 163, 168, 170, 174–75, 196
   UK 1–5, 8–10, 12–13, 14–15, 26, 27–28, 31, 36–38, 39, 47–60, 70, 76, 87, 93, 95, 101–2, 116–17, 119, 121, 122–23, 131, 139–40, 142, 143, 144, 145–48, 151, 152–53, 166–67, 171, 172–73, 177, 193–94, 195–97, 214
British Islam *see* Britain
British Muslims *see* Britain

Brotherhood 27–28, 50, 71, 83, 84, 85–87, 100, 108, 142
business 2–3, 4–5, 15–16, 26, 31, 45–46, 48, 50, 55, 56–57, 59–60, 71, 102–3, 105, 119, 120, 137, 145–46, 162–63, 164, 166–67, 172, 173–74, 191–92, 196–98
  businesspeople 32, 58, 105, 160–61, 162, 171, 190
  entrepreneur 6–7, 55, 61, 72, 162, 166–67, 174–75
  management 52–53

challenges 12, 13, 29–30, 58–59, 86, 87, 94, 108, 118–19, 127, 131, 141, 144, 146, 160, 181, 195, 197, 201, 202, 204, 205, 208
change 6, 23, 24–25, 29–31, 45–46, 48–49, 53–54, 60, 61, 79–80, 109, 124–26, 138–40, 143, 149, 165, 172–73, 174–75, 176, 178–79, 180, 197–99, 202, 203, 213–14, 217
charisma *see* ego
charities *see* organisations
citizenship 1–2, 3–4, 5–6, 26–27, 32, 36, 54–55, 82–83, 129, 137–38, 162–63, 192–93, 213–14
class 3–4, 24, 29–30, 31, 32–33, 37, 39, 81–82, 118, 129, 142, 150, 165, 194, 205, 206
  middle 23, 24, 30, 32–33, 82, 99, 104, 120–21, 151–52, 169
  working 1–2, 31, 32, 37, 40, 45–46, 53–54, 57, 82, 96, 120–21
coconut 23–25
collective 2, 15–16, 33–34, 39, 40, 52, 58–59, 81, 87–88, 94, 95–96, 102–3, 105, 109, 118, 119, 124–25, 130, 138, 142–43, 144–45, 149–51, 152, 155, 160, 169, 175–76, 177, 192–93, 196–97, 201, 202, 203, 216–17
colonisation 2–5, 7–9, 15–16, 24, 25–30, 35, 38–39, 45–46, 49, 55, 58–59, 60, 85, 98, 99, 106, 115, 117, 129, 131, 139–40, 141, 142–43, 149, 154, 162, 168, 170–73, 178–79, 182, 203–6, 213–15
community 1–2, 26–28, 32, 37–38, 46, 50, 53–55, 56–58, 59–61, 76, 78, 79–80, 87–88, 93–94, 97–98, 99–100, 102–7, 108, 109, 117, 120, 121, 130, 137, 140, 141, 143–44, 149–52, 166–67, 174, 189–90, 191, 192–93, 195–96, 197, 198–99, 201–2, 203, 206, 213, 215, 216–17
  Muslim 3, 4–7, 9, 12–13, 36, 37–39, 40, 51, 54–55, 58–59, 73, 76, 79–81, 85–86, 93, 94, 101, 102–5, 137, 141–47, 149–50, 151–52, 153, 160, 165, 170, 181, 182, 196, 213
  Ummah 15–16, 26, 37, 76, 78–79, 81, 85, 127, 137, 140–47, 180, 190, 197, 214–15

conflict 28, 47, 83, 161, 172, 175–76
conformity 8, 15–16, 23, 27–28, 29–36, 52, 139, 162–63, 165, 167, 168, 214
consensus 9, 15–16, 59–60, 192
consumerism 6, 32–33, 35, 36, 38–39, 49, 53, 98–99, 119, 122–23, 125, 126–27, 128–29, 151, 153, 154, 160, 161, 162, 164, 166–68, 174, 175–76, 181, 216
conviviality 9, 120, 126, 152, 196
counter-extremism *see* extremism
crime 2, 5, 11, 15–16, 47–49, 51–52, 59–60, 94, 127, 199, 200, 202
crisis 51, 70, 72–73, 76, 87, 118, 123–24, 129
Critical Race Theory *see* race
culture 2–3, 7–8, 9–11, 15–16, 24, 25, 26–28, 32–34, 38–39, 40, 51, 53–55, 59–60, 70, 72–74, 76, 77, 79, 80, 81, 82–83, 85, 87, 94, 99, 101–3, 106, 108, 116, 119–20, 121–22, 125, 126, 127, 130–31, 144–46, 147–48, 150–51, 152, 153, 154–55, 160–83, 196, 202, 203, 204–5, 206–7, 213, 214, 217–18
  multiculturalism 1, 8–9, 95, 96, 102

da'wa 80, 83–84, 180
decolonisation 3–4, 9, 15–16, 58–59, 75–76, 117, 123, 125–29, 132, 177, 190, 201–2, 203–8, 216–18
democracy 5–7, 14, 47, 192–93, 195
diaspora 2, 3, 6–7, 26–29, 35, 60, 71–72, 96–97, 119–20, 137, 151, 158, 168, 169, 177, 207–8, 214, 216
discrimination 28, 37–39, 48–49, 77, 82, 96–97
diversity 1, 6–7, 11, 56, 59–60, 85, 107, 137–38, 139, 147–48, 158, 159, 206, 208

education 4, 5, 6, 7, 8–9, 14–15, 24, 32–33, 36, 38–39, 48, 51, 72, 84–85, 139, 146, 147–48, 154, 179
ego 14–15, 45–46, 99–100, 101, 102–3, 117, 119, 120, 122, 123, 144, 152, 155, 164–65, 169, 172, 189, 191, 192, 196, 197, 206, 207–8, 215, 217
  charisma 45–46, 217
elders 26–27, 28, 37, 108, 121–22, 141–42, 145–46, 150, 151–52, 192–93
emotions 9, 11, 12, 14, 28, 71, 72, 78, 80–81, 93, 101, 103–4, 109, 116, 132, 138, 149, 151, 166, 169, 171, 175–76, 197, 202, 203, 204–5, 215
empires 2–3, 7–8, 35, 39, 45, 49, 57–58, 60, 75, 129, 149, 154, 170, 173, 204–5, 207–8, 215, 217–18
entrepreneur *see* business
environmentalism 3–4, 6–7, 15–16, 47, 115–17, 120–26, 129–32, 168, 206

ethnicity *see* background
ethnonormativity 27–28
Euro-America 2, 3–4, 9, 15–16, 28, 32, 35, 50, 70, 71–72, 75–76, 77, 87–88, 94, 100, 118–19, 120, 123–24, 127, 136, 144–45, 203, 204–5, 206–7
eurocentrism 2–3, 7, 8–9, 29, 38–39, 52–53, 72, 73–74, 77, 78, 94, 98, 101–2, 105, 106, 117, 120, 123, 126, 142–43, 168, 181, 204, 206–7
Europe 1–4, 7, 10, 15–16, 24, 31–32, 33, 36, 39, 47, 50, 52, 55, 71, 75, 79, 80–81, 94, 95–98, 100–1, 116–17, 119, 124, 126, 137, 151, 153, 214, 216
extremism 93–94
    counter-, 2, 8, 10, 11, 30, 46–51, 53–55, 75–76, 96–97, 142–43, 159, 196, 197, 203
    terrorism 1, 4, 47, 49, 53–54, 58, 60–61, 85, 96–97, 99, 128, 138, 203

faith 4, 9, 11, 15–16, 24, 26, 51, 76–77, 82, 85, 87–88, 94, 98, 100–3, 108–9, 124–26, 129, 130, 138, 140–41, 145, 151, 154–55, 169, 189, 195–96, 202, 206, 215, 216–17
    belief 3–4, 7, 10–11, 78, 99–100, 104–5, 153, 155, 179, 182, 183, 200, 205
family 7–8, 10–11, 26, 34, 73, 79, 87, 101, 103–4, 107, 121, 123–24, 126, 127, 130, 137, 142–43, 144, 145–46, 151, 153, 159–60, 166, 177, 190, 205, 214–15
far-right 2, 50, 77–78, 80–81, 82, 84, 95–96, 174
fasting 117, 124, 125, 126, 127–29, 189–90, 196, 206–7, 217
feminism 70–78, 82–83, 84, 86, 87, 167, 174, 201, 206
food 6–7, 33, 39–40, 116–17, 125–27, 128, 129, 137–38, 145, 146, 147–48, 151, 160–61, 162, 163–64, 189, 194, 196–97
France 9, 31, 48–49, 52, 53, 54–55, 59–60, 154, 166–67, 178–79, 214
    French Muslims 4–5, 36–37, 48–49, 93, 117, 118–19, 139, 145–46, 151, 171, 179, 216

gender 3–4, 6–8, 10, 25, 29–30, 32–33, 38–39, 71, 72–74, 75–76, 78, 104–5, 117, 118, 194, 205, 206
generations 4, 6, 15–16, 26–28, 40, 96, 99–100, 101, 108, 120, 130, 137, 143, 144, 145–46, 148, 150, 151, 155, 169, 189, 192, 208, 213–14
God 10–11, 60, 74, 78, 95–96, 100, 104–5, 106, 107, 108–9, 115, 116, 122, 123, 124, 125, 127, 129, 130, 131, 136, 142, 146, 154–55, 160–61, 166, 178, 181, 182–83, 197, 198–99, 200, 205–8, 214, 215, 217

governance 15–16, 39, 58–59, 117, 123–24
halal 83, 116–17, 126–27, 153, 160–61, 166–67, 179, 214–15
hardships 108, 124, 182–83, 190
healing 3, 9–10, 12–13, 15–16, 45–46, 76, 81, 87–88, 94, 95–96, 101, 108–9, 115, 123–24, 129–31, 146–47, 155, 158–59, 177, 179, 180–81, 190, 192–93, 195, 205, 215–17
hegemony 2–4, 7–9, 15–16, 32–33, 35, 53, 57–58, 74–75, 78, 85, 117, 127, 160, 205
heritage 3–4, 5, 26, 27–28, 58, 105, 108, 127, 137, 141, 144, 147–48, 150–51, 180, 196, 207
heterotopia 9, 191, 193
hierarchies 7–8, 24, 25, 28, 36, 74, 85, 99, 103, 119, 123, 154–55, 165, 192
hijab 10, 45, 48–49, 53, 59–60, 71, 84, 93, 138, 154, 158, 160–61, 165–68, 173–74, 176, 181–82, 191
history 7, 14, 15–16, 26–27, 28, 46, 57–59, 76–77, 97–98, 132, 136, 137–38, 139, 147–52, 154, 173, 178–79, 180–81, 204, 215, 216
hub *see* organisation
human rights *see* rights
humanitarian 4–5, 15–16, 48–49, 52–53, 56, 101, 160, 172

identity 5, 11, 23, 24–25, 26–27, 28, 29–30, 33, 34–35, 51–52, 54–55, 61, 76, 99–100, 102–3, 105, 107, 108, 129, 130, 131, 137, 142–43, 144, 147, 154–55, 162, 167, 177, 180, 183, 193–94, 204, 205, 206, 213, 214–15
immigrant *see* migration
India *see* South Asia
Individualism 9, 39, 46, 85, 99, 106, 118, 124, 143, 174, 191
inequalities 6–7, 40, 45–46, 108, 146, 205
influencer 5, 10–11, 15–16, 32, 33, 45, 52–53, 54–55, 56–57, 142–43, 158, 159, 160–70, 171, 172–76, 177, 178, 179, 200, 215
institutions 2, 5–6, 15–16, 37, 49, 51, 59–60, 78, 84, 94, 95–96, 101–2, 108, 109, 118–19, 137–38, 140, 149–50, 154, 167, 196, 201–2, 216
interpretation 10–11, 26, 48–49, 74–75, 77, 78, 94, 95–96, 118, 128, 168, 177, 182, 199–200
islamophobia 2, 4, 10, 24, 47–51, 56, 57–58, 59–60, 71, 73, 75, 76–81, 84, 93, 96–97, 99–100, 104–5, 138, 140, 142–43, 144–46, 174, 181–82, 199–200

leadership 6–7, 45, 55–56, 61, 73, 83, 100, 106, 117–20, 121, 123–25, 128, 162–63, 172–73, 192, 200, 214–15 liberation 3-4, 9, 35, 39, 51-52, 53, 71-72, 78, 83, 86, 117, 130, 131, 149, 160-61, 165, 166, 167, 169, 179, 204-5, 206, 207-8, 214-17

management *see* business
margins 2, 8, 9, 13, 33, 40, 47, 56-57, 58-59, 71-72, 76, 78, 81, 82-83, 84, 87, 99-100, 106, 107-8, 117, 130-31, 137, 141-42, 149, 165, 168, 183, 190, 197, 199, 215-16, 217
marriage 34-35, 38, 72-73, 80, 98, 99, 100, 120-21, 145-46, 151, 160-61, 166, 196-97
masculinity 70-75, 77-78, 83, 85, 87, 201
media 2, 5, 7-8, 10, 26-27, 47, 48, 50, 51, 54-55, 75-76, 93-94, 95-96, 100, 122-23, 128, 139, 140, 144-45, 190, 194, 198, 216
  social 2-3, 5, 6, 10-11, 12-13, 15-16, 33-35, 37-38, 45, 50, 52-55, 60, 70, 72-73, 76, 82, 95-96, 98-99, 101, 102, 106, 127, 128, 142-43, 144, 149, 158-83, 191-92
mental health 2-3, 10, 12, 15-16, 29-30, 34-35, 47, 48-49, 51, 73, 83, 87-88, 94, 96-98, 101-6, 109, 175-76, 194
metacolonisation 2-3, 8-9, 25, 28-30, 33-34, 39, 46, 53, 61, 71-72, 94, 98-100, 107-8, 117, 137, 139, 150, 168, 172, 183, 207-8, 214-18
migration 1-2, 6-7, 8-9, 10, 12, 14, 24, 25, 26-27, 32, 33, 47, 58, 71, 78, 80-81, 84, 96, 147-48, 150, 162, 177-78
minority 1-2, 3-4, 6-9, 24, 25, 26-27, 29-30, 50, 54-55, 56, 58-61, 73, 78, 80-81, 82, 94, 96-98, 101-2, 108, 128, 136, 139, 149, 169, 199, 213-14, 215
misogyny 7-8, 10, 15-16, 70, 71-72, 77, 87-88, 93, 155, 181, 202
modernity 2, 3, 8-9, 35, 36, 39, 72-73, 98-99, 117-20, 123-24, 127-29, 132, 136, 142-43, 147, 150, 167, 169, 175-76, 180, 189, 190, 191, 194, 204-5, 207-8
mosque 2, 4, 5, 25, 33, 80-81, 93, 104, 116-17, 122, 124-25, 136-38, 139, 141-43, 145-46, 147-50, 152-53, 181-82, 189, 193, 216
Muhammad *see* prophet
multiculturalism *see* culture
music 26-28, 37, 48-49, 107, 117, 131, 138, 153, 160-61, 168, 178-79, 183

neoliberalism 2-4, 5, 6-9, 13, 23, 35-36, 38-39, 45-46, 49, 52-53, 55, 72, 73, 75, 77, 83, 99, 102, 106, 108, 120, 122-23, 132, 150, 155, 160-61, 162, 164-67, 172, 175-76, 179, 190, 195, 202-3, 204-5, 207, 214, 215, 217
NGO *see* organisations
norms *see* standards

objectification 60-61, 128, 160-61, 167
organisations
  charities 4-6, 10, 15-16, 26, 33, 37, 45-46, 48-49, 52-53, 56-57, 59-60, 70, 100, 101, 103-4, 116-17, 119, 122-26, 140, 141, 143, 144-46, 155, 160, 170-73, 190, 193, 196-97, 200-1, 214-15
  hub 5, 10, 54, 72, 80-81, 103-4, 105, 147, 152, 171, 178, 189, 191-95
  NGO 4-5, 124-25
orientalism 60-61, 151, 167, 168, 178

Pakistan *see* South Asia
para-social 132, 165-66, 174
patriarchy 2-4, 13, 35-36, 38-39, 52, 87, 155, 167, 172, 179, 206, 214
police 2, 37-38, 48, 50, 75-76, 99-100
poverty 5, 6-7, 10, 32, 35, 52, 54-55, 128, 141, 160, 171-72
  ethical 2, 51-52, 172-73, 198
power 3-4, 6, 7-8, 9, 11, 24-25, 26-27, 28, 29-30, 31, 34-35, 37-40, 45-46, 52, 53-55, 56-61, 71, 72-73, 74-75, 78, 80-82, 83, 85, 87, 93-94, 98, 100-1, 107-8, 118-19, 120, 124, 128, 129, 130-31, 132, 139-40, 144, 147, 149, 154-55, 160, 164-66, 169, 173, 174-75, 177, 179, 183, 190, 194, 195, 196, 197, 200, 201-2, 203, 205, 206-8, 213-17
prayer 56, 79, 105, 106, 115, 116, 117, 120-21, 124, 130, 132, 136-37, 145, 147-49, 159, 163, 173, 189-90, 200, 201, 206-8
professionalism 25, 29, 33-34, 54-55, 58-59, 82, 100, 118, 124-25, 126
prophets 26, 56, 71, 74, 78-79, 83, 84-85, 108, 124, 128, 130-31, 164, 199, 202, 203
  Muhammad 74, 75-76, 77, 78, 84-85, 122, 123-24, 125, 126-27, 142-43, 177, 183, 189, 197, 200, 201, 207

Qur'an 4-5, 26, 52-53, 58-59, 74-75, 78, 84-85, 115, 120, 122, 125, 148, 155, 160-61, 193, 198, 206

racial abuse *see* abuse
racism 1-2, 6-8, 24, 29, 31-32, 35, 37-39, 45-46, 48-49, 51, 52, 54-55, 59-60, 71, 75, 76, 78, 80-81, 84, 87-88, 95, 96-98, 99-100, 101, 102, 128-29, 139-40, 141, 143, 145-46, 155, 160, 169, 181-82, 199
  critical race theory 76-77, 205
  race 3-4, 24, 29-30, 32-33, 38-39, 50, 59-60, 76, 80-81, 96-97, 104-5, 129, 150, 165, 170, 194, 205, 206, 217
Ramadan *see* fasting

INDEX

religion 5, 11, 15–16, 26, 35, 40, 46–47, 49, 52–53, 78, 85, 100, 104–5, 123, 126–27, 142–43, 145, 153, 155, 181, 204–7
religious authority *see* authority
representation 2, 4, 11, 15–16, 45–46, 51, 54–55, 56, 58–61, 96–97, 147, 154, 160–61, 166–67, 174, 176, 177, 178–79, 180, 214
resistance 3–4, 9, 12–13, 49, 52, 78, 94, 95–96, 107–8, 120, 128, 130, 131, 137, 139–40, 142–43, 146–47, 149, 155, 165, 167, 199, 206, 207–8, 213–14
rights
   human and civil 2–3, 4, 6, 14, 29, 48, 52, 53–55, 58–59, 60, 95–96, 142–43, 204–5
   men's *see* alt-bro
   women's rights *see* women
rituals 10–11, 25, 35, 95–96, 99, 143, 162–63, 164, 191, 206–7

sacred 100, 108, 109, 124, 131, 178, 181–82, 183, 216
salafi 40, 50
secularism 9, 31–32, 33, 49, 73–74, 75–76, 80–81, 117, 129, 136, 137, 174, 178
self-esteem 34, 37, 51, 95, 96–97, 98, 106, 149, 158–59, 164, 193–94
sexual abuse *see* abuse
social engineering 2, 15–16, 52, 53–54, 55, 164
social media *see* media
socio-economic *see* background
soup kitchen 10, 171, 190, 191–92, 194
South Asia 1–2, 6–7, 8–9, 24–25, 26–28, 30–31, 32–33, 37, 38, 39, 57, 58, 71–72, 79, 96–97, 103–4, 120–22, 126, 127, 145, 147–48, 151–52, 168, 170
   Bangladesh 1, 31, 40, 45, 127, 144, 145, 150, 153
   India 24, 26–27, 36–37, 151, 153, 169, 170, 176
   Pakistan 1–2, 26, 35, 36–37, 59–60, 82, 95, 145, 146, 150–51, 153, 162–63, 168, 169, 171–72, 180
spiritual abuse *see* abuse
spirituality 7–8, 9, 15–16, 26, 77, 80–81, 94, 95–96, 101, 102–3, 105, 106–7, 108, 115, 116, 120, 122, 123–24, 125–26, 129, 130, 131, 132, 151, 152, 171, 177, 178, 180, 182, 183, 189, 191–92, 198–99, 200, 204–5, 206, 207–8, 215, 216–17
standards 2–3, 15–16, 33, 36, 37, 38–39, 52–53, 85, 98, 107, 126, 165, 168, 202, 204–5, 217
   norms 3–4, 7–8, 27–28, 30–31, 33–36, 38–39, 40, 45, 49, 51, 52, 53–54, 72, 76, 94, 97–98, 99–100, 106, 124–25, 126, 141, 142–43, 160, 162–63, 164–65, 166, 179, 182, 191, 193, 206, 208, 213–14
stewardship 6–7, 15–16, 87, 115, 117, 120–25, 132, 192, 196–97, 208, 217
sufi 45–46, 49, 56, 106, 191, 193
surveillance 2, 48–49, 94, 98–99, 162–63, 181–82

terrorism *see* extremism
therapy *see* mental health
traditions 5, 6, 10–11, 12, 27–28, 36, 39, 47, 52–53, 58–60, 70, 76, 84, 105, 106, 108, 116–17, 121–22, 124, 126, 136, 138, 146, 149, 177, 178, 179, 191, 196, 200, 204, 206–7, 208
trauma 6–7, 15–16, 26, 71–72, 79–81, 96–97, 98, 99–100, 101, 102–3, 104–5, 106, 107, 109, 130, 149, 169, 215, 217
trust 5, 9, 10, 11–12, 55, 56, 100, 102–3, 106, 131, 132, 152, 165–66, 182, 190, 194, 195, 198, 200, 203, 206–7, 208
   entrustment 87, 115, 144–45, 173, 196–97, 208, 217

UK *see* Britain
Ummah *see* community
USA *see* America
utilitarian 124–25, 174–75
   anti-utilitarian 11, 204–5

veganism 116–17, 124, 126–27
violence 2–3, 10, 46, 49, 50, 73–75, 76, 86, 96
visibility 2, 6, 57–58, 73–74, 82, 87, 99–100, 104, 106, 139, 149–50, 160, 164–65, 166–67, 201, 214
volunteering 5, 6, 24, 51, 103–5, 109, 124, 140, 144–45, 151, 170–72, 190, 192–94, 196, 201
vote 1, 24, 40, 55, 58–59

westernization 26–28
   supremacy 28, 35, 132, 206–8
   white 2–3, 7–9, 23, 25, 38–39, 46, 78, 79, 81–82, 86, 131, 179, 205–8, 214
women 2, 5, 23, 35, 70, 72–78, 82–83, 85, 96, 100, 101–2, 103–4, 105, 120–22, 128, 167, 169
   Black women *see* Black
   Muslim, 29, 33–34, 36, 52, 76–77, 79, 84, 93, 98, 105, 115–16, 123–24, 129, 139, 143, 154, 160–61, 165, 166–68, 174, 180–81, 182, 194, 200
   rights 71, 107–8
worship 11, 108, 118, 146, 153, 154–55, 164, 181–82, 189